Judgment and Action

Judgment and Action

Fragments toward a History

✦

Edited by Vivasvan Soni
and Thomas Pfau

NORTHWESTERN UNIVERSITY PRESS
EVANSTON, ILLINOIS

Northwestern University Press
www.nupress.northwestern.edu

Printed in the United States of America

10 9 8 7 6 5 4 3 2 1

Library of Congress Cataloging-in-Publication Data

Names: Soni, Vivasvan, 1968– editor. | Pfau, Thomas, 1960– editor.
Title: Judgment and action : fragments toward a history / edited by Vivasvan Soni and Thomas Pfau.
Description: Evanston, Illinois : Northwestern University Press, 2018. | Includes index. | "The essays gathered in this volume emerged from an ongoing series of symposia organized at Duke University and Northwestern University, with faculty from across the United States and beyond, under the broad rubric of 'Fundamental Concepts in the Humanities.'"
Identifiers: LCCN 2017036636 | ISBN 9780810136328 (cloth : alk. paper) | ISBN 9780810136311 (pbk. : alk. paper) | ISBN 9780810136335 (e-book)
Subjects: LCSH: Judgment. | Judgment (Aesthetics) | Act (Philosophy)
Classification: LCC BF447 .J832 2018 | DDC 153.46—dc23
LC record available at https://lccn.loc.gov/2017036636

CONTENTS

INTRODUCTION

Vivasvan Soni

The essays gathered in this volume emerged from an ongoing series of symposia organized at Duke University and Northwestern University, with faculty from across the United States and beyond, under the broad rubric of "Fundamental Concepts in the Humanities."[1] The need for such a series arose from our growing sense that certain concepts indispensable to humanistic scholarship—concepts such as action, judgment, beauty, image, happiness, the human (Beckwith, this volume), autonomy (Nazar, this volume), will, and personhood—had become deeply suspect if not downright unintelligible in the current constellation of interpretive methods and critical approaches, even as they continue to be deployed surreptitiously with little awareness of the long and complex history of their transmission. Moreover, our work and that of a number of others in this area has led us to the conclusion that this conceptual amnesia, and the spirit of critique that views these concepts as hopelessly tainted, is not a thing of yesterday, but part of the enduring legacy of modernity.[2] The conceptual impoverishment wrought by modern theoretical paradigms (perhaps one of the more surprising legacies of modernity) is the systematic effect of deeply ingrained assumptions and methodological decisions so taken for granted that they have become invisible to us.

Changes of this scope and scale, whose consequences are so intertwined and far-reaching, cannot simply be wished away or undone at a stroke. Tracing the subtle pathways by which these concepts lose their purchase on us, and reconstituting the social and conceptual horizons in which they become intelligible again, require a sustained and comprehensive approach, an ambitious task that cannot be undertaken by any of the essays here for reasons of space. The purpose of this collection is a more modest one: to illuminate, from multiple disciplinary, period, and theoretical perspectives, the rich and imbricated history of the concepts of judgment and action; to draw attention to critical sites from which we may begin the work of rethinking these concepts; to urge the ongoing relevance of these concepts for humanistic inquiry; to point to some of the historical reasons that these particular concepts have fallen from grace; to situate the local vicissitudes of these concepts within a broader intellectual-historical trajectory that alone renders them intelligible. In short, the essays collected here may be viewed as fragments toward a history of ideas, not a history that would bind these concepts to an ever more thickly elaborated historical context, as is so often the case today, but one that would look to the past in order to recapture the normative force of the ideas themselves.[3]

Why begin a project of this kind with the concepts of judgment and action, when there are so many others that call out for attention? And why pair these two concepts, which are in some ways so different from one another? As I will make clear below, and as most of the essays in this collection make evident, it is almost impossible to think judgment and action apart from one another, so closely are they intertwined. An act of judgment is perhaps the most fundamental and basic kind of action, and no "doing" deserves to be dignified with the name of action if it does not issue from a judgment. But more importantly, if the purpose of the project is to restore to humanistic scholarship those concepts without which its intelligibility and relevance are compromised, then there could not be two more important concepts than judgment and action. The labor of interpretation is essential to all humanistic disciplines, and every interpretation is an act of judgment. Yet the work of interpretation and judgment has been profoundly called into question by contemporary hermeneutic methods in the humanities, which incline either toward contextual determination of meaning or the suspension of judgment altogether.[4] Furthermore, if we are to recognize the ongoing relevance of humanistic work, its ability to intervene and act meaningfully in the world, then we will have to learn that action is not simply the performance of a deed, but also requires the intelligibility of the deed, which can only be secured through an act of interpretation and judgment. As McGowan's essay reminds us: "Actions . . . are always subject to judgments of meaning, of whether they are significant or valuable" (McGowan, this volume; see also Hauerwas, this volume). And Hannah Arendt, in her account of action in the Greek *polis*, explained that the deeds of a hero could not have enduring effects without the forms of speech that both interpreted them and gave them substance beyond the fleeting and punctual motions of a moment. Indeed, among twentieth-century thinkers, it was Arendt more than any other who discerned how important it was to recover the concepts of judgment and action, not only for political thought but for humanistic learning more broadly. Without seeking to replicate Arendt's own reconstruction of these concepts, our project shares her diagnosis of their unfortunate eclipse and attempts to chart new ways to rethink these concepts and render them relevant for our present. We hope, then, that the essays in this collection will be useful to scholars across the humanistic disciplines, especially those who are most troubled by the so-called crisis in the humanities and those who object to the squeamishness about the concepts of judgment and action that has been the bequest of post-structuralist forms of "theory" since at least the 1980s.

The essays in this volume have been written by theologians, literary scholars, political theorists, classicists, and philosophers. The concepts of judgment and action do not allow themselves to be confined to a single disciplinary domain; they are pertinent for literary analysis, political theory, systematic theology, philosophy, ethics, aesthetics, and many others. But despite the divergent fields represented here, there are also significant overlaps in the thematic foci of the essays, as one would expect. For this reason it makes no more sense to organize the essays by discipline than it does to organize them strictly according to the concepts of judgment and action. To guide the reader through the collection, we have elected to group the essays around the preponderant themes that govern their analyses, themes that are relevant to multiple disciplines and draw further attention to the reason the concepts of judgment and action find themselves in such disarray in the contemporary humanities. The four themes are interiority/contemplation, ethics, politics/community, and aesthetics/image.

Although the "critique of subjectivity" is firmly established in the contemporary humanities, the first group of essays make the case that robust notions of interiority and contemplation are vital to rethinking judgment and action.[5] The danger of this insistence on the inward life is that we imagine a subjectivity radically cut off from others, exhibiting or claiming a bad autonomy all but synonymous with a willful disregard for community. The third group of essays corrects this misperception by showing that judgment and action cannot be solipsistic, but are in fact only intelligible in the context of communities, through interactions with multiple others. Likewise, the essays in the second group challenge the notion that judgment and action emanate from a "punctual self" (to borrow Charles Taylor's term), but they do so from the perspective of ethics. Judgment and action, they argue, are best understood not as discrete events but as constitutive of and emerging from character that is narratively extended in time and imbricated in its social world. Finally, as Pfau's essay shows, a traditional aesthetics had been comfortable conceiving the image as provoking judgment and action; however, contemporary aesthetic thought makes little room for judgment, let alone for a robust concept of action. The essays in the fourth group each interrogate an image or set of images to reveal the structure of judgment and action implicit in various contemporary aesthetic experiences. In the process, what we normally understand by judgment and action are significantly reconceived.

I said above that the essays in this collection can be viewed as notes toward a history of ideas, with a view to reconstituting the normative claims such ideas make on us. It is nearly impossible, in the current conjuncture, to articulate the legitimacy of this kind of project, for reasons that have to do with the very conceptual legacy of modernity that has blocked access to the ideas in the first place. A history of ideas has long been out of favor. To think, as Hegel once did, that ideas are "efficacious" (*wirklich*), that they possess an animating power that can become real, actual, or effective in the world, smacks today of metaphysical mysticism or, worse, simple naïveté.[6] Post-Nietzschean moderns would rather philosophize with a hammer. To be sure, ideas may be treated in the mode of discourse analysis, as strictly textual entities to be combined, manipulated, observed, and dispassionately analyzed, rather than inhabiting (and being inhabited by) subjects for whom they constitute a fundamental mode of access to the world. Alternatively, they may be deconstructed or exposed as the bearers of ideology. Then again, from the perspective of a no-holds-barred naturalism, ideas may seem no less fickle, ephemeral, or insubstantial than the subjects in whom they have their home, their flimsy fictionality obscuring the matter at hand, namely matter in its materiality. Cumulatively, these post-Hegelian approaches have given rise to the assumption that concepts and ideas can be invented willy-nilly as the need arises and dispensed with as soon as they no longer serve our ends. They seem to bear only a tenuous and adventitious relation to the material world they purport to organize and comprehend. Rather than ideas, it is the perpetual quest for the inchoate and noncognitive bedrock of materiality, in its many guises, that has guided humanistic scholarship for some time now, whether that materiality is thought to be affect, desire, the body, the economy, history, the unconscious, the materiality of the book, the materiality of language, the social, big data, the lighting up of neurons in fMRI scans, and so on; as though Hegel had not shown decisively that there is nothing more abstract than matter, nothing less substantial than the nothingness of Being.

If intellectual history in this context comes to seem like an antiquarian enterprise, it is because the one who studies ideas looks like someone who has become entranced by the tremulous patterns of froth on the wave of a tsunami, believing superstitiously that these hold the clue to the tremendous power that sweeps everything before it. The action, it is supposed, lies elsewhere, namely, at the quantifiable molecular level that accounts for the wave's sheer force (*kinesis*) rather than at the level of its organizing principle (*eidos/forma*) that allows us to grasp the phenomenon as a wave in the first place. Moreover, if concepts and ideas can effortlessly be conjured up or refashioned as needed to serve the occasion, what reason is there to attend to the historical process that brings them into being? Perhaps most troublingly, the method by which we approach the history of ideas requires that we set aside normative considerations, and view ideas with a clinical detachment that is less a neutral act of observation than a methodological dictate that preemptively denudes them of their significance.

The essays in this collection take a different approach, proceeding from the premise that we are *moved* by ideas. A history of ideas that is not merely antiquarian must remain attentive to the claims ideas make on us, to how and why we are moved by them. Otherwise, the methods that estrange us from their moving power will have become a self-fulfilling prophecy, draining them of the substance and force that they were supposed never to have possessed in the first place. Every one of the essays in this collection proceeds from the assumption that the concepts of judgment and action matter urgently to us and that attention to some aspect of their history can illuminate the hold they have over us.

Concepts such as judgment and action are especially vulnerable to the methodological prejudice against ideas and their history, and it is hardly surprising that we struggle to think them or make a place for them within contemporary historicist and materialist paradigms according to which idealism of any kind must be denounced.[7] Judgment and action are operative only in the realm of a certain ideality, and where this ideality is granted no legitimacy, they quite simply cease to exist as such. Without the immaterial ideas of end, purpose, and intention which guide it, action does not simply become disoriented and purposeless; it loses the name of action and becomes indistinguishable from mere motion or behavior. Alasdair MacIntyre's observation that "there is no such thing as 'behavior,' to be identified prior to and independently of intentions, beliefs and settings" and that "the concept of intelligible action is a more fundamental concept than that of an action as such" still rings true.[8] Likewise, without the immaterial ends and reasons that shape it, judgment becomes indistinguishable from the mere expression of an opinion or the execution of a decision, whose grounds are inscrutable or nonexistent. It is no wonder, then, that contemporary accounts so often treat action as no more than a species of motion and judgment as simply another name for decision or opinion, since the ideality that distinguishes them is considered a gratuitous inference lacking the requisite methodological warrant or an objective technique of measurement. We will not arrive at a satisfactory account of judgment and action until we can acknowledge the idealism without which these concepts cannot come into view in the first place. I have said that we are moved by ideas, but it is time to correct that formulation. We become agents capable of acting deliberately and thinkingly in the world only when ideas make our movements into more than motion (McGowan), when through their very insubstantiality they transform motion into action, when, that is to say, we judge. Idealism, then, is not a misguided faith in the mysterious moving power of ideas; it is rather the recognition that without ideas and the noumenal realm as a whole, action and judgment have no meaning whatsoever. To explore the history of concepts such as judgment and action demands a commitment to a certain idealism, however disavowed or concealed. What we stand in need of today is less a phenomenology than a noumenology.

Even if we grant that there is a certain ideality to both judgment and action, grouping the two concepts together under the rubric of ideality might appear to elide a crucial difference between them. Judgment, we suppose, is fundamentally a cognitive operation, even when it manifests itself in the form of a judicial decision,[9] whereas action signals our engagement with others and the world. Aristotle taught us that active and contemplative lives favor different virtues, and for Hannah Arendt, perhaps the most consequential thinker of both judgment and action in the twentieth century, this translates into a near-antithesis between the two concepts as they preside over their separate spheres. Action, for her, is future-oriented; it begins something new. The one who acts is the one who initiates, who sets things in motion, though she is not in control of the meaning of her action or its execution.[10] Judgment, by contrast, concerns or, at the very least, is informed by the past; there is always a retrospective dimension to it. Even though Arendt calls judgment "the most political of man's mental abilities,"[11] the one who judges is not the actor but the spectator or the historian.[12] The meaning of an action is determined after the fact, by the judgment of those who witness the event. However, if we have chosen to gather the essays from the Judgment and Action Symposia into a single volume, it is from a conviction that the concepts are deeply imbricated with one another, that it is impossible to think the one without the other. It is not just that judgment is itself a species of action; rather, judgment is quite simply the way that the mind acts in the world *as* mind. Judgment, Kant tells us, "is the faculty for thinking the particular as contained under the universal."[13] It joins together the heterogeneous orders of universal and particular, abstract and concrete, rule and example, mind and world, thought and action, thereby making *considered* action possible. Judgment "is the point at which thought touches on the world."[14] Put differently, action, if it is something more than the reflexive, convulsive, or unconscious movement of a body, is always an act *of* judgment. All action seeks to make a difference (Klinger; McGowan), and the work of creating, producing, or making difference, of differentiating, distinguishing, and discriminating, is precisely the purview of judgment.[15] Judgment and action are also connected by way of the question of ends or purposes, which themselves become especially problematic within modern theoretical paradigms. Meaningful action is only possible in relation to ends, and judgment is concerned not only with discerning the means to those ends but also, through its evaluative labor, with constituting those ends themselves.

Even though we did not ask contributors to thematize the deep interrelationship between judgment and action, a number of the essays spontaneously articulate some of the relays between the concepts, because it is almost impossible to speak in a sustained way of one without the other. It is perhaps not surprising that Klinger's pragmatist reconceptualization of judgment has recourse to the category of action; for him, judgment is "the basic act of making a difference," so that one cannot begin to think judgment except as a form of action. Klinger argues that Richter's painting makes the act central to both the production of form and the enactment of judgment: "The critical strategic move by which Richter achieves this suspension [of aesthetic principles] is his choice of the *act* as the relevant unit of the painterly process—the *single distinction* and difference, judgment at its most basic or, as Richter mostly says, *form*." O'Donovan's essay is concerned to track the "inward migration" of judgment, from what he believes is its primary sense, as the judicial decision of a public official. In his view, judgment refers to the public action of passing sentence before it refers to a particular kind of cognitive operation. Once again, the sense of judgment as public and indeed political action rather than simply inward cognitive resolution comes to the fore; he even refers to judgment as a kind of performance and highlights its prospective rather than merely retrospective dimensions. Menke, too, argues that "judgments have a performative force," explaining that "judgment constitutes *actions*: actions are consequences of judgments—to act means to implement a judgment." In Soni's reading of Shaftesbury, judgment is essential to the process of constituting the ends that guide action. But perhaps the most important way in which judgment is an action in its own right, rather than simply being the precursor to an action, is through its production and acknowledgment of community. Judgment, as several of the essays point out, is unusual in that it is not content with simply being a solitary mental operation; judgments solicit the engagement and even the agreement of others; their very enactment is generative of community (see Menke; Klinger; Nazar; Zerilli). A judgment cannot but act in and on the world; it is not a solipsistic mental activity; this is part of what distinguishes it as judgment.

Most of the essays on action also highlight that concept's reliance on judgment, and all of the essays draw attention to the ideality of action. Sarah Beckwith describes how Macbeth "tutor[s] himself in the denial of his own agency" by seeking "to eradicate thought altogether" and "removing any possibility of judgment and understanding from [Lady Macbeth's] ability to discern his action." For Stanley Hauerwas, "our character constitutes our agency," and "character suggest[s] the kind of person we must be to be a person of wise judgment." Likewise, Reydams-Schils, in order to make the case for the value of Stoicism's account of action, discovers in the Stoics "the notion of a mediating self," whose "primary function is to allow a human being . . . to weigh traditional value judgments against the radical transformation of these in Stoic ethics. . . .This self constitutes the mental space in which . . . one can check one's reactions and test one's impressions." And although John McGowan's essay is interested in conceptualizing collective action, he begins with William James, for whom "the self is the source of action" and "selves undertake actions that are meaningful to them, that link up to their judgment of what is desirable." The self's judgment, however, is not undertaken in isolation from others, but is "complexly related to what others judge to be meaningful or valuable." In short, these essays all suggest that no discussion of action could get off the ground without the space of ideality or noumenality that is constituted by the self (Pfau). Indeed, Hauerwas, McGowan, and Pfau all endorse MacIntyre's claim that the concept of intelligible action is more basic than that of action itself, and the idea that judgment and action both require the giving of reasons runs through many of the essays. Nowhere is the ideality of action more apparent than in the essays by Pfau and Beckwith, where action itself takes an especially contemplative and ideational form that proves transformative of the agent, be it as an act of visual attention (Pfau) or as one of remorse and forgiveness (Beckwith). If remorse and visual attention are not marginal cases but somehow paradigmatic forms of acting, as these essays suggest, then it is no wonder that for a modernity in which these states of ideation are merely fleeting ticks on a neural scan, it is so difficult to conceptualize action. As Pfau explains:

> Hence it cannot surprise that the concept of "attention" should no longer engage modern and, especially, contemporary philosophy. . . . What kind of "evidence," after all, could there ever be that someone is properly "attending" to something or someone, other than her verbal assurances that she is doing so? . . . For the modern skeptic, the first order of business thus becomes disentangling something as specious as inner states, such as attention, from the propositional language employed by individuals *claiming* to inhabit some such state. . . . Naturally, once inner states are deemed to lack objective, measurable criteria for their verification, it is but a small step to deny them any reality and legitimacy as topics for philosophical inquiry.

To the extent that action, as distinct from either motion or behavior, is dependent on its relation to such inner states, its legitimacy as a concept is also threatened, if not simply declared null and void, as any number of contemporary theoretical paradigms attest.

The idealism or ideality of judgment and action: the moment we acknowledge it, we can hear the objections like the voice of conscience. Decades of hermeneutic suspicion have trained us to ferret out and disavow idealism at every turn. Yet such an approach often reflects more an ethos of compliance with disciplinary and methodological imperatives than that which arises as a considered judgment about given phenomena or issues. However, it would be foolish to make light of the critiques of idealism. If the ideality of judgment and action requires taking into account an individual's deliberations, intentions, motivations, purposes, resolutions, then perhaps the greatest danger is that, Quixote-like, these become utterly divorced from the world in which they mean to intervene, forming a self-satisfied, self-confirming, self-referential circle of ideas that have no effects (or none of the expected effects) on any situation, and no relevance to the deliberations, intentions, and purposes of others. This view of judgment and action threatens to be solipsistic and self-certifying, thus leaving the individual trapped in a cocoon of his or her ideations. The world of ideas appears curiously frictionless, seeming to require no effort to invent and reinvent, while the world of judgment and action *resists* us at every turn, foiling our best-laid schemes, disappointing our hopes, and making a mockery of our attempts to impose our will on it. It is hard to avoid the tendency to overvalue the individual's cognitive capacities and what can be achieved through them, to imagine that we have greater control over others' wills and the outcome of our deeds than we do. We easily forget that ideas can be conditioned by historical circumstance, wanting rather to claim them as our own. The appropriative impulse and fantasy of control sometimes implicit in idealism, the desire to make the world over in the image of one's mind, has even led to accusations of totalitarianism. But the litany of idealism's pernicious delusions hardly ends there. The self that has become an atomized subject, cut off from the world and wrenched free of the communities that sustain its flourishing, is not only unable to comprehend the normative force of its judgments and actions, but also risks becoming disconnected from that which is closest to it: its body, its desires, its affections, the unconscious or noncognitive forces operative within it. It can overestimate the powers of reason, or violently seek to impose its own version of reason on the world and even on itself. In short, its Olympian or Promethean attitude might entail an antitragic stance, a refusal to acknowledge the limits of the human, as it takes flight into its unreal realm of ideas. For all these reasons, and no doubt a number of others, idealism has been not just an aberration to avoid, but a dangerous and destructive illusion to be combated at every turn. In keeping with the spirit of the times, our theoretical impulses have been anti-idealist to the core.

The hazards of idealism I have outlined above are real, and I do not mean to diminish or dismiss them by caricature. We must always remain vigilant against them. But the reader will not find them reflected in this collection of essays. On the contrary, most of the essays in this volume are explicitly concerned to develop accounts of judgment and action that can respond to such concerns and ward off these very kinds of objections. One of the strengths of the essays assembled here is that each develops the concepts of judgment or action in ways that do not leave them vulnerable to the critiques leveled at a naive idealism, even as they remain committed to the effective force of ideas. Indeed, given how hard these essays labor to stave off such criticisms, and how much this effort constitutes something of a unifying theme for our volume, it is worth dwelling at some length on the different forms that their resistance takes. Perhaps most directly, a number of the essays acknowledge the force of the noncognitive or the nonpropositional and seek to understand how judgment and action must take account of their interplay with cognitive factors.[16] Thus what draws Thomas Pfau to the image is that it promises "a nonpropositional form of knowledge" found "in a moment of incontrovertible presence": "On this model, action is an integral part of a narrative movement that begins with the apprehension of a conceptually inexhaustible fullness (*pleroma*) such as gives itself in images." In a similar vein, Menke insists that "the aesthetic reconception of judgment consists in understanding the *act* of judging in aesthetic matters as being itself an aesthetic—a 'dark,' 'unconscious'—doing." His essay situates itself in the aporia between conceiving judgment as force and the giving of reasons, demanding that we never reduce or elide this aporia. "Sensation, passion, pathos" must have their due. We have already seen that for Klinger, judgment is form, but in his account, form is prior to ideas: "Ideas can be triggered by form, but form cannot in turn be founded through ideas." And Zerilli turns to Arendt's interpretation of Kantian aesthetic judgments precisely in order to find an alternative to both the highly cognitivist version of judgment found in neo-Kantian political theorists and the radically noncognitivist view of judgment found in affect theorists. Whether or not these essays succeed in negotiating the tension between ideality and nonideality, then, it would be a mistake to think that there was a frictionless ideality or idealization at work in them. Rather than reducing or eliminating this tension, each of the essays seeks to inhabit it and to unfold its effects on our thinking of judgment and action.

Although McGowan's and Yeomans's essays are not principally concerned with the noncognitive dimensions of action, both take it upon themselves to navigate a similar tension between competing, even incompatible accounts of action, namely first-person, subjectivizing, and idealizing accounts of action—which emphasize purpose, intention, and meaning—and those that are undertaken from a third-person perspective. Instead of privileging the idealizing account over the nonidealizing or vice versa, both essays argue for a fundamentally pluralist view of action that would preserve both kinds of accounts, even though they are incompatible, in a "stereoscopic vision" (Yeomans). Yeomans does so by seeking a Hegelian synthesis of Hannah Arendt's and Robert Kane's theories of action, while McGowan attempts to give an intersubjective account, rather than a purely subjective (William James) or objective (Austin and Searle) one, by way of Wittgenstein. Nazar's literary reading of the problem of judgment in Rousseau and Adam Smith, while on the face of it quite different from Yeomans or McGowan, offers a strikingly similar result. Rousseau serves as a lesson in the dangers of an overly idealizing account of judgment, whereas Smith shows how we are constituted as moral agents through the eyes of others while nevertheless being able to achieve an autonomy of judgment through this process. If the buffered, self-enclosed, or disembedded self is one of the problems of an idealizing account of action, it would seem that the Stoic self could serve as its paradigmatic instance. Reydams-Schils, building on the rich body of recent scholarship on Stoicism, undertakes to show that the Stoic self is an "extended" rather than a buffered self, "in which the distinction between self and others becomes blurred." "The Stoic notion of self does not come with a radical sense of individuality or subjectivity." A combination of four factors shapes each individual's identity, including both cognitive and noncognitive elements. In particular, the "good emotions (*eupatheiai*)" have a more significant role in Stoic conceptions of responsibility than is usually acknowledged. The ideality of action and judgment, then, need not imply a self so wrapped up in its own ideas as to be oblivious to the social world that partially constitutes it.

The danger of overrating the self and its capacities for action is the topic of the essays by Beckwith and Hauerwas, as well as of Wetzel's response to Hauerwas. We have seen that, for Beckwith, the disavowal of thought is Macbeth's way of disowning responsibility for his actions. But paradoxically, one form that this disavowal takes is imagining that the *will*, unchecked by reason, is more powerful than it is. Action under such conditions is not just unthinking but criminal: "The refusal of remorse may well involve a vast overestimation of the role of the will. Macbeth shows us that picture of the will as murderous." The mistake is to imagine that we control the consequences of our actions. Rather, "we are the deed's creature. What Macbeth is blinding himself to is the shaping role of the agent's deeds in forming, in building a character." Ultimately, then, "vision, not choice, is a central dimension of moral agency." Hauerwas, too, in his exploration of the differences between Eichmann and Bonhoeffer, wants to "focus on character [rather than] discrete decisions." Bonhoeffer's reading of the Psalms teaches him "that he cannot be sure . . . whether he is wholly in his acts." Even though Hauerwas insists, following MacIntyre, that "the basic concept is not action, but intelligible action," there are nevertheless limits on that intelligibility: "But if we are not wholly present in our acts does that mean our very attempt to give narrative coherence to our lives may be an invitation to self-deception?" The ethical self that Hauerwas imagines is a chastened self, its inwardness liturgical rather than introspective. But for Wetzel, in his response to Hauerwas, this chastened self is not chastened enough, and Hauerwas's focus on narrative and the intelligibility of action fails to concede fully the unintelligibility of Christian redemption. O'Donovan's essay narrates the interiorization and idealization of judgment. While judgment remained purely public, determining and discriminating, it threatened an "overjuridicalization of society," but it acquires a certain legitimacy as it becomes more reflective: "The judgment that occurs in the mind . . . is without offense." But this interiorization of judgment is not an invitation to judge without restraint. Like Menke, O'Donovan argues that judgment, while inevitable, should be undertaken reluctantly, and, like Beckwith in her account of tragic action, he believes that there is something tragic in the need to judge when we would rather continue inquiring. The realm of ideality is not immune from the tragic constraints of finitude. With Soni's essay, we return strengthened to the ideality of the self, without surrendering any of the insights gleaned about its limitations. Soni reads Shaftesbury's "Soliloquy" as a response to Locke's account of action, in which our doings are simply the promptings of our desires or "uneasiness," with almost no room for deliberation and judgment. However, Locke does acknowledge the power of "hesitation," which Shaftesbury then develops into the rich, interior, and dramatic space of soliloquy that Soni's essay explores. Although soliloquy perhaps risks enclosing the self in its own cognitive processes, Shaftesbury guards against this in a number of ways. A dramatic soliloquy, even if it is a conversation with oneself, always has another (or oneself as another) as its addressee. In fact, in Shaftesbury's account, there is no self to speak of before the practice of soliloquy. The self is only constituted as self and only acquires a will through its dialogue with itself in soliloquy. If, as Beckwith argues, a naked will divorced from reason is murderous, Shaftesbury's "Soliloquy" is a study of the process by which we give ourselves reasons, reasons that are more than simply Reason as a calculative or computational faculty, but substantive reasons that are the grounds, ends, and purposes we must fiction for our actions. Like Pfau and Beckwith, for whom vision is inseparable from agency, Soni insists that judgment is impossible without imagining and fictioning ends for oneself. O'Donovan warns that there is a tragic aspect to any judgment, but to refuse to fiction the ends that enable judgment, Soni argues, can only result in indecision and inaction, the tragic consequences of which are on display in *Hamlet*.[17]

We hope that this collection of essays will suggest the urgency and immensity of the task that confronts us if we are to seek alternatives beyond the powerful conceptual legacy of modernity. At a time when even the humanities feel the allure of modern methodological imperatives whose reductionist logic tends to erode our conceptual resources, we ought to remind ourselves that one of the distinguishing characteristics of humanistic scholarship is the hermeneutic labor that allows us to reactivate and reexperience the conceptual intricacy of worlds not our own, and to recognize their persistent critical relevance to our present. The essays in this volume provide various historical and conceptual starting points for undertaking this work with the ideas of judgment and action. Yet at the same time, none of the essays is oblivious to the lessons to be learned from modern critical methodologies and from the many poignant critiques leveled against idealism. Cumulatively, the work presented in this volume encourages us to reengage with the history of ideas as an integral feature of humanistic inquiry, though without thereby succumbing to the pitfalls of a naive idealism. However, it will be apparent from reading these essays that the task is barely begun. Each of the concepts explored here is tied to innumerable others, and the fact that it is difficult to address any one in isolation further attests to their intrinsic fecundity. Since the Symposia on Judgment and Action, a subsequent symposium has taken place at Northwestern on the concept of beauty, and similar work is ongoing in a number of other quarters as well.[18] This collection of essays, then, is one contribution to what will have to be a sustained, comprehensive, and collective effort to dislodge the stranglehold of modern conceptual paradigms.

Notes

The editors wish to thank Jessica Hines for her meticulous proofreading of this volume and Steven Moore for preparing a detailed and thorough index.

1. Menke did not participate in the symposia, but his essay was solicited by the editors after he gave a talk at Northwestern on the topic of aesthetic judgment. Wetzel's essay was a response to Hauerwas's talk at the Action Symposium and is included here for the clarity and force of its intervention.

2. On these questions, see, among others, Thomas Pfau, *Minding the Modern: Human Agency, Intellectual Traditions, and Responsible Knowledge* (Notre Dame, Ind.: University of Notre Dame Press, 2013); Vivasvan Soni, *Mourning Happiness: Narrative and the Politics of Modernity* (Ithaca, N.Y.: Cornell University Press, 2010); Vivasvan Soni, "Energy," in *Fueling Culture: 101 Words for Energy and Environment*, ed. Imre Szeman, Jennifer Wenzel, and Patricia Yaeger (New York: Fordham University Press, 2017); Vivasvan Soni, "Introduction: The Crisis of Judgment," *Eighteenth Century: Theory and Interpretation* 51, no. 3 (2010): 261–88; Hannah Arendt, *The Human Condition* (Chicago: University of Chicago Press, 1958); Alasdair C. MacIntyre, *After Virtue: A Study in Moral Theory*, 2nd ed. (Notre Dame, Ind.: University of Notre Dame Press, 1984); Hans-Georg Gadamer, *Truth and Method*, translation rev. Joel Weinsheimer and Donald G. Marshall, 2nd rev. ed. (New York: Crossroad, 1989); Max Horkheimer, *Eclipse of Reason* (New York: Oxford University Press, 1947); Martin Heidegger, *Parmenides*, trans. André Schuwer and Richard Rojcewicz (Bloomington: Indiana University Press, 1992); G. E. M. Anscombe, "Modern Moral Philosophy," *Philosophy* 33, no. 124 (1958): 1–19; Cora Diamond, "Losing Your Concepts," *Ethics* 98, no. 2 (1988): 255–77; Iris Murdoch, *The Sovereignty of Good* (London: Routledge, 1971).

3. For a thoroughgoing critique of the contextualist premise that has dominated recent intellectual history, see Peter Gordon, "Contextualism and Criticism in the History of Ideas," in *Rethinking Modern European Intellectual History*, ed. Darrin M. McMahon and Samuel Moyn (Oxford: Oxford University Press, 2014).

4. Soni, "Introduction."

5. However, it should be noted that the themes of interiority, subjectivity, and contemplation recur throughout this volume. In addition to the essays by Soni, O'Donovan, and Reydams-Schils, see especially those by Beckwith, Nazar, and Pfau.

6. One should also recall here Weber's claim that *The Protestant Ethic and the Spirit of Capitalism* is "a contribution to the understanding of the manner in which ideas become effective forces in history." See Max Weber, *The Protestant Ethic and the Spirit of Capitalism*, trans. Talcott Parsons (New York: Charles Scribner's Sons, 1976), 90.

7. See especially Pfau, *Minding the Modern*; Soni, "Introduction"; Arendt, *Human Condition*.

8. MacIntyre, *After Virtue*, 208–9.

9. However, O'Donovan's essay in this collection reverses this assumption, arguing that the public, judicial sense of judgment is prior to the cognitive one.

10. Arendt, *Human Condition*, 9, 177–78.

11. Hannah Arendt, "Thinking and Moral Considerations," in *Responsibility and Judgment*, ed. Jerome Kohn (New York: Schocken, 2003), 188.

12. Hannah Arendt, *Lectures on Kant's Political Philosophy*, ed. Ronald Beiner (Chicago: University of Chicago Press, 1982), 3–5, 15, 45–47, 51–55, 59–63.

13. Immanuel Kant, *Critique of the Power of Judgment*, ed. Paul Guyer, trans. Paul Guyer and Eric Matthews (Cambridge: Cambridge University Press, 2000), 5:179.

14. Soni, "Introduction," 275.

15. John Locke, *An Essay concerning Human Understanding*, ed. Roger Woolhouse (London: Penguin, 2004), 153.

16. Though I group them together in my discussion here, the noncognitive and nonpropositional are by no means identical, and there are important differences among authors in this collection about the relative weight we should accord to each. I do not mean to obscure these differences, and urge the reader to remain alert to them.

17. For a reading of *Hamlet* in relation to the problem of judgment, see Vivasvan Soni, "Believing in Ghosts, in Part: Judgment and Indecision in *Hamlet*," in *Shakespeare and Judgment*, ed. Kevin Curran (Edinburgh: Edinburgh University Press, 2017).

18. The essays from the Beauty Symposium are collected in a special issue of *Republics of Letters*, http://arcade.stanford.edu/rofl_issue/volume-5-issue-1-0. In addition to the participants in these and future symposia, and those mentioned in note 2 above, two recent manifestos of intellectual history, one in a more Benjaminian vein and the other inspired by Arendt, argue in their different ways for a more normative and philosophically inclined approach to intellectual history. See Gordon, "Contextualism," and Sophia Rosenfeld, "On Lying: Writing Philosophical History after the Enlightenment and after Arendt," in *The Worlds of American Intellectual History*, ed. Joel Isaac et al. (Oxford: Oxford University Press, 2016).

Part I

✦

Interiority/Contemplation

Interiority and the capacity for contemplation have often been implicated in the paralysis of judgment and action. The conventional readings of three iconic texts from the early modern period suggest that a rich, deliberative inner life, rather than fostering judgment and action, creates labyrinths of the mind detached from the world, in which we risk losing ourselves forever. As Hamlet struggles with himself in soliloquy after soliloquy to resolve upon revenge, he worries that the "native hue of resolution / Is sicklied o'er with the pale cast of thought . . . los[ing] the name of action." The hyperactive imagination of Don Quixote, overstimulated by solitary reading of romances, leads him to hilariously aberrant judgments and actions. And Descartes's retreat into interiority makes the world shimmer like a mirage and forces him to question his judgment that other people exist. From Byron's *Manfred* and Coleridge's reading of *Hamlet*, to Carl Schmitt's indictment of deliberative democracy and his diagnosis of "political romanticism," this tradition of interpretation has endured. Nothing could be easier than to blame the crisis of judgment and action on interiority and contemplation.

Soni's essay argues that Shaftesbury's "Soliloquy" is one of the first in the early modern period to make the opposite case, namely that interiority, contemplation, and deliberation—the ability to talk to oneself—are essential for forming resolutions and acting on them, for being able to think and act in nonmechanical ways. Recognizing that the capacity for judgment is imperiled by Locke's model of the mind in the *Essay concerning Human Understanding*, Shaftesbury finds in Locke's discussion of hesitation an opening to establish a place for judgment, which he develops into the practice of soliloquy. Soliloquy reveals the remarkable fact that natural language opens a space of transcendence necessary for judgment.

Grappling with the biblical injunction against judgment ("Judge not lest ye be judged") and the tragic recognition that judgment is inevitable, O'Donovan argues that the target of the biblical prohibition is the political and juridical sense of judgment, which is primary. However, adhering to Aquinas's commentary, he tracks an inward migration of the term in Greek antiquity: "As the act of judgment migrates to the inner world of private thought, then, it brings with it something of its original public ambience; the life of the mind comes to be conceived as a *forum internum*, an 'inner courtroom.'" For O'Donovan, the inward migration of judgment serves as a restraint on it, and it is only within the mind that the right to judge can be defended: "The judgment that occurs in the mind, as it is essentially reflective, is without offense." Not unlike with Shaftesbury, the deliberative and dialogic practice of prayer becomes the ideal site for judgment.

Reydams-Schils's essay asks what we can learn from Stoic conceptions of agency. She finds, similarly, that the Stoic self "constitutes [a] mental space" that can mediate between itself and the world. Such mediation is required for judgment and action. But the mental space of the Stoic self is not radically autonomous, sheltered from the world and other people, as has often been thought; it does not constitute a "buffered self" in Charles Taylor's sense of the term. "The self in Stoicism sees human beings as essentially embedded in the reality surrounding them." Moreover, "the Stoic notion of self does not come with a radical sense of individuality or subjectivity." Rather, it "relies on the notion of an *extended* self in which the distinction between self and others becomes blurred." Reydams-Schils thus prepares the way for the next group of essays, in which an ethical perspective challenges the notion of a punctual self as a plausible foundation for meaningful and robust conceptions of judgment and action.

How to Hit Pause

Language, Transcendence, and the Capacity for Judgment in Shaftesbury's "Soliloquy; or, Advice to an Author"

Vivasvan Soni

> Nothing is so improving, nothing so natural, so *con-genial* to the liberal Arts, as that reigning Liberty and high Spirit of a People, which from the Habit of judging in the highest Matters for themselves, makes 'em freely judg of other Subjects.
>
> —Shaftesbury, "A Letter concerning the Art, or Science of Design"

Soliloquy is a dignified art. Arriving on the scene at times "of great pitch and moment," it pauses the headlong and nearly irresistible flow of dramatic action, allowing the protagonist a chance to muse, reflect, and resolve. Unlike its counterpart in science fiction films, in which time and motion are temporarily frozen as though we had hit pause on the DVD player while the protagonist mutely seeks to alter the course of physical motion in progress, soliloquy achieves its hiatus not through some unexplained technological ingenuity but rather through the simple capacity I have to engage myself in conversation: I pause by speaking. In watching a soliloquy, we are witness to a mind capable of going to work in the world, of intervening reflectively in it, not one that is simply victimized by it or reflexively reacting to it. It is not by accident that Shakespearean drama rises to its philosophical heights at moments of soliloquy, whether it be Hamlet wrestling with the most basic of existential questions or Edmund questioning the arbitrariness of social conventions ("Why bastard?"). Yet soliloquy is also the most palpably artificial of drama's artifices. A theatrical soliloquy is never quite a soliloquy, one alone speaking to herself; the spectators are the addressees of the speech. In the world beyond the theater, where is soliloquizing to be found? Who among us would admit to the practice, much less engage in it in public as theatrical protagonists do? If I see someone talking to themselves on the street, I assume they're talking on a cellphone, else I would worry about their mental health. Prayer is perhaps the everyday practice that comes closest to a form of soliloquizing, but it removes the taint of talking to myself by having a presumed addressee. There is something at once banal, grandiose, and unnerving in the practice of soliloquizing. Yet it is precisely in this peculiar practice that Shaftesbury means to locate a robust and primordial capacity for judgment, against empiricism's threat to render judgment obsolete. What is so remarkable about the ability to talk to myself "vivâ voce" (as Shaftesbury puts it), that it can serve as the practice which will attest to our capacity for judgment? After a brief detour through empiricism, in order to explain why judgment cannot be adequately theorized in that discourse, I will try to discern why Shaftesbury discovers so much promise in soliloquy as a locus for countering the crisis of judgment generated by empiricism.

The great virtue of empiricism is that it insists on explaining phenomena according to the logic of efficient causation. However, such explanations allow no place for judgment, and taken on their own terms, there is no reason they should. While these explanations are valuable for many purposes—indeed, they comprise the entire realm of scientific inquiry as we know it today—they fail to account adequately for the phenomena of human motivation, as Bacon had already recognized: "It is also not bad to distinguish four causes: Material, Formal, Efficient and Final. But of these the Final is a long way from being useful; in fact it actually distorts the sciences *except in the case of human actions*."[1] In the *Essay concerning Human Understanding*, Locke significantly revises his own account of motivation in chapter 2.21 in order to explain it according to the logic of desire and efficient causation. But he also recognizes that this reductive account of motivation is inadequate for explaining crucial aspects of human behavior. He strives without success to develop a more robust space for the practice of judgment, conceiving it as the experientially evident but unaccountable capacity we have to suspend the prosecution of any and all desires (242).[2] Nevertheless, along the way, his attentive phenomenology compels him to acknowledge that basic aspects of cognition, perception, and willing are impossible without judgment. In the absence of the discriminating and constitutive work of judgment, we would be unable to distinguish ideas from one another (chapter 2.11); unable to perceive three spatial dimensions (chapter 2.9); and, above all, unable to constitute the ends that motivate and guide our actions, thereby turning us into the victims of our own desires (chapter 2.21). Despite this acknowledgment of the indispensability of judgment for cognition, however, Locke recognizes that the anarchic fictioning power of judgment threatens to destabilize the empiricist project itself and, by the end of the *Essay*, he attempts to squeeze judgment to the margins of epistemology, the "twilight zone" of probabilistic knowledge (chapter 4.14). Locke at once created the conditions for a crisis of judgment and provided several openings by which the indispensable role of judgment might be reasserted.[3]

Now, Locke's reductive account of motivation has three separate aspects: the explanation of behavior by desire and efficient causation; the elision of any space for judgment; the refusal to allow agency to ends-oriented thinking. In my story, aesthetic theory, a discourse that is distinctive to the eighteenth century, emerges precisely as a response to the nexus of problems engendered by the reductive account of motivation in empiricism. In particular, some notion of aesthetic disinterest serves as a counter to theories that suggest behavior should be explained only by desire and self-interest (Shaftesbury, Hutcheson, Kant); and the teleological purposiveness of aesthetic categories like the beautiful, the sublime, and the new serve as a surrogate for the self-constitution of ends (Addison and Steele, Hutcheson). However, the elision of the space of judgment goes largely unremedied in this broad discursive formation. Some notion of taste, sensory responsiveness or instinctive aesthetic perception, generally substitutes for the work of judgment.[4] Even Kant, who is more attentive to the operation of judgment than nearly anyone else in the century, still conceives of aesthetic judgment as a suspension of judgment with respect to the object, and Schiller's *Letters on Aesthetic Education* continue rigorously in this tradition of evading judgment that gives birth to modern aesthetics. Perhaps only Shaftesbury, among theorists of the period, offers a rich and viable account of judgment as the key element for responding to empiricism's reductive account of motivation, in his "Soliloquy." Unlike Mandeville, who presses Locke's economistic model of mental functioning to its limit, Shaftesbury inhabits the countercurrents of Locke's thought, emphasizing aestheticizing moments such as wit and hesitation that mitigate the reductive empiricist account of desire and motivation. In this essay, I want to describe the remarkable way in which Shaftesbury asserts the absolute priority of judgment for the constitution of the self and for cognition in general, by way of the practice of soliloquy.[5]

Shaftesbury is acutely aware of the crisis of judgment, and his thinking is formulated more or less directly as a response to it. He focuses his attention on the moral, political, and social dimensions of the crisis, largely ignoring the cognitive, epistemological, and perceptual aspects of the problem prominent in empiricism. Situating himself in the chink through which the possibility of judgment glimmers in chapter 2.21 of Locke's *Essay*—namely the capacity of the mind to hesitate, to suspend any and all desires in order to reflect on them and decide which to act on—Shaftesbury will attempt, in "Soliloquy," to pry open this space, to develop on its foundation a robust account of how and why the practice of judgment is necessary in the moral life.[6] His method of soliloquy provides a model for how to cultivate a mental discipline of judgment (though perhaps running the risk of the solipsism and self-reflexivity of the *cogito*). In addition, Shaftesbury offers a fuller analysis of the crisis in his historico-political excurses, and he invents a number of other solutions to the problems generated by the crisis of judgment, solutions that will play an important role throughout the eighteenth century. For example, in "Sensus Communis" he attempts to find an objective, social replacement for the cognitive work of judgment by way of a dialectical, agonistic, market-based social theory that is typical of the later part of the century. He is also one of the earliest to enlist the assistance of the aesthetic, especially beauty, as a way of responding to empiricism's reductive account of motivation. Toward the end of this essay, I will turn briefly to Shaftesbury's aesthetics to show why beauty is an inadequate solution to the crisis of judgment, but for most of the essay, I want to focus on his complex account of soliloquy as a foundation for the practice of judgment.

Locke had located the possibility of judgment in our capacity to hesitate, our ability to suspend any and all desires in order to reflect on them:

> We have a power to *suspend* the prosecution of this or that desire, as everyone daily may experiment with himself. This seems to me the source of all liberty. . . . During this *suspension* of any desire, before the *will* be determined to action, and the action (which follows that determination) done, we have opportunity to examine, view, and judge, of the good or evil of what we are going to do. (*Essay*, 242; see also 254)

But is it possible to hesitate? How would we do it? How would we know a hesitation if we saw it? If you have an economic model of the psyche, in which desires collide with one another until the force of one comes to dominate the others, then the notion of hesitation makes no sense. It is the one thing that is impossible, because it implies a temporary cessation of the system itself. The system of desires moves as one; the self is seamlessly integrated with its world, both material and social.[7] Being itself is an undifferentiated unity of happening and force, in which the very notion of a differentiation of waves, fluxes, intensities is simply a convenient heuristic we impose to find sense where there is none. Even if we think we detect a pause or interruption in the system, it is simply conditioned by the state of the flux at a given moment. There may be pauses or cessations of motion produced by the movement of the system, but the system itself cannot be paused in its ineluctable flow. An equilibrium of forces is not a hesitation; it is simply the state of the system at a given point in time. It would be improper to speak of hesitation, a deliberate pause in order to reflect on and possibly even change the state of the system. On this reading, the notion of hesitation is elusive at best, the ghost in the machine or a vestige of humanist nostalgia lingering in Locke's empiricism.

But this economic model is only one model of the mind, which the mind gives to itself to account for its own functioning. In "Soliloquy," Shaftesbury offers us a different model—one that I will call "theatrical" for reasons that will quickly become apparent[8]—a model in which hesitation is possible and takes on a material and visible form rather than being the abstract, fleeting, elusive, and nearly unidentifiable hiatus of the mind that it was for Locke. For Shaftesbury, the possibility for hesitation and judgment begins with *division*, because as long as the self is one with itself and its world, it is impossible to even conceive what hesitation might mean.[9] I must be divided from myself at the very outset, not in order to produce a space of "disinterest" or "critical distance" (terms too dignified for this fundamental and archaic process), but in order simply that there might be some vantage from which it is possible to pause the machine, in order that something like hesitation and judgment might be possible at all. The division here is not between an already constituted self or subject and a world it transcends. It is a division that takes place *within* the "self" that is as yet indistinguishable from the world it inhabits:[10]

> I assert the contrary; and say, for instance, That we have each of us Our Selves to practise on. "Mere Quibble! (you'll say:) For who can thus multiply himself into two Persons, and be his own Subject? Who can properly laugh at himself, or find in his heart to be either merry or severe on such an occasion?" Go to the Poets, and they will present you with many Instances. Nothing is more common with them, than this sort of Soliloquy. A Person of profound Parts, or perhaps of ordinary Capacity, happens, on some occasion, to commit a Fault. He is concern'd for it. He comes alone upon the Stage; looks about him, to see if any body be near; then takes himself to task, without sparing himself in the least. You wou'd wonder to hear how close he pushes matters, and how thorowly he carrys on the business of Self-dissection. By virtue of this Soliloquy he becomes two distinct Persons. (1.99–100)[11]

Shaftesbury talks as though the self already exists and then divides itself in two. But properly speaking, there is no self yet. Depending on how you look at it, there is only undifferentiated Being,[12] or the self completely immersed in the frivolous and witty chatter of its social world,[13] or an inchoate morass of desire that has not even achieved articulacy:[14] "One wou'd think, there was nothing easier for us, than to know our own Minds, and understand what our main Scope was; . . . But our Thoughts have generally such an obscure implicit Language, that 'tis the hardest thing in the world to make 'em speak out distinctly. For this reason, the right Method is to give 'em Voice and Accent" (1.107). It requires work to introduce the slightest gap or differentiation into the seamlessness of being, social-being or desiring-being, in order to make hesitation possible. Shaftesbury's profoundest insight is that this work is fictive work or the work of fictioning ("Go to the Poets . . ."). If fictioning or *poiein* signify making, then the most fundamental making is this dividing into two (not of myself, since there is no self there yet), this making-two where there was only one before.[15] Only through this act of fiction or division can any kind of interruption or difference be introduced into the unity of being,[16] can anything like a "self" separate itself out from the world.[17] It may sound as though Shaftesbury is invoking the concepts of "consciousness" and "self-reflection" here. He is certainly moving in their vicinity, and even invokes the metaphor of a "vocal Looking-Glass" to describe the act of soliloquy (1.108).[18] But he means nothing so metaphysically freighted; he has in mind the very mundane observation that "I" have the ability to engage "myself" in conversation, not just in my head, but out loud *as though I were talking to someone else*: "We might peradventure be less noisy and more profitable in Company, if at convenient times we discharg'd some of our articulate Sound, and spoke to ourselves vivâ voce when alone" (1.100). Shaftesbury recognizes that there is something awkward and even a little uncanny about this practice, because it forces us to acknowledge that we are not quite ourselves when we engage in it, that we are only in the process of becoming selves, but that is perhaps why this discipline of talking to ourselves is necessary. In this ability to pause and engage ourselves in conversation, *to pause by engaging ourselves in conversation*, Shaftesbury wants to locate the concrete materiality of hesitation that forms the space of judgment in Locke.

In order to demonstrate the possibility of soliloquy and self-division, Shaftesbury turns to the fictions of dramatic "Poets," who exemplify the practice in its most robust and fully articulated form. The scene he describes is one in which the protagonist reflects on a deed already done, takes responsibility for it after the fact, and experiences remorse. Soliloquy is effectively a bodying forth of conscience.[19] But in this retrospective evaluation, it would be difficult to speak of a hesitation, only a desire to retract the deed and wish it otherwise. However, there is a protagonist famed for hesitating upon the point of action, whose name has become nearly a byword for the practice of soliloquy, and he haunts this essay throughout: Hamlet.[20] When Hamlet asks himself whether "to be or not to be," it is not a question of remorse but of resolve, a question of what course of action to determine on, or even *the* existential question about whether it is worth being at all. As Shaftesbury's later discussion of how we should organize our desires makes clear, at the heart of this essay is a meditation not merely on questions of conscience, remorse, and retrospective judgment, but on questions of how we resolve to act and how we make judgments that determine us to act.[21] Only judgments concerning a future course of action allow us to appreciate the extent to which fictioning is an integral part of the work of judgment.

The fictioning necessary to enable judgment is clearly visible in Hamlet's famous soliloquy. Without it, Hamlet would undoubtedly kill himself: "'Tis a consummation / Devoutly to be wished" (*Hamlet*, 3.1.64–65).[22] But something stops him. Only by imagining things about which he could never possibly have any knowledge, things that remain firmly ensconced in the realm of fiction, does the space of the "perchance" and the possibility of other decisions open up, the sense that things might be otherwise which is the condition of every judgment:[23] "Who would fardels bear, / . . . / *But that the dread* of something after death, / The undiscovered country, from whose bourn / No traveler returns, puzzles the will" (3.1.77–81, my emphasis). Even the finality of death threatens to dissolve under the strain of Hamlet's metaphorical associations, as its brute facticity begins to morph and mutate into a second life, animated by the fictioning power of the imagination: "To die, to sleep, / To sleep, perchance to dream—ay, there's the rub" (3.1.65–66). The fact of death remains unaltered, but its meaning and how we act in relation to it changes profoundly through his imaginative reframing: Hamlet's choice of life over death is based on a metaphorical recasting ("to die . . . to sleep . . . to dream") which is the enabling condition of his judgment.[24] His decision "to be" rather than "not to be" is only possible through the fictive capacity of dreams and imagination, the metaphorical connection that links death to sleep to dreams. Indeed, for Hamlet, the ability to hesitate, and hence to judge, comes from imagining the dreams that might haunt the sleep of death: "For in that sleep of death what dreams may come / When we have shuffled off this mortal coil / Must give us *pause*" (3.1.67–69, my emphasis). We acquire the ability to hesitate—to pause, reflect, and determine through judgment a course of action—when we imagine that we dream.[25]

Hamlet's lofty existential question is not the only one that calls out for the practice of soliloquy and judgment. We could similarly engage ourselves in conversation about the most quotidian of decisions. To take one crude example, suppose I am at a restaurant with a group of friends and someone at the table orders a basket of french fries. How do I decide whether to eat them or not? I might have arrived at the restaurant so hungry that I am impelled to eat them. Perhaps it is simply a Lockean unease that moves me. This is always a possibility and can never be excluded from consideration. Or I might be so absorbed in conversation that I reach out and begin to eat them unthinkingly, for reasons too inchoate to specify: the pleasure of the taste I anticipate, social habit, a mild hunger, simple reflex, mimicry of others' behavior. In all these cases, I am moved; I am one with my world, and it would be improper to speak of a *judgment* taking place. Only when I pause and engage myself in soliloquy—not when I simply act out of desire, habit, or reflex—am I authorized to speak of judgment in the fullest sense. Only then am I free; only then do I act freely. I can imagine innumerable conversations I might have with myself in this situation. I have heard how good the chef at this restaurant is, and I wonder if the french fries here are noticeably better than those I've eaten at other places. I don't like french fries, but I'm hungry and have several meetings after this one, so I'd better eat. I have read somewhere about scientific studies proclaiming the unpleasant things that will happen to you if you eat fried foods regularly, but I don't make a habit of this, so I might try a few. Or I'm not the kind of person who eats french fries, so I'm not going to touch these. Or perhaps, I'm not the kind of person who wants my eating habits to be determined by the latest fads generated by the misinterpretation of scientific research. The variations on reasons I can give myself are endless. You may remember or imagine the conversations you have with yourself in similar situations, conversations that often happen in the blink of an eye.[26]

The situation I am describing is entirely banal, and deliberately so, but there is, all the same, something to be marveled at in the sheer ability I have to engage in conversations of this kind. Even in this mundane example, the conversations I can have with myself about my decision are multifaceted, and they give evidence of some rather remarkable cognitive abilities. Indeed, it requires a good judge to discern the immense work behind what seems effortless, and this is as true of our everyday judgments as it is of the finest works of art (Shaftesbury, *Characteristics*, 1.145). One is tempted to speculate on the biological origins of such abilities, but for our purposes, such speculation is irrelevant.[27] What is important for now is to recognize the many levels at which the ability to imagine, fiction, and narrate are necessary to enable even a relatively trivial form of soliloquizing. First, and most significantly, it requires the ability to divide myself into two, the act by which I imagine myself as separate both from myself and the world. There are not two of me, except through the act by which I imagine that there is someone else there whom I can engage in conversation, someone who can listen to me and judge my reasons. Without this fundamental act of fictioning, Shaftesbury recognizes that there can be no such thing as judgment, self, consciousness, or world. The capacity for soliloquy is a precondition for all of these. Second, in order to engage myself in conversation about different courses of action, I have to imagine that different courses of action are possible, that things can always be otherwise.[28] This is true in the trivial sense that I imagine more than one course of action in order to deliberate about it ("to eat or not to eat"). Otherwise, there would be no soliloquy, nor any occasion for it. But it is also true in more complex and interesting ways. I make assumptions about what will happen if I behave a certain way; I make predictions about being able to manage my future behavior; I imagine what I might be doing tonight or over the next few years. All of these require some relation to futures imagined otherwise, and hence to the capacity for imagining, fictioning, narrating. Third, I tell myself stories about the kind of person I want to be, and imagine how a particular action in the present accords or does not accord with this sense of myself. Thinking of myself as a particular kind of person does not require me to reimagine the future per se, but it does require some work of fictioning to construct such a self. This fiction can then be combined with narratives about different outcomes (the second point), leading to an even more elaborate work of fictioning. Finally, I can give myself ends, goals, or purposes, and then wonder how my actions will assist or undermine those ends.[29] We will discuss this aspect more fully in a moment, since it is central to Shaftesbury's conception of how soliloquy works. There are perhaps even other ways in which fictioning, imagining, and narrating the future otherwise are integral to any judgment I make, but these four already convey some sense of how indispensable fictioning is for soliloquizing and what a multilayered activity it is. It demands cognitive powers of an extraordinary order.

I have described in some detail the practice of soliloquizing Shaftesbury prescribes (and the many forms of fictioning this practice requires), in order to produce and pry open the elusive space of hesitation that Locke had identified as a precondition for a judgment that transcends the mere economy of desire. Through soliloquizing, the transient time of a pause or hesitation acquires concrete form and structure, rather than remaining internal and abstract. But the fictioning practice of soliloquy that makes hesitation and judgment possible is not just a precondition for judgment. For all his polite and antimetaphysical approach to philosophizing, what Shaftesbury describes here is nothing less than a scene of originary judgment, in something like the sense that Hölderlin means it in his essay "Judgment and Being." Judgment is *Ur-teil*, the originary partition that divides being from itself, the self from itself, allowing us to pause and reflect on each; this originary partition is achieved through fiction, the fictive doubling of the self within the self that allows them to then be related to one another. If we recall Locke's distinction between wit and judgment in the *Essay* (153)—the former being the metaphorizing ability to see similarity in difference, the latter being the ability to discern difference in the midst of similarity—then the doubling division produced by soliloquizing fiction is not just the witty precondition for judgment but the judgment that makes all other judgment possible. Where Locke had separated the cognitive powers of wit and judgment, associating the former with a superficial fictionalizing and aestheticizing cognition and the latter with an earnest analytic precision, Shaftesbury's description of the practice of soliloquy allows us to see that the division, distinction, and differentiation of judgment cannot occur without the fictioning of wit. Fiction, metaphor, and narrative do not only synthesize, combine, and construct; they also divide, differentiate, and, indeed, judge. To imagine the world otherwise than it is, as we do in soliloquy, is already to have wrenched ourselves out of the world, to have transcended it in some way, to have constructed something against which we might *compare* it.[30] In short, to engage in the work of fictioning is *already* to have begun the labor of judgment.

Shaftesbury conceals the momentousness of his philosophical intervention here beneath the form of an urbane essay offering advice to an author. Without fanfare, without advertising it as such, he describes the originary scene by which a self comes into being through the fictioning judgment by which it divides itself from itself: "What he endures in this Operation [of soliloquy] is for no inconsiderable End: since 'tis to gain him a Will, and insure him a certain Resolution; by which he shall know where to find himself; be sure of his own Meaning and Design; and as to all his Desires, Opinions, and Inclinations, be warranted one and the same Person to day as yesterday, and to morrow as to day" (1.116). Through this process, the self achieves a certain *transcendence* on its world, a certain freedom from it to be able to both think about the world and act within it. The transcendence achieved here is a "finite" transcendence, a transcendence achieved by purely immanent and intraworldly means; it lies simply in the ability we have to imagine that we are more than one and to imagine other futures. It arises from the capacity of fiction to double, fold, or split the world, to make worlds where there was only one.[31] Is such a thing possible? Can there be transcendence and freedom, or do we just imagine them? This is precisely the problem Kant had attempted to solve, with his distinction between the phenomenal and noumenal worlds. From a purely empiricist or scientific perspective, the guiding assumption is that everything must be accounted for according to the mechanism of efficient causation, including all imaginings, all desiring and willing, all thinking and all decisions. This is simply what it means to do science: to account for phenomena in this way, through the language of mathematics which establishes relations. But the scene of soliloquizing Shaftesbury imagines here is "prior" to any scientific attitude, because it is required both for there to be anything like a world for the sciences to think about and for any ability to think about the world that exceeds the merely computational, that is to say, for action to be possible at all. To be sure, there is a mystery here. It remains to be seen whether and how a scientific perspective might account for such imagining, transcendence, and freedom, or whether indeed it might explain them away. But the phenomenological experience of soliloquizing transcendence that Shaftesbury describes, and our experience of it *as transcendence*, is undeniable. The mysterious and all but inaccessible noumenal world that Kant theorizes is, in Shaftesbury's account, made "manifest" every time we engage in the reason-giving and fictioning judgment that is the essence of all soliloquy. It is the precondition of any thinking intervention in the world. If the ability to soliloquize is not born of freedom (which is to say there is no soliloquy, only the semblance or appearance of it), but is conditioned by the mechanism of the world of which I am simply a part, then it is still the case that nearly every aspect of my conscious cognition functions through the delusions it gives itself about its ability to hesitate, to engage itself in conversation, and to act in the world.

Convalescing in Naples toward the end of his life, Shaftesbury commissioned a painting by Paolo de Matteis called *The Judgment of Hercules*.[32] The painting is effectively a representation of the very practice of soliloquy that Shaftesbury describes in his essay. In it, Hercules stands pensively, poised between Virtue and Pleasure, as each tries to persuade him to follow her example. In his description of the painting in the *Characteristics*, Shaftesbury asks us to think of the scene as Hercules's dream, confirming that this is an act of self-division analogous to that found in soliloquy (3.231). The painting thus depicts Hercules at the moment that he has divided himself into three, already an act of judgment as we have seen, that will demand a second act of judgment to choose between the competing claims of virtue and pleasure. Hercules turns toward Virtue, who holds his attention with animated discourse, but his body leans over toward a supine Pleasure supplicating him with her ignored gaze.

Is hesitation visible in the painting? Can it take phenomenal form? Nothing is less certain. The painting may portray a moment of hesitation, but we only know there is hesitation from Shaftesbury's supplementary discourse on it, "A Notion of the Historical Draught or Tablature of the Judgment of Hercules," which animates the scene with the soliloquy that gives it meaning. According to Shaftesbury, Hercules must be understood to be poised at the moment of decision, inclining toward Virtue without having fully committed himself yet:

> It shou'd appear by the very Turn, or Position of the Body alone, that this young Hero had not wholly quitted the balancing or pondering part. For in the manner of his turn towards the worthier of these Goddesses, he shou'd by no means appear so averse or separate from the other, as not to suffer it to be conceiv'd of him, that he had ever any inclination for her, or had ever hearken'd to her Voice. On the contrary, there ought to be some hopes yet remaining for this latter Goddess Pleasure, and some regret apparent in Hercules. (3.220)[33]

How will Hercules decide between these contending parties? We might imagine him torn between two opposing forces that pull in different directions, as the metaphor of "the balancing . . . part" suggests, just as we might imagine that when the self divides itself in two by judgment in order to judge, it produces an agonism within itself in which the stronger party will win out and determine the self's course of action. This is precisely the model of the mind that Locke had offered before he described the moment of hesitation, and it is the model of a purely immanent and emergent "judgment" that will be so seductive to a dialectical social theory later in the century, from Kant and Schiller to Hegel: history itself as the world's court of judgment in Hegel's account.[34] Judgment here is construed as mere negation and conflict, out of which something determinate may or may not emerge. Shaftesbury himself is tempted by this model in "Sensus Communis," offering an account of a "public sphere" where the free operation of ridicule (a form of negation) allows the truth to emerge of its own accord.[35] But this model remains economistic and computational, a mere balancing or accounting of forces (1.42), not the theatrical model that "Soliloquy" promises. The question remains: can we distinguish an economic from a theatrical model of judgment, and how will Hercules decide? The painting shows clearly that neither goddess threatens to force Hercules; they take turns offering their reasons, and it is these reasons that Hercules must ponder and *evaluate* (not weigh or balance, since we will see that these reasons are incommensurable fictions). We encounter here the limit of painting to depict soliloquy, indeed the failure of *The Judgment of Hercules* to show the judgment of Hercules. The reasons for Hercules's judgment are given elsewhere by Shaftesbury himself, in the "Moralists" and in "Soliloquy," as well as in the "Inquiry" in a nonconversational idiom. *Only* language and conversation are adequate to the giving of reasons. We are finally in a position to understand why the Lockean hesitation that opens the space of judgment cannot be just any hesitation, pause, cessation, interruption, or hiatus; *it must take the form of conversation*.[36] Soliloquy is not one form among many for the exercise of judgment; there is no practice of judgment worth the name which does not, in some way, take the form of soliloquy.[37]

When Shaftesbury recharacterizes the Lockean space of judgment as a space of conversation and soliloquy rather than merely a space of hesitation, it is difficult to take the full measure of the profound shift that he means to effect. At stake are not simply different procedures by which we make judgments but radically incommensurable regimes of causality and radically incompatible models of the mind. Shaftesbury explains the difference through a risky analogy that compares the mind to a watch:[38]

> If a Passenger shou'd turn by chance into a Watchmaker's Shop, and thinking to inform himself concerning Watches, shou'd inquire, of what Metal, or what Matter, each Part was compos'd; what gave the Colours, or what made the Sounds; without examining what the real Use was of such an Instrument; or by what Movements its End was best attain'd, and its Perfection acquir'd: 'tis plain that such an Examiner as this, wou'd come short of any Understanding in the real Nature of the Instrument. (1.181)

The "passenger" in this example is in the same situation we are in when we examine the painting of the *Judgment of Hercules*, studying the posture of the bodies, the gestures of the hands, and the color of the clothing in order to gain some insight into Hercules's judgment. We simply miss the point, since there is no way to infer from these phenomenal characteristics to the practice of judgment. Similarly, the passenger might learn an immense amount about the physics of gears and springs, the properties of various metals, the mechanical principles that determine the relations between the different parts, but there is simply no way to make an inference from these to the purpose of the watch or the *reason* for its existence. If I study the mechanics of watchmaking, I can learn much about this object as an interlocking set of parts that interact with each other in particular causal ways. Such an analysis allows me to *describe* with great accuracy and precision the various ways in which all the parts move, but it can offer no help in discerning which is the significant part of the system, namely the watch face, and it can offer no language to explain why or for what reason this part is significant, namely to tell me the time so I will not be late for my next appointment. For a physical analysis of the watch, all its parts are equally (un)interesting: I might pay attention now to the flywheel, now to the winding mechanism, now to the mathematical ratios by which the hands turn in relation to one another, now to the watch's weight or ability to conduct electricity. But nothing in such an analysis can tell me what makes a watch a watch: its ability to keep me apprised of the time. Even though the telling of time is as regular and rule-governed as anything could be (and this is the brilliance of Shaftesbury's example), there is nothing in the language of mathematics that would allow me to describe its purpose, end, or function, rather than its mere functioning. Mathematics has no language for purpose. Yet the purpose of the watch is simply and straightforwardly expressed in ordinary language: to tell time. Part of the reason that mathematics cannot express what is so easily explained in ordinary language is that the language of mathematics is designed to express *quantitative* relationships, but there is nothing quantitative about the purpose of telling time, even though time itself is eminently quantifiable. The language of mathematics expresses *determinate* relations between given things, and the purpose of a watch is not determinate in that way. The purpose of the watch is not given in the object itself, but something I project into it by a judgment I make about its end. This judgment I make about purpose is what allows me to home in on the face of the watch as its most significant part, and to ignore the rest of the machine's functioning as irrelevant to my purposes. This is precisely what turns the watch into a meaningful object for me, rather than merely a mechanism I can dissect, analyze, and describe. The radical disjunction between the reason for the watch's existence and the physical explanation of its functioning becomes apparent when I focus on the face of the watch to the exclusion of all else. Ultimately, it does not matter to me whether, behind the face, there is a cesium atomic clock, a complex system of cogs, a cheap electronic circuit, a burning candle, or dripping water, as long as I can read the time. Nor does it matter whether the time is shown through electronic digits, turning hands on a dial, or a level indicator. The *body* of the object is irrelevant to the purpose of the object, as long as the body is sufficient to the purpose, and there are many, perhaps innumerable, ways for it to be sufficient for its purpose. What Shaftesbury means us to see with this example is that, while the materiality of the object has some bearing on its suitability for its purpose—I may need the accuracy of a cesium clock and a cheap electronic watch may be utterly useless to me, or I may need the portability of a wristwatch not easily achieved by dripping water or a burning candle—the purpose of an object is an ideality I project onto it, and only through this projection does the thing acquire any significance whatsoever.

I call this ideal projection a "judgment" because it has several key features of a judgment, though they often go unrecognized or unremarked. First, it creates value where there was none, and it allows us to discern the important from the unimportant, the relevant from the irrelevant. Second, it is concerned with the work of forging ends. Third, it is only possible through a certain fictioning capacity. And fourth, it can always be made otherwise. These last two features are simply another way of saying that the meaning or end of an object is given not in the object itself but only through the idealizing projection of judgment. This will become clear if we press the example of the watch into further service. In most cases, my judgment that the purpose of the watch is to tell time will be the right one, *but not always*. If I am making an assumption about the one who made the watch, then I might be wrong because this watch might have been made to mimic an antique object for decorative purposes. Or if I am making an assumption about the purpose of the watch in a particular situation, I might be wrong because right now I need to use this object as a projectile in self-defense, or I need its conducting capacities to close a circuit urgently, or I need the metal in this watch to build something far more valuable to me. In short, no object has purpose except insofar as I bring purpose to it through the idealizing projection of judgment.[39]

Through the example of the watch, Shaftesbury is able to achieve a transformative commentary on Locke's account of motivation in chapter 2.21 of the *Essay*. In the first edition of the *Essay* (1690), Locke had accounted for motivation through the notion of some good for the sake of which we act: "Good then, the greater Good is that alone which determines the will."[40] We are determined to act through the notion of some purpose or end that motivates us, "that for the sake of which" we do something, as Aristotle explains. However, in the second edition of the essay, Locke revised his account significantly:

> It seems so established and settled a maxim by the general consent of mankind, that good, the greater good, determines the will, that I do not at all wonder, that when I first published my thoughts on this subject, I took it for granted. . . . But yet upon a stricter inquiry, I am forced to conclude that *good*, the *greater good*, though apprehended and acknowledged to be so, does not determine the *will*, until our desire, raised proportionably to it, make us *uneasy*, in the want of it. (234)

We might indeed have ideas of purposes or ends, Locke concedes, but he refuses to allow them any motive force in the psyche; something more is needed. At this point, he develops his mechanical or economic model of the psyche, which accounts for motivation purely through efficient causation, the motive force of what he calls "uneasiness" or desire, as though this were somehow a more satisfactory model. The impetus for this change can be traced at least to Locke's Baconian legacy, and Bacon's methodological injunction to disregard final causes.[41] At the same time, Locke himself recognized some of the inadequacies of this model when he noted our capacity to hesitate and suspend the motive force of any and all desires in order to judge which ones to act on. However, in Locke's account, the capacity to hesitate had emerged unaccountably, and its power over desire remained mysterious. Was it simply one force interacting with the others in the psyche, or did it have a different status altogether? What Shaftesbury allows us to see is that, when we remain at the level of desire and efficient causation, and even when we introduce the notion of hesitation as simple cessation of activity or of the impulsive force of desire, we resemble the passenger who inquires about the physics of the watch without understanding its purpose:

> Shou'd a Philosopher, after the same manner [as the passenger inquiring about the watch], employing himself in the Study of human Nature, discover only, what Effects each Passion wrought upon the Body; what change of Aspect or Feature they produc'd; and in what different manner they affected the Limbs and Muscles; this might possibly qualify him to give Advice to an Anatomist or a Limner, but not to Mankind or to Himself: Since according to this Survey he consider'd not the real Operation or Energy of his Subject, nor contemplated the Man, as real Man, and as a human Agent; but as a Watch or common Machine. (1.181)

Only when we conceive hesitation as the practice of soliloquy can we begin to understand how we might be motivated by purposes, ends, and reasons rather than desires, because only ordinary language and not the language of mathematics has the capacity to articulate purposes. When we begin to talk to ourselves in soliloquy, we can formulate ends, purposes, and reasons, which have nothing to do with the inarticulate push of desiring, and such ends and reasons have a motive power as a moment's reflection will show ("as everyone daily may experiment with himself," Locke says). In short, what the capacity for self-conversation allows us to do is not merely something as crude as suspending the press of desire, though it does this too; rather, *by the use of so-called natural language*, it wrenches us out of the phenomenal realm of efficient causation, into a noumenal realm of final causation where we are able to give ourselves ends, purposes, and reasons—desires may be among the considerations that shape these, but they will not be determinative—and act on them.[42] As much as an aura of mystery surrounds this observation, leading us to wonder *how* such an operation is possible, we should not be tempted to explain the observation away through a dogmatic insistence on the primacy or exclusivity of efficient causation, since the ability to soliloquize, give ourselves reasons, and act on them is the most indisputable of everyday facts that we can all confirm for ourselves every time we act reflectively and judgingly in the world. I would almost call this a phenomenological observation, since it involves a reflection on the process of our cognition as we form our resolutions to act, but it would be more accurate to call it a noumenological observation, since we enter here into the space of reasons which no phenomenology, only language in its nonphenomenality, can articulate and constitute. Hence the mute inanity of the painting of *The Judgment of Hercules*, which can only point us toward Shaftesbury's essays and the *reasons* they articulate for Hercules's judgment.[43]

Shaftesbury implies, by the end of the watch example, that the right way to consider a person is not as a desiring machine, but with a view to their purposes or ends which transcend the machinic assemblage of desires, since it was only by knowing the purpose of the watch that we understood it *as watch*, not by knowing the physical properties of the machine. But at precisely this moment, he breaks the analogy between the watch and the human being, even though it was the watch that had revealed to us the importance of thinking in purposive or ends-oriented ways: "Since according to this Survey he consider'd not the real Operation or Energy of his Subject, nor contemplated the Man, as real Man, and as a human Agent; but as a Watch or common Machine." What makes for the difference between the human being and the watch, since they both have purposes, and the very audacity of introducing the watch example was to show that, *just as with the watch*, it makes no sense to consider the human being apart from its purpose?[44] There are at least two important differences that make the watch a mechanism, despite its embodiment of purpose. First, if desires are to be considered the mechanism of the psyche, we cannot simply calculate their effects on behavior because they are never straighforwardly given; they can be shaped, altered, transformed, even destroyed by the process of judgment and soliloquy, just as judgment itself is shaped by and premised on desire. A person is not just a mechanism in which, once we are given all the desires, we can calculate the outcome, because examining and giving reasons change the desires themselves:

> For instance, if Superstition be the sort of Fear which most oppresses; 'tis not very material to inquire, on this occasion, to what Parts or Districts the Blood or Spirits are immediately detach'd, or where they are made to rendevouz. . . . But when the Grounds of this superstitious Fear are consider'd to be from Opinion, and the Subjects of it come to be thorowly search'd and examin'd; the Passion it-self must necessarily diminish. (1.182–83; see also 190, 197)

In this example, the process of engaging in soliloquy, the examination of the grounds and reasons for a passion, can have the effect of diminishing (but presumably also intensifying) the passion itself.[45] What is important here is that Shaftesbury is not interested in the eradication of desire (though the eradication of some desires may be necessary), nor is he interested in some crude opposition of Reason and desire. Desires are an essential part of the organism, and they *help* interest, motivate, and orient us.[46] Judgment *organizes* desires, but to do that, there must be desires for it to organize. By themselves, desires are disorganized and not purposive; they simply push us around this way and that. We may know what desires we have, but we do not know what we want until we have deliberated on it through the process of soliloquy.[47] One function of judgment, then, is to arrange, evaluate, and give purpose to desire, to decide which desires to act on *and which ones not to act on*, and this is what it means to craft oneself as a self: "As long as we enjoy a Mind, as long as we have Appetites and Sense, the Fancys of all kinds will be hard at work; and whether we are in company, or alone, they must range still, and be active. They must have their Field. The Question is, Whether they shall have it wholly to themselves; or whether they shall acknowledg some Controuler or Manager" (1.198; see also 1.192). On this model, the function of judgment is executive, but it does not operate according to some abstract and monolithic Reason or rationality which dominates and enforces its law. It is the very opposite of force, as we see in the *Judgment of Hercules*, where neither goddess threatens to or could bully Hercules into her point of view. Judgment works, then, not through Reason, but the giving of reasons and the articulation of purposes, in the plural, through the give-and-take of the conversation I have with myself (and others). Only the "gentle sway" of reasons, my ability to take them all and *consider* them on my own terms, can provide an alternative to force; only in the giving of reasons and the articulation of purposes does something like the possibility of freedom come into view, as an alternative to the economy of forces that otherwise determine everything. The giving of reasons integral to the practice of soliloquy is no abstruse metaphysical enterprise, but the most quotidian of experiences that occurs every time I talk to myself about how I will act in a particular situation. There are no rules or formulas for these conversations, since the field of things I might consider is potentially infinite, as are the kinds of reasons and purposes I might offer. We are like artists confronting a blank canvas; there are many ways that we might begin to articulate our reasons, and there can be no thought of running through the full range of possibilities available for consideration. Part of the art of judgment is recognizing the salient considerations in this instance, so that we might begin painting.

The second, and even more important, feature that distinguishes the watch from the person is that the watch cannot make its own purpose, whereas the human being can, and it is precisely the process of making oneself into a self through the giving of purposes that is at issue in the practice of soliloquy. Shaftesbury told us that the one who considered the person as a mechanism "consider'd not the real Operation or Energy of his Subject." "Energy" refers to the distinction Aristotle makes between *energeia* and *kinesis* in the *Metaphysics* (1048b.18–34). "Energetic" actions are those in which the end of the action is indistinguishable from the process itself, whereas "kinetic" actions are those in which the end is separate from the process and achieved only at the conclusion of the process.[48] When Shaftesbury transfers the notion of "Energy" to subjects rather than actions, he cannot mean simply that the end or purpose lies within the subject since, as I have already explained, no object has its purpose simply given within it in this way: the end is always a projective judgment. What Shaftesbury means, then, is not that the human being has its end given within it, but rather that we are the kinds of beings (there may be others) that make our own ends (though never just as we please, and often badly). We need not do so, but it is difficult to imagine what a life without ends-making would look like, or *why* we would even want to live it. Indeed, asking why already puts us in the realm of purposive reasoning: if we wanted a life stripped of ends, we would have to refuse the "why" question at every turn. We would have to follow every whim and passion as it came uppermost in our minds, with no regard for organizing our lives into anything like the "coherence" of a narrative.[49] Allowing ourselves to be buffeted around by every wayward whim of the psyche, we could not even be said to be persons who are distinct and separated off from the mechanism of the world. We become individuals only when, through the process of self-division, soliloquy, and fictioning judgment, we are able to give ourselves purposes where there were none before. At stake in the crafting of purposes is not principally the making of a better self (though that concerns Shaftesbury too) but the making of a self at all, someone for whom better and worse can even begin to matter:[50]

> We hope also that our Patient (for such we naturally suppose our Reader) will consider duly with himself, that what he endures in this Operation is for no inconsiderable End: since 'tis to gain him a Will, and insure him a certain Resolution; by which he shall know where to find himself; be sure of his own Meaning and Design; and as to all his Desires, Opinions, and Inclinations, be warranted one and the same Person to day as yesterday, and to morrow as to day. (116)

There is a nearly Nietzschean sense of aesthetic self-constitution here, except that the aesthetic (as we will see in a moment) has not yet been divorced of its ethical import; its purpose is precisely to ensure that the forging of ends is consonant with the demands of ethics (163, 208).

We have now established that Shaftesbury describes the practice of judgment as one in which we craft purposes for ourselves by giving reasons. But one of the most powerful critiques of the Enlightenment and modernity that we have inherited is the "critique of instrumental reason" developed by the Frankfurt School. Is Shaftesbury's model of judgment not the very epitome of instrumental reason, then, since he conceives reason as oriented toward the making and attaining of ends? Is this not the instrumentalization or functionalization of human life that the critique of instrumental reason was meant to put us on our guard against? Worse still, is Shaftesbury's account not incoherent, since his ethics is often directed against virtuous behavior undertaken merely for the sake of reward, against any instrumental or utilitarian account of ethics?[51] In fact, not only is Shaftesbury's account coherent, but we have much to learn from it in terms of developing a more complex and supple critique of instrumentality. One of the great dangers of a "critique of instrumental reason," and indeed of the many critiques of teleological thinking that abound in poststructuralist forms of critical theory, is that they afford us no way to distinguish any form of ends-oriented reasoning from mere instrumentality.[52] In both cases, there is an end specified, and we use certain means to achieve those ends. I use a hammer to bang in a nail; I exploit the labor of others to enrich myself; I act in certain ways to further my happiness. All these forms of activity require a certain coordination of means and ends, and therefore a certain instrumentality. So, if we radicalize the critique of instrumental reason, all these forms of purposive activity become suspect as ends-oriented or teleological. The alternative, then, from at least Kant onward, has been to find modes of action which are purely formal, self-reflexive, and not oriented toward ends, which are concerned with process and procedure alone. The bracketing of ends, the taboo on positing ends of any kind, is one form of the crisis of judgment, and it has become de rigueur in most of the forms of critical theory we are familiar with: any form of substantive thinking about ends is off-limits and tantamount to ideology, crass moralism, metaphysics, or "ontotheology." But to give up on ends-oriented thinking entirely, as I have been trying to argue, would require us to abandon the most basic kinds of purposive activities out of which we fabricate our lives; in the extreme instances, it requires the abandonment of any substantive judgment and therefore any possibility of acting thinkingly in the world.

However, one of the architects of the critique of instrumental reason, Max Horkheimer, while he is certainly prone to the danger I have described of eliding the distinction between ends-oriented reason and instrumental reason, still manages to preserve something of the distinction in his impressive study *Eclipse of Reason*. The first chapter of *Eclipse of Reason* ought to be read in its entirety alongside Shaftesbury's own account, for the exemplary diagnosis it offers, but I will offer a brief synopsis here. Horkheimer begins by explaining how a premodern conception of objective reason differs from the subjective reason that comes to displace it in modernity:

> The degree of reasonableness of a man's life could be determined according to its harmony with this totality. Its objective structure, and not just man and his purposes, was to be the measuring rod for individual thoughts and actions. . . . *The emphasis was on ends rather than means*. The supreme endeavor of this kind of thinking was to reconcile the objective order of the "reasonable," as philosophy conceived it, with human existence, including self-interest and self-preservation. . . . The theory of objective reason did not focus on the co-ordination of behavior and aim, *but on concepts—however mythological they sound to us today*—on the idea of the greatest good, on the problem of human destiny, and on the way of realization of ultimate goals.[53]

The account might as well be Shaftesbury's, with the reference to "harmony" that is such an important feature of Shaftesbury's analysis, the focus on ends, and the uncomfortable recognition of the fictive ground on which judgments are based ("concepts—however mythological they sound to us today"). The effort to distinguish instrumental reason ("the co-ordination of behavior and aim") from ends-oriented reason ("the idea of the greatest good," etc.) is also in evidence here, but the grounds for this distinction remain opaque. How are the aims toward which behavior is coordinated in any way different from ends such as the greatest good? Once we have an end such as the latter, do we not coordinate our actions in such a way as to achieve it? It is precisely the ability to distinguish between these two kinds of ends-oriented action that the critique of instrumental reason promises to deliver without being able to do so.

Once the distinction between defensible ends and a mere instrumentality becomes elusive, all forms of ends-orientation begin to seem suspect. Speaking of the practice of critical theory, Horkheimer says: "On the contrary, it is suspicious of the very categories of better, useful, appropriate, productive, and valuable, as these are understood in the present order, and refuses to take them as nonscientific presuppositions about which one can do nothing."[54] The qualification "as these are understood in the present order" makes clear that some version of these ends are desirable and necessary, though they must be transformed in some way. But what is wrong with the ends themselves? Is it simply the fact of existing within the present order, in which case the problem lies not with the ends or instrumentality but with the social order? And how are the problems with that social order to be judged if not instrumentally, by way of some set of purposes or ends? How can the ends be transformed to make them more appropriate or defensible? Without any ability to distinguish between instrumental and noninstrumental versions of "better," "productive," and "valuable," the critique threatens to consume any account of ends-orientation as merely instrumental. An example of this excessive critique can be found in the *Dialectic of Enlightenment*, when Adorno and Horkheimer compare the man of science to the dictator: "The man of science knows things in so far as he can make them. In this way their potentiality is turned to his own ends" (9). One wonders what, in the abstract, can be wrong with making and shaping things for our own ends, and how it is even possible to live without doing so. The effect of a critique that will concede no orientation according to ends, a critique that cannot offer a defense of certain ends as preferable to others, is that only formal, abstract, and nonsubstantive uses of reason can be endorsed: "In a historical period like the present true theory is more critical than affirmative, just as the society that corresponds to it cannot be called 'productive'" ("Traditional and Critical Theory," 242). For such a negative dialectics, freedom has to be understood as liberation from purposiveness (*Dialectic of Enlightenment*, 157), a noninstrumentalized thinking becomes a reflection on itself (25), and concrete suggestions for action become taboo ("the author is not trying to suggest anything like a program of action" [*Eclipse of Reason*, vi]).

Despite the proximity of my diagnosis to Horkheimer's (and Adorno's), the critique of instrumental reason does not offer us a helpful way to distinguish between a degraded instrumentality and a valuable, indeed indispensable, orientation toward ends. The only way beyond these impasses of the critique of instrumental reason is through a robust account of the practice of judgment, of the kind I have been trying to extract from Shaftesbury's "Soliloquy" essay. Such an account of finite judgment will have to satisfy several conditions. It must allow us to specify substantive ends without recourse to notions such as "objective reason" that are no longer available to us. It must embrace the fictions on which any judgment is founded. Yet the process of judgment, and even the construction of appropriate fictions, must not be construed as arbitrary; it has to be grounded, not in Reason, but in the giving of reasons. The conditions that an account of judgment must satisfy are easy to state, but it is difficult to find a working account that satisfies them.

Can Shaftesbury teach us how to save the possibility of an ends-oriented reason, while still retaining the valuable critique of instrumentality that both he and the Frankfurt School share? I believe the answer is embedded in Shaftesbury's "Soliloquy" essay, but it cannot lie in the distinction between means and ends, and the ways in which those are coordinated. Any such attempt will result in the abandonment of ends-orientation altogether, because an ends-oriented reason coordinates means to ends just as instrumental reason does. Whether I want to hammer in a nail, make a corporation more efficient, hire a contract killer, or want to have been judged happy, I will have to reason about the means that are necessary for that particular end and act in certain ways to try and achieve it. Yet the first three would surely be classified as instrumental reasoning, whereas the fourth ("the greatest good") is, even for Horkheimer, appropriate as an end if considered in the right way. In order to arrive at a tenable distinction between those uses of reason that Horkheimer calls "instrumental" and those he calls "objective," we must consider the explanatory regimes within which the coordination of means to ends and the constitution of ends are undertaken. In particular, we must attend to the fundamental shift from explanations in the mode of efficient causation to explanation in the mode of final causation that is made possible by the fictioning judgment that opens the space of soliloquy. To see what I mean, let us turn to Shaftesbury's watch again. To understand the watch from the perspective of efficient causation is to describe the laws of physics by which the various gears and springs move in relation to each other. (In fact, such a description will already require a *judgment* about which aspect of the physical description is salient.) Now, we have already seen that the language of efficient causation, the language of mathematics, does not even have a way of expressing something like the "purpose" of the watch, and must stand mute in relation to that purpose, which can only be accounted for in the mode of final causation.[55] So a first problem with explaining the watch in the mode of efficient causation is simply that it misses entirely the point of the watch as an object. This by itself is not an ethical problem. Indeed, the development of mechanics to a certain level of sophistication is necessary before accurate timepieces can be made. The issue is rather that we fail to understand something fundamental about the watch, the reason anyone would want to make such a thing in the first place, if we do not situate it in relation to the world of human purposes and ends. Instrumentality or, more precisely expressed, explanation in the mode of efficient causation, is obtuse to the "for-the-sake-of" or the "why" of the watch.

However, there is a second problem with explaining the watch in the mode of efficient causation, which begins to touch on the ethical concerns articulated by the critique of instrumental reason. It arises when we assume that an explanation in the mode of efficient causation actually does give us a purpose to which we are compelled to subject ourselves, rather than one which we might reject, deliberate about, or organize otherwise. One need only think here of the myriad descriptions of the way in which the human body is subjected to the rigid regimes of factory time and industrial process, without considering the adequacy of those regimes to human ends and purposes. An early instance of this, nearly contemporaneous with Shaftesbury, is found in Swift's description of the Lilliputians trying to make sense of Gulliver's relationship to his watch:

> Out of the right fob hung a great silver chain, with a wonderful kind of engine at the bottom. We directed him to draw out whatever was at the end of the chain, which appeared to be a globe, half silver, and half of some transparent metal. . . . And we conjecture that it is either some unknown animal or the god that he worships: but we are more inclined to the latter opinion, because he assured us . . . that he seldom did anything without consulting it. He called it his oracle, and said it pointed out the time for everything in his life.[56]

To say that the watch is "the god that he worships" is, in this instance, to say that Gulliver accepts the purpose supposedly dictated by the watch without deliberating about it or questioning it, as he easily might. For example, we could imagine him wondering: "Why should I subject myself to the mechanical temporality of this watch? Wouldn't my life be better if I sometimes ignored it? What is the right relationship between attending to the strictness of clock time and being able to free myself from it?" These are the questions of deliberative and soliloquizing judgment that are elided when the purpose of the watch is treated as given by the explanation in the mode of efficient causality. Obscuring such questions involves a misunderstanding or misapplication of the explanation by efficient causality, *which can never give any purpose*, but it is one that is all too common; the history of violence it has given rise to in terms of subjecting the rhythms of human time to clock time are too well known to need rehearsing. As the sciences daily expand their explanatory reach and seek to explain everything observable in the mode of efficient causation, it is vital to acknowledge the value, salience, and validity of this enterprise, and to encourage its extension as far as possible, at the same time as we must refuse the misapplication of this explanatory mode—the assumption that it can generate purposes or ends—at every turn.[57] The sciences, for all their remarkable achievements which continue to astound us every day—like the newest model of a cesium clock, which divides a second into quadrillionths and is possibly accurate enough to test the theory of relativity[58]—must stand in mute obeisance at the door of human purposes.[59]

There is a third problem with explanations by efficient causality, but it cannot be disclosed by the example of the watch, because it involves applying such explanations to beings who are not only motivated by purposes but who also have the capacity to make those purposes for themselves: beings like us. This is precisely the point where Shaftesbury had diagnosed the breakdown of the analogy between the watch and the human being (1.181), and even Bacon recognized the continuing value of explanations by final causation. Today the sciences are pressing ever further and deeper in the direction of explaining human behavior in the mode of efficient causality, though this project, as we have seen, can be traced at least to Locke's *Essay*. But we must be very cautious about how we specify the problem. There can be no question of calling a halt to this endeavor; indeed, it must be encouraged to proceed as far as possible. We have only the vaguest comprehension of it possibilities and limits at the present moment. The problem, then, cannot lie in the simple fact of applying such explanations, as far as they go and with the appropriate limits, to human behavior. It must lie elsewhere, and there are at least two facets to it. First, no explanation of my action in the mode of efficient causation can or should prevent me from using my freedom, if I have it, to exercise my judgment in the determination of my ends. Second, it is unclear how or whether the language of efficient causation might be translated into the language of final causes, and if it were to become possible, what its effects might be. It cannot be ruled out that a translation might be possible. However, such a translation can have no effect on the practice of soliloquizing judgment. Moreover, under the current conditions of knowledge, the sense of violence that we have in the application of explanations by efficient causation to forms of behavior ostensibly motivated by final causes—the sense of an instrumental reason run amok—lies in part in the crude and forcible application of simplistic efficient-causal explanations to forms of thinking and action to which it does not seem adequate, with no demonstration of either the possibility or legitimacy of translation between these causal regimes that appear so fundamentally incommensurable.[60]

I have thus far avoided any appeal to the aesthetic in my description of the practice of soliloquizing judgment as Shaftesbury understands it. This originary judgment, or originary partition (*Ur-teil*) as Hölderlin has it ("Judgment and Being"), which first opens a world to us and discloses a self to us in its self-division, requires no appeal to the category of the aesthetic or to any faculty of aesthetic judgment. It is judgment per se, though it could be said to have an aesthetic component to it insofar as it only works through the fictions that enable it. My account is faithful to Shaftesbury's argument in that, even though much of the essay is about the critical reception of works of art by princes, critics, and the public at large, Shaftesbury turns to the aesthetic proper only after a lengthy description of the process of self-constitution through soliloquy.[61] Although Shaftesbury is often considered to be one of the first architects of modern aesthetics,[62] one would be hard pressed to find anything like a conventional aesthetic theory in the *Characteristics*. Shaftesbury's reflections on beauty are scattered throughout the text, and interwoven with his thoughts on moral action, religion, benevolence, the social contract, and so forth. This is not simply an effect of his allergy to systematic philosophizing.[63] Although Shaftesbury is forging concepts that will be indispensable for a subsequent aesthetic tradition—like sensus communis and aesthetic disinterest[64]—his own writing resembles earlier treatises on the arts like Aristotle's *Poetics*, which took the form of technical advice for practitioners rather than meditations on the beautiful as such.[65] In "Soliloquy," Shaftesbury undoubtedly addresses in a sustained way the role of the arts in society, but liberty and judgment are his main concerns, not beauty. When the discussion does turn to beauty late in the essay, what is in question is the constitution of the self—its projects and ends, its capacity to resolve and act morally—revealing just how directly the nascent interest in the aesthetic responds to the problems emerging in chapter 2.21 of Locke's *Essay*. For Shaftesbury, long before Nietzsche, the aesthetic object of greatest interest is the self.[66] Poised between a Stoic virtue ethics, which needed no recourse to the aesthetic,[67] and a Nietzschean aestheticism purged of any relation to virtue or morality, Shaftesbury can help us understand how the discourse of the aesthetic comes into being as an unsuccessful attempt to establish a notion of judgment and value in the wake of empiricism.

The practice of soliloquizing judgment is not rule-bound. It cannot be if it is to remain judgment. If a rule were given according to which a judgment must be formed, then the so-called judgment would simply be a form of computation, indistinguishable from the merely instrumental use of reason. With this in mind, the purpose of beauty in this essay is a strange and paradoxical one: to give us a rule that does not appear to be a rule, or to offer an end that will ultimately turn out to be no end at all. The purpose of beauty is purpose itself, which is to say that beauty serves to relieve us of the burden of judging purpose.[68] Its function is not to aid judgment or offer advice, so much as to constrain or radically curb the free exercise of judgment.[69] Confronted with the anarchic, fictioning power of judgment to make its own ends, a power that can in the last instance only be adequately constrained by the habits and practices atrophying under the conditions of modernity, Shaftesbury balks.[70]

The emergence of aesthetic discourse at this moment is the panicked reaction to the discovery of the free fictioning power of judgment, as it is disclosed in Shaftesbury's confrontation with Lockean empiricism. We have seen that Shaftesbury has a rich and robust account of judgment as perhaps *the* most fundamental process of cognition, since it is what makes us into the ends-oriented beings that we are. But the aesthetic does not dictate or confirm for judgment some intrinsic end that we have, as it does in the case of Addison and Steele or Hutcheson. Rather, it restricts the use of judgment by specifying a *formal* rule or condition that the ends of judgment must satisfy in any circumstances whatsoever. The love of beauty ingrains in us a commitment to the principle of harmony, which is meant to keep the free exercise of judgment within proper bounds (194–95). The formal condition that Shaftesbury introduces to constrain the exercise of judgment is at once unnecessary and insufficient: unnecessary because there will be situations in which harmony, order, and self-consistency will be the wrong criteria to use; insufficient because the purpose of the condition is to ensure the coincidence of virtue and beauty, and to allow the love of beauty to serve as a propaedeutic to virtue, which it manifestly cannot do.[71] The premise underlying Shaftesbury's alignment of virtue and beauty is that, if we forge ourselves poetically in ways that are consistent, harmonious, and orderly, we will inescapably have become virtuous:[72]

> Such a Poet is indeed a second Maker; a just Prometheus, under Jove. Like that Sovereign Artist or universal Plastick Nature, he forms a Whole, coherent and proportion'd in it-self, with due Subjection and Subordinacy of constituent Parts. . . . The moral Artist . . . will hardly, I presume, be found unknowing in Himself, or at a loss in those Numbers which make the Harmony of a Mind. *For Knavery is mere Dissonance and Disproportion*. And tho Villains may have strong Tones and natural Capacitys of Action; *'tis impossible that true Judgment and Ingenuity shou'd reside, where Harmony and Honesty have no being*. (129–30, my emphasis)

Shaftesbury aligns the villain with "mere dissonance and disproportion," judgment with harmony, but it is all too easy to imagine characters who make an *art* of crime and atrocity.[73] The tether for judgment that Shaftesbury seeks, in the form of the perception of beauty, cannot provide the determinate and concrete end he desires. In making ourselves, acting according to the dictates of harmony and proportion cannot guarantee that we will act well or live well, and, moreover, there will be times when it is *necessary* to defy those dictates in order to act well and live well. Only good judgment, not some formal criterion specified in advance, can discern when those times will be.[74]

Having provided perhaps the most thoroughgoing and compelling account of the foundational character of judgment for cognition, Shaftesbury himself avoids or feigns the avoidance of judgment at decisive moments in the essay. The conclusion is riddled with failures of judgment. Most notably, having accorded philosophy—by which he means his "honest Home-Philosophy" of soliloquy (1.224)—the role of absolute arbiter of judgment (1.184), he retracts or at least strongly qualifies that position at the end. Whereas in the earlier passage, philosophy was accorded the privilege of "giv[ing] to every inferior Science its just rank," now there is a fragmentation of disciplines: "The main matter is to keep these Provinces [religion and philosophy] distinct, and settle their just Boundarys" (1.222). This is not simply an equal division. While philosophy is allowed to exercise judgment in private, judgment is required to defer to the authorized forms in public: "'Tis agreed on all hands, that particular Persons may design or paint, in their private Capacity, after what manner they think fit: But they must blazon only as the Publick directs. . . . Naturalists may, in their separate and distinct Capacity, inquire, as they think fit, into the real Existence and natural Truth of Things: But they must by no means dispute the authoriz'd Forms" (1.223; see also 1.220). This drastic contraction of the realm of judgment is not consonant with the rights of soliloquizing philosophy to sit in judgment on any discipline whatsoever, to accord it its boundaries and assess its value.[75] There can be no clearer abdication of judgment than this. But we need not have waited till the end of the essay to find this out, because Shaftesbury warns us at the very beginning of the essay that he will refuse judgment. The essay had billed itself as "Advice to an Author" in its subtitle, and advice is the very mode in which good judgment is imparted or shared. But, in the self-reflexive gesture that characterizes all formalism,[76] Shaftesbury declares at the outset that he will withhold advice, or, at best, only offer advice about how to give advice: "My Pretension is not so much to give Advice, as to consider of the Way and Manner of advising" (1.98). If beauty had held out the promise of determining our judgment, that is a promise it simply cannot deliver on.[77] And we should be glad it cannot. Because in the moment it did, it would have usurped our capacity for judgment. The hazard and opportunity of judgment is that, in the last instance, it can rely on nothing but itself.

Notes

1. Francis Bacon, *The New Organon*, ed. Lisa Jardine and Michael Silverthorne (Cambridge: Cambridge University Press, 2000), 102, my emphasis.

2. All references, except for one below to the first edition of 1690, will be to John Locke, *An Essay concerning Human Understanding*, ed. R. S. Woolhouse (London: Penguin, 1997).

3. See also Thomas Pfau, *Minding the Modern: Human Agency, Intellectual Traditions, and Responsible Knowledge* (South Bend, Ind.: University of Notre Dame Press, 2013), 221–22.

4. Dabney Townsend, "Shaftesbury's Aesthetic Theory," *Journal of Aesthetic and Art Criticism* 41, no. 2 (1982): 205–13, at 210.

5. Douglas J. Den Uyl argues that "the central text for Shaftesbury's moral philosophy—and I believe the central text in all of his writings—is the *Soliloquy* and not, for example, the *Inquiry Concerning Virtue or Merit*." Den Uyl, "Shaftesbury and the Modern Problem of Virtue," *Social Philosophy and Policy* 15, no. 1 (1998): 275–316, at 283. See also Lawrence E. Klein, *Shaftesbury and the Culture of Politeness: Moral Discourse and Cultural Politics in Early Eighteenth-Century England* (Cambridge: Cambridge University Press, 1994), 48–50. Although those who prefer systematic philosophy turn to the *Inquiry*, Klein privileges "The Moralists" (118, 124).

6. On Shaftesbury's relation to Locke, see Pfau, *Minding the Modern*, 227–48; Klein, *Shaftesbury and the Culture of Politeness*, 15, 28, 40, 65; and Karen Valihora, *Austen's Oughts: Judgment after Locke and Shaftesbury* (Newark: University of Delaware Press, 2010), 32.

7. On the lively debates about "compatibilism," the notion of a self completely integrated with its world, between the time of Hobbes and Locke, see Jonathan Kramnick, *Actions and Objects from Hobbes to Richardson* (Stanford, Calif.: Stanford University Press, 2010), 27–60.

8. On the tense relationship of philosophy to theater, see Martin Puchner, "The Theater in Modernist Thought," *New Literary History* 33, no. 3 (2002): 521–32. However, Puchner does not take up the important example of Shaftesbury.

9. On dialogue as self-division and the subsequent restoration of coherence through reason, see Michael Prince, *Philosophical Dialogue in the British Enlightenment: Theology, Aesthetics, and the Novel* (Cambridge: Cambridge University Press, 1996), 14. Hina Nazar is also attentive to the importance of dialogue and deliberation for judgment in the period: *Enlightened Sentiments: Judgment and Autonomy in the Age of Sensibility* (New York: Fordham University Press, 2012), 2–3.

10. It should be noted that Locke himself is alert to this underlying meaning of judgment as division, separation, differentiation, distinguishing, discernment, in chapter 2.11 of the *Essay*.

11. Quotations from Shaftesbury are taken from Lord Shaftesbury (Anthony Ashley Cooper, Third Earl of Shaftesbury), *Characteristicks of Men, Manners, Opinions, Times*, ed. Douglas Den Uyl, 3 vols. (Indianapolis: Liberty Fund, 2001).

12. Later in the century, Friedrich Hölderlin will describe judgment as the originary partition (*Ur-teil*), that which introduces difference or division into the seamless unity of being, though he does so in a more ontologized idiom: "Judgment and Being," in *Essays and Letters on Theory*, ed. and trans. Thomas Pfau (Albany: State University of New York Press, 1988).

13. Klein explains well how the discipline of soliloquy, practiced at length in Shaftesbury's notebooks, is essential for constituting a social self whose autonomy is not consumed by its own sociality (*Shaftesbury and the Culture of Politeness*, 70–90). The philosopher of sociability does not eschew interiority, but sees it as the precondition for a healthy sociability. However, on the dangers of this Stoic model of judgment, which relies on a lengthy suspension of judgment, see Thomas Pfau, "The Letter of Judgment: Practical Reason in Aristotle, the Stoics, and Rousseau," *Eighteenth Century: Theory and Interpretation* 51, no. 3 (2010):

289–316, at 294, 296. Pfau argues that for Shaftesbury soliloquy is "intrinsically social and dialogic" (*Minding the Modern*, 239).

14. This is the Lockean model before hesitation is introduced.

15. On the generative, replicative, and even reproductive character of beauty, see Elaine Scarry, *On Beauty and Being Just* (Princeton, N.J.: Princeton University Press, 1999).

16. By conceiving *différance* as originary, Derrida thereby occludes the fictioning work of judgment required to produce it.

17. It has been too easy to conceive this separation as a fall or alienation. It is a precondition for any thinking relation to the world, and to desire its eradication signals a discontent with the condition of finitude itself.

18. The emblematic drawing that opens "Soliloquy" also depicts two boys holding mirrors. On the care with which Shaftesbury conceived these emblematic illustrations, see Felix Paknadel, "Shaftesbury's Illustrations of *Characteristics*," *Journal of the Warburg and Courtauld Institutes* 37 (1974): 290–312. See also his description of this drawing, especially of the fashionable mirror in the central image that reflects nothing (307–8).

19. Paknadel claims that "two boys on each side [of the illustration at the head of the essay] represent good and evil conscience" ("Shaftesbury's Illustrations," 307). In her essay "Thinking and Moral Considerations," Hannah Arendt also describes conscience as emerging from self-dialogue: in *Responsibility and Judgment*, ed. Jerome Kohn (New York: Schocken, 2003), 183–87.

20. Surprisingly, *Hamlet* is only mentioned once in passing in Shaftesbury's essay, though with high praise (1.171). In this context, see Theodore Ziolkowski, *Hesitant Heroes: Private Inhibition, Cultural Crisis* (Ithaca, N.Y.: Cornell University Press, 2004). Unlike many commentators, Ziolkowski sees Hamlet's delay as a reasonable response to irruption of the irrational into the play, in the form of the ghost (79–82). For him, Hamlet's hesitation "exposes . . . the epistemological anxieties of the age" (94–95). But, more importantly, he situates Hamlet in a longer tradition of heroes who hesitate, while arguing that the hesitation progressively lengthens and intensifies to the point of "total inaction" in romanticism (5). This confirms from a different perspective my claim of a deepening crisis of judgment in the early modern period.

21. One of the limitations of Arendt's account of judgment is that she conceives it as always retrospective rather than prospective. See Hannah Arendt, *Lectures on Kant's Political Philosophy*, ed. Ronald Beiner (Chicago: University of Chicago Press, 1982), 7.

22. William Shakespeare, *Hamlet*, ed. Robert S. Miola (New York: Norton, 2011).

23. For Arendt too, thinking concerns invisible or nonphenomenal entities ("Thinking," 162, 175).

24. In the case of this soliloquy, it would be a mistake to think that Hamlet dithers on the point of action and finds himself suspended in indecision between being and nonbeing. In fact, in the course of this speech, he gives reasons to favor being over nonbeing and then follows that course of action. However, it is probably Hamlet himself, in this very speech, who is responsible for the characterization of his judgment as indecision, leading to a long tradition of interpretation: "Thus conscience does make cowards of us all, / And thus the native hue of resolution

/ Is sicklied o'er with the pale cast of thought, / And enterprises of great pitch and moment, / With this regard, their currents turn awry, / And lose the name of action" (3.1.83–88). Margreta de Grazia has traced the emergence, in the eighteenth century, of the interpretation of *Hamlet* as a play about tragic inaction, arguing that the initial reading of the figure of Hamlet was more comic: "*Hamlet*" *without Hamlet* (Cambridge: Cambridge University Press, 2006). In a sense, then, the emergence of this interpretation of *Hamlet* can be seen as one more symptom of the crisis of judgment, one that continues to have an afterlife in contemporary theory in the argument between Schmitt and Benjamin over Hamlet's indecisiveness and the (in)decision of the baroque sovereign. See Walter Benjamin, *Origin of German Tragic Drama*, trans. John Osborne (London: Verso, 1985), 65, 71; Carl Schmitt, *Hamlet or Hecuba? The Intrusion of Time into the Play*, trans. David Pan and Jennifer Rust (New York: Telos, 2009). For a full reading of *Hamlet* in relation to the problem of judgment, see Vivasvan Soni, "Believing in Ghosts, in Part: Judgment and Indecision in *Hamlet*," in *Shakespeare and Judgment*, ed. Kevin Curran (Edinburgh: Edinburgh University Press, 2017).

25. It is becoming increasingly clear that our everyday interpretation of language depends on such fictioning judgment. In an interview on the phenomenon of mondegreens, linguist Mark Liberman explains: "When we understand what someone says, it's always at least partly a hallucination. . . . There's a piece of what we understand that comes from the sound that comes in our ear [but] there's a piece of what we understand that comes from the expectations in our brain." See Alina Simone, "The Spread of Mondegreens Should Have Ended with the Internet—But It Hasn't," *The World in Words*, Public Radio International, November 20, 2014, www.pri.org/stories/2014-11-20/spread-mondegreens-should-have-ended-internet-it-hasnt.

26. The imagined conversations I am describing here constitute an example of a fully articulated practice of judgment, much like that undertaken by Elizabeth Bennet, when changing her mind about Darcy. See Vivasvan Soni, "Committing Freedom: The Cultivation of Judgment in Rousseau's *Emile* and Austen's *Pride and Prejudice*," *Eighteenth Century: Theory and Interpretation* 51, no. 3 (2010): 363–87. But a thoroughgoing account of judgment will require us to distinguish a number of intermediate cases, between this fully articulated practice and the quasi-instinctual reaching out for the fries under the impulsion of desire (Lockean unease), described at the beginning of the paragraph. For example, I might make a conscious decision to eat the fries, but without reflection (Schmittian decisionism). Or I might have formed a principled resolution or a habit not to eat french fries, made through a fully articulated practice of judgment in an earlier moment, but one which I do not repeat now. Or, I do not hesitate in this case, but recognize that I could have, so that this can be designated a "judgment" in the sense of occupying the site of a potential judgment, but one that was not realized as a fully articulated practice.

27. Daniel Gilbert argues that the ability to think, imagine, fiction, and simulate the future is perhaps the most important development connected to the evolution of the human brain and its disproportionately sized frontal cortex: *Stumbling on Happiness* (New York: Vintage, 2005), 4–27. Gilbert is most interested in the many errors of affective prediction about happiness this gives rise to, inclining him to a certain presentism in his interpretation of happiness. As I will

explain elsewhere, judgment always opens itself to the possibility of radical error, very different from the infallibility of computation, but this is no reason to abandon or do without it (nor is that possible). From an evolutionary perspective, the strategy of imagining the future and making judgments on this basis appears to have been unusually successful.

28. On the significance of this requirement for judgment, see Vivasvan Soni, "Judging Inevitably: Aesthetic Judgment and Novelistic Form in Fielding's *Joseph Andrews*," *Modern Language Quarterly* 76, no. 2 (2105): 159–80.

29. Although Howard Caygill is interested in the productive or constitutive dimension of judgment, he is inexplicably critical of its manifestation as ends-constitution in Shaftesbury: see Caygill, *Art of Judgment* (Oxford: Blackwell, 1989), at 38 and 48, respectively.

30. Rousseau tells us that "to compare is to judge." See Jean-Jacques Rousseau, *Emile; or, On Education*, trans. Allan Bloom (New York: Basic Books, 1979), 270.

31. The fictioning judgment which divides me from myself and enables soliloquy is a nearly uncategorizable thing, neither subjective nor objective (since it precedes the distinction of subject and object and makes them possible), neither true nor false (since it is an act of making two out of one), neither reflecting nor determining (it might be termed constituting).

32. On the importance of the painting and his treatise about it ("A Notion of the Historical Draught") to Shaftesbury, see J. E. Sweetman, "Shaftesbury's Last Commission," *Journal of the Warburg and Courtauld Institutes* 19, nos. 1–2 (1956): 110–16, at 111, 113. Sweetman describes Shaftesbury's last commission to de Matteis, a portrait of Shaftesbury as a dying philosopher, in which the text of the "Notion" was to be clearly visible, along with a sketch for the painting.

33. By a curious coincidence, Rancière's recent *Aisthesis* opens with a reading of another eighteenth-century Hercules poised at a moment of inaction, namely his reading of Winckelmann's reading of a Hercules torso. See Jacques Rancière, *Aisthesis: Scenes from the Aesthetic Regime of Art*, trans. Zakir Paul (London: Verso, 2013), 1–20. It is worth wondering why the classical action hero should, at this moment, become a figure of reflection. But in Rancière's reading, Hercules's inaction does not represent the reflective pause that will issue in a judgment. What is important for him is the apotheosis of inactivity, indecision, indeterminacy, another example of the suspension of judgment that I have argued partly characterizes the crisis of judgment today.

34. See Georg Wilhelm Friedrich Hegel, *Hegel's Philosophy of Right*, trans. T. M. Knox (London: Oxford University Press, 1967), 216.

35. Elsewhere, however, Shaftesbury describes this economic and agonistic model of conversation as "controversy," productive for the book trade, but operating through force, not reason (3.11).

36. The logic of conversation Shaftesbury describes, especially the way in which this differs from force through the capacity to hesitate, is nearly identical to Milton's account in *Paradise Lost*:

> He [Satan] ended, and his words replete with guile
> Into her [Eve's] heart too easy entrance won:
> Fixed on the fruit she gazed, which to behold

Might tempt alone, and in her ears the sound
Yet rung of his persuasive words, impregned
With reason, to her seeming, and with truth.
. . . .
yet first
Pausing a while, thus to herself she mused. (9.733–44, my emphasis)

Quotation taken from John Milton, *Paradise Lost: An Authoritative Text, Backgrounds and Sources, Criticism*, ed. Scott Elledge (New York: Norton, 1975). Eve's pause distinguishes persuasion through reason from persuasion through force. Following Fish, Prince suggests that *Paradise Lost* should be viewed as a philosophical dialogue, one more example of the importance of the genre between 1650 and 1750 (*Philosophical Dialogue*, 25 and 12).

37. It must be recognized, however, that Shaftesbury's soliloquy is not opposed to dialogue with another. Indeed, it confuses or refuses that distinction since soliloquy here is never quite soliloquy; it is always dialogue with another, who may or may not be myself.

38. The example of the watch introduces Shaftesbury's own act of soliloquizing in the essay, a presumed act of self-disclosure in which we learn almost nothing about him. Soliloquy is about reasoning with oneself, not about revealing or making public a private interiority.

39. Two things should be noted about this idealizing projection of judgment. First, it explains why we think of meaning as "spiritual," that is to say, a thing of the mind independent of the materiality of the object, though there is nothing mystical or otherworldly about this spirituality. It refers simply to the purposes we endow things with. Second, though meaning is not simply given by the object, it is not completely arbitrary, and it is constrained by the materiality of the object. Thus judgments can be good or bad, better or worse, even when judgment is a fictioning projection. In most ordinary circumstances, someone who thought the purpose of a watch was anything other than telling the time would be mistaken, and there are ends which this particular object cannot serve, not matter how much I may will it so. For example, I could not use the watch as a writing implement or a means of transportation.

40. John Locke, *An Essay concerning Humane Understanding: In Four Books* (London: Thomas Basset, 1690), 124.

41. On Locke's Baconianism, see Neal Wood, *The Politics of Locke's Philosophy: A Social Study of "An Essay concerning Human Understanding"* (Berkeley: University of California Press, 1983).

42. I only wish to make the case for the possibility of this alternate mode of causation as a way of accounting for certain actions. I do not mean to suggest that it accounts for all behavior. There are clearly many unconscious processes at work in the body, that operate in the modality of efficient causation, and the efficacy of drugs that alter mental states shows that the mind is in no way immune from this form of causation. Nor do I mean to speculate about how these two forms of causality interact with or relate to one another. (Indeed, how to understand their interaction is precisely the problem that an argument such as this one poses.) Finally, it is not even the case that it is *always* better to operate in the mode of final causation. To subject every aspect of our bodily functioning

to conscious control would be both impossible and undesirable. For now, it is enough to establish the possibility of final causation, and that it operates according to a different logic than efficient causation.

43. For a contrasting account of the plenitude of images, see Thomas Pfau's essay in this volume. But it is important to note that what animates these images are the texts of Tolstoy, Hopkins, and Pfau himself, suggesting once again the priority of language over the image for comprehending nonphenomenality. However, on the relation of language and transcendence, see Pfau, *Minding the Modern*, 474.

44. Kramnick shows that the example of the watch surfaces in compatibilist accounts in the period as a way of erasing the differences between physical objects and minded ones (*Actions and Objects*, 45). For the ongoing importance of the watch in eighteenth-century aesthetic arguments about design, see Jonathan Loesberg, *A Return to Aesthetics: Autonomy, Indifference, and Postmodernism* (Stanford, Calif.: Stanford University Press, 2005), 27, 58.

45. For Epictetus, the very naming of something diminishes our attachment to it: "If you are fond of a jug, say, 'It is a jug that I am fond of'; then, if it is broken, you will not be disturbed." Epictetus, *The Discourses; the Handbook; Fragments*, ed. Christopher Gill, trans. Robin Hard (London: J. M. Dent, 1995), 288. It is also worth noting that the rhetorical form of the advice Epictetus gives here and throughout the handbook is about the kinds of things one should say to oneself in particular situations. In other words, it is a set of prescriptions for how to undertake soliloquy. He also recognizes the value of delay or hesitation (300). See also Klein, *Shaftesbury and the Culture of Politeness*, 89, on the importance of language for reasoning with one's desires. Pfau explains more fully why "the Stoics' conception of judgment is anchored in a philosophy of language" ("Letter of Judgment," 298).

46. This is one reason that, as Dabney Townsend explains, Shaftesbury's notion of judgment cannot easily be understood in terms of the later concept of aesthetic disinterest: "Shaftesbury's Aesthetic Theory," 206, 211. See also Den Uyl, "Shaftesbury and the Modern Problem of Virtue," 301, for the notion of beauty as engagement rather than disinterest; Klein, *Shaftesbury and the Culture of Politeness*, 56. Similarly, Nazar sees sentiment and autonomous judgment as being aligned rather than opposed in the period (*Enlightened Sentiments*). By contrast, Valihora still reads Shaftesbury's account of judgment in terms of distance, impartiality, and objectivity (*Austen's Oughts*, 38, 40).

47. See Townsend, "Shaftesbury's Aesthetic Theory," 212.

48. See Vivasvan Soni, "Energy," in *Fueling Culture: 101 Words for Energy and Environment*, ed. Imre Szeman, Jennifer Wenzel, and Patricia Yaeger (New York: Fordham University Press, 2017).

49. Coherence need not imply a strong sense of subordination to a single unifying principle. There are many forms that the coherence of narrative can take. Coherence only refers to the active work of organization. However, Shaftesbury himself inclines toward a stronger notion of coherence, unity, or harmony. Susan M. Purviance argues that the unity of a life is never actually achieved, but a guiding idea or project: "Shaftesbury on Self as a Practice," *Journal of Scottish Philosophy* 2, no. 2 (2004): 155–63, at 155. Prince appropriately raises the question of how Shaftesbury can insist on unity when the *Characteristics* resists

unification and systematic theorization, answering that Shaftesbury has two competing criteria, a skeptical one based on ridicule and a Platonic one based on unity and decorum (*Philosophical Dialogue*, 28). See also Klein, *Shaftesbury and the Culture of Politeness*, 114–15.

50. See Den Uyl, "Shaftesbury and the Modern Problem of Virtue," 310.

51. See ibid., 289; Prince, *Philosophical Dialogue*, 54; Klein, *Shaftesbury and the Culture of Politeness*, 53; Valihora, *Austen's Oughts*, 38.

52. For perhaps the most recent critique of ends-oriented thinking and action from an aesthetic perspective, see Rancière, *Aisthesis*, xiv–xvi.

53. Max Horkheimer, *The Eclipse of Reason* (New York: Oxford University Press, 1947), 4–5, my emphasis; see also Theodor W. Adorno and Max Horkheimer, *Dialectic of Enlightenment*, trans. John Cumming (New York: Continuum, 1972), 104.

54. Max Horkheimer, "Traditional and Critical Theory," in *Critical Theory: Selected Essays*, trans. Matthew J. O'Connell et al. (New York: Continuum, 1989), 207.

55. One of the critiques of mathematization, within this theory, is that it renders everything equivalent and fungible, thereby subordinating it to the logic of the market. See Adorno and Horkheimer, *Dialectic of Enlightenment*, 7, 10, 25. However, from the perspective I am describing, the problem with a mathematical description of any system is not its rendering equivalent of incommensurables. As Jacques Derrida has shown, exchange value will always haunt use value, so it makes no sense to find value in things sheltered from the vagaries of exchange: *Specters of Marx: The State of the Debt, the Work of Mourning and the New International*, trans. Peggy Kamuf (New York: Routledge, 1994). The problem is rather the evacuation of purposiveness required by any model of efficient causation.

56. Jonathan Swift, *Gulliver's Travels*, ed. Albert J. Rivero (New York: Norton, 2001), 29.

57. For a contemporary example of the misapplication of explanatory modes, drawn from the field of "positive psychology," see Vivasvan Soni, "Introduction: The Crisis of Judgment," *Eighteenth Century: Theory and Interpretation* 51, no. 3 (2010): 261–88, at 264.

58. Adam Cole, "The World's Most Precise Clock Could Prove Einstein Wrong," *All Things Considered*, National Public Radio, August 22, 2013, www.npr.org/2013/08/22/214186448/the-worlds-most-precise-clock-could-prove-einstein-wrong.

59. Horkheimer and Adorno rightly emphasize this dimension of the problem. See Horkheimer and Adorno, *Dialectic of Enlightenment*, 85; Horkheimer, *The Eclipse of Reason*, 175. I should emphasize that my claim is not meant to authorize *interference* in the work of science to make it serve particular ends. As far as possible, the work of science must be allowed to continue autonomously without such interference, to pursue its mode of explanation to the limit, though judgment and speculation about ends will always operate at the margins to shape, in more or less narrow ways, the kinds of research undertaken.

60. On this point, see especially Pfau, "Letter of Judgment," 291, 295. He explains that judgment is called for by the antagonism between efficient-causal and final-causal explanations.

61. Pfau recognizes the inadequacy of the aesthetic in Shaftesbury. For him, it is the supplement necessary when Aquinas's *synderesis* is replaced by Shaftesbury's "natural Affections" (233). However, I would suggest that prior to the foreclosure that occurs in the aesthetic turn, the "Soliloquy" essay allows significant room for shaping the will through inward reflection. See also Soni, "Judging Inevitably," for a fuller account of how aesthetics forecloses the possibility of judgment in Shaftesbury.

62. "Shaftesbury's aesthetic theory was one of the first and most influential produced by an English-speaking philosopher": Michael B. Gill, "Lord Shaftesbury [Anthony Ashley Cooper, 3rd Earl of Shaftesbury]," *The Stanford Encyclopedia of Philosophy* (Fall 2011 ed.), ed. Edward N. Zalta, http://plato.stanford.edu/archives/fall2011/entries/shaftesbury/. See also Jerome Stolnitz, "On the Significance of Lord Shaftesbury in Modern Aesthetic Theory," *Philosophical Quarterly* 11, no. 43 (1961): 97–113, at 97; Townsend, "Shaftesbury's Aesthetic Theory," 205; Richard Glauser and Anthony Savile, "Aesthetic Experience in Shaftesbury," *Proceedings of the Aristotelian Society*, suppl. vol. 76 (2002): 25–54, at 25. Terry Eagleton also situates Shaftesbury at the beginning of his account of the aesthetic in *The Ideology of the Aesthetic* (Malden, Mass.: Blackwell, 1990). By contrast, Jorge V. Arregui and Pablo Arnau contend that Shaftesbury is the first important critic of aesthetics in modernity: "Shaftesbury: Father or Critic of Modern Aesthetics?," *British Journal of Aesthetics* 34, no. 4 (1994): 350–62. However, if this were the case, it is unclear whose aesthetic theory Shaftesbury would be responding to.

63. On the antisystemic form of Shaftesbury's writing, and its intimate connection with his critique of reductive accounts of behavior, see Den Uyl, "Shaftesbury and the Modern Problem of Virtue"; Klein, *Shaftesbury and the Culture of Politeness*, 69; Pfau, *Minding the Modern*, 246. Shaftesbury himself is quite blunt about the virtues of systematic philosophizing: "The most ingenious way of becoming foolish, is by a System" (*Characteristics*, 1.180).

64. The notion of sensus communis found in the essay of that title, which is the cornerstone of Shaftesbury's critique of Hobbes, will be taken up by Kant in his notion of a "universal voice" that speaks through us in aesthetic judging. On the shifting political valences of the concept in this period, see Sophia Rosenfeld, *Common Sense: A Political History* (Cambridge, Mass.: Harvard University Press, 2011). She also notes the way that this concept comes to serve as a standard for judgment (30, 43). Stolnitz credits Shaftesbury with identifying disinterest as a key feature of aesthetic perception ("On the Significance of Lord Shaftesbury"). Although Hutcheson is indebted to Shaftesbury in developing his notion of the aesthetic sense, Townsend warns us not to project this notion back into Shaftesbury himself ("Shaftesbury's Aesthetic Theory," 208). See also Den Uyl, "Shaftesbury and the Modern Problem of Virtue," 301–2; Valihora, *Austen's Oughts*, 41–43.

65. Klein situates Shaftesbury's writing in the context of a genre of advice literature, which took upon itself to disseminate a culture of politeness (*Shaftesbury and the Culture of Politeness*, 102).

66. See Stolnitz, "On the Significance of Lord Shaftesbury," 103; Arregui and Arnau, "Shaftesbury," 357–58; Valihora, *Austen's Oughts*, 35, 37. Eagleton claims that the new subjectivity more generally is modeled on the aesthetic object

in this period (*Ideology of the Aesthetic*, 20, 41). Purviance describes the unusual status of Shaftesbury's conception of the self in the British context ("Shaftesbury on Self as a Practice"). In the *Birth of Tragedy*, Nietzsche urges us to craft ourselves as works of art, rather than thinking of ourselves as artists, focusing on the loss of self-consciousness involved in the process: see Friedrich Nietzsche, *The Birth of Tragedy; The Case of Wagner*, trans. Walter Arnold Kaufmann (New York: Vintage, 1967), 37. This is just one of the ways his aesthetic constitution of the self differs from Shaftesbury's.

67. Jennifer A. McMahon has argued that Stoicism does have a conception of decorum and of the beauty of the soul, borrowed by Cicero from Panaetius, which is important for the development of eighteenth-century aesthetics. But she acknowledges that her notion of a Stoic aesthetics is an unusual one. See McMahon, "Beauty as Harmony of the Soul: The Aesthetic of the Stoics," in *Greek Research in Australia: Proceedings of the Eighth Biennial International Conference of Greek Studies 2009*, ed. M. Rossetto, M. Tsianikas, G. Couvalis, and M. Palaktsoglou (Adelaide: Flinders University, 2011), 33–42.

68. Caygill, by contrast, sees beauty as questioning the legitimacy of judgment (*Art of Judgment*, 16–17, 35).

69. The problem with giving a rule by which to judge beauty cannot lie in the mere fact of constraint, since we have seen that judgment always operates with constraints. The problem is rather that one form of constraint is inflexibly applied to all situations equally, eliding the work of judgment about whether this constraint is appropriate or not. An aesthetic of harmony is certainly one form of the aesthetic, but so is an aesthetic of disharmony, disruption, and the *judicious* breaking of symmetry. See Stolnitz, "On the Significance of Lord Shaftesbury," 111.

70. See Stolnitz, "On the Significance of Lord Shaftesbury," 113; Prince, *Philosophical Dialogue*, 42.

71. See Pfau, *Minding the Modern*, 240. Later in the century, Austen will make this incisive critique of a Shaftesburian aesthetics in the person of Marianne in *Sense and Sensibility*, insisting that only good judgment, not any aesthetic criteria, can serve to guide the faculty of judgment. See Vivasvan Soni, "Preface: Austen's Critique of Aesthetic Judgment," in *Jane Austen and the Arts: Elegance, Harmony, Propriety*, ed. Natasha Duquette and Elisabeth Lenckos (Bethlehem, Pa.: Lehigh University Press, 2014).

72. Loesberg traces the argument relating harmony to morality back to Samuel Clarke (*Return to Aesthetics*, 34). He also reconstructs the arguments by which Shaftesbury links aesthetics and morality (38–40).

73. In contemporary terms, one might think of a character like Hannibal Lecter, or Lacan's Antigone. It is not coincidental that such characters begin to fascinate in the romantic period, for example, Byron's Manfred. Austen's Willoughby is a less extreme example, but operates in a similar way.

74. There are times when Shaftesbury recognizes the inadequacy of a formal rule specified in advance as a criterion for good judgment. For example, only good judgment, not any rule, will allow us to discern the difference between good and bad forms of enthusiasm in the "Letter Concerning Enthusiasm" and between good and bad forms of ridicule in "Sensus Communis."

75. See Prince, *Philosophical Dialogue*, 34.

76. "Self-reflexive" in this context does not mean reflecting on the self, as in soliloquy. It refers, rather, to the way Shaftesbury refuses to offer substantive advice but only gives advice about how to give advice. This gesture is replicated elsewhere, and typical of how judgment is evaded. See my "Introduction: The Crisis of Judgment" for more examples.

77. My purpose, in making this case, is not to suggest that we should "do without art," as Steven Connor has recently argued. See "Doing without Art," *New Literary History* 42, no. 1 (2011): 53–69. His project of liberating modes of perception from cognitive interference is, paradoxically, aligned with eighteenth-century aesthetic theories, though he presents this as an anti-aesthetic gesture (64, 67).

"Judge Not" and "Judge for Yourselves"

Oliver O'Donovan

The presenting question about the category of judgment is its ambivalence: why is it an activity that we are sometimes warned against, sometimes encouraged to undertake? To begin with, we must make some cursory observations on the scope of the term.

Philologically, the word "judgment" suggests an activity undertaken by a public official. In all the languages, ancient and modern, that have contributed to or been shaped by Judeo-Christian culture (with the exception, unique so far as I know, of German), the abstract noun "judgment" is derived, as in English, from a verb meaning "to judge" and a concrete noun referring to the one authorized to be the subject of the verb, "the judge." In some languages the verb generates the concrete noun (as in the Greek κρίνω, κρίτης, and the Hebrew טָפַשׁ, טֹפֵשׁ); in others the concrete noun generates the verb (as in Latin *iudex, iudicare*). But in all cases the abstract noun "judgment" speaks of the activity of the authorized person, the "judge," and the function of the judge's court. Without doubt the political sense is basic. (The German *Urteil*, which means a "determinative apportionment," is no exception to that generalization.)

Yet already in antiquity the word "judgment" had extended its range in two directions. It had extended it *outward* from the political to the public. Judgment takes place not only in the court, but in society at large. So in a Hebrew proverb we read that *reputation* is what judges a man, as a crucible tests silver or a furnace proves gold (Prov. 27:7). In Greek antiquity, meanwhile, the term had migrated from the courtroom *inward*, acquiring a partly independent reference to thoughts formed in the mind. The first person I know of who described this philological development and found it worthy of reflection was Thomas Aquinas, who devoted the six articles of question 60 in the *Secunda secundae* of the *Summa Theologiae* to the topic of *judicium*, asking first whether it was the "act of justice." He replied that it was because strictly understood it referred to the act of a judge. However, the primary sense of the word had been expanded, he noted, to include any act of reason, so that in the secondary sense judgment was an act of prudence.[1] With this separation of the judgment of the mind from the judgment of the court there went, of course, a loss of the reference to a restricted and authorized performance. Just judgment is supremely in the power of a ruling authority, who has the responsibility of "putting his hand between us both"; the wider sense of judgment as prudence lies in the competence of anyone who has a mind sufficient for it.[2]

It is with this inward migration of the term that we shall be chiefly concerned in what follows, and our exploration may be seen as an annotation on Thomas's discussion, which I begin by summarizing.

Judgment is not an Aristotelian term, but Thomas's account of justice will, in general, be founded on Aristotelian categories, especially the distinctions between "general" and "special" justice and between "commutative" and "distributive" justice.[3] Justice is situated in the architecture of the *Summa* as one of the four cardinal virtues which the world beyond the sphere of revelation could know and practice. Judgment is, on the other hand, a biblical term, translating the Hebrew מִשְׁפָּט, which, though sometimes simply a term for justice, is most typically a noun of action. In asking, therefore, whether judgment is "the *enactment* of justice," Thomas asks, by implication, how the Aristotelian conception of justice as a virtue can be expanded to accommodate the biblical conception of judgment as a performance. With that expansion comes the question, equally biblical, of the moral character of this performance. Looked at broadly, the long treatise on justice, containing sixty-six questions (compared with ten on prudence, eighteen on courage, thirty on temperance), bears strong indications of a major reconstructive enterprise, Christianizing and politicizing Aristotle's idea of justice as an individual virtue. The first sign of this is given in the first question of the treatise (q. 57), which is *de jure*, "on right," another non-Aristotelian term. The question on judgment then follows prominently in fourth place, after two definitional questions on justice and injustice respectively.

Situating the virtue within political community requires that Thomas focus more clearly than Aristotle could on the character of judgment as a public enactment. Hence the first article, as we have seen, beginning from the problematically broad application of the term, establishes its central focus on the act of the judge. Outside the paradigm use, he declares, the term is applied by analogy to all kinds of correct determination, speculative or practical, and may be applied to acts of knowledge, love, and other virtues. He turns, in the second article, to the biblical warnings against judgment. These are concerned with the many temptations to misjudgment, which happens not only by moral misperception of rights and wrongs, yielding "perverse judgment," but by unauthorized assumption of the prerogative of judgment, "usurping judgment," and by conclusions not grounded in sufficient certainty, "rash judgment." So seriously do these warnings restrict our right to judge that Thomas has to devote a third article to showing that we can, in fact, sometimes have sufficient certainty to reach a judgment at all. In the course of this he remarks that ungrounded suspicions entertained in the mind but not expressed in speech or action are like other kinds of inner temptation, such as lustful desire not expressed in fornication, so that the problem of misjudgment may be addressed in part by restraint in utterance.

Given the problem of uncertainty, he asks in his fourth article whether it is more praiseworthy to judge with excessive generosity, assuming the best possible scenario which cannot always be true, than to seek veracity at the risk of being overharsh. He answers with typical finesse that in judging *people* it is better to err in that way, but in judging *facts* only veracity counts. Someone lies dead with a dagger through his heart, and you can't nuance that fact charitably; you can only call it by its proper name. But when you find out who did it, you may assume the most sympathetic motives that could have produced the action. A fifth article then enters into the necessary place of written law in a judicial decision, which is, of course, to ensure that the decision is a collective, coherent one, reflecting the authoritative formulations of the community, and the sixth returns to where the first began, reemphasizing that judgment is an act under political authority as well as of political authority, both authorized and authorizing.

Besides reflecting on this important discussion in Thomas, what follows may also be seen as self-annotation, for in my book *The Ways of Judgment* I proposed, as a definition of public judgment, that it was an *act of moral discrimination that pronounces upon a preceding act or existing state of affairs to establish a new public context.*[4] An act of moral discrimination, first of all, dividing right from wrong. The pretension of judgment is to resolve moral ambiguity and to make the right and the wrong in a given historical situation clear to our eyes. But since it is invoked in a situation of contested right and wrong, it clarifies not only *what* is right and wrong, but also *who*. Even when a judgment takes the form of a simple finding of fact (e.g., the testator was of sound mind when the will was made), it establishes one party's claim and sets aside another's. It is an intellectual act, and in the Hebrew scriptures it often appears as an expression of "wisdom" appropriate to a ruler. The famous story of Solomon and the two women (1 Kings 3:16–28) is intended to display how the wisdom conferred by God on princes resolves the obscurities of conflicting claims.

In the second place, however, it *pronounces on a preceding act*, or on an existing state of affairs brought about by action. It is not *anticipatory*, occupying itself with what will be the case in the future, but reflective on a concrete reality that obtains already. Nor is it *deliberative*, occupying itself with what is to be done. There is a clear difference between a judgment and an arbitration. When parties seek a creative resolution to a conflict and resort to an arbitrator, the successful outcome of the procedure is simply a plan to which they can all consent: if a wealthy person dies intestate, a division of the estate must be agreed on; if the arbitrator comes up with a plan that all accept, there is no further question to ask about what happened, who is in the right, and so on. But a judgment has to reach a "verdict" (*ueredictum*), which is a truthful statement about some reality. This must be a *concrete* reality, not a generalization. It is not a "judgment" that the square on the hypotenuse of an isosceles triangle equals the sum of the squares on the other two sides. It is a judgment that *this* triangle is isosceles.

In the third place judgment establishes a public context, a practical context in which succeeding acts, private or public, are to be performed. The fact that an act must be by definition retrospective (e.g., the act of remembering) does not mean that it must be undertaken without a forward-looking deliberative object. No human actions are ever undertaken without a deliberative object; they differ, however, as to whether their objects are *purely* deliberative, as in "setting out on a journey"—or incorporate a reflective object, too. The deliberative object of an act of public judgment is the securing of an order in which we may act and interact as members of a community. Judgment aims not simply to be true, but to be valid. The truth declared is meant to determine all future relations of right both for the contesting parties and for wider society.

These three aspects constitute judgment as an act with a Janus-like aspect, looking backward and looking forward. A public judgment pronounces retrospectively on, and determines prospectively for, actions within the community that authorizes it. Some acts performed by public authority are not acts of judgment because they make no reflective pronouncement: the government signs a contract with one company rather than another, the prime minister appoints this politician rather than that one to a cabinet post; there is no suggestion that the disappointed company or politician has done anything wrong. Some acts performed by public authority are not acts of judgment because they determine no future relations of public right: the health secretary issues warnings to the public about safe levels of drinking, but we have exactly the same discretion over how much we drink as we had before. This double aspect makes judgment subject both to criteria of *truth* and criteria of *effectiveness*. These two sets of criteria apply equally and at once to one and the same act. A well-made judgment is a statement that is true, and *as such* a deed that is effective.

This brief account of judgment as a public act I take to be the central and paradigmatic use of the term. But it generates an extensive analogy of acts which are called judgment, both within the sphere of public performances, within the sphere of private communications, and within the sphere of interior thoughts. When an employer conscientiously pays the proper insurance contribution for an employee, he may be said, in a secondary sense, to make a "judgment" that this payment is required of him, corresponding to the "judgment" of the lawmakers, enshrined in employment law, which makes that payment due. And we may speak, in a yet further analogy, of a "judgment" on the part of the employees' association demanding that the employer pay what he is liable for. And why not also of "judgments" reached tacitly in the mind of a third party, for example, the judgment that the employees' association is right to demand the payment, the judgment that the employer is right to think it due, and maybe even the judgment that the legislators are right to require it?

But when we follow the analogy of judgment through its migration into the mind of an observer, how much of the formal description is still valid? This much, at least, I would maintain of the interior as of the external act of judgment: it is Janus-faced, simultaneously retrospective and prospective, and the prospective aspect is determinative, settling not simply what shall be, but what shall be *right*. Unspoken private judgments are more than mere opinions about what is the case, and they are more than mere purposes about what should be brought about. We "entertain" opinions, as we entertain passing guests; we also revise them and discard them. But we are said to "form" judgments, as we are said to "form" purposes, and they become the scaffolding on which we proceed to erect our further thoughts and actions. We do not speak of "judgments" in connection with purely speculative opinions, even opinions about concrete facts; we speak of them when there is something we must settle practically, when we find ourselves having to take one side or another in an argument in order to find a position where we can stand our ground. Yet we believe our judgments are true, as we do not believe our purposes are true. Judgments, we may say, are *decided opinions*, opinions we have resolved on as we resolve on an action, and we commit ourselves to them in such a way as to make them difficult to change. We treat them as clear and unarguable foundations for further projects of thought and action, as ground that will bear our weight.

As the act of judgment migrates to the inner world of private thought, then, it brings with it something of its original public ambience; the life of the mind comes to be conceived as a *forum internum*, an "inner courtroom." The courtroom is as such, of course, pure metaphor; thought about thought depends on a repertoire of such images in order to get a purchase on itself. Yet metaphors differ in their ontological weight; some are avowedly pictorial, while others are underpinned by real analogies. This metaphor rests on the real and constant interplay of interior and exterior discourse. There are essential lines of connection between the mind's recognition of truth and the tongue's public utterance of it. The double application of the term "judgment" highlights the inseparable, if complex, connections between tasks of thought and practical tasks of imposing rational order on public life.

There is a second step in the inward migration of judgment, from intellectual *act* to intellectual *power* and to moral *quality*. Judgment comes to refer to a virtue, which may be acquired, and perhaps lost, which may be given concrete expression in an act, but is supposed to be immanent in the subject. Here we encounter most sharply the problem of the ambivalence of judgment, for while judgment as an act may be either good or bad, judgment as a moral quality is spoken of only in a favorable sense, while other dispositions in relation to judgment are referred to always unfavorably. Unless I am mistaken, one does not call anyone "judgmental" without making a criticism (though to my surprise the *New Shorter Oxford English Dictionary* does not make this observation), but when we talk of judgment as a virtue and judgmental habits as vicious, what aspects of judgment do we praise or blame? Judgment as a virtue is related to the *reflective* side of the act; one who displays judgment is praised for capable reflection, and since capable reflection is truthful reflection, no one has "judgment" who does not have a tendency, by and large, to discern the truths of contested states of affairs. On the other hand, when we speak of proneness to judge as a vice, it is the determinative-discriminative aspect that comes to the fore. The judgmental person is not blamed for judging *mistakenly*, but for judging *inopportunely* (Thomas's *judicium temerarium*), for trying to settle matters not ripe for settling, for discriminating between righteous and unrighteous where discrimination is not fitting, speaking when there is no call to speak, and so on.

At this point we are ready to frame a hypothesis, which we shall qualify in the course of what follows: since the offense of judgment lies in its determinative-discriminative aspect, it is located in the *public* performance of judgment. The judgment that occurs in the mind, as it is essentially reflective, is without offense. The critique of judgment, on this understanding, is focused on public performance, the exercise of judgment in government. It intends to impose stringent conditions of authorization and of procedure for the successful performance of judgment as a political act. It gives voice to a concern about the overjuridicalization of society—*summum ius, summa iniuria*, as the Ciceronian tag expressed it. Freedom and peace require restraint of the juridical functions of society, politically circumscribing both the authority to perform them and the occasions for their performance.

This hypothesis may claim some support from what I wrote in *The Ways of Judgment*, where my interpretation of the warning against judgment was almost entirely focused on distinguishing the sphere of political action from the wider field of public communications. Marked out by practice of judgment, politics was a "definite something," with a defined beginning and a defined end. The vis-à-vis of political life and social life required that there should be much in society that does not involve judging. "The ways of judgment are more specified than the ways of life, and the possibilities open to judgment are more limited than the possibilities of life. . . . Judgment is a special activity that must be taken up and put down; there is a time for practising it and a time for abstaining from it."[5] To understand the notion of justice, I argued, we should be able to follow Aristotle in distinguishing a "general justice" over against a "special justice," governed by the special principles of "politics." Without a sense of this difference, articulated by the warning "Judge not!," the notion of the common good became sucked into a political constructivism with no place left for ordinary, human social communications, of food, wisdom, affection, and so on, leaving no worthwhile mode of human cooperation except jurisdiction. The corrective to this mistake lay in the role of the Church, which, as a "postpolitical society," refrained from judgment not because it was uninterested in it, but because it had felt the need for it, had cried to God for it, and had seen it revealed in Christ.

With these contentions entered in my name, I have a certain obligation to examine this hypothesis. But I did not presume to say that these considerations *exhaust* the scope of the warning against judgment. The question remains open as to whether there is room for an analogous warning addressed to the mental exercise of interior judgment. This appears to be the view of Thomas Aquinas, who in listing the things that we are warned against in the saying "Judge not!" includes not only failures of authority and objective errors of justice, but failures of reason which can befall mental as well as juridical performances: judgments about other peoples' secret thoughts, for example, or about the acts of God, or judgments formed in bitterness.[6] To test our hypothesis we must explore the nature of private judgment further, asking what force the idea of a court within the mind can have, and whether it invites the same caution against swallowing everything into itself as the court in the public realm does. And since the sources of the idea of the *forum internum* are originally theological, I need hardly apologize for pursuing this question, in keeping with my own engagements as a theologian, largely out of the Christian scriptures.

"Judge not, that you be not judged." This famous apophthegm, forming part of the collection of teachings preserved in the Sermon on the Mount of Matthew's Gospel, has at least three layers of context that we need to be aware of. In the first place it belongs to a series of remarks (Matt. 7:1–12) following the general form "What we put in, we get out." "With the judgment you pronounce you will be judged," its expansion runs, "and the measure you give will be the measure you get." A few lines later we have "Ask, and it will be given you; seek, and you will find; knock, and it will be opened to you." And at the conclusion of the section: "Whatever you wish that men would do to you, do so to them; for this is the law and the prophets." A fourth unit in the same section warns, "Do not give dogs what is holy, and do not throw your pearls before swine, lest they trample them under foot." In this instance what we put in is indifference to the aptness of our communications to time and circumstance; what we get out is a corresponding indifference to their value.

The discouragement of judgment fits very well into a general motif, familiar in ancient traditions of moral teaching, which raises the challenge of objectivity against a sense of privileged uniqueness in the unreflective perspective of the agent. It invites us, by an act of imaginative reversal, to see ourselves, the subject of our acts, as their object, and to see the objects of our acts as the subject of similar acts toward ourselves: the neighbor as the self, the self as the neighbor's neighbor. But this motif can be deployed in a variety of ways, and in the context of the Sermon on the Mount it is more than an invitation to use our imaginations. It is associated with a definite prediction of future judgment. The reversal of roles is not a thought-experiment, but a coming act of God, which will overturn the existing state of affairs on which we rely. That theme dominates the first unit of the Sermon, the famous set of blessings on the oppressed which we call the Beatitudes, and it forms its conclusion in the parable of the two houses built on rock and sand. The saying about judging, then, treats judgment as a status that is bound to be inverted. The relative positions of judge and judged will be turned through 180 degrees, and all judgments will be judged by events.

There is a third and further layer of context which makes the judge an especially telling example of the threat of reversal. Public truth has a perilous standing in the light of the radical future of God's purposes. The judge's role is exposed not only because it is, like any role, reversible, but because it is public. The privileged position of the *secret* is a recurrent theme in the recorded teachings of Jesus. The parable of the seed growing secretly (Mark 4:26–29) is a decisive key to Jesus's teaching on the Kingdom of God. What God's plan intends has not yet appeared, but it shall. Realities that seem beyond question are liable to revision and disproof. Christian thought is often characterized as suspicious of public illusion. But this is a very different suspicion from that reserve in the face of appearances which historians of philosophy typically attribute to the influence of Plato. There is no permanent dichotomy of inner truth and outward illusion. Rather, the inner truth makes its way inexorably toward a final emergence into outward view, when illusion shall be dispelled. "Nothing is hidden that shall not be revealed" (Mark 4:22). There is not one realm of appearances, but two, that of the present and that of the future. The confidence that the future will bring all to light throws the present appearance into doubt. That is the ground for treating public authority as supremely exposed to the warnings of reversal; another and more final authority is shortly to appear and to occupy the public realm.

The critique of public appearance is not focused only on the agency of government. If for the modern political imaginary whatever is not private is political, and government is the supreme bearer of public meaning, in Jesus's imaginary the public space was more richly and variously populated. Rulers and princes jostled for authority alongside landowners, rich merchants, holy men, and teachers. The most faithful interpreter of the Sermon on the Mount, that "James" who authored a short general letter that is preserved in the New Testament, applied these warnings first and foremost to those with intellectual authority. One should not, he urged, be in any hurry to occupy a teaching role and "be judged with greater strictness." The power of public speech, terrifyingly full of danger to self and others, incurs vast responsibilities (3:1–12). Like Jesus, James is concerned especially with the responsibility for negative speech: we are not to call our brother "fool," the one warns us (Matt. 5:22); we are not to "disparage" one another, writes the other (James 4:11).

To judge publicly is to discriminate between parties, making a clear distinction between those who are, and those who are not, justified. Somebody leaves every courtroom humiliated. That is what gives the act of public judgment its dangerous aspect. And since, as Christians have believed, no condemnation of ours can be final, since the judgment of every judgment has been reserved for the time of God's great reversal, there is a peril in judging. One presumes to humiliate someone whom God may vindicate. The division made for all practical and public purposes between the innocent and the guilty, the resolution of ambiguities in epistemic conditions that do not allow of easy resolution, these constitute false pretenses to the role of God. The critique of judgment, then, is essentially a *skeptical* critique, a denial of the possibility of knowing everything that a truthful judgment needs to know.

Precisely this skepticism motivates the turn from exterior to interior. It is within the mind that a certain human competence to judge rightly can be ascertained and defended. Augustine, to whom we owe much of the exploration of interior judgment in the Western tradition, is typical in finding possibilities of certainty in the conditions of consciousness itself—a line of thought notoriously extended in a later age by Descartes. True thought reached out from those central certainties, which generated, but did not conclude, interrogations about the world and its realities. Interior judgment is a comprehensive, presiding, surveying activity which embodies a sense of future time and possibility in a knowledge that its objects are contingent and changing. The conditions of true judgment included a sense of inward necessity and awareness of the reality of God. The right place for judgment to be exercised was in prayer, where the discourse of the mind with the voice of God became explicitly dialogical, and the secret thoughts of the heart could be corrected by the promptings of the Holy Spirit.[7] But if true judgment exposed the secrets of one's own heart, it also produced a thoroughgoing realism about the inaccessibility of others' thoughts. No one in the ancient world wrote more eloquently about the exposed and hazardous position of the judge sitting in court.[8]

We may know, and reflect on, the judgment of God that will be given on our own judgments. That is the logic of the inward migration. Not that we may know all that God in his judgment knows, of course, but we may know the difference between what we can know and what only he can know. The inner space, which in the Hebrew scriptures had been primarily a space of *deliberation*, a place where dangerously inverted people denied the all-seeing rule of God and planned to overthrow the public order of right ("The fool hath said in his heart . . . ," Pss. 14, 53), now comes to include a great deal of *reflection* on reality. That is why, as is often noticed, the inner space bulks larger in Christian thought about thought, accommodating within itself all the possible reflective contents of moral knowledge. But why is it a judgment and not merely a reflection? Why is the inner space not simply a cavernous storehouse, as famously depicted by Augustine, but a forum?[9]

First of all, it is because the content of the reflection is *evaluative*. Its task is to "value the things that matter most" (δοκιμάζειν τὰ διαφέροντα), as Saint Paul expressed it (Phil. 1:10). The inner space is not cut off from practical reason, but assembles the resources of moral appreciation that will provide an adequate foundation for it. In the second place, the turn from the exterior to the interior is already, as we saw Thomas observe, an act of restraint. Restraint is action, not only inaction. In transplanting the act of judgment out of the sphere of action into the sphere of reflection, it avoids judging by means of a definite and resolute judgment. The inward migration of judgment is therefore not an abandonment of judgment, but a mutation of it in the light of God's future judgment, not only restraining, but also enriching and focusing the human power to judge.

This reflective turn is essentially a turn to *knowledge of the self*. "Why do you not judge what is right for yourselves?" Jesus asked on one occasion (Luke 12:57). Judging "for" yourself is the best that the English translators could do with ἀφ' ἑαυτῶν, "out of your own resources," making the point, as the parable that illustrates it shows, that instead of waiting for God to judge what we have done, we may anticipate it, by acting in the light of it. We make friends with our accuser before he takes us to court, we pay our debts before they are exacted from us, repair our broken relations before they catch up with us. So judging "out of our own resources" is judging *ourselves*, arraigning our projected acts before the seat of divine judgment. The relation to the self is no longer immanent, as when we act with a sense of certainty or confidence, but reflective, and not only reflective but reflexive, turned in a focused attention on ourselves, assuming an objective view of ourselves that may approximate, at least, the view of God, whose knowledge of us is the basis of our self-knowledge.

This analogy between self-knowledge and God's knowledge is one reason for retaining the term "judgment" for this inward act of restraint. In its negative form, "Judge not, that you be not judged!," it may seem to allow a strategy of passive avoidance, screening out every judgmental thought or word from the mind or tongue, resolutely believing the best about everybody all the time, and, when evidence points the other way, not wanting to know. Whether that psychological strategy is really possible, or whether every policy of "See no evil, hear no evil, speak no evil" reaches a breaking point when judgment rushes in like a storm tide through a broken dike, I do not presume to say. What is certain is that this strategy has no place for self-knowledge, but is motivated by fear of it. But what is urged on us negatively and passively in the warning "that you be not judged" is urged on us as a positive demand in the question "Why do you not judge for yourselves?" We are bound to develop a reflexive-judicial inner view of ourselves.

But this self-knowledge is qualified as a *knowledge of time*. A judgment must be appropriate to the moment of its making, timely and opportune, and that condition applies to thoughts that take on the character of judgment by reaching some kind of a concrete conclusion. The knowledge of time, for beings who exist and act in time, is a concrete knowledge. We know time either as "now" or as "then," a future or a past in a certain relation to "now."

The year 1776 is not for us, as it was for Lincoln, fourscore and seven years ago; 2050 is for us, and was not for our grandparents, within the lifetime of some who are now born. We know both these times differently, and we know ourselves differently in relation to these times. Knowing time and knowing self are closely intertwined. To know *when* is to know the here and now that comprises our own sphere of memory and possibility. So to make a judgment, even a mental judgment, *as a timely act*, is to introduce a reference to our subjective knowledge of ourselves. A judgment aims to reach a true conclusion about objective reality, to be sure, but it does so *in relation to* the here-and-now of the one who forms it. And if it is a true judgment, its truth must include the truth of that here-and-now. The self-knowledge that brings us to the recognition of our own liability to judgment may entail a further recognition of our unfitness to judge here and now.[10] The truth of any judgment includes the truth of its subject-object relation. To say "I cannot tell" may be the truest judgment on an object available to us, true, at least, in its grasp of the inaccessibility of the object to a conclusion from this particular vantage point. If judgment implies a falsehood about the position of the one who makes it, no objective truth it may succeed in speaking can be more than equivocally true. In the famous saying of Jesus about the accusers of the adulterous woman, "Let him who is without fault among you cast the first stone" (John 8:1–11), the reason for suspending judgment was the unfitness of the judges to pronounce it, a condition which, in his radical application, appeared universal. We should be clear how wide the scope of Jesus's remark really is. We are commonly reminded of it, and appropriately, when capital punishment is discussed, and sometimes, not inappropriately, when sexual faults are discussed, but its implications extend to criminal judgments of every scale, to civil judgments, even to those informal judgments which may seem essential to the workings of our institutions, such as the granting or refusal of bank loans, the grading of students' examinations, and so on.

Of the two criteria we identified for public judgment, then, interior judgment is subject not only to the first, the criterion of truth, as any act of cognition must be, but to the second, that of effectiveness. An interior judgment may be ill-timed, even if there is no moment at which it is given spoken expression. Simply as a conclusion in the mind, it will determine attitudes and limit further inquiries, leaving no room for revision and new discovery. "Do not judge before the time!" (1 Cor. 4:5), Saint Paul warns us. Even if there is an element of restraint in keeping judgment to ourselves, yet it is still an act of *making up* the mind, of coming to a resolution. And that is why we cannot be content with the hypothesis we first proposed, that internal judgment is not liable to offend as public judgment is. It is possible for a mind to rush precipitately to conclusions, and so prejudice its subsequent reflection on experience. Not every faulty judgment is a prejudiced judgment. We tend, by the very nature of our learning, to get a great deal wrong before we begin to get a few things right, and that is eminently true of our knowledge of ourselves. Yet we can open ourselves to learning more, or we can close ourselves against it. "Prejudice" means invoking closure on our course of learning at the wrong moment, before we are in a position to do so.

Knowledge of self and knowledge of time: as a thought-experiment we may imagine these elements of knowledge supervening upon a state of mind from which they are wholly absent. Let us call this state of mind "the moral point of view." It is not, in all probability, a state of mind we can attribute to anyone all the time, but it is one which we can recognize ourselves as having occupied at some time. It arises from the perception of good and evil in the world, the order God has made and the opportunities that order affords us, both for fulfillment and for destruction. It does not treat the world as value-free, but embraces it as good, at the same time as it shuns the evils that mar it. It knows birth as good, death as evil, joyfulness as good, hunger as evil, kindness as good, and harshness as evil. Such a view of the world in its grand moral lines, with its orderly goods and disorderly evils, is entirely positive so far as it goes, but it goes no further than generic categories. *Particular* actions and events fit into the moral point of view only as they are classified as instances of those categories. So this morality is, as we have dubbed it, a "point of view"; it occupies a position of a spectator in the theater or football stadium, surveying what unfolds, living by contemplation of others' lives. The power of experience is poured into tears and laughter, cheers and denunciations, manifold appreciations of the ebb and flow of typical events which stage themselves, anger, sorrow, delight, amusement, all blending into an affective world-experience that is essentially aesthetic rather than agential. Knowledge of the world swallows up any knowledge of the moment of living.

The reason that everything in the moral point of view is generic, nothing particular, is that understanding the moral meaning of a particular involves an experience of ambiguity and moral irresolution which can arise only as we do our own living, when what we encounter is not yet recognizable as an instance of a known good or evil, but simply a *next* thing, different from all previous things, requiring interpretation *ab initio* in active engagement—our own and not someone else's, at this point of time and not earlier or later. The interpretation of a particular is achieved, of course, by understanding it in terms of the various kinds to which it may be subsumed; but to encounter it as a particular is not to encounter it as a unit of meaning already interpreted, but as a still-unanswered question, and to encounter it, not in the wide world over which we cast our comprehensive gaze, but before our feet, on the very ground we step onto, demanding a focused and concentrated attention.

The happy state of the moral point of view is liable to be broken up even if we do not, of our own reflection, penetrate beyond it. Self-knowledge, if not cultivated, bursts in unforewarned in the form of acutely uncomfortable self-consciousness. We become aware of our acting self through the peremptory voice of conscience, which seems to speak with immediate certainty about ourselves and to impose immediate judgments. If we are wise, we shall recognize that this peremptory self-knowledge is incomplete, that its judgment is not well-formed, and that we still need to inquire about ourselves and to take note of truths about ourselves other than those that the lightning-flash of conscience brings to our notice. But that demands interrogation and thought, not only about ourselves but about others with whom we have interacted. It demands that we understand ourselves through our likenesses and unlikenesses to others. All of which we may be too lazy or too frightened to engage on. What if we do not take up this task of questioning ourselves, but remain in the contradiction between our observer's view of the world and the painful immediacy of our self-awareness? There is only one way of resolving this tension other than by seeking true self-knowledge, which is to project the painful awareness of ourselves back onto the moral order we are accustomed to contemplate. We mistake the judgment of conscience for a general truth about the objective world. What we refuse immediately in ourselves, we suppose to be a typical reality in the world, and we judge others with the same immediacy as we are tempted to judge ourselves.

We are speaking here of what is often called "projection." It may make the phenomenon clearer if we draw out a contrast between projection and sympathy. Sympathy is a way of learning to see others as ourselves, imagining that we were in their place, and it is an essential part of understanding others' moral agency. The question of another's reasons for acting, "Why did he do that?," has to be passed through the filter of a question about ourselves: "Why might I, if I were situated otherwise than I am, do such a thing?" But this is an inquiry which requires probing and learning; it is not an immediate delivery of insight. If we keep asking why Macbeth murdered Duncan, we come to an answer only as we learn something we never knew about what might drive us, too, to treachery. It is not simply a question of illuminating Macbeth out of our own experience, but of illuminating ourselves out of Macbeth's experience. We never simply occupy Macbeth's skin, see through Macbeth's eyes. The insight delivered by sympathetic engagement with his history is the sketching of another history in which we and not Macbeth are the agents. That is the nature of good sympathy, preserving the difference between one and another agent even as it teases out the likenesses.[11]

One who has sought fuller reflective self-knowledge and understood that there are differences as well as likenesses does not waste time judging others' actions except when they impinge directly on the practical moment he or she has to face. If it is a question of doing justice or doing charity, there may be need for a decision, however inadequate, about someone else's deeds; otherwise, why judge? One who has brought to others' acts a projection of immediate self-consciousness, on the other hand, absorbs the agency of others, treats it as an extension or reflection of his or her own, praises or criticizes the other as a surrogate for confirming or restraining his or her own practical inclinations. In matters of sex this pattern of misjudgment is generally well recognized. Bathsheba takes off her clothes to bathe; David, observing her and unable to distinguish her mind from his own—a typically monarchical problem!—has the illusory sense of being involved, as though she were taking off her clothes *for him*. So he stumbles on the inclination to adultery in himself and projects it onto her: he has her stoned, or else seduces her. The first outcome we would commonly describe as "judgmental"; the second may be no less judgmental, in fact. In seeking Bathsheba's collusion for his evasion of what would commonly be considered honest behavior, he projects his own suppressed self-censure onto society and its norms.

Underlying the judgment of projection there is a terror of losing control of our agency. We behave as though by pouring judgments into the air as riotously as rifle-fire we could bring ourselves under control. In most informal social contexts we dislike judgmental behavior intensely, though in certain more formal public contexts—politics and religion especially—we affect to admire it and treat those who judge others' faults most severely as demonstrating high "ideals," as we like to say. In this way we acknowledge our own tendency to project judgments onto the world in general, and we seek to keep a space open for it. It is a measure of the extent to which the political and religious realms are viewed by us as alien realms. We do not really believe in political and religious actors as human actors; they are bearers of demonic possibilities, fit objects for the projection of what we idolize and fear within our own practical powers.

The warning against judgment is a warning against the moral point of view, which can become dangerously restful. The turn to the self is not simply a turn to moral *reflection*, but a resolute *focusing* of moral reflection on our own responsibility to act. Reflection is to be ordered to deliberation—that is what "judging for ourselves" means. "Today if you will hear his voice, harden not your hearts," warned an ancient psalm (95:7). There is a task of today, "each day while it is still called today," as the earliest Christian commentator on that psalm wrote (Heb. 3:13), that of bringing reflection to bear upon ourselves, opening the way to act. "Are those that are saved few?" Jesus was asked, and he answered: "Strive to enter by the narrow door!" (Luke 13:24). To luxuriate in a reflective view of the moral world is to lose sight of our agency and its outstanding tasks. To warn against judgment is to warn against that worst possibility of self-loss.

Let us draw these explorations to a close. A warning against judgment is a warning against premature closure of inquiry. The work of inquiring thought is a work of empirical and reflective reason, gathering information about contingencies, exploring their meaning discursively, overcoming perspectival limitations, and the greater the object, the greater the work. To reach the point of judgment is to put an end to that work, to prescind from what might fruitfully be explored further. That such moments should be reached is, of course, an indispensable condition of practical existence. That they should dominate the public realm is an inevitable implication of the infinite possibilities of concealment. No common life would be possible were all open questions to be held open indefinitely. So public judgment, like death, is one of the necessities of mortal life. But like death, it must be approached nervously and with a sense of inadequacy (*cum humilitate et timore*), taken up only as it is required by the position we find ourselves in (*si necessitas judicandi immineat propter officium*).[12] Properly undertaken, it is a diversion from, not a fulfillment of, our human potential. And when the juridical function comes to be seen as the whole content of public life, as in the universalized culture of "rights," it becomes unbearably oppressive.

Yet the logic of *inquiring thought* demands that open questions be kept open. And the inherent tension between inquiring thought and practical decisiveness is what gives the necessity of judgment its aspect of tragedy. That is why the shadow of judgment is cast beyond the paradigm case of political life onto every situation where thought and action can be in tension, even into the interior life of the mind, since there, too, decisions may be made and reflections cut short. If the warning against judgment could not be applied across the spectrum, it would raise a question about the analogy of judgment itself. Judgment may occur wherever reflection is cut short, and wherever reflection is cut short, presumptuousness and immaturity can misdirect thought.

Yet to these cautions, typical of the traditions of ancient wisdom, the Gospels have something positive to add, for they speak of a final destiny in judgment that is not merely a negative horizon, but a promise. Judgment as an eschatological event is not confined to the activity of God himself, but the saints and the redeemed are associated in it with God: "You shall sit on twelve thrones, judging the twelve tribes of Israel" (Luke 22:30). The inner tension in the human mind between reflection and decision is offered a horizon of resolution. "The spiritual man judges all things, and is judged of none," as Saint Paul wrote. Fulfillment must never be seized hold of preemptively; it has to be reached slowly, in the time appointed for it. So we are summoned back from the apocalyptic viewpoint to the moment that confronts us now, where our view is not universal and decisiveness still wrestles against reflectiveness. But we may anticipate it. We may engage in a judgment that is already timely, a judgment centered on ourselves and our immediate practical situations. World and time are already offered to us as reconciled in the gift of a self that may act. The opportunity for self-judgment offers a mediation between the poles of reflection and decision, expanding our understanding precisely as we focus it on the tasks we are given to perform.

Notes

1. Thomas Aquinas, *Summa Theologiae* (hereafter *ST*) 2–2.60.1: *Nomen judicii, quod secundum primam impositionem significat rectam determinationem iustorum, ampliatum est ad significandum rectam determinationem in*

quibuscumque rebus, tam in speculativis quam in practicis . . . et sic judicium est actus rationis. Sic ergo judicium est quidam actus justitiae sicut inclinantis ad recte judicandum, prudentiae autem sicut judicium proferentis.

2. Ibid. ad 2: *homo spiritualis . . . habet inclinationem ad recte judicandum de omnibus secundum regulas divinas, ex quibus judicium per donum sapientiae pronuntiat*; ad 3: *in his quae pertinent ad justitiam requiritur ulterius judicium alicujus superioris, qui utrumque valeat arguere et ponere manum suam in ambobus* (Job 9:33); ad 4: *ideo judicium quod importat definitionem justi pertinet ad justitiam secumdum quod est principaliori modo in praesidente.*

3. Q. 58.5,7 and q. 61.1. Thomas's incorporation of these two distinctions into an account of the body politic is another example of his bold reworking of Aristotle within the terms of Christian society.

4. Oliver O'Donovan, *The Ways of Judgment* (Grand Rapids, Mich.: Eerdmans, 2005), 7.

5. Ibid., 32.

6. *ST* 2–2.60.2 ad 2: *Dominus prohibet judicium temerarium quod est de intentione cordis vel de aliis incertis, ut Augustinus dicit. Vel prohibet ibi judicium de rebus divinis, de quibus, cum sint supra nos, non debemus judicare sed simpliciter ea credere, ut Hilarius dicit. Vel prohibet judicium quod non fit ex benevolentia, sed ex animi amaritudine, ut Chrysostomus dicit.*

7. The influence of 1 Cor. 2:15 ("The spiritual man judges all things, but is judged of no one") runs throughout Augustine's handling of the topic. I must acknowledge my obligation to the doctoral work of Ron Haflidson at the University of Edinburgh on Augustine's handling of this theme from his youth to his maturity.

8. *City of God*, 19.6.

9. *Confessions* 10.

10. Cf. *ST* 2–2.60.1 ad 1. *Aliud autem est dispositio judicantis, ex qua habet idoneitatem ad recte judicandum.*

11. These questions with regard to Macbeth are taken up more fully by Sarah Beckwith's essay in this volume.

12. *ST* 2–2.60.2 ad 3.

Stoic Agency and Its Reception

Gretchen Reydams-Schils

1

In the seventeenth century, the heyday of the revival of Stoicism, Pascal expressed a clear ambivalence about this current of thought. We have a record, as the text presents itself, of a conversation from 1655 between Pascal and his director of conscience at Port-Royal, M. de Saci (*Entretien de M. Pascal et de M. de Saci, sur la lecture d'Épictète et de Montaigne*, allegedly recorded by Fontaine, the secretary of de Saci). Pascal appears to know his Epictetus quite well, but in a dialectical move he plays out Montaigne against the Stoics, only to have them both surpassed by Christian teaching. Pascal praises Epictetus for being "among the philosophers of the world who have best understood the duties of man."[1] Epictetus, according to Pascal, "never tires of repeating that the whole study and desire of man should be to perceive the will of God and to pursue it." And to those who hanker after external goods, Epictetus has this to say, Pascal claims: "I find in Epictetus an incomparable art for troubling the repose of those who seek it in external things, and for forcing them to acknowledge that they are veritable slaves and miserable blind men; that it is impossible that they should find anything else than the error and pain which they fly, unless they give themselves without reserve to God alone" (405). Epictetus, then, can be commended for turning human beings away from the errors in their ways and toward God. Pascal even goes so far as to acknowledge that there is some type of humility to be found in Epictetus, in the latter's recommendation that human beings "should conceal good resolutions, especially in the beginning" (394).

Yet despite these powerful insights, the current of thought exemplified by Epictetus falls prey to diabolical pride (*superbe diabolique*), Pascal avers, because of its unwarranted confidence in the ability of human reason, as free and in our power, to reach the lofty goals of virtue, holiness, and companionship with God. In addition to pointing out this fundamental flaw, Pascal rejects the Stoic views that the human soul is a portion of the divine substance, that sorrow and death are not evils, and that suicide is permitted under certain circumstances.

To Epictetus's unwarranted trust in the power of human reason, the "skepticism" of Montaigne, in Pascal's eyes, provides a necessary antidote.

Moreover, embedded in what Pascal presents as a response to Stoicism, we find Montaigne utterly rejecting "that stoical virtue (*cette virtue stoïque*) which is depicted with a severe mien, fierce glance, bristling locks, and wrinkled and moist brow, in a painful and distorted posture, far from men in a gloomy silence, alone upon the summit of a rock: a phantom, he says, fit to frighten children, and which does nothing else with continual effort than to seek the repose which it never attains" (401).[2] So Stoicism is not only presented as having too much faith in human reason; it is also seen as harsh and antisocial, and as striving toward a goal that is impossible to attain.

Pascal attacks Montaigne's position in turn, however, for succumbing to moral laxity, and thus Epictetus's and Montaigne's viewpoints end up canceling each other out. These views lead to an impasse for which only Christianity can provide a way out with its doctrines of original sin, revelation, and grace—the latter especially as revealed in the two natures of Christ. The context of the debate with M. de Saci—who, to put it mildly, is not convinced of the advisability of reading philosophers such as Epictetus and Montaigne—reveals that these true insights are meant to be anchored in the writings of St. Augustine, who was the primary source of influence (also through his polemic against Pelagianism) for the Jansenist movement centered at Port Royal.

Augustine, then, appears to be at the heart of a current in Christianity that has been highly critical of Stoicism (though, of course, we need to be cautious not to take every aspect of the Jansenist hardening of the Augustinian line at face value). Moreover, while the critique leveled against Stoicism may have one of its primary points of origin in Augustine's writings, it also started to lead a life of its own, detached from that original context. And if that critique still holds in some form or another, Stoicism would appear not to be very promising for any current attempts to retrieve a more robust notion of human agency. So how could a deeper awareness of what Stoicism stands for, resulting also from the revival of research on Hellenistic philosophy of the last few decades, change such a perception? And would it be desirable to undo the conceptual amnesia that came about through the cultural dominance of the Augustinian and related criticisms?

2

A Unified Self as a Mediator

Work on the notion of (the) self has become quite prevalent in recent scholarship, and in a wide range of disciplines, not least because of Foucault's work, as in his *Le souci de soi* (1984) and the lectures published as *L'herméneutique du sujet* (1981–82, published in 2001).[3] But even if the notion has, perhaps, become too capacious and ubiquitous to be of much philosophical use any longer, I would still contend that of all the models for the human soul and action in ancient philosophy, the Stoic one presents the strongest version of selfhood. And because it is pre-Cartesian (and pre-Nietzschean and pre-Freudian, for that matter), the self in Stoicism sees human beings as essentially embedded in the reality surrounding them, in what Christopher Gill so aptly calls an objective-participant relationship.[4]

Contrary to its Platonic and even Aristotelian counterparts, Stoicism (with the possible exception of Posidonius) endorses a monist view of the human soul and does not rely on irrational parts or functions to account for the passions and irrational behavior. Human beings are said to come into the full use of reason at age seven or fourteen. But that stage does not yet entail the perfection of reason. For the Stoics either reason functions properly or it does not, and the latter case, not some kind of inner conflict, accounts for irrational behavior. If we feel torn between conflicting motivations, our reason in fact oscillates more rapidly than we can perceive between alternating judgments and courses of action. Thus the Stoics posit a unified psychological model.

Second, this unified soul, itself corporeal, is fully embedded in the human body, in the ordered structure of the universe, and in a web of social relations (the "participant" component, in Gill's wording). The first-century Stoic Hierocles renders this relation between soul and body as follows:

> Since an animal is a composite of body and soul, and both of these are tangible and impressible and of course subject to resistance, and also blended through and through, and one of them is a sensory faculty which itself undergoes movement in the way we have indicated, it is evident that an animal perceives itself continuously. For by stretching out and relaxing, the soul has an impact on all the body's parts, since it is blended with them all, and in making an impact it receives an impact in response.[5]

And Seneca, likewise, states that "one's constitution (*constitutio*) consists of a ruling power in the soul which has a certain relation towards the body" (*Epistles* 121.10). So the Stoics see human beings as unified wholes of soul and body, in which each is completely blended with the other.

At the next level of reality a human being, according to the Stoics, is completely integrated into the order of the universe (an aspect of Stoicism to which Foucault did not pay sufficient attention).[6] Human reason is literally made of the same substance as the divine principle that structures all of reality. Moreover, for the Stoics, as is especially clear in the *Prefaces* of Seneca's *Natural Questions*, ethics and the study of nature mutually reinforce each other. Human beings who strive toward maximal consistency in their rationality are meant to see such a consistency and rationality confirmed in the world around them, and especially in the heavens.

The features of the Stoic theory I have listed so far are, I would argue, not yet sufficient to attribute to them a robust notion of self. Strictly speaking, the mere Stoic "theory of action," in contemporary philosophical parlance, would not yield a self either. One can describe the Stoic view of human action, for which Brad Inwood's work still constitutes the authoritative account, in objectively normative and third-person terms (the "objective" component of Gill's phrase), as the proper interaction between the four aspects of the human mind (or of the "ruling principle" of the soul, *hêgemonikon*), namely, reason (*logos*), impression (*phantasia*), assent (*sunkatathesis*), and impulse (*hormê*).[7]

But there is another perspective on human action that is prevalent especially in the later Stoics from the Roman imperial era: the first-person point of view of lived reality. The emphasis on interiority and the importance of reflexive pronouns is very striking in these accounts, as, for instance, in Seneca's shorthand phrase "knowledge of nature and self" (*sui naturaeque cognitio*, *Epistles* 82.6). A robust role for this reflexive language does not require a reified self, "the" self in the sense of an entity in its own right, over and above the aspects of the soul which the early Stoics posited.[8] Conversely, the absence of such a distinct entity does not entail that the language of "self" is not doing some serious philosophical work.

It is the case, however—and this is difficult for us to wrap our minds around—that the Stoic notion of self does not come with a radical sense of individuality or subjectivity.[9] The Stoic Panaetius (second century BCE) provides the best avenue for understanding how the Stoics could allow for differences in individual outlooks without positing an irreducible individuality and personal point of view. As Cicero attests in his *On Duties* (1.107–17), Panaetius posits four factors that shape the identity of each human being, and these factors include but are not limited to what we would now consider social roles: (1) the nature all human beings have in common, which is characterized by rationality; (2) each person's individual disposition—bodily, temperamental, and mental; (3) the circumstances that govern one's position in life; and (4) individual choices having to do with how to lead one's life. The first factor is common to all human beings and grounds the other three; the second leaves room for individual differences. The third factor, as well as the second, one could argue, are aspects of life that are given and predetermined; the fourth, by contrast, allows for choice, but in light of what one is given to work with in terms of one's disposition and circumstances. The combination of these four factors leaves room for quite a range of different outlooks and positions in life, and these positions for the Stoics are integral to leading a philosophical life (a point to which we will return below).

The main reason the Stoics require us to think about the self without resorting to subjectivity in any later or contemporary sense is that this self is never its own end and does not stand in opposition to the world around it. Hence I posit the notion of a mediating self.[10] Its primary function is to allow a human being, in the midst of so-called ordinary concerns and occupations, to weigh traditional value judgments against the radical transformation of these in Stoic ethics, which posits virtue in the guise of perfected reason as the only good. This self constitutes the mental space in which, for instance, as Epictetus recommends, one can check one's reactions and test one's impressions. If something announces itself as good, is it truly? Would the judgment that it is good be based on the opinion of one's father-in-law, for instance, or the goal of human life as defined by philosophy?

If the self primarily has this mediating function, then it does not make sense to talk about an "impersonal" or "ideal" self. The closer human beings get to the ideal—a point that arguably holds for Plato and Aristotle as well—the less distinctive they become. Or in Stoic terms, in their perfected reason all sages are alike to one another and to the divine principle, but through their different situations in life, which require different balancing acts, they do present different manifestations of virtue.

Finally, the secondary literature in recent decades has approached this theme via the notion of the will. One could emphasize, for instance, the voluntarist aspects of Seneca's ethics, or examine Epictetus's notion of "moral choice" (*prohairesis*) from this angle.[11] But these aspects of the Stoic views can also be explained as arising from the perceived need for self-control, or with the help of the contemporary notion of intentionality (in itself an anachronism).

Action and Contemplation

Absolutely indispensable for a correct understanding of the Stoics' notion of agency is their groundbreaking view of the relation between action and contemplation. The far-reaching implications of this view are still in the process of being (re)discovered in current scholarship. It is rather an understatement to say that in both Plato's and Aristotle's works there remains an unresolved tension between *praxis* as an active, political life in communities and some form of pure thought aimed at in *theôria* (a burden they passed along to the Christian tradition). Hannah Arendt, in *The Human Condition*, is right in diagnosing this tension as creating a major challenge for a robust notion of agency.[12] But the Stoic response to this challenge is missing entirely from her account, and Stoicism itself is barely present, and then only through the mistaken stereotypical view that it recommends "abstention from the whole realm of human affairs."[13] The Stoic view on action and contemplation, which is as bold as it is succinct, has been preserved by Diogenes Laertius in this formula: "Of the three kinds of life, the contemplative, the practical, and the rational (*logikos*), they declare that we ought to choose the last, for that a rational being is expressly produced by nature for contemplation and for action."[14] So for the Stoics the "rational life" (*bios logikos*) encompasses both contemplation and action. As Thomas Bénatouïl has argued convincingly, with this claim the Stoics do not have a so-called mixed life in mind, with alternations between action and contemplation. Rather, what they imply is that action and contemplation always go together and mutually inform each other and, moreover, that contemplation is *for the sake of* a better way of being in the world.[15] Another way of phrasing this point is that the Stoics, unlike Aristotle, posit no distinction between practical reasoning and a higher mode of reason.

The standard Stoic view states that the sage will participate in politics (as well as marry and have children; see below) and thus play his part in the life of communities. If someone has a special aptitude (for which the theory of roles developed by Panaetius would allow; see above), this person can devote him- or herself to philosophy in the narrow sense, or if circumstances are not propitious, a sage can withdraw from political functions (sometimes this can also happen involuntarily, as in exile). But, the Stoics are adamant on this point, even in such situations a sage, or someone aiming to become one, will not abdicate his political responsibilities, but will, for example, teach, devise laws, or develop constitutions.[16] For the Stoics, "theory"—rather as in our use of the word—stands for the content of philosophical doctrines, in itself quite powerless if not accompanied by the right actions. And, as indicated above, they do acknowledge a special role for the contemplation of the order in the universe, as manifested especially by the heavenly bodies. But there is literally no flight from the world possible for a Stoic, a world that at its highest level constitutes the *cosmopolis* as the community of the gods and humans of which one always remains a citizen.[17]

In sum, according to the Stoics, whether one devotes most of one's time and efforts to philosophy in the strict sense or, at the other end of the continuum, finds oneself in the thick of demanding political responsibilities, both modes of life would entail the combination of theory and praxis. The Stoic philosopher never abdicates her responsibility to the community in which she finds herself; the Stoic politician does not assess how he is doing by the standard of success as traditionally defined. But still more importantly this mode of being, of continuously reorienting traditional values in the light of the true good, allows for what one could call a heroism of everyday life. A Homeric hero may need a fight, an extraordinary cause, or a monster, but for a Stoic, in his recasting of Odysseus or Heracles, the challenges of so-called ordinary life, in which a spouse or child are as fragile and can break as easily as a clay pot, are worthy of philosophy's attention and care.

Sociability

The idea of the cosmopolis as the community of gods and human beings is based on another groundbreaking innovation, which also accounts for the mutual implication of action and contemplation. As we have seen, according to Pascal, Montaigne claims (as does Hannah Arendt; see above) that the Stoic lives "far from men in a gloomy silence, alone upon the summit of a rock." Yet Seneca claims that "no school [other than the Stoics] is kinder and more gentle, none more full of affection for human beings nor more attentive to the common good" (*De Clementia* 2.5.3). Who is right, and what is the justification for Seneca's claim?

For the Stoics rationality, both at the divine and at the human level, is intrinsically social, and the importance of this view and what it entails cannot be overestimated. Aristotle's statement that a human being is by nature a political animal still leaves room for a crucial ambiguity from the Stoic point of view.[18] Are we talking here about the nature humans have in common with other animals, or their distinctive nature as rational beings? Moreover, the emphasis on the contemplative life in book 10 of Aristotle's *Nicomachean Ethics* undermines the importance of sociability, not only at the level of the *polis* but even at the level of the more intimate relationship of friendship. If at the end of book 9 Aristotle seems to have posited friendship as essential to the pursuit of philosophy (9.9, 1170b10–19), in his discussion of contemplation he ends up stating that "the philosopher, even when by himself, can contemplate truth, and the better the wiser he is; he can perhaps do so better if he has fellow-workers, but still he is the most self-sufficient" (10.7, 1177a33–77b1).[19] So it appears that at the pinnacle of contemplation, when one finds oneself in a direct relation with the divine, as in the final moment of Augustine's conversion (*Confessions* 8.12), one leaves even friendship behind. Admittedly Augustine returns to his friend Alypius, or shares his experience of divine communion with his mother (*Confessions* 9.10). But a Stoic does not need such a moment of *return* to the web of social relations because he or she never abandons it in the first place, not even when being alone.

By contrast with Aristotle, the Stoics posit that human sociability has some features, such as parental care for offspring, in common with certain animals, but that it is ultimately grounded in the divine rational principle, which, in its providential function, has ordered all of reality (Cicero, *On Ends* 3.62ff.). There exists an inescapable and fundamental kinship between all human beings because they literally all have their origin in the divine principle. The self is intrinsically relational, and human beings are meant to imitate the divine care for the world (whereas it is difficult to reconcile the notion of Providence with Aristotle's concept of an Unmoved Mover).

But the Stoics do not limit sociability to the kinship of all with all. Contrary to Plato in his *Republic*, and more in line with Aristotle on this specific point, they do not hold that more intimate and traditional relationships stand in the way of the common good; rather, sociability expresses itself first and foremost in those relationships, which are indeed, in the final analysis, to be harmonized with the universal perspective, but not as a result of bypassing those relationships altogether. Hence the Stoic view that the sage will not only participate in politics, as discussed above, but also marry and have children.

One of the most striking instantiations of this point of view is Epictetus's response to a Roman official (*Discourses* 1.11) who could not stand witnessing the suffering of his sick daughter and turned away from her. The same Epictetus who is notorious for such prima facie harsh comparisons between a wife or child and a clay pot (as in *Enchiridion* 3, 11, 14) tells the official that he should have stood by his child and taken care of her himself. Overcoming the fear of death here serves not the turn toward a higher level of reality, as in Plato's *Phaedo*, but rather one's responsibility toward others.

From a contemporary point of view, we may want to posit that a genuine commitment to others requires that we register their loss as a real calamity and true evil, that, in other words, we give vulnerability its full due rather than arm ourselves against it. The strength of the Stoic view, however, becomes apparent especially in cases in which excessive emotions and grief would actually impede our commitment to others, as, for instance, with the Roman official who could not handle the risk of emotional vulnerability at all, and hence turned away from the suffering of his child. Other recurring motifs in Seneca's consolations also address problems with excessive mourning, such as the potential neglect of one's responsibilities toward other members of one's circle, or even the inability to honor the memory of the deceased. Viewed from this angle, the Stoic stance amounts not to evasiveness and detachment, but rather to a form of emotional courage in one's relations with others.

Moreover, this responsibility is not a matter of mere impersonal duty, but allows for genuine affection. It is often overlooked that the Stoic battle against the passions and their ambivalence about pity also leaves room for good emotions (*eupatheiai*), which are compatible with or supervenient on the correct functioning of reasoning.[20] The good emotion joy is the counterpart to the passion of excessive elation, caution is the counterpart to fear, and wish to desire (the sage has no use for a positive counterpart to distress). And as it so happens, the subkinds of "wish" are all forms of affection toward or caring for others. There is no reason to assume that these good emotions would be tepid or mere shadows of what we would consider genuine affection. If the above claims hold, we are indeed very far removed now from the Stoic as a gloomy and asocial phantom. Or as Plutarch recorded about the Stoic notion of friendship:

> If a single sage anywhere at all extends his finger prudently, all the sages throughout the inhabited world are benefited. This is their amity's work; this is the end in which for their common benefits the virtues of the sage issue . . . the amazing benefit which sages receive [from] the virtuous motions of one another even if they are not together and happen not even to be acquainted.[21]

Authority and Agency

One more feature of Stoic agency that cannot be captured by any contemporary analytical sense of a "theory of action" pertains to its relation with authority. Epictetus can always be relied on to provide succinct and pointed renderings of an issue: "Remember that it is not merely desire for office and wealth which makes men abject and subservient to others, but desire also for peace, and leisure, and travel, and scholarship. For it makes no difference what the external object be, the value you set upon it makes you subservient to another."[22] The Stoics warn against making one's reason and faculty of judgment subservient to another even if that other happens to be a teacher of philosophy. We have ample evidence to show that the Stoics cast the role of a teacher or philosophical school in conscious opposition to other modes of doing philosophy in Antiquity.[23] The founders of Stoicism—Zeno, Cleanthes, and Chrysippus—did not claim the status of sagehood for themselves,[24] their successors cautioned against potential excesses of worshipping founders as opposed to thinking for oneself, and they did not promote (semi-)permanent attachments to schools. The ultimate goal of Epictetus's teaching was for his pupils to make insights their own and to apply these in whichever social context to which they would eventually return. Thus for the Stoics the lifelong conversation with oneself takes precedence over the relation with an authority figure such as a teacher. The idea that Zeus has entrusted us to ourselves as an inalienable duty, that is, one that cannot be transferred to anybody else (Epictetus, *Discourses* 2.8.21–23), underscores the notion of agency as both empowerment and responsibility.

3

If we return to the conversation of Pascal with which we started, three principal criticisms appear to have been leveled against Stoicism (and Augustine probably constituted a watershed moment in the Christian tradition's critical attitude—a topic that would merit renewed investigation, even though there are also many positive influences of Stoicism to be detected in Augustine's writings).[25] First, the Stoic ideal of self-possession has come across as egocentric and as coldly, if not downright cruelly, detached. This criticism already occurred during the time of the Stoics themselves—Seneca addresses it, for instance, in his *On Mercy* 2.5.2, precisely in a context in which he distinguishes between the virtue of mercy, a reasoned state, and pity as an irrational emotional response. Second, the ideal the Stoics propose has been seen as unattainable for human beings, and hence as useless in the final analysis (as in Seneca, *Epistles* 92.27; but this critique would apply to all forms of becoming godlike in ancient philosophy). Last but not least, the ideal seems to presuppose an unwarranted Promethean confidence in human rationality and the ability of human beings to be the agents of their own happiness; or, in other words, the Stoics have an implausibly strong notion of human agency coupled with a rejection of any radically transcendent concept of the divine.

Yet, on closer scrutiny, the Stoics themselves have answers to all these charges. As indicated already above, they constituted the only school of thought in antiquity that made sociability intrinsic to rationality, and their theory of "good emotions" left ample room for affection. The main challenge here is to conceive of a type of sociability that is not centered on the opposition between self-centered behavior and a type of altruism that respects the other qua other (a much later notion, and hence an anachronism when applied to the Stoics), but rather relies on the notion of an *extended* self in which the distinction between self and others becomes blurred.

On the second point, the Stoics themselves were aware of the scarcity of the sage (see above). Perhaps none had ever existed, but the most common stance appears to have been that there were a few instances, among which Stoics also ranked Socrates. But as Plato's Socrates already pointed out in the *Republic* (502b), it makes all the difference in the world if only one instance of a sage can be found. Moreover, despite a radical "all-or-nothing stance" according to which even someone with very minor flaws would still fall short of goodness, just as someone just below the water's surface would still be drowning (Plutarch *On Common Conceptions* 1063A-B = SVF 3.539 = LS 61T), the Stoics did see value in moral progress. In fact, as has often been noted, the writings of the later Stoics tend to focus on the common run of human beings who are still muddling through. What has been noticed less, however, is that the rarity of the Stoic sage, and the fact that Stoic masters did not claim this status for themselves or for their own teachers and thus adopted a low-authority profile, reinforced their pupils' individual agency and responsibility.

Yet the central paradox of human agency in Stoicism, which keeps the latter from turning into a Promethean self and for which the Stoics were often attacked in antiquity, is that, succinctly put, the utmost freedom consists in aligning one's own reason with the divine providential reason that through fate has ordered all of reality. It is true that Epictetus, for instance, in the famous opening passage from the *Handbook*, starts out with the fundamental distinction between "that which is up to us" and "that which is not." But it is also the case, as Pascal rightly noted, that the correct, rational use of impressions, the only thing up to us, reveals the inextricable connection between human and divine reason, and presents human rationality as a gift of divine Providence (as in *Diss.* 1.1 and 3), that is, precisely *not* as the ground of its own being and freedom. A brief comparison with Boethius's *Consolation of Philosophy* reveals a similar approach, this time set in more Platonic terms: Boethius too claims that the more human beings detach themselves from worldly concerns, and the closer they get to the divine, the more free and empowered they become (5.2). And if there remains, indeed, a certain optimism about human nature in the Stoic position that all human beings have the potential to grow into the full use of their reason that will lead to happiness, this optimism is balanced, again, by the scarcity of the sage. Similarly, the claim that human nature does not come with intrinsic liabilities, such as, for instance, the two lower-soul parts known as spirit and appetite in Platonism, is offset by the power and pervasiveness of the two main corrupting influences the Stoics do acknowledge, namely the wrong-headed influence of others and the inherent attraction of externals. To reach the good life in Stoic terms remains a formidable challenge.

4

Among contemporary philosophers Alasdair MacIntyre has been very critical of Stoicism, thereby underestimating the potential of this current of ancient philosophy for what has now come to be known as virtue ethics. MacIntyre objects to the Stoics that (1) they focus too much on the individual to the detriment of the social aspect of human existence in communities; (2) their philosophy is not teleological; (3) and it is rule-based, and hence not a true virtue ethics.[26] These charges are untenable, as other scholars have also pointed out.[27]

History, or, more precisely, the availability of Stoic sources, may have a lot to do with the distorted picture that has come down to us. To this day, the study of the early phase of Stoicism is a difficult and highly technical matter because only fragments of the works have survived. Of the later Stoics, only Seneca wrote in Latin and was well-known throughout the Middle Ages; but Cicero, especially his *On Ends*, needs to be taken into account as well. The rediscovery of the views of other later Stoics, such as Epictetus and Marcus Aurelius, had to wait until the retrieval of the Greek tradition and the new editions of the Renaissance. And given how difficult the access to Early Stoicism is, it took even longer, roughly to the second half of the twentieth century, to rediscover the full range of the connections between later Stoics and the more technical aspects of original Stoicism.[28]

The first edition of MacIntyre's *After Virtue* came out in 1981. At that point scholars still had to rely primarily on von Arnim's collection of the fragments of Early Stoicism, the *Stoicorum Veterum Fragmenta*, which provides only the Greek and Latin and does not spell out any connections. Moreover, the standard view of the writings of the later Stoics claimed that these represented mere popular moralizing, that they were thin in philosophical content and not necessarily faithful to key Stoic notions. But by the date of the publication of *After Virtue*, a major revival in the study of Hellenistic philosophy, including Stoicism, was well under way. In 1987, Anthony A. Long and David Sedley published their groundbreaking two volumes of key fragments of the Hellenistic philosophers, now thematically arranged, with translations and succinct commentary, as well as bibliography.[29] These two volumes became catalysts for a new wave of highly intensified research on Hellenistic philosophy, leading to results and insights that were simply not available yet when MacIntyre wrote his seminal work. In this crucial sense too, history matters.

In contrast to Alasdair MacIntyre, Charles Taylor, in his *A Secular Age* published about twenty-five years after MacIntyre's work (2007), is markedly more historically sensitive to the defining features of Stoicism.[30] Taylor is fully aware of the fundamental differences between Stoicism in antiquity and its reemergence in neo-Stoicism in the late sixteenth and seventeenth centuries, as in the primary case of Lipsius. The "reconstructivist" agenda of neo-Stoicism, to use Taylor's term, emphasizes activism and free will and relies on a fundamental assumption of the malleability of human nature, of society, and, through science and a mechanistic view of the universe, ultimately of the world around us. But this agenda has no counterpart in original Stoicism. (Stoicism, in fact, has legitimately been criticized for not advocating for the abolition of slavery, given its assumption that all human beings in their rationality have the capacity for virtue.)

Descartes's ethics too shows traces of an influence of Stoicism, especially in his notion of a provisionary moral dwelling in his *Discours de la méthode* (ch. 3; see also his correspondence with Princess Elisabeth of Bohemia and *The Passions of the Soul*).[31] But as Taylor acknowledges, in Descartes's worldview the gap with Stoicism widens even more, in the sense that Descartes no longer sees the rational self as fundamentally embedded in a given divine and rational order that permeates the entire cosmos. According to the terms used in this essay, Descartes does away with the objective-participant aspect of the Stoic self.

Moreover, more work needs to be done to understand the exact relations between the Stoic elements in Descartes's ethics and the strong Platonic-Augustinian influence on his metaphysics and mind-body dualism.[32] Though I cannot prove the point fully within the confines of this essay, Descartes's Stoicism could, I suggest, be read as turning the Augustinian critical and reductionist rendering of Stoicism on its head, by using this version as something not to be rejected, but to be embraced fully. If a (mistaken) Promethean Stoic self emerged from Augustine's *City of God*, Descartes is reclaiming it. But if this is the case and Taylor's reading of Lipsius's neo-Stoicism is on the right track, we still do not have an explanation as to *why* Lipsius chose to read the Stoics in this manner, or *what led* Descartes *to this* selective appropriation of the Stoic tradition. The reason, in other words, cannot be found in Stoicism itself.

Yet there is also more than a soupçon in Taylor's account that something in the Stoic self, in its attempt at eliminating the passions and its emphasis on self-sufficiency, was amenable to being turned into what he calls the modern notion of the "buffered self," a self that is too far gone in its detachment and its attempt to bypass the world and a higher order. If the overview of this essay has any plausibility, however, that charge cannot be laid at the doorstep of the Stoics. The true connection may be somewhere else, namely in the fact that the Stoics minimize the importance of external authority in the mediation of wisdom (see above), and this stance could have had a major influence on the resistance to what was perceived as the Church's dogmatism and abuses of power in the early modern and modern periods. But as I indicated already, the Stoic low-authority approach still posits a self that is embedded in the order of the world and is fully relational, the self as a mediator, never becoming an end in itself (as Taylor himself points out earlier in his account [p. 27]).

In an earlier work, *Sources of the Self*, Taylor picks up the idea that "radical reflexivity," or the focus on inwardness and self-awareness, is essential to Augustine's *Confessions*.[33] This potential rapprochement between Augustine and the Stoics in light of Descartes's use of both traditions needs, again, to be viewed from the proper perspective. The Stoics may indeed have been too close for comfort to Augustine (and not just in his earlier, so-called ethical phase, but throughout his career, as his opponents did not fail to point out): *neither* Augustine *nor* the Stoics endorse a kind of radical reflexivity that would lead to a disengaged stance; both versions of self are open to the divine and to manifestations of its providential agency (albeit in very different forms). Augustine's *Confessions*, for all the crucial differences—not the least of which, of course, is the doctrine of grace—can legitimately be seen as the heir of the Stoic view that philosophy writes itself, in Seneca's *Letters* and Marcus Aurelius's *Meditations*, as a human being's struggle with everyday, ordinary challenges such as ill health, running into difficult and disagreeable people, preferring play to homework, struggling with lust and other flaws, restlessness, and dissatisfaction. It is not a Platonist like Plotinus, who according to Porphyry's biography refused to provide details of his life in the body (*Life of Plotinus* 3), but the Stoics who would have given Augustine a model to transform in his *Confessions*.

In sum, a lot more work remains to be done to retrieve the results of recent research on Stoic agency and to undo this conceptual amnesia. The impact of Stoicism on early Christianity is in the process of being reassessed. In light of this process, we need a better sense of where and how exactly the outlines of the critique of Stoicism emerged. To what extent, if any, did Stoic ethics and its notion of agency survive underground, so to speak, in the Middle Ages? How did Stoicism in the revival of the late sixteenth and seventeenth centuries become aligned with different positions? Last but not least, what distinctive contributions can Stoicism make to a robust notion of agency in a contemporary context—contributions that are not limited to the interest in cognitive therapy or a version of cosmopolitanism? Once we start looking beyond the surface of Augustine's critique of the Stoics, starting with Augustine's own work, the story largely remains to be written.

Notes

1. Blaise Pascal, *Minor Works*, trans. O. W. Wight, vol. 48, Part 2, Harvard Classics (New York: P. F. Collier & Son, 1909–14), 392–405, at 393–94. Subsequent citations appear in the text above. See also from his *Pensées* 98 (80), 100 (467), 140 (466), 144 (360), 146 (350), and in general headings IX and X, 279 (690), 407 (465), 745 (18b). For a detailed analysis of the parallels between this text and Epictetus, Montaigne, and Augustine's *Confessions*, see Pierre Courcelle, *L'entretien de Pascal et Sacy, ses sources et ses énigmes* (Paris: Vrin, 1960). But another set of parallels remains to be developed, namely, that between Pascal's criticisms of Stoicism and Augustine's, with the latter especially in the *City of God*, books 9, 14, and 19.

2. See Michel de Montaigne, *The Complete Essays of Montaigne*, trans. Donald M. Frame (Stanford, Calif.: Stanford University Press, 1976), 1.26, "On the Education of Children" (section on philosophy).

3. Michel Foucault, *L'herméneutique du sujet: Cours au Collège de France, 1981–1982*, ed. Frédéric Gros (Paris: Gallimard / Le Seuil, 2001), and *The History of Sexuality*, vol. 3, *The Care of the Self*, trans. Robert Hurley (New York: Vintage, 1988).

4. Christopher Gill, *Personality in Greek Epic, Tragedy, and Philosophy: The Self in Dialogue* (Oxford: Oxford University Press, 1996), 10; see also his *The Structured Self in Hellenistic and Roman Thought* (Oxford: Oxford University Press, 2006) and Anthony A. Long's groundbreaking essay "Representation and the Self in Stoicism," in *Companions to Ancient Thought*, vol. 2, *Psychology*, ed. Stephen Everson (Cambridge: Cambridge University Press, 1991), 102–20.

5. Hierocles 4.38–48, slightly modified = LS53B5–6, in Anthony A. Long and David N. Sedley, *The Hellenistic Philosophers*, 2 vols. (Cambridge: Cambridge University Press, 1987).

6. On this point, see the illuminating critique by Pierre Hadot, *Philosophy as a Way of Life: Spiritual Exercises from Socrates to Foucault*, ed. Arnold Davidson, trans. Michael Chase (Oxford: Blackwell, 1995), ch. 7, 206–13. One could object to Hadot in turn, however, that he did not pay sufficient attention to the fundamental differences between the Platonist and the Stoic conceptions of philosophy as a way of life.

7. See Brad Inwood, *Ethics and Human Action in Early Stoicism* (Oxford: Clarendon, 1985).

8. Contrary to Brad Inwood, *Reading Seneca: Stoic Philosophy at Rome* (Oxford: Clarendon, 2005), 321–52; see also Gretchen Reydams-Schils, "Review of B. Inwood: *Reading Seneca: Stoic Philosophy at Rome*," *Phoenix* 61.1–2 (2007): 186–89, and "Authority and Agency in Stoicism," *Greek, Roman, and Byzantine Studies* 51 (2011): 296–322.

9. See Gill, *Structured Self*, 325–407.

10. See Gretchen Reydams-Schils, *The Roman Stoics: Self, Responsibility, and Affection* (Chicago: University of Chicago Press, 2005), ch. 1.

11. For the first emphasis, see Inwood, *Reading Seneca*, 132–56; for the second, see Michael Frede, *A Free Will: Origins of the Notion in Ancient Thought* (Berkeley: University of California Press, 2011).

12. Hannah Arendt, *The Human Condition*, 2nd ed. (Chicago: University of Chicago Press, 1998), 7–21.

13. Ibid., 234.

14. Diogenes Laertius 7.130, in Robert D. Hicks, ed., *Lives of Eminent Philosophers*, vol. 2 (Cambridge, Mass.: Harvard University Press, 1931).

15. See Thomas Bénatouïl, "Theôria et vie contemplative du stoïcisme au platonisme: Chrysippe, Panétius, Antiochus et Alcinoos," in *The Origins of the Platonic System: Platonisms of the Early Empire and Their Philosophical Contexts*, ed. Mauro Bonazzi and Jan Opsomer (Leuven: Peeters, 2009), 3–31.

16. See Reydams-Schils, *Roman Stoics*, ch. 3.

17. See Katja M. Vogt, *Law, Reason, and the Cosmic City: Political Philosophy in the Early Stoa* (New York: Oxford University Press, 2008).

18. For a recent reassessment of this issue, see also Adriel Trott, *Aristotle on the Nature of Community* (Cambridge: Cambridge University Press, 2014).

19. Aristotle, *Nichomachean Ethics*, trans. W. D. Ross, in *The Basic Works of Aristotle*, ed. Richard McKeon (New York: Random House, 1941).

20. Margaret Graver, *Stoicism and Emotion* (Chicago: University of Chicago Press, 2007).

21. Plutarch, *Comm. Not*. 1068F–1069A, in Harold Cherniss and William C. Helmbold, eds., *Plutarch's Moralia*, vol. 13, part 2 (Cambridge, Mass.: Harvard University Press, 1957).

22. Epictetus, *Diss*. 4.4.1, in William A. Oldfather, trans., *Epictetus*, vol. 2 (London: Heinemann; Cambridge, Mass.: Harvard University Press, 1925).

23. Reydams-Schils, "Authority and Agency in Stoicism."

24. René Brouwer, "Sagehood and the Stoics," *Oxford Studies in Ancient Philosophy* 23 (2002): 181–224.

25. On the topic of Augustine's relation to the Stoics, see Marcia Colish, *The Stoic Tradition from Antiquity to the Early Middle Ages*, vol. 2, *Stoicism in Christian Latin Thought through the Sixth Century* (Leiden: Brill, 1990); and Sarah Byers, *Perception, Sensibility, and Moral Motivation in Augustine* (Cambridge: Cambridge University Press, 2013). The latter, one could argue, takes an extreme view of the positive influence of Stoicism on Augustine and does not pay sufficient attention to Augustine's critique of Stoicism. But Byers is right in pointing out that even in the polemic against the Pelagians (as in *c. Iul*. 4.15.76) Augustine still reserves praise for Stoic ethics (125, n. 132).

26. The same mistake can be found in Robert J. O'Connell, "*De libero arbitrio I*: Stoicism revisited," *Augustinian Studies* 1 (1970): 49–68, at 65.

27. See for instance Anthony A. Long, "Greek Ethics after MacIntyre and the Stoic Community of Reason," *Ancient Philosophy* 3 (1983): 184–97; and David Burchell, "Civic Personae: MacIntyre, Cicero and Moral Personality," *History of Political Thought* 19.1 (1998): 101–18. I owe this succinct rendering of MacIntyre's main objections to Paul Scherz, "Technology and Subjectivity in the Thought of Alasdair MacIntyre and Michel Foucault" (Ph.D. diss., University of Notre Dame, 2014).

28. For a good example of this type of work on Seneca, see Jula Wildberger, *Seneca und die Stoa: Der Platz des Menschen in der Welt*, Untersuchungen zur Antiken Literatur und Geschichte 84, nos. 1–2 (Berlin and New York: de Gruyter, 2006).

29. Long and Sedley, *Hellenistic Philosophers*.

30. Charles Taylor, *A Secular Age* (Cambridge, Mass.: Harvard University Press, 2007), 90–145.

31. On this point, see two excellent analyses by Donald Rutherford: "On the Happy Life: Descartes vis-à-vis Seneca," in *Stoicism: Traditions and Transformations*, ed. Steven Strange and Jack Zupko (Cambridge: Cambridge University Press, 2004), 177–97, esp. 188–93, and "Reading Descartes as a Stoic: Appropriate Action, Virtue, and the Passions," *Philosophie Antique* 14 (2014): 129–55.

32. Stephen Menn, *Descartes and Augustine* (Cambridge: Cambridge University Press, 1998).

33. Charles Taylor, *Sources of the Self: The Making of Modern Identity* (Cambridge, Mass.: Harvard University Press, 1989), 130–31. For a critical response to this claim, see Thomas Pfau, *Minding the Modern: Human Agency, Intellectual Traditions, and Responsible Knowledge* (South Bend, Ind.: University of Notre Dame Press, 2013), 120–21.

Part II

Ethics

Among the dominant tendencies in modern ethical thought since the eighteenth century has been the desire for calculability, whether in Smith's sentimentalism, Bentham's utilitarian calculus, or Kant's categorical imperative. By contrast, poststructuralist thought, when it has attended to the ethical rather than dismissing it, has insisted on an experience of the aporia (irreconcilable, conflicting imperatives) as the irreducible core of an anti-programmatic ethics. Between algorithmic computation and undecidability, there is little or no room allowed for the exercise of independent judgment or genuinely creative action in ethical matters, unlike an Aristotelian virtue ethics for which judgment (*phronesis*) was the crucial intellectual virtue. The essays in this second group reflect on some of the ways that the capacity for judgment and action might be threatened in the realm of ethics, and what might be necessary to reinvigorate our atrophying capacity for judgment and action. At the heart of all three essays is a meditation on the self as a character that is narratively extended in time, and imbricated in its social world rather than existing apart from it.

Surprisingly, the target of Hauerwas's critique is not any of the ethical paradigms I mention above, but Alasdair MacIntyre's virtue ethics. MacIntyre is one of the key architects of a contemporary virtue ethics, and one would not expect him to be vulnerable to this sort of critique. Indeed, Hauerwas accepts several of his premises, including that it is important to focus on character rather than discrete ethical situations, that character concerns "wise judgment," and that "intelligible actions are more basic than the notion of action qua action." But he critiques MacIntyre from a Christian theological perspective, arguing that without a "thick narrative" of the virtues, it is impossible to make sense of why Eichmann and Bonhoeffer respond so differently to the Holocaust. Bonhoeffer's actions cannot be made intelligible without the Christian God. In Wetzel's response to Hauerwas's essay (see appendix), he takes this a step further, arguing that "whatever the nature of the redemption . . . , it is not a redemption paid out in the coinage of intelligibility." "It isn't the Christian narrative that saves, Hauerwas reminds us, but Christ."

Beckwith, too, explores agency and its limits through a single character. She argues that Macbeth can only perform his murderous deeds because he "is tutoring himself in the denial of his own agency" and that in Macbeth, "Shakespeare is showing us a mind losing the concept of human action." To expose Macbeth's dangerous sophistry, she begins from Aquinas's insight that "actions . . . proceed from a deliberate will," grounded in reasons, not causes. By refusing to think at all, Macbeth is able to rewrite his reasons as though they were "causes [he] experiences as compulsions, extrinsic to its own will," thereby "turning his action into behavior." Just as Arendt thought that the capacity to promise and forgive were essential conditions for action,

Beckwith argues that our recognition of having acted rather than merely reacted can be restored through remorse, and the painful reflection it forces on us.

Finally, Nazar begins with the critique of autonomy that pervades the contemporary humanities, a critique that in her view jeopardizes the capacity for independent judgment. However, she does not seek a naive restoration of autonomy in order to enable judgment, because she is cognizant of the ways that certain forms of autonomy imply a self severed from the social world and obtuse to the perspective of others. Instead, she studies two models of autonomy and judgment from the eighteenth century, Rousseau's *Émile* and Adam Smith's *Theory of Moral Sentiments*. She shows that Rousseau offers a model that is indeed vulnerable to contemporary concerns about autonomy. By contrast, Smith proposes an alternative account of autonomy, an autonomy that is able to retain its independence while still remaining attentive to the social embeddedness of the self. Thus "Smith's account of judgment aligns the quest for moral independence with the dynamics of interdependence, and paves the way for an understanding of autonomy that is hospitable to our common intuitions regarding the individual's social embedment." This enables the Smithian judge to be open to the judgments of others, without being determined by them. By showing that one cannot see for oneself without engaging the eyes of others, Nazar prepares the way for the next group of essays, which examine judgment and action under what Arendt would call the "condition of plurality."

How to Be an Agent
Why Character Matters

Stanley Hauerwas

1. Back to the Beginning

> If "God's will" means "God's voluntary action" then it is a synonym for God himself; for what is a person but his voluntary action? Finite persons, indeed, such as we are, are so imperfectly integrated that they have no full possession of themselves and are not wholly in their acts; but such qualifications seem meaningless when transferred to God, and in any case play no part in the religious fact.[1]

I begin with this quote from the great English philosophical theologian, Austin Farrer, because Farrer was able to say what Christians should say about action, as well as who is capable of acting, with a remarkable economy of expression. Farrer's ability to put the matter so succinctly was the hard-won result of having thought about these issues for years. He had previously explored questions surrounding action and agency in his Gifford Lectures, *The Freedom of the Will*, which were delivered in 1957.[2]

Farrer's observation is important first and foremost because he suggests that how God is understood has implications for how we understand ourselves. It is easy to miss the significance of this presumption. It is easy to miss the significance of such a move because the metaphysic associated with discussions of God's existence has not been associated with action as the fundamental metaphysical term. Yet Farrer seems to be following Aquinas by suggesting that action is the basic metaphysical notion for any account of what it means for God to be God. As David Burrell will later argue, an argument that supports Farrer's account of voluntary action and in particular Aquinas's understanding of God as pure act, a metaphysics of action is at the heart of Aquinas's understanding of God.[3]

I begin with these remarks to signal that I will explore the concept of action for the role the concept can and, perhaps, must play in Christian theology. By focusing on the formation of Christian character I hope to suggest how the relation of God, the self, and agency can be or, perhaps better, should be understood. This is not a new theme for me. Indeed, it has been at the heart of what I have been about for what is now quite literally a lifetime. But by exploring Farrer's observation that we are finite creatures who are not in full possession of ourselves and "not wholly in our acts" I hope to force myself to think thoughts I should have contemplated more thoroughly than I have in the past. I have been so intent on trying to show how the virtues help us better understand what being Christian entails that I may have not paid sufficient attention to our capacity to deceive others but most of all ourselves.[4] In particular I want to investigate how even if we are never fully in our acts we nonetheless must be sufficiently who we seem to be to discover in what ways we are not who we seem to be. Our agency depends on our being people of character, and character depends on the development of those habits we call the virtues, which are necessary for us to discover we have not done what we thought we were doing.[5]

In order to set the context for how I am approaching the question of action, I think it will be helpful to give a brief account of my early work. In 1968 I completed my dissertation at Yale University. The dissertation, as dissertations tend to do, bore a "dramatic" title, "Moral Character as a Problem for Theological Ethics." That admittedly mundane title at least indicated that the focus of the dissertation was on how to understand how our lives acquire a history, a character, which reflects as well as enhances our agency.

The focus on character was my attempt to articulate an alternative to the emphasis in ethics on discrete decisions that at the time dominated ethical theory. Joseph Fletcher's *Situation Ethics*, a book in which a rather crude form of act-utilitarianism was defended as the expression of the love ethic of Christianity, was the center of discussions in Christian ethics. I had read Aristotle. There was simply nothing in Fletcher about character and the virtues, nor did he spend any time trying to develop an account of practical reason. Fletcher was not alone in ignoring the significance of the virtues. Broader work in philosophical as well as theological work in ethics devoted little space to explore the role of the virtues in the moral life.

Any account of the significance of character and the virtues I assumed had to attend to Aristotle's distinction between *techne* and *phronesis*, which, as Joseph Dunne would later argue, is based on Aristotle's prior distinction between making and acting.[6] I took Fletcher to be the exemplification of the kind of technical rationality that Aristotle thought would defeat the kind of agent we must be if we are to acquire the habits that make us virtuous. Aristotle was surely right to argue that any account of the virtues would depend on an account of action in which the end and the means are inseparable.[7] There seemed no place in Fletcher's account of moral choice for the difference a person's character might make for how what we do and how we do it are crucial for making us moral agents.[8]

Rather than focusing on individual virtues I thought I needed to explore how character is best understood.[9] I assumed that character suggested the kind of person we must be to be a person of wise judgment and therefore capable of acquiring the virtues. In order to develop an account of character, however, I thought I needed a thicker account of agency if I was to give expression to Aristotle's essential insights. Such an account I mistakenly assumed could be had by drawing on the developing work in philosophy loosely associated with what was called "action theory." I was attracted to action theory because the account of agency I found there seemed to offer a way to avoid the unhappy alternatives of libertarian and determinist accounts of agent causality.[10]

Accordingly I defined character as "the qualification of a person's self-agency through their beliefs, intentions, and actions, by which a person acquires a moral history befitting their nature as a self-determining being."[11] That I had little sense of what needed to be said to sustain an account of character and the virtues is evident by the fact I called my understanding of character a "definition." Even more problematic was my assumption that I could give a defense of "self-agency" on grounds that an account of action qua action was sufficient to sustain the claim that we are "self-determining" beings.

I tried to defend the account of agency I thought I needed to sustain the significance of character by asserting that "to be a person is to be an autonomous center of activity and the source of one's own determinations: all we know, all we will, all we do issues from that very act by which we know what we are."[12] I was not clear whether agency was somehow prior to character or whether character is the form our agency takes. I, therefore, tried to have it both ways by claiming that character entails the presumption that we can act in a manner that determines our lives without the loss of ourselves in those determinations.[13] Only later did I come to realize that character is not the qualification of our agency, but our character constitutes our agency.

That way of putting the matter was made possible by MacIntyre's *After Virtue*. Reading MacIntyre made clear to me the mistake I made in *Character and the Christian Life*. The mistake was to try to defend an account of agency to sustain what it means for us to take ownership of what we do on grounds that first-person avowals of action cannot be described in third-person language. I was, in short, trying to defend action qua action as a logically primitive notion.[14] I knew actions begged for narrative display, but I did not realize that action qua action cannot be made intelligible unless we acknowledge the narrative that renders the action intelligible. MacIntyre's argument, however, in *After Virtue*, is that intelligible actions are more basic than the notion of action qua action. It follows, therefore, that an unintelligible action is a failed candidate to be counted as an intelligible action. To lump intelligible and unintelligible actions under the general classification of action is to invite conceptual confusion.[15]

Once it is acknowledged that the basic concept is not action but intelligible action, the question then becomes, What narratives do actions presuppose?

It is only through a narrative that the interrelationship between the intentional, the social, and the historical can be displayed. The agent's intentions, which may or may not be "conscious," locate what has been done, or better, determine what has been done given how the descriptions of the actions have a place in that person's history. The agent's account of how the actions "fit" in their narrative must also be located for their role in the history in which the agent exists; and this makes possible the placing of the action in the social context in which the action took place.[16] Thus MacIntyre's conclusion: "Narrative history of a certain kind turns out to be the basic and essential genre for the characterization of human actions."[17]

Yet it must also be the case that an intelligible action entails a narration that must remain open to renarration. That surely is an implication of Farrer's suggestion that as finite creatures we are imperfectly integrated, which means we lack full possession of ourselves. If, as Farrer suggests, we are not fully present in our acts, how can we be sure that what we do is actually what we do? But if we are not wholly present in our acts, does that mean our very attempt to give narrative coherence to our lives may be an invitation to self-deception? The question then becomes whether we are ever capable of acting in a manner that makes possible the self-knowledge that seems necessary to be a person of character. The question can be turned around to ask: given our lack of presence in our actions, how can we develop the character that makes it possible for us to hold ourselves as well as be held accountable for who we are?

One way to explore these questions is to investigate how what we think we have done can be and even must be redescribed retrospectively. We live our lives prospectively, but surely we only come to understand what we have done and who we have become by what we have done retrospectively. Our lives are constituted by ongoing negotiations necessary for our ability to locate what story or stories have shaped as well as been shaped by our agency. It is, however, very difficult to even know how to address these issues without attending to something like biographical exemplification.[18]

MacIntyre, however, has relentlessly attempted to expose the fundamental philosophical presuppositions that shape the political and social practices that may constrain our ability to understand who we are now.[19] By directing attention to MacIntyre's diagnosis of the pathologies of our current practices I hope to show how his account helps us understand better why current ways of understanding agency are so limited. I will also try to enrich MacIntyre's account of agency by contrasting his understanding of how a "theoretical" person he identifies as "J" can be held responsible for doing great harm when contrasted with a life such as the life of Dietrich Bonhoeffer. By directing attention to Bonhoeffer, and in particular his poem "Who Am I?," I hope to show what a life looks like when lived in a manner that would be unintelligible if the God we worship as Christians does not exist.

2. MacIntyre's Account of the Case of J

One of MacIntyre's achievements, an achievement I think not appropriately appreciated, is his ability to show how contemporary social realities can be obstacles for any attempt to understand moral concepts and arguments necessary for a recovery of the moral life found in Aristotle and Thomas Aquinas.[20] In an essay titled "Social Structures and Their Threats to Moral Agency" he explores this problem by asking us to imagine "the case of J."[21] MacIntyre says that J as a name could be shorthand for *jemand*, because he chose the letter J to suggest that J could stand for anyone. Or at least J stands for anyone that inhabits space in the world in which we find ourselves.

MacIntyre characterizes that world as constituted by socially approved roles that are so well defined that responsibilities and role-structured behavior can be assumed to be morally unproblematic. Those who occupy the hierarchy of approved roles must try to meet the expectations of those roles because if they do not they will face the disapproval of others for being socially irresponsible. MacIntyre therefore tells us that J is a faithful citizen of such an order having been formed by the concepts that legitimate such an order. He had been taught that he owed to others the discharge of his duties and responsibilities that were inherent in the roles he assumed throughout his life. J is not philosophically inclined, but if he were MacIntyre suggests he might recognize that Plato's understanding of justice and Kant's account of duty express his assumption that by doing his duty he is doing what is necessary to be a moral agent (186).

According to MacIntyre, J occupies a number of roles. He is a father, a participant in various sport clubs, a former soldier, and a man whose working career was with the railroads. He was responsible for scheduling passenger and freight trains as well as making adjustments to schedules necessary when trains break down. Early in his career he had been mildly interested in what the trains might carry, but he was instructed by his superiors that he was to take no interest in such matters, so he acquired the habit of disinterest about such matters. That remained the case even when the passengers were Jews on their way to concentration camps. When he was later questioned about his indifference, he defended himself by claiming he was only doing his duty. He was innocent of the murder of the Jews because he had no knowledge of what was happening to the Jews because a person in his position was not to have such knowledge. MacIntyre's primary interest in J is to explore whether J's defense of himself is adequate (187).

MacIntyre thinks for most of us it would be obvious that such a defense is inadequate. We believe that J can be held responsible because he is a moral agent. As such he should have been aware of what was going on and therefore been held responsible for the predicable effects of his actions. MacIntyre notes, however, that such a judgment about J presumes on occasions one can and should put established standards in question. J's attempt to defend himself by claiming he was only fulfilling his responsibilities made him open to the challenge of why he assumed he had no reason to ask whether the established standards governing his role responsibilities were in fact the best standards (189).

If J is to be held responsible, MacIntyre suggests, J must have been able to understand himself as a moral agent because the condition for such an understanding is in fact that you are a moral agent. The question then becomes whether there are forms of societal structures that would prevent one from understanding themselves as a moral agent. Before trying to answer that question, MacIntyre explores what is required if we are to understand ourselves as moral agents. He argues that at least two conditions are necessary for such agency: (1) I must understand myself as well as present myself to others as someone with an identity other than the identity associated with the roles I occupy; and (2) I must understand myself not just as an individual but as a rational individual who has confidence in my critical judgments (189).

Such an account of moral agency, MacIntyre argues, requires a particular social setting in which accountability to particular others is in place, some participation in critical inquiry possible, and acknowledgment of the individuality of others and oneself are recognized as conditions necessary for sustaining moral agency. These conditions for moral agency make possible the ability to stand back from our engagements to assess what we may wrongly think we are doing.[22] Another way to put the matter is: truthfulness is required if we are to be rational agents who desire not to deceive or be deceived (194).

Rational agency cannot stand alone, however, but must be supplemented by the virtues. The virtues needed may vary given different historical challenges, but MacIntyre argues that there is a core notion of the virtues without which no other virtues can be possessed. MacIntyre gives the traditional names of integrity and constancy to the virtues he argues we cannot live without. At least we cannot live without them if we are to be rational agents. Integrity and constancy are the virtues that set inflexible limits to a person's adaptability to the roles they may find themselves occupying (192).

Individuals who possess the virtues of integrity and constancy will not only occupy some determinative set of roles, but they will also know how to think about the goods associated with those roles. In particular they will discover a tension between their understanding of themselves as moral agents and their role obligations. Such a tension is a good, requiring as it must a critical attitude between socially embodied modes of practice and our presumption that we are moral agents. According to MacIntyre the tension between role requirements and the virtues of integrity and constancy will vary from social order and from different times (194).

Having provided an account of rational agency, MacIntyre then asks what implications this understanding of agency should have for how J is to be morally assessed. He concludes that if J was a psychologically normal human being, which MacIntyre assumes he was, he must be held accountable for the murder of the Jews (195). But it must then be asked what J needed if he was to exercise the power of moral agency. In a somewhat surprising formal conclusion MacIntyre answers that J only needed through the power of moral agency to recognize that he had the power of moral agency.[23]

That is MacIntyre's way to suggest that though J did not exercise his capacity to understand his moral identity, he was to some degree distinct and independent from his social roles, which means in principle he could have exercised his responsibility (195). To so exercise his responsibility would have required J to have the confidence that his judgments reflect the natural moral law. The knowledge of such a law is that our judgments about the moral character of human beings requires participation in social relationships in which one's reflective judgments emerge from systematic dialogue with others. Without such milieus of relationships the exercise of moral agency will be undermined (196).

Yet MacIntyre fears that the social and political conditions he has identified as crucial to sustain moral agency are increasingly undermined by the compartmentalization that is so characteristic of modern social orders. For MacIntyre compartmentalization involves more than the differentiation of roles characteristic of every society. The compartmentalization characteristic of advanced industrial societies is based on the assumption that each sphere of social activity has its own role structure and is governed by its own specific norms, which are independent of other spheres. Social orders so constituted produce divided selves incapable of integrity or constancy. Integrity is impossible because the allegiance to any set of standards is assumed to be temporary. Constancy is problematic because any commitment to an unwavering directedness necessary to be constant is subject to changes of direction because the self must always be ready to adjust to different spheres (200).

MacIntyre argues that selves formed by the modes of compartmentalization characteristic of modern societies can and should be held responsible for their failure to be moral agents because our agency can never be dissolved entirely in the distinctive roles we play. Moreover, when an individual shifts from one role to another the individual as an individual cannot help but appear even if it is to manage that transition from one role to another. The selves characteristic of compartmentalized social orders in order not to confront the incoherence of their lives must develop habits of mind that enable them not to attend to what they would have to attend to if they would be capable of recognizing their own incoherence (203). Yet even those so constituted have resources in the incoherence of their lives that might make possible a reclaiming of their moral agency.

MacIntyre argues that there remains a profound difference between J and those determined by compartmentalization. The difference is quite simple. J has some awareness of his situation that those who inhabit compartmentalized societies do not. J's proud defense of his attention to duty that was characteristic of his role responsibilities is sufficient to hold him responsible for his failure to act to prevent murder. In contrast those whose lives reflect the compartmentalization of our social orders are unable to defend their lives in a similar manner. At best they are coauthors of their social and moral worlds, which means they lack any resources that would enable them to comprehend their lives as being capable of taking responsibility for who they are. J, in contrast, chose not to move beyond his role-determined sense of responsibility.

MacIntyre ends his account of J and the effects of a compartmentalized social order by suggesting that a crucial question for those who would be moral agents is to "ask about your social and cultural order what it needs you and others not to know." MacIntyre argues that lives that reflect the compartmentalized social orders we inhabit cannot acknowledge the power of such a question. In that respect J, in contrast to the compartmentalized souls, has more moral resources by the very fact he was able to morally refuse knowledge that would make him responsible for refusing to know what he could have known. Even if J did not know what was to happen to the Jews, he is rightly to be held responsible for his role in their destruction. In fact, it is not just J that is guilty, but his whole social and cultural order (204).

MacIntyre's argument is subtle. One aspect of the subtle character of the argument is he never makes explicit the character of the argument. There are no doubt good reasons for that, but for my purposes it is important to name what MacIntyre has done. What he has done is to develop what many would identify as a natural law argument, that is, he is able to judge J responsible on grounds anyone should acknowledge qua human being. Yet the question remains, at least for me, whether MacIntyre's appeal to rational agency is sufficient to produce people with characters capable of resisting the effects of the compartmentalization he so astutely describes as our fate. Put differently, I worry that the thick narrative he argues is required for sustaining agency is not developed in his account of J.

The virtues he commends, integrity and constancy, are no doubt crucial for sustaining the habits necessary for the flourishing of people of practical reason. But it is also the case that integrity and constancy beg for further specification through narrative exemplification. Such exemplification, moreover, cannot be had without the identification of communities that represent alternative traditions to the social orders determined by the presumption that the moral life is available to anyone without training. MacIntyre's account of J as well as those suffering from the habits of compartmentalized social orders powerfully describes pathologies that make it difficult to sustain the practices necessary to produce people of character. But if it is also true, as Farrer suggests, that we are only "imperfectly integrated," then more must be said about what is required to sustain moral agency.

I noted above MacIntyre's observation that a narrative history of a certain kind is an essential genre for the characterizations of human actions. I am sure he is right about that, but I wonder if he has done justice to that claim in the manner he presents J. We do not get any idea of the thick narrative that has made J what he is. The conceit MacIntyre uses is not to give J a proper name. He is anyone, but MacIntyre knows his readers will think J is someone. J is Adolf Eichmann. Because he is Adolf Eichmann, we assume MacIntyre is right to hold J responsible on the grounds that he is a rational moral agent. MacIntyre never has to mention that Eichmann was a good German. To use that description—that is, Eichmann was a good German—would have made MacIntyre's account of J's refusal to take responsibility for whom the trains carried a moral failure not only by J, but he would have had to be more specific about the failure of the culture that produced J.

I should not want these remarks to be taken to be a decisive criticism of MacIntyre. I am only able to make them because of what MacIntyre has already given us. But MacIntyre is a philosopher who is determined to avoid as much as possible theological claims. I am, however, a theologian who thinks God has something to do with our being regarded as agents who can be held responsible for our character. In order to explore what such a suggestion might entail, I want to contrast MacIntyre's account of J with that of another German—Dietrich Bonhoeffer.

3. The Case of Bonhoeffer

The main details of Bonhoeffer's life are well-known. His life has been the subject of a number of excellent biographies.[24] The most recent work by Charles Marsh, *Strange Glory: A Life of Dietrich Bonhoeffer*, is particularly important for the story I will tell.[25] One of the great virtues of Marsh's biography is his reticence to explain how Bonhoeffer became the Bonhoeffer celebrated as the courageous opponent of Hitler's regime. It is not simply a matter of explaining how this man from the upper classes of Germany, this man who took great pride in being German, how his life was ended by the personal order of Hitler at Flossenburg Concentration Camp on April 9, 1945. The challenge is how to account for his life as a Christian.

Early in his life Bonhoeffer seems to have an uncanny sense of himself. He was raised in the high culture of the German upper classes. He was immensely talented and intelligent. He was, for example, quite musical. There were no limits to what he might do with his life. He could have followed his father into medicine or some other prestigious profession, but much to the surprise of his family by the age of thirteen he adamantly declared he would become a theologian. His family was conventionally Christian, so his decision to become a theologian may not have seemed completely surprising. What was unusual, however, was his insistence that he desired to be ordained. His commitment to be ordained suggested that he seemed to think to be a theologian meant you had to be a serious Christian.

His sense of self was also manifest by his response to his education at the University of Berlin. Berlin was the home of Protestant liberalism. Harnack was not only Bonhoeffer's teacher; he was also a friend of the Bonhoeffer family. Though Bonhoeffer admired Harnack, that admiration did not mean he had to agree with Harnack. Accordingly, Bonhoeffer saw the significance of Karl Barth's work and closely identified with Barth's theological project. Barth's influence was evident in Bonhoeffer's first dissertation, *Sanctorum Communio*, a book Barth described as a theological miracle because he did not see how such a book could be written at the University of Berlin.

Bonhoeffer came from a well-to-do family. His tastes were the habits of those whose lives do not suffer from financial necessity. He relished travel and good food, and he liked to live comfortably. Yet in his first pastoral appointment to the Lutheran church in Spain he discovered the poor. He not only discovered the poor, he thought the poor could not be ignored as those that represented the heart of the Gospel. That conviction was manifest during his studies at Union Theological Seminary in New York City, where he felt most at home when worshipping with African Americans.

Bonhoeffer was a proud German Lutheran, but that did not stop him from becoming a pacifist. He was quite critical of the traditional Lutheran division between the orders of creation and redemption. He saw these divisions, which were meant to secure the freedom of the church to preach the Gospel, as giving the state too much power. The Sermon on the Mount became central for his account of discipleship, which he developed as an alternative to what he described as the "cheap grace" that characterized the practice of Protestant Christianity. From Bonhoeffer's perspective the costliness of being forgiven had ironically been lost, in Protestantism, in the name of justification by grace alone.

Bonhoeffer was a worldly person, but he was deeply pious. Nowhere was that more evident than in the work he did to make the illegal seminary at Finkenwald a reality. Always ready to learn from others during his pastoral service in England, he had seen how priests were formed in the Community of the Resurrection. His profound engagement with scripture, and in particular the Psalms, informed how he went about the formation of those at Finkenwald who would become pastors in the Confessing Church.

Bonhoeffer seemed to have the confidence that comes naturally to those born to privilege. Yet he also had a gift for friendship.[26] He continued to write his former students from Finkenwald who were serving on the Russian front. His friendship with Eberhard Bethge was one Bethge himself thought unlikely, given Bethge's country-boy habits. But that did not deter Bonhoeffer, who claimed Bethge as a friend and included him in the Bonhoeffer family. His friendship with Bishop Bell of the Church of England was a testimony to their common love of God and the church.

Bonhoeffer's sense of self, his unwavering courageous intelligence, is perhaps nowhere more evident than in his early recognition of who Hitler was and in his opposition to the ascendance of Hitler. Bonhoeffer was politically astute, but the astute character of his judgments was shaped by his fundamental theological convictions. He saw the demonic character of the Third Reich early on because he knew that the attack on the Jews was a clear indication that the regime was idolatrous. With great courage in 1933 he delivered a radio address, an address he was not allowed to finish, that identified the threat Hitler represented to Germany. His opposition, of course, finally earned him prison and death.

Bonhoeffer was a German, but it would be hard to imagine anyone more unlike MacIntyre's J than Bonhoeffer. Bonhoeffer certainly accepted the duties that came with his roles in life. He was an exemplary pastor and teacher. But, as I hope my brief account of his life makes clear, he had a sense of self and agency that gave his life direction and purpose. If anyone could claim to be a "rational agent" in MacIntyre's sense, surely Bonhoeffer could be such a person. Yet while in prison he wrote a poem entitled "Who Am I?" that demands attention before attributing to him an overdetermined sense of agency. The poem reads:

> Who am I? They often tell me
> I would step from my cell's confinement
> Calmly, cheerfully, firmly,
> Like a squire from his country house.
>
> Who am I? They often tell me
> I would talk to my warders
> Freely and friendly and clearly,
> As though it were mine to command.
>
> Who am I? They also tell me
> I would bear the days of misfortune
> Equably, smilingly, proudly,
> Like one accustomed to win.
>
> Am I then really all that which other men tell of?
> Or am I only what I know of myself,
> Restless and longing and sick, like a bird in a cage,
> Struggling for breath, as though hands were compressing
> my throat,
> Yearning for colours, for flowers, for neighbourliness,
> Trembling with anger at despotism and petty humiliation,
> Tossing in expectation of great events,
> Powerlessly trembling for friends at an infinite distance,
> Weary and empty at praying, at thinking, at making,
> Faint, and ready to say farewell to it all?

Who am I? This or the other?
Am I one person today and tomorrow another?
Am I both at once? A hypocrite before others,
And before myself a contemptible woebegone weakling?
Or is something within me still like a beaten army,
Fleeing in disorder from victory already achieved?

Who am I? They mock me, these lonely questions of mine.
Whoever I am, thou knowest, O God, I am thine.[27]

Given my account of Bonhoeffer's life, some may find the first three verses of Bonhoeffer's poem more a pose than an expression of who he "really was." Of course, he is writing the poem in prison, which might make anyone, even Bonhoeffer, wonder about who they are. I do not think, however, that is what is happening with Bonhoeffer. Rather, I think he is giving expression to something he learned in his daily reading of the Psalms, a recognition that he cannot be sure, in Farrer's language, whether he is wholly in his acts. No doubt Bonhoeffer tried to put on a "brave face" for those who loved him, but it turned out the face he "put on" was who he was. At least we know that to be the case because of the way he went to his death.

In the letter to Bethge that accompanied this poem Bonhoeffer distanced himself from those who stressed the importance of introspection for discovering "who we really are." He had little use for such inwardness because he thought the creation of an "inner domain," a space hidden from view, to be a strategy to displace God from the world by creating a sphere of the "personal," "the inner," or "the private" where God might still be found.[28] Michael Northcott, however, argues that Bonhoeffer is not critiquing all appeals to "inwardness," but Bonhoeffer is reconfiguring what the "inner" entails by employing liturgical forms such as the lament Psalms to exemplify the language of the heart.[29]

Northcott's insight is confirmed by the last line of thc poem, which suggests that Bonhoeffer did not think, apart from God, we have the means to know the truth about ourselves. As Northcott observes, Bonhoeffer believed that we only acquire a true narrative of the self through incorporation into the body of Christ. That is why the poem presents a balance or even a tension between the account of the self as that "which other men tell of" and "what I know of myself." "Any lack of fit between these two is not so much resolved as set in perspective by the concluding recognition 'O God, I am thine.'"[30] That recognition—that is, the recognition that we are God's even more than we are ourselves—comes through spiritual disciplines that make possible an ownership of our lives to the extent that we are left with nothing to hide from God and even ourselves. To have nothing to hide is the condition that most nearly makes possible the correspondence between what we do and who we are.

4. Where Has This Gotten Us?

Above I stressed MacIntyre's contention that a narrative history is required for an account of human agency. That claim I take to be but an implication of the point that intelligible action is a more basic concept than action. I should like to think what I have done in this essay supports that contention. But if that is right, the problem then becomes what genre best exemplifies or expresses that crucial insight. The contrast between MacIntyre's J and my account of Bonhoeffer was meant to highlight that question, but the challenge remains to create the kind of reflection that not only formally helps us see the intrinsic relation between agents and action but practically help us to be what we see.

Of course it is not simply a matter of reflection. If our agency is determined by our character and our character names the habits and virtues that make our lives our own, then questions of formation cannot be avoided. MacIntyre's J had been schooled in the habits that were assumed to make a "good German." Bonhoeffer had received some of the same formation, but there was a narrative and correlative virtues that made what it meant for Bonhoeffer to be a good German quite different from J. Of course Bonhoeffer's resistance to Hitler might be attributed to his class presumptions, but that kind of reductive account cannot make sense of the narrative arc of his life. If we are to know how to better understand the formation of people of character, I suspect attention to lives like the life of Bonhoeffer is crucial.

Of course the story that is Dietrich Bonhoeffer is complex. The story of his life entails the interrelation of the story of Germany, the story of the rise of Hitler, the story of Bonhoeffer's family, and the story of how Dietrich Bonhoeffer found his way through these stories as well as other stories I have not highlighted. Bonhoeffer's "agency" is to be found in how he negotiated these complex narratives that made him Dietrich Bonhoeffer. That "agency" is surely to be found in the narrative that came to him through the church. His life makes no sense if the God we worship in Jesus Christ does not exist. Bonhoeffer was rightly suspicious of his public persona, but that suspicion is a given for Christians who must acknowledge that we are never "wholly in our acts."

Our inability to be wholly in our acts, however, is why we so desperately need to be incorporated into a community of practices that can provide the formation of our agency through a truthful narrative. Our character begins to be formed through what may appear to be insignificant actions which prove to be quite important because through them we become participants in a way of life that only makes sense if the God Christians worship exists. Charlie Pinches observes that Christians are told they must feed the hungry, share the Eucharist, stay faithful in their marriages, comfort the sick, venerate the cross, and seek the truth. Because Christians have the time to engage in such practices they learn how to use the action descriptions that hold this vocabulary of actions in place. It is through such a vocabulary that "Christians fill out their claim of Christ's Lordship and all it entails about the human world."[31]

Augustine begins book 10 of his *Confessions* with somewhat surprising reflections about whether he now knows himself better for having written the *Confessions*. He observes that many would like to think that they know who he is through the *Confessions*, but he doubts whether they or whether he knows better who he is.[32] Yet Augustine takes comfort in the fact that he knows something of God that he does not know of himself. He knows he is opaque to himself, but if he knows himself through the shining of God's light, God's glory, the darkness of his life will be made as the noonday sun. For finally we only know ourselves as we are known by God.[33] Augustine's claim that we know only as we are known I take to be the last word Christians have to say about our ability to be who God has created us to be.

We are never fully in our acts, but Christians believe we have been given a way of life that draws us beyond our limits, making us more than we could have ever imagined. Indeed, it has been imagined for us. Our character is forged through our conformity to Christ. This account of character subverts accounts of action qua action that presuppose autonomy. For to be Christian is to experience freedom in contingency; it is a freedom given and gained through submission to a Lord who was fully in his action on our behalf, that is, to die willingly on a cross that we might be free from the lies that threaten to consume us.

Notes

1. Austin Farrer, *Faith and Speculation* (New York: New York University Press, 1967), 57.

2. Austin Farrer, *The Freedom of the Will* (New York: Charles Scribner's Sons, 1958).

3. David Burrell, *Aquinas: God and Action* (London: Routledge & Kegan Paul, 1979), 146–75. For an illuminating account of Farrer's reflections on natural theology, see Robert MacSwain, *Solved by Sacrifice: Austin Farrer, Fideism, and the Evidence of Faith* (Leuven: Peeters, 2013). MacSwain's account of the influence of Diogenes Allen on Farrer is not only of great scholarly interest, but also a contribution to helping us better understand the grammar of faith.

4. I should like to think that our penchant for self-deception has, however, never been far from my understanding of the moral life. See, for example, David Burrell's and my chapter, "Self-Deception and Autobiography: Reflections on Speer's *Inside the Third Reich*," in my *Truthfulness and Tragedy: Further Investigations into Christian Ethics* (Notre Dame: University of Notre Dame Press, 1977), 82–100. I have always assumed that our desperate desire to make sense of our lives is at once the source of our goodness and our ability to live the lie.

5. The role of habits for agency is a complex subject that deserves more attention than I have given it in this essay. For a more extended analysis see my chapter

"Habit Matters: The Bodily Character of the Virtues" in my book *Approaching the End: Eschatological Reflections on Church, Politics, and Life* (Grand Rapids, Mich.: Eerdmans, 2013), 158–75. In this chapter I explore what Jennifer Herdt characterizes as the "mystery of habituation," that is, how habits acquired through imitation become habits that make us virtuous.

6. Joseph Dunne, *Back to the Rough Ground: "Phronesis" and "Techne" in Modern Philosophy and in Aristotle* (Notre Dame: University of Notre Dame Press, 1993), 244.

7. Aristotle's understanding of the relation of the ends and the means is complex as he sometimes seems to suggest that the end is simply a given, but his account of the relation of the means to the end suggests that the means to achieve the end will transform how the end is understood. Crucial for me is his claim that we deliberate about what is up to us, which means persons of character will confront challenges that those without character cannot even imagine. Aristotle, *Nicomachean Ethics*, trans. Terence Irwin (Indianapolis: Hackett, 1999), 1112a–12b. For my more extended discussion of Aristotle see Charles Pinches's and my *Christians among the Virtues: Theological Conversations with Ancient and Modern Ethics* (Notre Dame: University of Notre Dame Press, 1997), 3–54.

8. Also missing from Fletcher's understanding of the moral life was the role of language. Fletcher seemed to assume that descriptions fell from the sky. Crucial for me was Joseph Kovesi's important but still sadly overlooked book, *Moral Notions* (New York: Humanities, 1967).

9. The relation of character and the virtues is a fascinating question that depends on one's views about the unity of the virtues. The presumption that to have any virtue requires that you have all the virtues clearly cannot be sustained, but exactly because the different virtues are acquired across time does not mean a person of virtue may be understood to "have character." To "have character" at the very least means they can be trusted to be who they seem to be, that is, they have acquired a moral history that means what they do and do not do "makes sense."

10. I find it interesting that at the time Dr. Anscombe's article "Thought and Action in Aristotle" was probably more important to me than *Intention* (Oxford: Basil Blackwell, 1957), because if I had attended to *Intention* I might have avoided the mistake of thinking an account of agency could be sustained in terms of what makes an action an action.

11. Stanley Hauerwas, *Character and the Christian Life: A Study in Theological Ethics* (Notre Dame: University of Notre Dame Press, 1994), 11. The original quote uses the masculine pronoun, which I find painful to read. Because it is my prose I assumed I could give myself permission, I could exercise my agency, to change the masculine pronouns. *Character and the Christian Life* was originally published by Trinity University Press in 1975. The University of Notre Dame edition has the new "Introduction."

12. Hauerwas, *Character and the Christian Life*, 18.

13. Ibid., 21.

14. For the best critique I know of action theory see Charles R. Pinches, *Theology and Action: After Theory in Christian Ethics* (Grand Rapids, Mich.: Eerdmans, 2002), 11–33. Pinches argues that action theory in its many variations was bound to fail because the attempt to extract particular actions from the rich

narratives that characterize our lives cannot help but result in distortions (27). Pinches also provides an extremely rich account of Aquinas on acts. Unfortunately Aquinas's account of acts is not closely studied, which often results in a failure to understand that Aquinas (as well as Anscombe) well understood that a number of descriptions may be true of an act.

15. Alasdair MacIntyre, *After Virtue*, 3rd ed. (Notre Dame: University of Notre Dame Press, 2007), 209. I think it quite interesting that in *Minding the Modern: Human Agency, Intellectual Traditions, and Responsible Knowledge* (Notre Dame: University of Notre Dame Press, 2013) Thomas Pfau calls attention to this passage in *After Virtue* in critique of Hume (pp. 297–98). Pfau quite rightly draws attention to the significance of speech for the intelligibility of actions.

16. In his extremely useful account of practical reason, Mark Ryan puts the matter this way: "Agency is embedded in the life of a particular community, and practical inferences are licensed within communities of shared goods or reasons. This is the 'politics' component of the three interrelated concepts—agency, practical reason, and politics." Mark Ryan, *The Politics of Practical Reason: Why Theological Ethics Must Change Your Life* (Eugene, Ore.: Cascade, 2011), 99. Ryan's and Pinches's books are complementary.

17. MacIntyre, *After Virtue*, 208.

18. Narcissism threatens but I cannot resist calling attention to my memoir, *Hannah's Child: A Theological Memoir* (Grand Rapids, Mich.: Eerdmans, 2012) and, in particular, the afterword to the second edition. There I reflect on how often in the memoir I must confess I began engagements, such as going to divinity school, clearly not knowing what I was doing but later came to "own" what I had done. Of course that "owning" was not the same as my original engagement because what I had done was now understood as part of a different narrative.

19. "Who we are now" is a phrase meant to suggest allusion to Nicholas Boyle's great book *Who Are We Now? Christian Humanism and the Global Market from Hegel to Heaney* (Notre Dame: University of Notre Dame Press, 1998). Boyle suggests the modern sense of who we are, an account he thinks best articulated by Heidegger, is that our power to make our future is by choosing a tradition and heritage. We create our past in the image of the future. "We have a fate because, like Nietzsche, we are a fate. Out of the contingencies of that 'fate' Existence chooses its particular destiny, the events it willingly shares with 'its collectivity, its people.' " Boyle observes that the flaw in this account is how it ignores that historicity is a gift from others (223). Later Boyle contrasts this Heideggerian view, a view he thinks shared by political conservatives and postmodernists, with Christianity. According to Boyle "the Christian belief that our identity becomes visible to us in an act of historical interpretation, in the words by which a past is given to us is related to a future of our own making" (318).

20. See, for example, MacIntyre's essay "Moral Philosophy and Contemporary Social Practice," in his *The Tasks of Philosophy*, vol. 1 (Cambridge: Cambridge University Press, 2006), 104–24.

21. Alasdair MacIntyre, *Ethics and Politics: Selected Essays* (Cambridge: Cambridge University Press, 2006), 2:186–204. Page numbers will appear in the text.

22. The image of "standing back" from ourselves can be quite misleading because it seems to suggest I have a self somehow "behind" the self that makes me who I am. There is no question that a critical relation to oneself is one of the

hallmarks of a person of character, but that critical relation to ourselves cannot be guaranteed by assuming that a formal relation with ourselves is always possible. The critical perspective we must have is finally a function of the basic narrative that constitutes our lives over time.

23. The formal character of MacIntyre's argument is reminiscent of his account of the good life in *After Virtue*, that is, "The good life for man is the life spent in seeking for the good life for man, and the virtues necessary for the seeking are those which will enable us to understand what more and what else the good life for man is" (219).

24. Of course the most important biography remains Eberhard Bethge's *Dietrich Bonhoeffer: A Biography*, rev. ed. (Minneapolis: Fortress, 1999).

25. Charles Marsh, *Strange Glory: A Life of Dietrich Bonhoeffer* (New York: Knopf, 2014).

26. For an analysis of Bonhoeffer's poem, "The Friend" see my "Friendship and Freedom: Reflections on Bonhoeffer's 'The Friend,'" in my *Working with Words: On Learning to Speak Christian* (Eugene, Ore: Cascade, 2011), 270–86.

27. This translation of the poem is by John Bowden. The poem is to be found in *Who Am I? Bonhoeffer's Theology through His Poetry*, ed. Bernd Wannenwetsch (London: T&T Clark, 2009), 13. The poem is accompanied by a fine exegetical article by Michael Northcott, "'Who Am I?': Human Identity and the Spiritual Disciplines in the Witness of Dietrich Bonhoeffer," 11–29. The poem was originally published in Dietrich Bonhoeffer, *Letters and Papers from Prison* (New York: Simon and Schuster, 1997), 347–48.

28. Bonhoeffer, *Letters and Papers from Prison*, 344.

29. Northcott, "'Who Am I?,'" 16–17.

30. Ibid., 18.

31. Pinches, *Theology and Action*, 229.

32. Augustine, *Confessions*, trans. F. J. Sheed (Indianapolis: Hackett, 1993), 10.3.

33. Ibid., 10.5–6.

Losing the Name of Action

Shakespeare, *Macbeth*, and Speech as Action

Sarah Beckwith

> Being human is the power to grant being human. Something about flesh and blood elicits this grant from us, and something about flesh and blood can also repel it.
>
> —Stanley Cavell, *The Claim of Reason*

For a while in the literary academy the word "human" never appeared without its little straitjacket of scare quotes, as if those would save us from the fear of giving voice to the word. It has been the dogma of the academy for quite some time that talk of the human *automatically* invited universalism or essentialism, that it was *automatically* exclusionary and implied an arrogant presumption of the place of humanity in the world and in nature.[1] The savage institutional, economic, social, and political structures and habits that sustained such arrogance are rightly to be eschewed. I do not underestimate the long, unfinished labor of contesting an insular yet viciously successful hegemony.

It is perhaps no wonder that we are troubled so much for the word for our kind, the human. For we live in a society that sometimes seems incapable of knowing what a human life is worth. John Berger suggests that this is because it cannot afford to: "If it did, it would either have to dismiss this knowledge and with it dismiss all pretenses to democracy and so become totalitarian: or it would have to take account of this knowledge and revolutionize itself. Either way it would be transformed."[2] Then perhaps our scare quotes are an inchoate hedging, helping us avoid our aspirations to be human, which is, of course, a task, not a given.[3] In that task we live, as Stanley Cavell is fond of saying, between acknowledgment and avoidance.

But who were we trying to scare away with those scare quotes? The scare quotes—a marked feature of literary theory in the height of its poststructuralist grip—were supposed to put us at an ironic distance from the word, protected by the little punctuation marks. The first usage of *scare quotes* is 1960.[4] The *Oxford English Dictionary* describes scare quotes as "quotation marks used around a word or phrase when they are not required, thereby eliciting attention or doubts." Scare quotes then are not a piece of grammar but rather a rhetorical maneuver to suggest that the very usage of the word is a problem without this ironic distancing.

When I say "legitimate rape," I want to put it in scare quotes because I do not share Representative Todd Akin's dangerous lunacy. In that instance I am showing that I am using Akin's language and not mine. The quotation marks are in this instance citational. There the distancing seems fully appropriate. But from whose usage, whose particular usage, am I distancing myself when I say "the human" and make those little signals with my hands? Those who used to do this so frequently (and may I say so irritatingly) might say: Well, I am distancing myself from those who are assuming that the white Western liberal subject speaks for the human; I am showing that I understand this to be a usurpation. Only I think the two cases are not analogous. Akin's term "legitimate rape" shows that he does not understand what rape is. Whereas the person distancing himself from the putative haughty humanist or the unwitting sexist or racist is relying on a shared understanding of the human when he thinks he is only guarding against one usage of that term. In that sense he has not quite done what he thinks he has done. The human is not the haughty humanist's term in the way that "legitimate rape" was Todd Akin's crazy solecism. He has in fact depended on the shared understanding of this term and then used the scare quotes to try to highlight a reduced usage of it. In this sense his scare quotes are not citational at all. So whom is the scare quoter distancing himself from? What is *he* scared of? And who is he scaring off?[5]

The rejection of *all* talk of the human has left the humanities pathetically enfeebled and almost defenseless against the combined but formidable onslaughts of the corporate university, the business model of education, and its own consequential abandonment of the common reader. Shakespeare offers us a way of talking about the human—not as he "invented" it—and not as either a metaphysically grounded or biological entity distinguished as such by the protocols of science, not as a definition that excludes nonrational creatures, but as a form of life to which we are fated.[6] He understood the "importance of being human" (as Cora Diamond has put it) in our most basic and our most sophisticated linguistic and ethical competencies. In particular his tragedies are involved in an exploration of how it is internal to being human to wish to escape from this condition, and the cravings, ruses, compulsions, the costs and consequences of this avoidance.[7]

The invocation of Shakespeare is no panacea, no guarantee against these corrosions absent a patient description of how we take on the exposure and risk of human form, human expressiveness individually. This essay will explore the idea of a "common humanity" in Shakespeare and its home in the mutual responsiveness, recognition, and responsibility, but also repudiation and rejection of the human in our dealings with each other, and in the genre of tragedy. In particular I will be pursuing the idea of pity and remorse as a "form of conviction" (Wittgenstein) in *Macbeth*. I will be particularly interested here in the way that the Scottish play, when approached in a certain spirit, helps us both sharpen and deepen our understanding of, and indeed *through,* remorse. Such specifications, while not working through arguments, are nevertheless conceptual; they help us get a grip on questions of action and human agency that are all too liable to become dry, narrow, and attenuated.[8]

Shakespeare cherishes the human, and this is nowhere more obvious than in his profound analysis of the process of dehumanization. (I will ask again at the end of this essay whether this is the right name for what is happening to Macbeth, but I will let this stand for now.)

1. Losing the Name of Action

We can smell trouble when at the beginning of act 1, scene 7, Macbeth refers to the imminent murder of Duncan as "it." And he surrounds his "it" by a conditional "if," and more, a subjunctive, "were": "If it were done" (1.7.1).[9] It is as if he imagines the future precipitously as the past, moreover, a past in which a deed has been done with no apparent doer. In a few short words he has removed himself from the picture. Against the contorted rhythm of Macbeth's obfuscations, Shakespeare sounds the beat of the deed: done, done, done, three times in one-and-a-half lines, with the last sounding with an off-beat stress. And then another conditional followed by a string of complex evasions: now the murder is an "assassination," and he is imagining a world where deeds have no consequences. Since this cannot be the world of human action, Macbeth is denaturing himself, imagining he is more or less than human, and exiling himself from the shared meanings on which his words depend.

In her brilliant book *The Human Condition*, Hannah Arendt discussed action as necessarily irreversible, unpredictable, and boundless. To do and to suffer are opposite sides of the same coin, she claims, and an act begins a story whose consequences are "boundless," caught up in the reactions and responses of others who are moreover unpredictable, whose "full meaning can reveal itself only when it has ended."[10] That a deed once performed cannot be taken back is what tragedy focuses on: the irreversibility of action. So now in the nasty compactness of "surcease" (another evasion) and "success" he tries to short-circuit the very logic of action. He is imagining a deed, "this blow" (1.7.4), that would be entirely sufficient to itself, bringing with it purely the consequences he desires. So the deed would be his alone to define, carved out of the world of the responses of others. And now Macbeth talks on emphasizing *here*: "that but this blow / Might be the be-all and end-all—here" (1.7.4–5). That this is a crazy, cock-eyed impossibility is shown in the unstoppable spill over to the next line: "but here, upon this bank and shoal of time" (1.7.6). Macbeth is tutoring himself in the denial of his own agency, in the avoidance of the very nature of the deed he is about to commit, and what that deed makes him. In separating his own agency from the deed, in denying the very nature of the deed he is committing, he is traducing the very nature of human action.

For Macbeth is here denying some very basic facts of human nature, facts not fixed by custom or convention, facts so obvious they might go unnoticed, "such as, for example, the fact that the realization of human intention requires action, that action requires movement, that movement involves consequences we had not intended, that our knowledge (and ignorance) of ourselves and of others depends upon the way our minds are expressed (and distorted) in word and deed and passion; that actions have histories."[11]

When we next see Macbeth speaking alone we see him apparently in the grip of an apparition. Is the dagger he sees before him a fatal vision that is "sensible to feeling" (2.1.36–37), or is it a dagger of the mind? Whatever it is, the dagger is a "thou," given personality, intimacy even; it is a thing that addresses him and that he addresses. It is marshaling him along a path he is already traveling: "thou marshall'st me the way I was going" (2.1.42). He doesn't need a marshall, then—he was already traveling that path. But the marshall is a companion, a guide, and it takes the edge off his agency, his responsibility to be guided in this way. Macbeth, I want to say, is turning his action into behavior. "I go, and it is done" (2.1.62). Once again he elides his own agency in the act, imagining that he is drawn by the imaginary dagger, instructed by the whole of nature itself, and finally summoned by the bell that invites him to heaven or hell. James Calderwood has brilliantly said of these lines: "The whole speech marvelously illustrates the workings of a self-protective consciousness as it projects its inner impulses to create a behaviouristic world to whose stimuli it can then respond."[12]

This slip from action to behavior is important. For in representing his action as a response to a set of stimuli—the bell, the world of nature, the dagger itself—he begins to think of them as *causal* and abandons the entire domain of responsibility that is internally connected to what a human action is, and where talk is properly of reasons, not causes.[13] For we don't know what action has been done without understanding the intentions with which it was done, without an answer, potential or actual, to the question "Why did you do that?"

In the *Prima Secunda* of Thomas Aquinas's great *Summa Theologiae*, Aquinas contemplates human actions "proper to man as man": "Those actions are properly called actions that proceed from a *deliberate* will [my italics]. And if any other actions are found in man, they are called actions of a man, but not properly human actions, since they are not proper to a man as man" (I–IIae, q. 1.1, resp.). An action according to Elizabeth Anscombe in her modern classic, *Intentions*, is purposive and can always be answered by the question "Why are you doing that?"[14] Notice here that the claim is by no means that the intention controls the meaning of the action—as an editor, translator, and friend of Wittgenstein, Anscombe was hardly likely to make that blunder. For Aquinas what follows from his deeply Aristotelian understanding of action is that we are the deed's creature. What Macbeth is blinding himself to is the shaping role of the agent's deeds in forming, in building a character. In denying the natural logic of man and woman and deed, Macbeth is denying his own humanity.

The dagger marshals him, as if in a dream. Soon he will be melodramatically conjuring himself as Tarquin and pleading with the very earth not to respond to him. The path to murder is to deny all responsiveness to the world and the world to you. Macbeth requires the earth's deafness ("Hear not my steps which way they walk" [2.1.50]), and the world's darkness ("Let not light see my black and deep desires" [1.4.51]) as a presage to his act. And as he seeks the world's blindness and indifference, as he covets the darkness that he imagines will render his deeds invisible, the very physical integrity of his person cracks up. His eye will wink at his hand (1.4.52). The invisibility to himself that he covets, call it soul-blindness, will result not merely in a blackening out of self—"to know my deed 'twere best not know myself" (2.2.76)—but an intense isolation and self-deadening. It is a presage of the deadening that will come at the end of the play. There surcease and success have reached a different accommodation; there the succession of days, "tomorrow and tomorrow and tomorrow" (5.5.18) annihilates novelty. The evil man's world is a solipsistic world. He can "take things from others, but he can receive nothing from them."[15]

Were Macbeth able to do what he desires—to extricate his murder from all consequences save that of his own succession to the crown, to define the exact limits and contours of the act unilaterally—it would not be human action. And so in Shakespeare's understanding he has to deny and avoid his own humanity in order to perform actions that logically must have the consequences of human actions. Macbeth is beginning to have merely the illusion of sense, and that is why his nihilism is the logical end point, for he has stopped making any sense at all, has stupefied himself.

How does Macbeth stupefy himself? We witness this process immediately after as well as before the murder. When Macbeth describes how he could not say "Amen" when he overhears the prayers of the grooms he is about to murder, Lady Macbeth responds: "These deeds must not be thought / After these ways; so, it will make us mad" (2.2.36–37). Macbeth, being afraid "to think what (he) ha(s) done," must not think at all. When he hears that Macduff has "fled to England," he wishes entirely to eradicate any gap there might be between the conception and execution of a deed, such that "The very firstlings of my heart shall be / The firstlings of my hand." "Be it thought and done" (4.2.147). His wish is to eradicate thought altogether, to remove the very possibility that there could be a conceivable answer to the question "Why are you doing that?" He renders himself thoughtless: this is the "sweet oblivious antidote" (5.3.44) that he ministers to himself.

Closely allied to his willful thoughtlessness, his self-stupefaction, is his desire for isolation. "We will keep ourself / Til suppertime alone" (3.1.43). "Why do you keep alone?" (3.2.8) asks Lady Macbeth, who has encouraged his oblivion, his thoughtlessness: "Things without all remedy / Should be without regard" (3.2.11–12). He tells her that "there shall be done / A deed of dreadful note" (3.3.44–45). (Again his use of the passive tense averts his own agency in the murders he has ordered.) To her inquiries about what it is that is to be done, he asks not for her consultation, but for her applause after the fact: "Be innocent of the knowledge, dearest chuck / Til thou applaud the deed" (3.3.45–46). And his next address, turning away from his wife, is to the night, to blind the day, scarf up its eye to his future actions. Lady Macbeth is reduced to being a retrospective cheerleader for nameless, authorless deeds, deeds he will not and cannot now share because to share them—in prospect or retrospect—might be to name them. (And how innocent of the knowledge *could* she applaud the deed? Macbeth is removing any possibility of judgment and understanding from her ability to discern his action.) Once again we can see the separation of reason from will, the denaturing of action, and the concomitant destruction of intimacy and community. Wishing not to know his deed or his self, he can scarcely afford the risk of human company, the risk of being known by anyone else. "It will have blood" (3.4.123), he says. What is the it? He has now conceived himself as wading in a river of blood so deep that to continue across is all the same as to return, negating the point of action to a bloody and terrible sameness, to whose horror he is nonetheless numb (3.4.138). His deeds "must be acted ere they may be scanned" (3.4.140). In what sense, then, are they human acts at all in his diseased and confused imagination?

I am suggesting here that Shakespeare is showing us a mind losing the concept of human action.[16] Shakespeare has not lost this concept. How else can he keep its contours so firmly, so relentlessly before us? And how might it be recovered?

2. Lady Macbeth's Cry

The recovery of the concept of deed and doer in the world of human action may come through remorse, whose characteristic voice is "My God, what have I done?" *or*—it is Lady Macbeth's terrible cry, uttered while sleepwalking—which I can only now and forever hear in the shattering, soul-searching, soul-touching cry of Judi Dench.[17]

Lady Macbeth has conjured the stopping up of "the access and passage to remorse" (1.5.42) so that the compunctious visitings of nature cannot shake her murderous purpose (1.5.43). But we can only feel remorse over what has the power to haunt us, and Lady Macbeth will feel her remorse once the access and passage to it is unstopped, in the unremitting horror of her awakening memory. There she will feel, as Emily Dickinson says in her brilliant poem on remorse, "A presence of departed acts / At window and at door."[18] It is in remorse that the doer recognizes the one wronged in all his or her particularity, in the recognition of what she has done. Remorse is to be distinguished from shame in that the focus is unerringly concentrated on the reality of the one wronged, not in his or her *general* humanity, but precisely in her or his uniqueness and irreplaceability. In remorse one recognizes what one has become simultaneously with the particular reality of the other. Raimond Gaita puts it this way: "A certain sense of her victim's individuality is internal to a murderer's understanding of the moral significance of what she did." "That," he says, "is part of what it is to be aware of the reality of another human being."[19] Gaita is not saying that we feel remorse *because* we see that something is wrong. He is saying that our natural dispositions to remorse and to pity are one of the determinants of our concept of remorse and of what a human being is. Gaita makes the analogy to what he calls Wittgenstein's astonishingly radical remark that "pity is a form of conviction that someone is in pain."[20] Pity, he is suggesting, is not a psychological state but, as he puts it, "*normative* for the description of the forms of our indifference to the suffering of others" (my italics).[21] We know pity not epistemically but through our most basic *responses* in healing, binding, wounding, hurting, comforting, and crying, in the fact that we look into someone's face when binding his wounds. In remorse, says Gaita, in a wonderful indictment of what passes for moral theory in philosophy, "he is not haunted by his principles; he is not haunted by the moral law; he is not haunted by the fact that he did what he ought not to have done. . . . He is haunted by the particular human being he has murdered."[22] Again, haunted is the right word. In Lady Macbeth's nightwalking scene the passages to remorse are utterly unstopped. She is haunted nightly by the old man who had so much blood in him, by the Thane of Fife's wife. She is haunted by *them*. It is a picture of the human not general at all but *this* particular one, in his or her uniqueness and irreplaceability.

How is she haunted by her deeds? How then does her remorse bring in the reality of the other? It cannot quite be said that it is a conscience awakening to what she has done, for she is, after all, sleepwalking. It is a despairing and permanent redoing of the act itself, only now the words she said—"a little water clears us of this deed"—are ironized by the carelessness with which she said them then, with their irreversibility, their boundless echo in her poor tormented soul. What's done cannot be undone. In that thought she can only now undo herself. For that undoing, announced by the offstage cry of women, there can be no time: "she should have died hereafter" (5.5.17).[23]

Remorse is one of the ways in which the concept of human action is recovered for it is in remorse that, bitingly, agonizingly, the very contours of the terrible deed, the very significance of the act performed, reemerge in the sense of the particular harm done. Raimond Gaita has said that remorse is a "disciplined remembrance of the moral significance of what we did."[24] So the doer, the deed, and the one harmed come into focus all together, inextricably and mutually. Raimond Gaita says this: "The terrible recognition of what we have become is the necessary condition of the recognition of the evil we have done."[25] If remorse has to do with understanding yourself and your action, what you have done to someone else, it is because it involves a self not carved out of its own self-definition, its own will, but rather an understanding that your actions are involved with the life of others, subject to their representation, an understanding that those actions define you, and that you are the deed's creature, the deed is not your creature.

There is no time to mourn Lady Macbeth, for Macbeth has abolished time. He assimilated himself to a timeless will, a will which has anaesthetized its own reasons and rationales and replaced them with causes it experiences as compulsions, extrinsic to its own will. To refuse remorse, as Rowan Williams has said, is to "refuse to think what it is to be a subject changing according to processes and interactions outside my own will."[26] The refusal of remorse may well involve a vast overestimation of the role of the will. Macbeth shows us that picture of the will as murderous. The stopping and unstopping of remorse is Shakespeare's way of retrieving the very concept of human action from a murderous will—Macbeth's—and from a picture of the will that is itself murderous and bound up with violence.[27]

3. Losing Our Concepts

In charting in *Macbeth* the internal relations between the concepts of action and remorse, the danger of losing the name of human action and recovering it again in the disciplined remembrance of past deeds, in which remembrances the doer perceives himself painfully as the evil doer he has become by virtue of his deeds, in charting the play's contours in these respects, I wish to allude to the notion of conceptual amnesia. My essay title, "Losing the Name of Action," comes, of course, from *Hamlet*. It comes at the end of the most famous soliloquy of all in that play, "To be or not to be." We might describe at least part of this famous soliloquy as Hamlet trying to force himself to be more like Macbeth, as he entertains the idea that conscience makes cowards of us, turning awry enterprises of great pith and moment so that they lose the name of action (so that they are impossible to act on, so that they can't properly be called actions). That play too is an astonishing exploration of action—who authors it or seeks to do so, quite how it escapes intention, how death supersedes all revenging plots in the face of which, finally, only readiness is all. But I've borrowed the phrase to suggest the work of conceptual amnesia. This is central to Thomas Pfau's recent book *Minding the Modern*, and it may be said to have its roots in Iris Murdoch's pithy and brilliant essay "Against Dryness," but it is also beautifully elaborated in the work of Cora

Diamond, and especially in her important essay "Losing Your Concepts."[28] Murdoch says in "Against Dryness," "We have suffered a general loss of concepts, the loss of a moral and political vocabulary. . . . We no longer see man against a background of values, of realities, which transcend him. We picture man as a brave naked will surrounded by an easily comprehended empirical world."[29] I don't have space here to explore the differences in conceptual amnesia as it is posited differently in the work of MacIntyre and Murdoch, which is part of what Cora Diamond undertakes in "Losing Your Concepts"; or to do more than allude to the riches on offer in Thomas Pfau's extraordinary book, a complex investigation of agency, its attenuation in modernity, and its related concepts. Both Cora Diamond and Niklas Forsberg distinguish the ways in which concepts can be lost. They can be lost historically—things change in such a way that we no longer understand certain ways of life; they can be lost philosophically, as Wittgenstein argues when, for example, he shows how our conceptions of inner life have been radically misconstrued.[30] For Murdoch conceptual loss involves *our* loss of conceptual realities, ones that derive from a conflict between ourselves and the pictures of the good life we strive to emulate. We strive to become the naked choosing wills pictured in our moral philosophy.[31] Murdoch wanted us to see that moral agency and our reasons for action were not properly conceived solely in terms of choice, that often choice is irrelevant (because someone's very being cannot conceive a choice where others might so conceive it, or because the very formulation of something as a choice is already morally degrading).[32] Further, as Niklas Forsberg has recently shown, the conception of human freedom as choice, the picture of the naked will in a supermarket of options, strips us of our reality and makes our attempts at self-understanding merely "regional."[33] The picture of the human as a naked will makes it hard to see, and easy to forget, the intricacy of the connections between conceptions of action, remorse, evil, and the central way in which our modes of describing and misdescribing what we do are bound up with our self-understanding. I have borrowed the phrase from Hamlet, "losing the name of action," to show Macbeth's conceptual amnesia. Macbeth has to work hard to stupefy himself, to dull himself to the concept of action. By imagining deeds without succession (a deep pun in the play) he is both denaturing the shared sense of what an action comes to, its reality, and at the same time losing his self-understanding in one and the same thought. (We tend to lose an understanding of the world and an understanding of ourselves together.) If he were to know his deed, it were best then not to know himself: right there is an acknowledgment of the horror of regicide and murder. But he cannot know his deed without knowing himself, that is, without understanding what his action entails. Shakespeare shows us the very process of conceptual amnesia in Macbeth's mind, as he shows how he loses his grip on both self, world, and action.

My brief exploration of remorse in relation to *Macbeth* has shown that it too is internally connected to questions of the very nature of a deed in the light of doer and the one harmed. With the concept of remorse, then, comes the concept of evil. When concepts of the will are dessicated, so too are concepts of evil. "Is there something in our experience that can . . . teach us what evil is? There is, I believe. It is remorse."[34] Macbeth has been called "an anatomy of evil" and "Shakespeare's most profound and mature vision of evil."[35]

In his brilliant chapter "Evil Done and Evil Suffered" in *Good and Evil: An Absolute Conception*, Gaita shows us how problematic certain conceptions of evil are in moral philosophy by virtue of a powerful thought-experiment, the kind of experiment that Murdoch might have had in mind in her essay "Against Dryness." He takes the example of the kind used by consequentialists: what if you could save ten people by shooting one? He claims that those who think that it is obvious that one should be shot to save ten have no sense of evil done or suffered. He imagines the response of one who is saved by virtue of the shooting of the one. I will give simply a short excerpt from his account:

> If he dies, I will live, because he died, and because there are nine others with me, each of the nine others will be able to say the same. Yet when he is dead, will I be able to console myself by saying that he died only one tenth for me? Though you think you must kill him not for me or for any of the others taken individually, when he is dead each of us must accept the fact that insofar as he was murdered for our sake, he died for us singly and individually. Each of us, in his singularity, is implicated in the evil of his murder. . . . If you must count, then let it be like this: one, one, one . . . and when there is no more "one" to be said, content yourself with that and resist the temptation to say: And they total ten whereas there is only one over there.[36]

Gaita is trying to get at the artificial separation of the very idea of evil done and evil suffered, and at the moral idiocy of choice in certain examples. "My example," he suggests, "shows that the most important philosophical question is not 'What ought to be done?' The most important question is how to characterize the situation and to capture the evil in it."[37] What Gaita has done by virtue of his superbly perceptive writing is to get us to see the situation posed by the consequentialists in a different light. The situation now comes under an altogether new description and renders absurd the strict parameters as it is conceived in the moral philosopher's "dilemma," parameters that entirely dissolve reality. For in imagining and protecting the surveying eye/I, viewing a range of options in a world of possibilities, the real dimensions of self and world are vanishing from view.[38] Gaita's point—and it is surely Shakespeare's point too in *Macbeth*—is that what we do, our actions, come under myriad descriptions, and these descriptions define us because they articulate the positions we are prepared to take and what we hold ourselves responsible for.[39] Gaita consistently helps us to see the inadequacies of the idea that moral agency involves a world of facts and attitudes we might take toward them. As Lars Hertzberg has said in a lucid commentary on Gaita's work: "As I read him, he considers the question of what I take to be the case and the way I respond to it to be inseparable aspects of the situation."[40] This is how vision, not choice, is a central dimension of moral agency and why the way we see the world is as revelatory of us as of the world we see, respond to, and describe in everyday life and in fiction.[41] In remorse the deed, the doer, and what is done are realized together in a biting, retrospective recognition. That is why seeing the shape of evil and the shape of love are coterminous, and that is why remorse shows us an encounter with "the reality of the ethical." That is also why the play as a whole does not share in the nihilism it exposes in its central protagonist but rather sees that pointlessness, that signification of precisely nothing, the tale only of sound, fury, and idiocy, as the logical end of the extinction of action, and this precisely not in a moralistic way but through our pity for what Macbeth has become.[42]

Under current ideas of action we tend to imagine that feeling pity for someone would mean that we are slackening our sense of what it is they have actually done, perhaps because we can think of holding someone responsible only in terms of blame. But *Macbeth* helps us to see that it might be precisely by virtue of our pity that we might hold Macbeth responsible for all that he has done and that we might also pity the creature he has become, indeed that our pity is part of the fabric of our moral imagination.[43]

What we need, Murdoch suggests against simplistic ideas of freedom of the will, and the will's agency in action, is a "renewed sense of the difficulty and complexity of the moral life and the opacity of persons." She finds literature a good home for the exploration of concepts, where vision is enlarged.[44] Seeing what is "most precious to us" is a task I see at the heart of Shakespeare's late tragedies. There what is precious is only realized through a recognition of loss.

4. The Thane of Fife Had a Wife: What Is Most Precious to Us

I take those last terms "most precious to us" from Macduff's response to Malcolm when he has received the news of his wife's and children's deaths. I want to dwell on this response for a while, and rehearse what Macduff is responding to in the play. This will show how the play continually refines and holds open to view not how to choose between different actions, "what ought to be done?"—here to cry like a woman or fight like a man—but rather how to hold a sense, a vision (in Murdoch's terms) of what is precious to us. It helps us see that moral judgment is about the *apprehension* of a world apt for valuing, rather than a choice between different values.[45] To explore Macduff's response we need to appreciate what it is a response to.

In Michael Boyd's recent RSC production of *Macbeth* at Stratford in 2012, the moral center of the play is the murder of Lady Macduff's children at the castle in Fife.[46] This scene was sometimes cut in eighteenth- and nineteenth-century productions. It is also often produced in a highly sentimental fashion (the boy is too sweet, and banal understandings of femininity—weak, not wise—get in the way of Lady Macduff's clear-sighted understanding of her own betrayal, isolation, and abandonment), corrupting the lucidity with which the scene was written. For here we encounter the courage of a young boy standing in for his father toward a wife and mother abandoned by her great warrior husband who will redeem the land. Only no such redemption is yet at hand. This is what it is to live in the Scotland of Macbeth. We know that Macbeth's Scotland is a land ruled by and through fear. The exchange with Ross and Lady Macduff at the beginning of this scene is vital. In the preceding scene we have just seen Macbeth in dismay at the news of Macduff's flight declaring that he will "surprise" Macduff's castle in Fife and seize his lands.

Now in the next scene we move to Fife and Lady Macduff is being brought the news from Ross that Macduff has fled the land. Her first question is to ask what had he done that he should flee? And she thinks his flight is madness, that he has become a traitor (to her and his children) by virtue of his fears. And to this Ross tries out the idea that she does not know whether it was wisdom or fear. Lady Macduff replies that it cannot be wisdom to "leave his wife, to leave his babes, / His mansions, and his titles in a place / From whence himself does fly?" (4.2.6–8). For her this is a sign that he cannot love them, for even the wren fights against the owl to protect the young ones in her nest: "All is the fear, nothing is the love" (4.2.12). A description apt for the denaturing of Scotland. Ross tries again the thought that Macduff is "noble, wise, judicious, and best knows / The fits of the season" (4.2.16–17). But he admits that the times are cruel "when we are traitors / And do not know ourselves, yet know not what we fear, / But float upon a wild and violent sea / Each way and none" (4.2.20–22). Not enough credence is usually given to Lady Macduff's apprehension of what wisdom here might come to, against the initially bland, superficial, and false consolations of Ross. And then Ross goes. And then a messenger comes in warning her to flee. And then he goes. It is left to her son to be the man. And he is, in this striking staging, the best man in the play, his actions and vision the least corrupted, his heart the purest. The scene anatomizes the effect of fear, or how liable it is to make us traitors even when we don't know what we fear, floating "each way" and therefore "none." To draw out the depth of Macduff's response to their slaughter this scene needs to be free of condescension, and needs to be as clear-sighted as Lady Macduff is within it.

Macduff's response to the slaughter of his entire family and household insists on the responsibility of responsiveness.[47] He is told by Malcolm that he must dispute it like a man. To Malcolm's morally feeble, instrumental words "Be comforted. / Let's make us med'cines of our great revenge" (4.3.215), he finds it enough to comment: "He has no children." And then:

I shall do so
But I must also feel it as a man;
I cannot but remember such things were
That were most precious to me. (4.3.223–26)

All Malcolm can think of is turning Macduff into the instrument of revenge against Macbeth. But Macduff is reminded of all that is precious in the world, the remembrance of which, the recovery of which, is what he thought he was fighting for, though he now, I think, realizes that he might have forgotten this. Macbeth has destroyed what is precious to him; he has destroyed what he cares about and values, so it is what is precious, what is valued that is here enlarged, put before us to care about. Macbeth too will eventually know that he has destroyed the things he can no longer look to have as honor, love, troops of friends.

Macbeth puts before us anatomy of evil whose contours can only come clear because of remorse, and the subsequent revelation of the shape of harm. In so doing it shows us what is at stake in the concept of human action, but also what gets lost by dry versions of what it is that human beings do, dry versions of the so-called dilemmas before them, and it shows us too how violent and murderous are pictures of the will absent the acknowledgment of others.

Being human is aspiring to being human, says Cavell. "Since it is not aspiring to being the only human, it is an aspiration on behalf of others as well."[48]

5. Tragedy

Macbeth has not rendered himself inhuman. But only a human being can behave inhumanly. This is why being human is not a given. "Being human is the power to grant being human." "What gives us *so much as the idea* that human beings think, can feel?"[49] Nothing, because it is not an idea. "I am not of the opinion that he has a soul."[50]

Before we reject the human, before we imagine we are posthuman, we should know what it means to cherish it.

We sometimes call on each other to treat each other as human beings. We seem to need reminders. Or we say, the way she humiliated him was inhuman, or the rapist sat on her to tie up his shoelaces after he raped her as if she was interchangeable with a log or a bench. Is there any other way to treat each other except as human?[51] But surely we—and not the rapist either—do not need reminders of the difference between a log and a woman?[52] Such phrases are rather a call to justice, a plea that she will fall into the realm of justice as a stone or log does not. They are a shamed acknowledgment that it is precisely in the realm of the human that people treat each other with a cruelty likely to madden us if we contemplate it too surely.

It is perhaps too comforting a thought to imagine that tragedy is about our finiteness, about what we can't know or do. If we see it that way we can avoid our irreducible, inevitable responsibility in adopting an attitude toward each other's souls. If we follow Cavell's logic, of the embeddedness of knowledge in acknowledgment and response, then the idea of our finitude might come as a relief from the perpetual burden of having to read each other, and having to express ourselves, of having to draw the connections we draw between body and soul.

Tragedy is therefore a good reminder for the humanities because it calls us back to our irreducible role in seeing each other as human, as task, not given. Criticism is making a work of art available to just response. If we justly respond to Shakespearean tragedy, can it help the humanities, help us, be humane?

Notes

1. For vital reflections on the question of the human as a question of *recognition* to which I return later in the essay, see Stanley Cavell, *The Claim of Reason: Wittgenstein, Skepticism, Morality, Tragedy* (New York: Oxford University Press, 1979); Cora Diamond, "The Importance of Being Human," in *Human Beings*, ed. David Cockburn (Cambridge: Cambridge University Press, 1991), 35–62; and more recently, Niklas Forsberg, *Language Lost and Found: On Iris Murdoch and the Limits of Philosophical Discourse* (New York and London: Bloomsbury, 2013).

2. John Berger and Jean Mohr, *A Fortunate Man: The Story of a Country Doctor* (1967; rpt. New York: Vintage International, 1997), 166.

3. "Being human is aspiring to be human . . . since it is not aspiring to being the only human, it is an aspiration on behalf of others as well." Cavell, *Claim of Reason*, 399.

4. Merriam-Webster defines scare quotes as "quotation marks used to express esp. skepticism or decision concerning the use of the enclosed word or phrase." See https://www.merriam-webster.com/dictionary/scare%20quotes, accessed June 10, 2017.

5. For details on Todd Akin's unfortunate statement see http://www.nytimes.com/2012/08/21/us/politics/rep-todd-akin-legitimate-rape-statement-and-reaction.html, accessed June 10, 2017. For some reflections on the question of the human, see Richard Eldridge and Bernie Rhie, "Introduction: Cavell, Literary Studies, and the Human Subject: Consequences of Skepticism," in *Stanley Cavell and Literary Studies: Consequences of Skepticism*, ed. Eldridge and Rhie (New York: Continuum, 2011), 5. See also Richard Eldridge, *Leading a Human Life: Wittgenstein, Intentionality, and Romanticism* (Chicago: University of Chicago Press, 1997).

6. See Harold Bloom for the idea of Shakespeare and the "invention" of the human, *Shakespeare: The Invention of the Human* (New York: Riverhead Trade, 1998).

7. This essay is part of a book on Shakespeare's late tragedies and ethics, called at the moment *Shakespeare's Private Linguists*.

8. Iris Murdoch, "Against Dryness," in *Existentialists and Mystics: Writings on Philosophy and Literature*, ed. Peter Conradi (Harmondsworth, U.K.: Penguin, 1997), for the dessication of the concept of human action at the hands of moral theory. For a brilliant recent exploration of human agency taking up some of Murdoch's perceptions, see Thomas Pfau, *Minding the Modern: Human Agency, Intellectual Traditions, and Responsible Knowledge* (South Bend, Ind.: University of Notre Dame Press, 2013).

9. This reference to his murder of Duncan or to his other murders as an unspecified "it" is a characteristic locution for Macbeth. See also 1.4.50, 2.1.62, for example.

10. Hannah Arendt, *The Human Condition*, 2nd ed. (Chicago: University of Chicago Press, 1998).

11. Cavell, *Claim of Reason*, 110. Here, importantly, he is getting at the depth of convention in human life.

12. James Calderwood, *If It Were Done: Macbeth and Tragic Action* (Amherst: University of Massachusetts Press, 1986). I have found this excellent study very helpful.

13. See J. L. Austin's beautifully understated but trenchant analysis in "A Plea for Excuses," perhaps one of the best essays ever written on the philosophy of action, in *Philosophical Papers* (Oxford: Clarendon, 1961); see p. 202 for our language helping us to mistake causes for reasons. For the transition from action to behavior and its disastrous *ethical* consequences, see Charles Taylor, *The Explanation of Behaviour* (London: Routledge and Kegan Paul, 1980); Thomas Pfau, *Minding the Modern*; and Peter Winch's still highly relevant *The Idea of a Social Science and Its Relevance to Philosophy* (London: Routledge and Kegan Paul, 1958).

14. "Intentional actions" are ones to which a certain sense of the question "why?" has application. See G. E. M. Anscombe, *Intentions* (Oxford: Blackwell, 1963), 11. I am using the Complete English Edition of the *Summa* translated by the Fathers of the English Dominican Province in 5 vols. (New York: Christian Classics, 1981).

15. Ilham Dilman, *Raskolnikov's Rebirth: Psychology and the Understanding of Evil* (Chicago: Open Court, 2000), 112.

16. On losing concepts, see Niklas Forsberg, *Language Lost and Found*, and Cora Diamond's seminal essay "Losing Your Concepts," *Ethics* 98, no. 2 (1998): 255–77. One of Forsberg's key points is that it may be hard to see when we might be losing our grip of a concept and speaking only under the illusion of sense because "words are worn and torn and so turned differently. . . . They are changed but not necessarily exchanged since words may look the same when their concepts change—and because this is so it is oftentimes hard to come to see that one may fail in the command of one's own language" (1).

17. Raimond Gaita, *Good and Evil: An Absolute Conception* (London: Macmillan, 1991), xxi. Judi Dench's outstanding performance as Lady Macbeth was in Trevor Nunn's production (with Ian McKellen as Macbeth) in 1976. My own attendance at this production at the Young Vic transformed my sense of the possibilities of theater utterly and forever.

18. Thanks to Thomas Pfau for the reference to Emily Dickinson's poem. It can be found in *The Complete Poems of Emily Dickinson*, ed. Thomas H. Johnson (San Francisco: Back Bay Books, 1976), 365. Raimond Gaita, "Ethical Individuality," in *Value and Understanding: Essays for Peter Winch*, ed. Gaita (London: Routledge, 1990), 118–48, at 137.

19. Gaita, *Good and Evil*, 52.

20. Wittgenstein, *Philosophical Investigations*, 4th ed., trans. G. E. M. Anscombe, P. M. S. Hacker, and Joachim Schulte (Oxford: Wiley-Blackwell, 2009), Remark 287: "How am I filled with pity *for this human being?* How does it come about what the object of my pity is? (Pity, one may say, is one form of being convinced that someone else is in pain.)"

21. Gaita, *Good and Evil*, 177–78.

22. Gaita, "Ethical Individuality," 127.

23. Lady Macbeth was going to die sooner or later. Lady Macbeth should have died at a more convenient time (to mourn her?). Both readings cauterize natural response.

24. Gaita, *Good and Evil*, 59.

25. Ibid., 63.

26. Rowan Williams, *Lost Icons: Reflections on Cultural Bereavement* (Edinburgh: T & T Clark, 2000), 109. This picture of the will is intrinsically bound up with the negation of time. An atemporal self does not have to be connected with the lives of others. Macbeth's reading of the weird sisters' equivocations as prophecies and predictions is an evasion of his temporal self.

27. See the epigraph by Iris Murdoch to *Existentialists and Mystics*: "Man is a creature who makes pictures of himself, and then comes to resemble the picture," from "Metaphysics and Ethics," 75.

28. Pfau writes: "To work with concepts . . . means to enter into an ethical—as opposed to a straightforwardly pragmatic—relation to the reality that these concepts *prima facie* allow us to apprehend" (*Minding the Modern*, 3).

29. Murdoch, "Against Dryness," 290.

30. Forsberg, *Language Lost and Found*, 62.

31. Murdoch's understanding of conceptual amnesia is superbly elucidated by Forsberg: see *Language Lost and Found*, 171.

32. For an excellent elucidation of Murdoch and the idea of choice, see Susan Wolf's essay "Loving Attention: Lessons in Love from *The Philadelphia Story*," in *Understanding Love: Philosophy, Film, and Fiction*, ed. Susan Wolf and Christopher Grau (Oxford: Oxford University Press, 2014), 369–86.

33. Forsberg, *Language Lost and Found*, 132; and for the idea of comprehension as merely regional, 133.

34. Raimond Gaita, *A Common Humanity: Thinking about Love and Truth and Justice* (London: Routledge, 2000), 4.

35. See G. K. Hunter, in the introduction to the Penguin edition of *Macbeth*; G. Wilson Knight in his essay "Macbeth and the Metaphysic of Evil," in *The Wheel of Fire: Interpretations of Shakespearean Tragedy* (1930; rpt., London: Routledge, 1989).

36. Gaita, *Good and Evil*, 68.

37. Cavell, *Claim of Reason*, part 3, pp. 247ff., for a brilliant critique of moral philosophy in terms of "what ought to be done."

38. Forsberg, *Language Lost and Found*, 171: "A loss of concepts is, at bottom, due to a lack, or a distorted form of self-understanding. This lack or these distortions are in turn related, but not reducible to misunderstandings of our language."

39. See Cavell, *Claim of Reason*, 324, Cavell's critique of Rawls, and his elucidation of specifically moral claims: "What you are said to do can have various descriptions; under some you will know that you are doing it, under others you will not, under some your act will seem unjust to you, under others not. What alternatives we can and must take are not fixed, but chosen; and thereby fix us."

40. Lars Hertzberg, "Gaita on Recognizing the Human," in *Ethics, Philosophy and a Common Humanity*, ed. Christopher Cordner (London: Routledge, 2010), 7–20.

41. Mark Doty, *The Art of Description: World into Word* (Minnesota: Graywolf, 2010), 65: "Description is an art to the degree it gives us not just the world but the inner life of the witness."

42. For Iris Murdoch understanding the reality of another person is the work of love, justice, and pity, all essential to the vision of Shakespeare's late tragedies. Gaita's vital commentary on this comment is that love, justice, and pity are *forms of understanding*, and not merely "conditions which facilitate understanding": see *A Common Humanity*, vii.

43. A point that Gaita makes about Oedipus in *Good and Evil.*

44. Murdoch, "Against Dryness," 293.

45. A point made in Yaniv Iczkovits, *Wittgenstein's Ethical Thought* (Basingstoke: Palgrave Macmillan, 2012), 145.

46. Michael Boyd's fabulously inventive production doubled the actors playing Macduff's children for the weird sisters, who appeared hanging down on nooses in the second appearance of the weird sisters (the first scene was cut). The production kept "the eye of childhood" resolutely to the fore.

47. "The responsibility of responsiveness" is a key idea in Cavell's interpretation of Wittgenstein and Austin. For the phrase in Cavell's work, see *A Pitch of Philosophy: Autobiographical Exercises* (Cambridge, Mass.: Harvard University Press, 1996), 126.

48. Cavell, *Claim of Reason*, 399.

49. Wittgenstein, *Philosophical Investigations*, Remark 283.

50. See "Eine Einstellung zur Seele," in Peter Winch, *Trying to Make Sense* (Oxford: Basil Blackwell, 1987).

51. The key discussion here is Cavell's discussion of the slaveholder in *Claim of Reason*, 372ff., and Gaita, *A Common Humanity.*

52. On treating persons as persons, with startlingly lucid and extended examples, see Cavell, *Claim of Reason*, and the discussion of "the vanishing of the human."

"The Eyes of Others"

Rousseau and Adam Smith on Judgment and Autonomy

Hina Nazar

Readers of this essay will likely agree that we have the right, as adults, to make choices that are based on our private deliberations and judgments rather than imposed upon us from without. Yet the concept of autonomy, which gives philosophical texture to this right, is highly controversial in the humanities today. Closely aligned with the critical philosophy of Immanuel Kant, autonomy is often thought to mobilize unrealistic, even dangerous, conceptions of the atomistic individual or the Sovereign Subject, to disregard the claims of the emotions and the ties of community, and to ignore the very obvious fact that subjectivity is a development of sociability.[1] Neo-Aristotelian and communitarian philosophers have also argued that ethical systems like Kantianism, which put a high premium on autonomy, work with a technical and rule-bound understanding of theoretical reason that preempts adequate consideration of the messy practice of moral judgment—the capacity, among other things, to make determinations of right and wrong by relating the particulars of a given moral scenario to general rules.[2] Charles E. Larmore contends, for example, that modern moral philosophy implies that "we have an adequate theory of some intentional human practice, if we can reconstruct the rules, both explicit and tacit, that characterize it."[3] As such, the moderns relegate judgment to the margins, since judgment often "transcends the explicit or tacit rules upon which it only partially depends."[4]

The aims of this essay are twofold: to challenge the argument that the modern commitment to autonomy necessarily sidelines the practice of judgment and to ask what happens to the concept of autonomy when this latter practice is accorded due importance. I will tackle these goals by considering the writings of two of Kant's most important Enlightenment precursors, Adam Smith and Jean-Jacques Rousseau, both of whom occupy the curious crossroads of eighteenth-century thought marked by the intersection of liberalism and sentimentalism.[5] While many scholars take Rousseau's famous definition of freedom in *The Social Contract* (1762)—that is, "obedience to the law one has prescribed to oneself"—to constitute his most important contribution to the discourse of autonomy (one that exercised enormous influence on Kant's later formulation), I will focus here on Rousseau's narrative about educating the autonomous man in *Emile* (1762).[6] Regarded by Rousseau himself as his "worthiest and best book," *Emile* explicitly ties the cultivation of moral freedom to that of a finely honed judgment.[7] Emile's tutor underscores that his pupil is to learn "less science than judgment," so that, as an adult, he will "no longer have need of any guide other than himself."[8]

To summon Adam Smith's writings in the context of an argument about autonomy is somewhat controversial, since, until quite recently, Smith was not known as much of a moral philosopher at all: his principal contribution in this context, *The Theory of Moral Sentiments* (1759, 1790), was all but eclipsed by his economic treatise *The Wealth of Nations* (1776). Furthermore, Smith's *Theory*, like his fellow sentimentalist David Hume's *Treatise of Human Nature* (1739–40) and *Enquiry Concerning the Principles of Morals* (1751), develops a psychological and social explanation of the origins of moral judgment, which appears, at least on the surface, to have little to do with moral obligation or freedom. Nonetheless, following the recent example of scholars such as Samuel Fleischacker and Michael Frazer, I will suggest that implicit in Smith's argument about judgment is a compelling account of moral freedom, understood as the exercise of independent judgment.[9]

In pooling together Smith's and Rousseau's writings, I do not seek to develop a sentimentalist alternative to rationalism per se.[10] As I suggest elsewhere, eighteenth-century sentimentalism and rationalism intersect in productive ways, even as the former highlights the centrality of sentiment within moral life.[11] I aim, rather, to explore the implications for autonomy—broadly construed as the condition of being "directed by considerations, desires, conditions, and characteristics that are not simply imposed externally on one"—of two related, but ultimately distinct, understandings of judgment.[12] The differences I have in mind have less to do with Smith's championing of modern commercial society and Rousseau's critique of it, since recent scholarship has done much to complicate the caricature of Smith as an apologist for laissez-faire capitalism.[13] I will be concerned instead with Smith's and Rousseau's very different attitudes toward public opinion and intersubjective exchange as factors influencing private moral judgment. Rousseau repeatedly refers to other people's opinions as a "poison" (*Emile* 178) that corrodes the integrity of judgment, though, as we will see, he reverses his position in relation to women so that "opinion is the grave of virtue among men and its throne among women" (365). For Rousseau, attention to the judgments and opinions of others (a form of attention that is valid for women but not for men) is the work of the relative self-love that he calls *amour-propre* and that most commentators translate as vanity. Rousseau contrasts *amour-propre* with *amour de soi*, the healthy instinct of self-preservation that is man's principal guide in a state of nature, a condition described at length in his *Discourse on the Origin and Foundations of Inequality among Men* (1755), or *Second Discourse*. Emile's education is designed to foster independence of judgment by forestalling the development of *amour-propre* and limiting social engagement until young adulthood. Whereas for John Locke, Rousseau's most important Enlightenment interlocutor in the field of educational theory, instruction in public opinion and judgment of it are coterminous developments, for Rousseau, a child who engages other people's judgments before developing his own becomes a slave to common prejudice. In *Emile* he asserts, "If you begin by instructing [your pupil] in public opinion before teaching him to appraise it, rest assured that, whatever you may do, it will become his, and you will never be able to destroy it" (187). Reinforcing this point, he observes, "As soon as one must see with the eyes of others, one must will with their wills" (84).

While the figure of other people's eyes accrues a distinctly negative charge in *Emile*, it has both positive and negative connotations in Smith's *Theory of Moral Sentiments*. Societal judgment, Smith argues, often serves as a paltry standard of right and wrong, since the world's eye is blinded all too often by the glare of wealth and fashion. At the same time, Smith accords value to the considered judgments of society—as embodied, for example, in the laws of justice—as whetting stones in the cultivation of private judgment. More radically, he suggests that independent moral judgment is really only possible in an interactive context. This counterintuitive claim flows out of Smith's understanding of the impartial standpoint that legitimates judgment, a standpoint that, he argues, is enabled by sympathetically or imaginatively engaging the judgments of other people. Delineating the process by which individuals judge the "propriety" or "impropriety" (Smith's context-sensitive reformulation of "right" or "wrong") of their own actions, Smith observes,

> We can never survey our own sentiments and motives, we can never form any judgment concerning them; unless we remove ourselves, as it were, from our own natural station, and endeavour to view them as at a certain distance from us. But we can do this in no other way than by endeavouring to view them with the eyes of other people, or as other people are likely to view them.[14]

Far from blinding one's vision, the eyes of others enable critical distance: other people's judgments are an important resource in mitigating personal bias and fostering impartiality.

Smith and Rousseau are both "sentimentalists" because for both, moral judgment is, in significant ways, a matter of inner sentiment. For neither, however, does this mean that judgment is the same thing as personal preference; if it were, it could not serve as a guide to conduct in a world shared with others. Both thinkers indicate that judgment has standards, and it is in their respective accounts of its standards that they part ways, specifying different directions not only for sentimentalism but also for a future liberalism. For Smith, as I have already begun to suggest, judgment gains validity in an intersubjective context. By contrast, Rousseau looks for the standards of judgment in what might best be described as a norm of nature, where "nature" connotes not only the physical world and its laws but also an inner human nature that is defined in sharp opposition to social influence. Justice and goodness, he argues in *Emile*, are "true affections of the soul enlightened by reason, and hence only an ordered development of our primitive affections" (235). On this account, the uncorrupted passions or "primitive affections," which are free from the taint of *amour-propre*, join hands with reason to yield moral conceptions.

I will suggest that the narrative about judgment developed in *Emile* engenders an understanding of moral freedom that is vulnerable to many recent criticisms of autonomy, and especially the criticism that autonomy presupposes a radical self-containment. By contrast, Smith's account of judgment aligns the quest for moral independence with the dynamics of interdependence and paves the way for an understanding of autonomy that is hospitable to our common intuitions regarding the individual's social embedment. As such, the *Theory of Moral Sentiments* anticipates recent attempts, especially by feminist theorists, to radically rethink the concept of autonomy by "socializing" it—that is, by theorizing it in conjunction with the thesis of the subject's social constitution.[15] In one such attempt, Marilyn Friedman argues that

> implicit in the idea of acting according to wants, desires, cares, concerns, values, or commitments that are one's own is the idea that one might have acted according to the wants, desires, cares, concerns, values, or commitments of *others* but did not do so. This implicit contrast is a part of what autonomy means. . . . Although autonomy is individuating in its effects on persons, it never loses its social rootedness.[16]

For Friedman, among other feminist thinkers, autonomy remains a crucial feminist ideal because of the unparalleled importance it accords to individual choice and judgment, and a key goal of feminist theory today must be to bring it into dialogue with feminism's long-standing interest in the social determinants of subjectivity and women's oppression.

Feminist attempts to rethink autonomy have as a necessary corollary a revaluation of the liberal philosophical tradition that institutes the modern rhetoric of self-direction. My reading of Smith and Rousseau is meant to be a contribution in this context. By placing the motif of context-sensitive judgment at the center of their moral theories, Smith and Rousseau produce an implicit challenge to those critics of liberalism who see liberal moral theory as hopelessly lost in the exigencies of theoretical reason. But these Enlightenment thinkers challenge liberalism's critics in different ways, and their primary difference has to do with their respective attitudes to sociability. It is to a fuller understanding of these attitudes and their implications for autonomy that I now turn.

The Social Contexts of Private Judgment

According to the Kantian philosopher Christine M. Korsgaard, the British sentimentalists initiated the modern revolution in ethics that culminated in the ideal of autonomy.[17] They did so by giving morality a radical inward turn and contesting the realism of earlier schools of moral philosophy. Whereas for the moral realists right and wrong are intrinsic properties of certain actions and motives, for the sentimentalists they are attributes that individuals ascribe to those actions and motives. According to Francis Hutcheson, David Hume, and Adam Smith, an action is understood to be good or bad not because it *is* good or bad but because *we* deem it to be so.[18] Moreover, the actions or motives we give a moral designation address us differently than do the objects of knowledge. Establishing a parallel between moral and aesthetic judgments, the sentimentalists argued that a beautiful landscape or a noble action is not *known* to be beautiful or noble but is, at least initially, *felt* to be so. The more considered judgments we make about beauty or goodness require that we examine, more fully, our feelings of approval or disapproval as opposed to the objects soliciting them. This is the gist of the sentimentalists' fact-value distinction, most famously delineated by David Hume in Book III of *A Treatise of Human Nature*:

> Take any action allow'd to be vicious: Wilful murder, for instance. Examine it in all lights, and see if you can find a matter of fact, or real existence, which you call vice. In which-ever way you take it, you find only certain passions, motives, volitions, and thoughts. There is no other matter of fact in the case. The vice entirely escapes you, as long as you consider the object. You never find it, till you turn your reflexion into your own breast, and find a sentiment of disapprobation, which arises in you towards this action.[19]

Anticipating moral constructivists such as Korsgaard, Hume argues that values are found within us rather than "out there" in the world.[20] As Korsgaard explains, "To talk about values and meanings is not to talk about entities, either mental or Platonic, but to talk in a shorthand way about relations we have with ourselves and one another."[21] For John Rawls too, constructivism—the position that I, following Korsgaard, see as originating in eighteenth-century sentimentalism—must be understood as an alternative to moral realism or to any belief in an objective (that is, extrasubjective or mind-independent) order of right and wrong. Moral principles, Rawls argues, cannot be justified by any "moral truth interpreted as fixed by a prior and independent order of objects and relations, whether natural or divine, an order apart from and distinct from how we conceive ourselves."[22]

While the sentimentalists gave morality a decisive inward turn, rendering it a "matter of feeling" (to borrow Hume's phrase) and analogous to aesthetics, they did not understand it to be a matter of personal preference. Taste, Hume underscores in his famous 1757 essay, "Of the Standard of Taste," has a standard. And the standard of that which is ineluctably subjective—namely, aesthetic taste and moral judgment—derives from *inter*subjectivity. I will be especially interested in this section in what this means for Smith, but it is worth noting up front that an intersubjective dynamic is built into the basic moral scenario that both Hume and Smith summon to describe the workings of judgment: this is presumed to require more than one person (real or imagined) to be possible at all. There is, to begin with, the actor or agent whose actions or intended actions are being judged; there is at least one judge or spectator of the action; and for Hume, there is also always a recipient of the action (Smith brings this third character into the picture only when talking about a distinct category of judgment, judgments of merit and demerit). Smith's is regarded as a more autonomy-friendly account than Hume's because it shuns consequentialism—judgments of propriety or impropriety consider the motives underwriting an action rather than its consequences—and it is for this reason that I focus on Smith as a representative of British sentimentalism.

In the *Theory of Moral Sentiments*, Smith argues that moral judgments are grounded in the sympathy of spectators.[23] Observing the behavior of others, we approve of a given action if, upon imaginatively transporting ourselves into the position of the agent, we sympathize with his motives. In the absence of such sympathy, we deem the agent's action inappropriate. Likewise, we judge our own actions by imagining how they might appear to an onlooker, and, ideally, to an onlooker who has no stakes in the consequences of the action. If we believe that an impartial spectator will sympathize with us, we judge our action to be appropriate and vice versa. Smith explains:

> We either approve or disapprove of the conduct of another man according as we feel that, when we bring his case home to ourselves, we either can or cannot entirely sympathize with the sentiments and motives which directed it. And, in the same manner, we either approve or disapprove of our own conduct, according as we feel that, when we place ourselves in the situation of another man, and view it, as it were, with his eyes and from his station, we either can or cannot entirely enter into and sympathize with the sentiments and motives which influenced it. We can never survey our own sentiments and motives, we can never form any judgment concerning them; unless we remove ourselves, as it were, from our own natural station, and endeavour to view them as at a certain distance from us. But we can do this in no other way than by endeavouring to view them with the eyes of other people, or as other people are likely to view them. (109–10)

While judgments have a sentimental basis, they are not sentiments alone. Sentiments become judgments by being reflectively endorsed from an impartial standpoint. Smith suggests that impartiality is relatively easy to establish vis-à-vis the actions and motives of others, in relation to which we naturally occupy the position of an onlooker—the figure of the spectator specifying critical distance. It is harder to cultivate in relation to our own actions and motives. To create the requisite distance, we must consider, at least to begin with, how our actions appear to others, who are bearers of standpoints other than our own. The judge, Smith elaborates, must be open "either to what are, or to what, upon a certain condition, would be, or to what, we imagine, ought to be the judgment of others" (110). Significantly, the judgments that become relevant in cultivating impartiality are not necessarily the actual judgments of others; they include our imagination of the hypothetical judgments of others, as well as our sense of how others *ought* to judge under certain circumstances, a point to which I will return later. Whatever the source of these other judgments, however, they are necessary to cultivating impartiality. The impartial standpoint, as such, does not specify a view from nowhere or entail transcending bias, as under ideal observer theories.[24] Instead, it enjoins that the judge complicate bias by reference to the real or imagined judgments of others under particular moral scenarios.

Society, on this understanding, is the sine qua non of moral judgment, as it is also of aesthetic discrimination. Both require a shifting of personal perspective that is made possible by engaging the viewpoints of others. The eyes of others, Smith argues, are a necessary mirror for self-review:

> Were it possible that a human creature could grow up to manhood in some solitary place, without any communication with his own species, he could no more think of his own character, of the propriety or demerit of his own sentiments and conduct, of the beauty or deformity of his own mind, than of the beauty or deformity of his own face. All these are objects which he cannot easily see, which naturally he does not look at, and with regard to which he is provided with no mirror which can present them to his view. Bring him into society, and he is immediately provided with the mirror which he wanted before. It is placed in the countenance and behaviour of those he lives with, which always mark when they enter into, and when they disapprove of his sentiments; and it is here that he first views the propriety and impropriety of his own passions, the beauty and deformity of his own mind. (110)

Morality, Smith contends, is coterminous with sociability. A man on a desert island, who has never known others, does not engage in the higher-order reflection of the judge. He perceives but does not reflect on his perceptions: "The objects of his passions, the external bodies which either pleased or hurt him, would occupy his whole attention. The passions themselves . . . could scarce ever be the objects of his thoughts" (110). In the absence of others, the primary perceptions would constitute subjectivity; it is only when (real or imagined) others are present that their *quality* matters, and the inner doubling of self-review begins.[25]

The importance Smith ascribes to the judgments of others in the constitution of self-judgment raises the question of how his account becomes relevant to debates about autonomy. At times, Smith seems to provide little more than an explanation of socialization: we come to judge of certain actions in such and such way because we see other people judging them in such and such way. To offer an account of socialization is, however, by no means Smith's principal intention, as can be gleaned from the revisions he made to the *Theory* after its first edition—revisions that, as the editors of the latter work point out, seek to distinguish between the impartial standpoint, the standpoint from which judgments should be made, and the standpoint of convention.[26] While society, Smith clarifies, is a mirror for the moral self, it is so only in the first instance. Hence, it is in society that man "*first* views the propriety and impropriety of his own passions." Over time, moral agents are capable of developing a relative autonomy vis-à-vis societal judgment by establishing ideals of propriety and rules of conduct for themselves that take precedence over established social norms. The judge must distinguish between the actual judgments of her community and what ought to be their judgment, on the basis of standards of judgment she has established for herself. In his revisions, Smith describes the commitment to such standards as the love of praiseworthiness over praise: "The love of praise is the desire of obtaining the favourable sentiments of our brethren. The love of praise-worthiness is the desire of rendering ourselves the proper object of those sentiments" (126). To the mature moral agent or "well-formed mind" (117), the second motive takes precedence over the first, and self-approbation, on the basis of one's own judgments, trumps approbation by others. While the just man, Smith observes, might crave the praise that is due to him, he "sometimes . . . neglects, and even despises it; and he is never more apt to do so than when he has the most perfect assurance of the perfect propriety of every part of his own conduct. His self-approbation, in this case, stands in need of no confirmation from the approbation of other men" (117).

Unlike the other British sentimentalists, Smith makes duty or a commitment to self-given moral principles a cornerstone of his moral theory. The sense of duty, he argues, is a "principle of the greatest consequence in human life" (162) because of the prevalence of self-deceit, a "fatal weakness of mankind" and "the source of half the disorders of human life" (158). A strong sense of duty enables individuals to act in accordance with their own reflectively endorsed principles even when it is inconvenient to do so. Smith explains:

> When our passive feelings are almost always so sordid and so selfish, how comes it that our active principles should often be so generous and so noble? . . . It is not the soft power of humanity, it is not that feeble spark of benevolence which Nature has lighted up in the human heart, that is thus capable of counteracting the strongest impulses of self-love. It is a stronger power, a more forcible motive, which exerts itself upon such occasions. It is reason, principle, conscience, the inhabitant of the breast, the man within, the great judge and arbiter of our conduct. It is he who, whenever we are about to act so as to affect the happiness of others, calls to us, with a voice capable of astonishing the most presumptuous of our passions, that we are but one of the multitude, in no respect better than any other in it. (137)

While Smith's rhetoric anticipates Kant's famously reverential invocation of the "starry heavens above me and the moral law within me" in the *Critique of Practical Reason* (1788), the *Theory* underscores that the moral law is not an a priori general rule.[27] Conflating the two is the mistake made by "several very eminent authors" who "draw up their systems in such a manner, as if they had supposed that the original judgments of mankind with regard to right and wrong, were formed like the decisions of a court of judicatory, by considering first the general rule, and then, secondly, whether the particular action under consideration fell properly within its comprehension" (160). Rules, Smith elaborates, are not handed down to us by God or by a supersensible reason but are ultimately founded in the sympathetic responses of impartial spectators—spectators, incidentally, who needn't be gendered male, as they are by Smith when he personifies conscience as the man within the breast. On this understanding, everyone is capable, at least in principle, of establishing general rules of morality on the basis of everyday experiences of judging: "Our continual observations upon the conduct of others, insensibly lead us to form to ourselves certain general rules concerning what is fit and proper to be done or to be avoided" (159). One implication here, which Smith develops sporadically rather than systematically, is that what is first formed "insensibly" must then be refined through active comparison with the rules and the particular judgments of others. A dialogic ethic is implicit in Smith's talk about impartiality and the formation of general rules: the mature moral agent seeks to know the judgments of others, not only as these are unconsciously imprinted in their eyes and demeanors but also as they become manifest in conversation and critical dialogue.

To continue with the Kantian connection summoned above, it is worth noting that in Kantian terms, Adam Smith understands moral judgments to be "reflective" rather than "determinant." For Kant, reflective judgments, of which the paradigmatic case is aesthetic judgments, are judgments for which a rule is not given but must be found.[28] He contrasts these with determinant judgments—for example, moral judgments—for which the rule is given a priori by reason. Political theorists like Hannah Arendt have argued that Kant's restriction of reflective judgments to the aesthetic domain is a major shortcoming of his critical philosophy, one that shortchanges its full potential as critique.[29] This is because critical thinking, like reflective judgment, entails "thinking without banisters"; it must shun the absolutism of determinant judgments and take as its object a "phenomenal world" of appearances or opinions rather than truths. I have argued elsewhere that the understanding of political judgment that Arendt develops by adapting Kant's aesthetics bears remarkable parallels to moral judgment as theorized by the British sentimentalists.[30] What Arendt shares with thinkers like Smith and Hume is not only an interest in aesthetics, and in reflective judgments over determinant truths, but also an understanding of the standards of judgment as a development of sociability. "The power of judgment," Arendt explains, "rests on a potential agreement with others, and the thinking process which is active in judging something is not, like the thought process of pure reasoning, a dialogue between me and myself, but finds itself always and primarily, even if I am quite alone in making up my mind, in an anticipated communication with others with whom I know I must finally come to an agreement."[31] In the *Lectures on Kant's Political Philosophy*, Arendt elaborates that judgment requires cultivating what Kant called the "enlarged mentality," and "to think with an enlarged mentality is to train the imagination to go visiting."[32]

Feminist theorists such as Seyla Benhabib have argued that Arendt's claims about political judgment can be extended to the moral sphere to yield an ethics that is at once universalistic and attentive to the claims of particularity, an ethics in which the validity of judgments is not established a priori by reason (as under Kant) but is the infinitely revisable outcome of private and public deliberation.[33] The discourse ethics to which Benhabib herself subscribes builds on Arendtian judgment to reformulate normativity:

> Instead of asking what an individual moral agent could or would will, without self-contradiction, to be a universal norm for all, one asks: what norms or institutions would the members of an ideal or real communication community agree to as representing their common interests after engaging in a special kind of argumentation or conversation? The procedural model of an argumentative praxis replaces the silent thought-experiment enjoined by the Kantian universalizability test.[34]

Other feminist thinkers, such as Jennifer Nedelsky, have highlighted the implications of Arendtian judgment for a revaluation of autonomy: instead of summoning the choices and deliberations of the isolated individual, autonomy, Nedelsky argues, is a capacity belonging to socially embedded agents, whose judgment must take account of the perspectives of others.[35]

If autonomy denotes the ability to make choices on the basis of one's own judgments then Arendt permits a radical revision of this norm, since judgment, as she describes it, "finds itself . . . in an anticipated communication with others."

I believe that we can see a comparable attempt to connect autonomy and sociability in Smith's writings on judgment.[36] In Smith's moral universe, the true lover of virtue is one who prioritizes self-approbation over public approval, who cares about the quality of her actions regardless of the applause bestowed on them. However, she judges those actions on the basis of a standpoint and of rules that are ultimately formed by engaging others. The eyes of others are crucial on this understanding of moral judgment. Sociability is the precondition of autonomy.

From Necessity and Utility to Goodness

In a 1756 letter to the editors of the *Edinburgh Review*, Adam Smith pointedly recommended Rousseau's *Discourse on Inequality* (published less than a year earlier) to the journal's Scottish readers.[37] Mr. Rousseau's treatise, Smith observes, is a spirited and eloquent work, and of interest to a British audience not least because it builds on British contributions to metaphysics and morals. Smith's praise becomes double-edged, however, because the native thinker he summons as Rousseau's closest precursor is one that he, alongside the other British sentimentalists, repeatedly singled out for criticism—that is, the consummate philosophical egoist or "profligate" Mandeville, as Smith calls him.[38] On Smith's description indeed, Rousseau emerges as little more than a Mandeville in sheep's clothing. Using a moving style and a "little philosophical chemistry," Rousseau, Smith contends, renders attractive all that is repugnant in Mandeville: "The principles and ideas of the profligate Mandeville seem in him [Rousseau] to have all the purity and sublimity of the morals of Plato, and to be only the true spirit of a republican carried a little too far."[39]

The parallel Smith draws is a seemingly counterintuitive one. The proud citizen of Geneva was a self-described lover of virtue, while Mandeville gleefully sought to expose virtue's seamy underside: the notorious thesis of the *Fable of the Bees* (1714–28) is that greed and vanity undergird the so-called social virtues. Smith concedes that the two thinkers differ in certain respects and highlights their distinct understandings of a hypothetical state of nature: while Rousseau glorifies the latter as enabling man's most complete self-sufficiency, Mandeville follows Hobbes to interpret it as a state of universal war. For Smith, however, this difference pales in comparison with what the two men share, which is a deep-rooted suspicion of society and all sociable impulses. Rousseau's and Mandeville's projects become powerfully welded, Smith argues, by their shared belief that

> there is in man no powerful instinct which necessarily determines him to seek society for its own sake: but according to the one, the misery of his original state compelled him to have recourse to this otherwise disagreeable remedy; according to the other, some unfortunate accidents having given birth to the unnatural passions of ambition and the vain desire of superiority, to which he had before been a stranger, produced the same fatal effect.[40]

It is easy to see why Smith would be hostile to any interpretation of society as a "disagreeable remedy" or "fatal effect," since his moral theory begins from the premise of sympathetic sociability, the idea that individuals are naturally inclined to imaginatively change places with others and to care about other people's perceptions of their actions. Unlike the philosophers of egoism and the social contract theorists, Smith is uninterested in the hypothesis of a state of nature because for him, as we have seen, there simply is no self without the other—or, at least, there is no self capable of the higher-order reflection morality requires. Even independent moral judgment, as he understands it, requires recourse to otherness in that it is made from a standpoint that has been shaped by social engagement.

But is Smith's characterization of Rousseau as a fundamentally antisocial thinker fair? In *Emile*, which appeared seven years after the *Second Discourse*, Rousseau emphatically asserts, "It is not good for man to be alone" (357). Like the later eighteenth- and nineteenth-century *Bildungsromane*, of which it is a prototype of sorts, the generically mixed *Emile*—part philosophical treatise, part educational manual, part novel—ends in marriage. Rousseau's eponymous pupil is by no means the savage he describes in the *Second Discourse*, who typically lives alone, exercising a rough justice through sporadic acts of pity for his kind, and satisfying his sexual needs in random sexual encounters. Nor is he the citizen of *The Social Contract*, whose individual will is entirely subsumed under the general will.[41] Instead, he is the autonomous moral man who lives alongside others but adheres at all times to his own judgments: "It suffices that, enclosed in a social whirlpool, he not let himself get carried away by either the passions or the opinions of men, that he see with his eyes, that he feel with his heart, that no authority govern him beyond that of his own reason" (255). Such a being, Rousseau contends, is not to be found in the world as it is but must be made from scratch. He is the product of a new kind of education, a natural education, which seeks to preserve some degree of the original freedom belonging to man, the freedom of man in the state of nature. Emile, Rousseau charges, "is not a savage to be relegated to the desert. He is a savage made to inhabit cities" (205).

Why is the freedom of the "savage" so attractive to Rousseau? In the *Second Discourse*, Rousseau explains that before he entered civil society, man was fundamentally self-sufficient, relying on neither the labor nor the good opinion of others: "The Savage lives within himself; sociable man, always outside himself, is capable of living only in the opinion of others and, so to speak, derives the sentiment of his existence solely from their judgment."[42] In contrast with civil man, whose very sense of self is contingent on the judgments of others, natural man thinks nothing of other people's opinions; he thinks only of himself and his own preservation. He is guided in what he does by the natural and freedom-preserving passion of *amour de soi*. In *Emile* Rousseau suggests, "Our natural passions are very limited. They are the instruments of our freedom; they tend to preserve us. All those which subject and destroy us come from elsewhere. Nature does not give them to us" (212). Above all, natural man is free from the unrealistic expectations of *amour-propre*, which demands that others accord us the same importance we accord ourselves. Against philosophical egoists such as Hobbes and Mandeville, Rousseau distinguishes between good and bad forms of self-love. In *Emile* he observes that "self-love, which regards only ourselves, is contented when our true needs are satisfied. But *amour-propre*, which makes comparisons, is never content and never could be, because this sentiment, preferring ourselves to others, also demands others to prefer us to themselves, which is impossible" (213).

The argument of *Emile* is that a child will mature into an autonomous adult, capable of using his own reason and judgment, only if childhood is a time of relative freedom from the claims of *amour-propre*. As Rousseau puts it, "Before instructing him in our sentiments, begin by teaching him to evaluate them" (187). Rousseau would agree with Adam Smith that in the absence of others, there are no moral conceptions whatsoever. But he deems such ignorance to be the best preparation for moral life, or life as an autonomous moral being. Until he is a young adult, Emile recalls the solitary Smith summons at one point in the *Theory*, the man on a desert island who has no need for higher-order moral reflection because he lacks access to the mirror that is society. Rousseau explicitly likens his pupil to the eponymous hero of Defoe's *Robinson Crusoe*, the only book Emile is allowed to read during childhood, the prohibition on books being part of Rousseau's program of protecting the child from investing in the opinions of others.[43] The state of the solitary, Rousseau underscores, is not Emile's final state or destination. Nonetheless, "it is on the basis of this very state that he ought to appraise all the others. The surest means of raising oneself above prejudices and ordering one's judgments about the true relations of things is to put oneself in the place of an isolated man and to judge of everything as this man himself ought to judge of it with respect to his own utility" (185).

For Rousseau, in other words, nonmoral judgments have a certain ineluctable priority over moral judgments. Interpreting this precedence principally as a matter of chronology, Ryan Patrick Hanley argues that *Emile* traces a "movement from the merely physical to the genuinely moral."[44] Rousseau's pedagogical prescriptions, Hanley suggests, aim at encouraging "the child to transfer his or her cultivated capacity for the judgment of physical relations to the judgment of moral relations."[45] Good discernment in one domain enables a like facility in the other domain.

My argument below is different: I suggest that Emile's education in the judgment of nonmoral relations does not prepare him for moral judgment because the two kinds of judgment are fundamentally different, a difference that is acknowledged by the British sentimentalists through their fact-value distinction. As sentimentalists like Hume indicate, in the case of nonmoral judgments, the judge relates to the object of judgment as a subject to an object. With moral judgments, there is no "object" of judgment other than our own feelings of approval or disapproval (or the feelings of others); the relationship is an intrasubjective or intersubjective one. The first relationship, to return to the ocular metaphor both Rousseau and Smith deploy, needn't mobilize more than one pair of eyes. The second implicitly summons more than one spectator. Moral judgment, as described by Smith, takes account of this plurality in its interpretation of impartiality. By contrast, Rousseau seeks to bridge incommensurable domains (the moral and the nonmoral) by forestalling the transformative potential of an encounter with others. Emile's transition from solitary to sociable savage is achieved only by severely truncating the meaning of sociability.

To develop this argument, it is useful to consider Emile's education as divisible into two broad phases. Following Rousseau, we might call the first stage, which embraces the period from birth until adolescence, an education through dependence on things rather than wills. While childhood is perforce a time of weakness and dependence, Rousseau explains that there are two kinds of dependence, with varying implications for freedom: "Dependence on things, since it has no morality, is in no way detrimental to freedom and engenders no vices. Dependence on men, since it is without order, engenders all the vices, and by it, master and slave are mutually corrupted" (85). Emile is dependent primarily on things until the second phase of his education, during which he is introduced into society, albeit under the guardianship of his tutor. It is only at the end of this phase, signaled by the news that he is about to become a father, that he is ready to assume full moral responsibility.

The first phase is a time of highly limited sociability. The child, Rousseau argues, should be placed on the path of freedom by protecting him from public opinion and all other-directed passions until he has reason and judgment of his own. While the world he inhabits is by no means a solitary one—his omnipresent tutor manages every aspect of his daily life—it is meant to be divested of moral consequences, since the child does not encounter other people as sources of authority or as bearers of wills that he can bend to his own. The tutor performs a vanishing act of sorts whereby he ceases to exist for his pupil as someone who might command or obey. Rousseau enjoins: "Do not give your pupil any kind of verbal lessons" (92), "command him nothing" (91). All the lessons the tutor would have the child learn seemingly emanate instead from an impersonal nature. These include not only knowledge of the natural world, obtained through the senses and the "first reason" that is the "reason of the senses" (125), but also an acknowledgment of personal limitation: "Let his haughty head at an early date feel the harsh yoke which nature imposes on man, the heavy yoke of necessity under which every finite being must bend. Let him see this necessity in things, never in the caprice of men" (91). Punishment, in particular, should appear to have nothing to do with the ill will of others: "Never present to his undiscriminating will anything but physical obstacles or punishments which stem from the actions themselves and which he will recall on the proper occasion" (85).

Rousseau is aware that a child brought up amid others, even in the small village society in which he places his pupil, can hardly be unconscious of other people. Indeed, various episodes in Books I to III of *Emile*, which trace its protagonist's education through things, complicate the assertion that the child is conscious only of things. Hence, Emile learns the meaning of property through an altercation with his gardener. He learns to estimate distances through running competitions with peasant boys. And he learns how magnetic forces operate through a humiliating encounter with a magician at a local fair. In each of these instances, the relative "I" is mobilized, yet Rousseau claims that his pupil is brought up until the age of fifteen only in dependence on things.

Rather than interpreting this as a straightforward contradiction, let us concede to Rousseau that his pupil is brought up mostly in dependence on things and that his encounter with wills approximates a dependence on things since it engenders learning primarily of a nonmoral sort (for example, knowledge of distances and magnetic forces). Jonathan Marks usefully glosses Rousseau's paradoxical remarks about Emile's dependence on things, citing the philosopher's suggestion that "if the laws of nations could, like those of nature, have an inflexibility that no human force could ever conquer, dependence on men would then become dependence on things again" (*Emile*, 85).[46] Rousseau, Marks argues, ascribes a certain inflexibility and impersonality to the tutor's will: it is not shaped by the pupil's demands, nor does it enjoin obedience. It simply *is*—a force to be felt rather than a perspective that Emile can recognize as a comparable standpoint on the world. As Rousseau himself elaborates, "Let the bridle that restrains him [the child] be force and not authority. Do not forbid him to do that from which he should abstain; prevent him from doing it without explanations, without reasonings" (91).

Dependent principally on things, Emile approximates natural man in the knowledge he acquires. This is "to know well the use of our strength, the relations of our bodies to surrounding bodies, and the use of the natural instruments which are within our reach and are suitable for our organs" (124). Above all, he comes to acknowledge two laws that will be crucial to his well-being over the course of his entire life: the laws of necessity and utility. As already noted, he learns of the first when he acknowledges that he is not omnipotent. He learns of the second with his growing recognition that the objects around him can be useful to him and that their value resides in their utility rather than in the importance others attach to them. Like his hero Crusoe, Emile attaches little value to the labor of a jeweler but a great deal of that of a carpenter.

At the age of fifteen, Emile is meant to be entirely independent in a nonmoral sense. His tutor proudly proclaims that "Emile has only natural and purely physical knowledge. . . . He knows the essential relations of man to things but nothing of the moral relations of man to man. . . . What is more useful to him, he takes more seriously; never deviating from this way of evaluating, he grants nothing to opinion" (207). This is the time, Rousseau argues, to safely induct the pupil into society, since he has sufficient judgment of his own to judge society's specious standards of judgment. It is also the time to directly solicit the latent voice of conscience, which Rousseau describes as a "rule prior to opinion [that] exists for the whole human species," an inner principle that comes into maturity, however, only by interacting with a developed reason.[47]

Yet Rousseau's account of the second phase of Emile's education implies that it is never quite safe for the "naturally free" individual to become a social participant: heteronomy continually threatens to undo autonomy. Emile's social interactions are heavily monitored by his tutor during this stage of his education, and they are monitored, more precisely, to prevent other people's judgments from influencing his own. As Rousseau's pupil transitions from the nonmoral to the moral domains, his judgment, it appears, remains truly his only if other people are encountered as something other than judges in their own right. Emile's introduction into society does little to modify what we might characterize as Rousseau's "ocularphobia," since he encounters the world of other people less as a domain of alternative judgments or points of view than as a space where essentially one person's power of vision matters—namely, his own.[48]

It is against the backdrop of Rousseau's discomfort with "the eyes of others" that we must interpret his claims about pity, which he characterizes as the first relative sentiment that links the individual to the species. Unlike Smith's capacious category of sympathy, which denotes "fellow feeling with any passion whatever" (*Theory* 10), pity preserves a particularly strong asymmetry between spectator and agent (in this case, sufferer). The pity Emile is encouraged to cultivate as soon as he enters the social world prompts him to feel tenderness for his species but also discourages him from seeing other people as equal interlocutors who might complicate his judgment of things, and especially his incipient sense of right and wrong. Rousseau describes pity as "the best-conceived sentiment that man can have about his species" (236) not only because it tempers the aggression that accompanies the birth of *amour-propre* but also because it has the paradoxical effect of reinforcing the boundary that divides self and other. Pity moves Emile outside himself and toward empathy with others, but it also prompts a self-return that is experienced as self-satisfaction: "If the first sight that strikes him is an object of sadness, the first return to himself is a sentiment of pleasure" (229). Keeping Emile happy in his own skin—pleased to be himself rather than another—pity maintains the hard-earned self-sufficiency he has gained through his dependence on things in the first phase of his education.

The sentiment of pity structures Emile's early interactions not only with the living but also with the dead. Rousseau indicates that the independent (in a nonmoral sense) young man is ready for books, especially histories, but he adds that Emile will be reading history as the history of pitiable humanity. Again, the emphasis is on preserving Emile's self-sufficiency, which should remain undisturbed as he encounters the great men of the past, whom he will view with a combination of tenderness and disdain, as pitiable creatures blinded by *amour-propre*. Emile, Rousseau underscores, will not find a mirror for himself in the history of his species; he will only find examples of what not to become: "Emile will hardly recognize himself in the strange objects which will strike his glance during these new studies. But he will know ahead of time how to dispel the illusion of the passions before they are born; and, seeing that in all times they have blinded men, he will be warned of the way in which they can blind him in turn, if ever he yields to them" (243). Unlike Smith's spectator-judge, whose vision is sharpened by engaging other spectator-judges—who, like himself or herself, combine blindness and insight—Rousseau's moral man gains in autonomy to the degree that others are perceived to be blind. History-reading contracts Emile within himself, prohibiting any identification with others: "As for my Emile, if in these parallels he just once prefers to be someone other than himself—were this other Socrates, were it Cato—everything has failed. He who begins to become alien to himself does not take long to forget himself entirely" (243). Even the historian, Rousseau warns, should not be encountered by the young reader as a role model or potential teacher, since, if his judgments become appealing to Emile, the latter will cease to judge for himself. Hence, "the worst historians for a young man are those who make judgments. Facts! Facts! And let him make his own judgments. It is thus that he learns to know men. If the author's judgment guides him constantly, all he does is see with another's eye; and when that eye fails him, he no longer sees anything" (239).

Rousseau's discussion of history-reading in *Emile* illuminates his understanding not only of pity but also of the imagination, which he takes to be one of the most powerful, active, and potentially dangerous human faculties. While Smith accords the imagination a central place in his moral theory—the sympathetic imagination permits the perspective-shifting that judgment requires—Rousseau is anxious about the imagination's transporting powers.[49] His principal worry in this context is that the imagination prevents one from accepting the principle of natural necessity or one's "natural" place in what he calls "the order of things." Hence, "it is imagination which extends for us the measure of the possible, whether for good or bad, and which consequently excites and nourishes the desires by the hope of satisfying them" (81).

Freedom and happiness, on this understanding, require maximizing personal strength, or, conversely, limiting desire and imagination: "The real world has its limits; the imaginary world is infinite. Unable to enlarge the one, let us restrict the other, for it is from the difference between the two alone that are born all the pains which make us truly unhappy" (81).

This is not to say that the imagination plays no role in Emile's education. It assumes greater importance in the second phase of this education, once Rousseau's pupil enters society. At this stage, Rousseau indicates, both the passions and the imagination are activated, and it is no longer possible to entirely sidestep them. Nonetheless, the imagination can and should be strictly monitored to protect the pupil's still-fragile self-sufficiency. The tutor appeals, for example, to Emile's imagination when he paints for him a deeply attractive ideal of womanhood. The principal aim of this fiction, however, is to keep Emile out of the reach of real women, all of whom seem to him to fall far short of the ideal. As such, he is able to sublimate the sexual feelings that, according to his tutor, increasingly threaten to undo his self-sufficiency and make him a victim of his passions.

There is, however, one instance in *Emile* in which Emile's imagination is solicited to move him outside himself rather than keeping him within the borders established by his dependence on things. This is the moment when the tutor reveals to his pupil the story of his tutelage in order to maintain it, albeit temporarily, on higher grounds—through Emile's consent, which, Rousseau suggests, is necessary once Emile becomes a young man. Subterfuge, on this account, can be used to render children docile, but a young man should be made so through gratitude and affection. It is imperative, then, that the story of Emile's education or his relationship with his tutor be a moving narrative, one that will lead him to willingly relinquish to his tutor the government of his passions until he is able to master them himself. This particular fiction must be "engraved" in "his memory in such a way that it will never be effaced" (321). The tutor indicates: "I shall choose the time, the place, and the objects most favorable to the impression I want to make. I shall, so to speak, call all of nature as a witness to our conversations. . . . I shall heighten the force of my reasoning with images and figurative language" (323). In sublime natural surroundings, the tutor artfully and eloquently claims his pupil as his life's work and as someone forever in his debt: "You are my property, my child, my work. It is from your happiness that I expect my own. If you frustrate my hopes, you are robbing me of twenty years of my life, and you are causing the unhappiness of my old age" (323). With no other relationship producing a distancing perspective on Emile's primary relationship with his tutor, the young man proves to be a willing subject of tutelage. He readily concedes to the older man the authority he claims: "You had this authority up to this time only due to my weakness; now you shall have it due to my will, and it shall be more sacred to me. . . . Make me free by protecting me against those of my passions which do violence to me" (325).

While Rousseau suggests that the tutor claims the authority to govern by consent only for a fixed period—that is, as long as Emile remains unmarried—it is unclear when his "higher" mode of tutelage ends. *Emile* concludes with a resounding reaffirmation of the tutor's authority. In Emile's last speech to his tutor he announces at once that he is about to become a father and that he needs his tutor-father as much as ever. While Emile looks forward to becoming the teacher of his unborn son, his own mentor will remain "the master of the young masters" (480), who are Emile and his wife, Sophie. Indeed, according to Emile, "As long as I live, I shall need you" (480).[50]

It appears that Emile's "autonomy" is a capacity that comes into play in all relationships other than the relationship between Emile and his tutor. The other principal relationship of Emile's adult life, with his wife, Sophie, is certainly very different: it reverses the hierarchy of the tutor-tutee relationship by casting Emile in the role of governor and Sophie in that of docile pupil. There is little in the way of interdependence here, since the marital bond is cemented by Sophie's dependence on her husband's judgment, a dependence that ensures that Emile will remain untroubled by the challenge of other people's distinct judgments. Marriage, as Rousseau understands it, is a union of unequal beings: "In the union of the sexes each contributes equally to the common aim, but not in the same way. . . . One ought to be active and strong, the other passive and weak. One must necessarily will and be able; it suffices that the other put up little resistance" (358). Women, on this account, lack the judgment and reason for autonomy.[51] Their virtue resides instead in adhering to the judgments of others, as embodied in the laws of modesty and chastity. While the eyes of others exercise a baneful influence on male morality, a woman must "give evidence of her virtue to the eyes of others as well as to her own conscience" (361). As Rousseau puts it:

> By the very law of nature women are at the mercy of men's judgments, as much for their own sake as for that of their children. It is not enough that they be estimable; they must be esteemed. It is not enough for them to be pretty; they must please. It is not enough for them to be temperate; they must be recognized as such. Their honor is not only in their conduct but in their reputation; and it is not possible that a woman who consents to be regarded as disreputable can ever be decent. When a man acts well, he depends only on himself and can brave public judgment; but when a woman acts well, she has accomplished only half her task, and what is thought of her is no less important to her than what she actually is. . . . Opinion is the grave of virtue among men and its throne among women. (364–65)

Whereas for Smith, the prevalence of self-deceit and the fallibility of human judgment make it imperative that individuals engage judgments other than their own, for Rousseau such an imperative is pertinent only to women. As the physically weaker sex, women are perceived by him to occupy a lower rung in the natural order of things than do men. They need male protection for themselves and their offspring, and men will be motivated to offer such protection only if women are universally respected and admired. For this reason, women should be educated not in autonomous judgment but in the arts of winning approval, especially the approval of their husbands: "Thus the whole education of women ought to relate to men. To please men, to be useful to them, to make herself loved and honored by them, to raise them when young, to care for them when grown, to counsel them, to console them, to make their lives agreeable and sweet—these are the duties of women at all times, and they ought to be taught from childhood" (365).

Sophie needs to cultivate the arts of pleasing because in the moral universe Rousseau describes only some individuals have the right to judge for themselves. Others are figured as inert objects of judgment—we are back here to Emile's childhood world of things—denied the possibility of looking back or judging in turn. Rousseau can bridge the gap between nonmoral and moral judgments only by blinding one sex so that the other sex remains untroubled by its judgments. Characterizing the trajectory of Emile's development as a move from dependence on things to independence in the midst of others, Rousseau is unable to give *inter*dependence any place in his final account of autonomy. Emile, as we leave him at the end of Rousseau's pedagogical narrative, is likely to remain untroubled by the judgments of most people—and not only those of his wife—because he is not in the habit of seeing others as judges or as bearers of alternative perspectives on human actions and motives. Ultimately, Rousseau's ocularphobia occurs at the expense not only of women but of perspective itself: excising the eyes of others (that is, others other than the tutor) from Emile's adult world brings the world of value into safe approximation with the world of fact, but it also severely limits the possibility of seeing otherwise, of seeing from somewhere else, or with someone else.

Through their different claims on behalf of judgment, Rousseau and Smith enable two divergent understandings of autonomy. By attempting to close the gap between nonmoral and moral judgments, Rousseau specifies autonomy to be a species of radical self-enclosure, reinforcing the arguments of communitarians and others that the autonomous liberal subject is a problematic, windowless monad. What the critics of autonomy ignore, however, is that the Enlightenment tradition of theorizing freedom exhibits considerable internal diversity. At the crossroads of sentimentalism and liberalism, we have accounts not only like Rousseau's but also like Smith's, and in the latter, independent moral judgment becomes inextricably linked to a perspectival ethos that validates difference and plurality. In quest of impartiality, the Smithian judge assumes the persona of a spectator in a world of other spectators. When it comes to judgment, as Hannah Arendt argues, "spectators exist only in the plural."[52] For both Arendt and Smith, judging spectators are always multiple because the integrity of judgment has to do with the standpoint one occupies, and there are always alternative standpoints one could occupy (and that others do occupy). Arguably, Smith's account of moral judgment remains incomplete, and it is up to later theorists such as Arendt to sharpen his distinction between the impartial standpoint and conventional wisdom by making critical debate an integral aspect of judging. Nonetheless, the *Theory of Moral Sentiments* is remarkable for its attempt to bring the ancient *topos* of judgment to the doorstep of the moderns, and for its suggestion that the private deliberative procedures for which each of us bears final responsibility would be impossible without others. At stake here is an understanding of autonomy that liberalism's critics and defenders alike would do well to acknowledge more fully.

Notes

1. For overviews of the principal criticisms of autonomy, see the editors' introductions to John Christman and Joel Anderson, eds., *Autonomy and the Challenges to Liberalism: New Essays* (Cambridge: Cambridge University Press, 2009); and Catriona Mackenzie and Natalie Stoljar, eds., *Relational Autonomy: Feminist Perspectives on Autonomy, Agency, and the Social Self* (Oxford: Oxford University Press, 2000).

2. The classic communitarian criticisms of the Kantian tradition include Charles Taylor, *Sources of the Self: The Making of the Modern Identity* (Cambridge: Cambridge University Press, 1989); Michael J. Sandel, *Liberalism and the Limits of Justice* (Cambridge: Cambridge University Press, 1982); and Alasdair MacIntyre, *After Virtue: A Study in Moral Theory* (London: Bristol Classical, 1981).

3. Charles E. Larmore, *Patterns of Moral Complexity* (Cambridge: Cambridge University Press, 1987), 20.

4. Ibid.

5. Larmore identifies Smith, alongside Hans-Georg Gadamer, as one of the few modern thinkers to seriously engage the motif of moral judgment, but he finds Smith's *Theory of Moral Sentiments* to be suggestive rather than substantive in this context. Smith's view, he argues, "never really advanced beyond the assertion that proper moral judgment should be seen as the expression of the moral sentiment that 'the impartial spectator' would feel." Larmore, *Patterns of Moral Complexity*, 18.

6. Jean-Jacques Rousseau, *The Social Contract and Other Later Political Writings*, ed. Victor Gourevitch (Cambridge: Cambridge University Press, 2006), 54.

7. Jean-Jacques Rousseau, *The Collected Writings of Rousseau: "Confessions" and Correspondence, including the Letters to Malesherbes*, ed. Roger D. Masters and Christopher Kelly, trans. Christopher Kelly and Judith R. Bush, vol. 5 (Hanover, N.H.: Dartmouth College Press, 1998), 475. In the *Dialogues*, Rousseau reinforces this assessment, characterizing *Emile* as his "greatest and best book." Jean-Jacques Rousseau, *The Collected Writings of Rousseau: Rousseau,*

Judge of Jean-Jacques: Dialogues, ed. Roger D. Masters and Christopher Kelly, trans. Roger D. Masters, Christopher Kelly, and Judith R. Bush, vol. 1 (Hanover, N.H.: Dartmouth College Press, 1990), 23.

8. Jean-Jacques Rousseau, *Emile; or, On Education*, ed. and trans. Allan Bloom (New York: Basic Books, 1979), 192, 50. All subsequent page number references are to this edition and will be indicated parenthetically.

9. Michael Frazer, "John Rawls: Between Two Enlightenments," *Political Theory* 35, no. 6 (2007): 756–80; Samuel Fleischacker, *A Third Concept of Liberty: Judgment and Freedom in Kant and Adam Smith* (Princeton, N.J.: Princeton University Press, 1999); and "Philosophy in Moral Practice: Kant and Adam Smith," *Kant-Studien* 82, no. 3 (1991): 249–69. For an overview of recent revaluations of Smith's moral theory, see Stephen Darwall, "Sympathetic Liberalism: Recent Work on Adam Smith," *Philosophy and Public Affairs* 28, no. 2 (1999): 139–64.

10. Comparisons of Smith and Rousseau remain few and far between. The only book-length study putting their writings in extended dialogue is Dennis Rasmussen's *The Problems and Promise of Commercial Society: Adam Smith's Response to Rousseau* (University Park: Pennsylvania State University Press, 2008). Shorter studies include Ryan Patrick Hanley, "Enlightened Nation Building: The 'Science of the Legislator' in Adam Smith and Rousseau," *American Journal of Political Science* 52, no. 2 (2008): 219–34; "Commerce and Corruption: Rousseau's Diagnosis and Adam Smith's Cure," *European Journal of Political Theory* 7 (2008): 137–58; "From Geneva to Glasgow: Rousseau and Adam Smith on the Theatre and Commercial Society," *Studies in Eighteenth-Century Culture* 35 (2006): 177–202; Spencer J. Pack, "The Rousseau-Smith Connection," *History of Economic Ideas* 8 (2000): 35–62; Norman Barry, "Hume, Smith, and Rousseau on Freedom," in *Rousseau and Liberty*, ed. Robert Wokler (Manchester: Manchester University Press, 1995), 29–52; Lucio Colletti, "Mandeville, Rousseau and Smith," in *From Rousseau to Lenin: Studies in Ideology and Society*, trans. John Merrington and Judith White (New York: Monthly Review Press, 1972), 195–216; and E. G. West, "Adam Smith and Rousseau's *Discourse on Inequality*: Inspiration or Provocation?," *Journal of Economic Issues* 5, no. 2 (1971): 56–70.

11. Hina Nazar, *Enlightened Sentiments: Judgment and Autonomy in the Age of Sensibility* (New York: Fordham University Press, 2012), chs. 1 and 2.

12. I take this definition of autonomy from Christman and Anderson, *Autonomy and the Challenges of Liberalism*, 4.

13. The literature here is vast. In addition to the work of Samuel Fleischacker, Ryan Patrick Hanley, and Dennis Rasmussen, notable reassessments of Smith include Emma Rothschild, *Economic Sentiments: Adam Smith, Condorcet, and the Enlightenment* (Cambridge, Mass.: Harvard University Press, 2001); Charles L. Griswold, *Adam Smith and the Virtues of Enlightenment* (Cambridge: Cambridge University Press, 1999); Jerry Z. Muller, *Adam Smith in His Time and Ours* (Princeton, N.J.: Princeton University Press, 1993); Spencer J. Pack, *Capitalism as a Moral System: Adam Smith's Critique of the Free Market Economy* (Aldershot: Edward Elgar, 1991); Emma Rothschild and Amartya Sen, "Adam Smith's Economics," in *The Cambridge Companion to Adam Smith*, ed. Knud Haakonssen (Cambridge: Cambridge University Press, 2006), 320–65; and Knud Haakonssen, *The Science of a Legislator: The Natural Jurisprudence of David Hume and Adam Smith* (Cambridge: Cambridge University Press, 1981).

14. Adam Smith, *The Theory of Moral Sentiments*, ed. D. D. Raphael and A. L. Macfie, The Glasgow Edition of the Works and Correspondence of Adam Smith, vol.1 (Oxford: Clarendon, 1976; rpt., Indianapolis: Liberty Fund, 1982), 110. All subsequent page number references are to this edition and will be indicated parenthetically.

15. See, for example, Jennifer Nedelsky, *Law's Relations: A Relational Theory of Self, Autonomy, and Law* (Oxford: Oxford University Press, 2013); Marilyn Friedman, *Autonomy, Gender, Politics* (Oxford: Oxford University Press, 2003); Mackenzie and Stoljar, *Relational Autonomy*; Diana Tietjens Meyers, ed., *Feminists Rethink the Self* (Boulder: Westview, 1997); and Seyla Benhabib, *Situating the Self: Gender, Community, and Postmodernism in Contemporary Ethics* (New York: Routledge, 1992). Marilyn Friedman offers a helpful overview of nonfeminist approaches to autonomy that converge, in important respects, with feminist revaluations of the concept. See Friedman, *Autonomy, Gender, Politics*, 87–91.

16. Friedman, *Autonomy, Gender, Politics*, 17.

17. Christine M. Korsgaard, *The Sources of Normativity* (Cambridge: Cambridge University Press, 1996). This section builds on the reading of British sentimentalism I give in *Enlightened Sentiments*, chs. 1 and 2.

18. Notwithstanding important parallels, Hume's and Smith's versions of sentimentalism are productively distinguished from Hutcheson's. The latter's moral sense theory indicates that perceptions of right and wrong are enabled by an inner moral sense that operates like the physical senses, instantaneously and independently of the will. By contrast, for the later sentimentalists, judgment is a deliberative process that requires reason, feeling, and imagination.

19. David Hume, *A Treatise of Human Nature*, ed. L. A. Selby-Bigge, with text revised and variant readings by P. H. Nidditch, 2nd ed. (Oxford: Oxford University Press, 1978), 468–69.

20. On constructivism and its difference from moral realism, see Carla Bagnoli, ed., *Constructivism in Ethics* (Cambridge: Cambridge University Press, 2013); Christine M. Korsgaard, "Realism and Constructivism in Twentieth-Century Moral Philosophy," in *The Constitution of Agency: Essays on Practical Reason and Moral Psychology* (Oxford: Oxford University Press, 2008), 302–26; Korsgaard, *Sources of Normativity*; and John Rawls, "Kantian Constructivism in Moral Theory," *Journal of Philosophy* 77, no. 9 (1980): 515–72.

21. Korsgaard, *Sources of Normativity*, 138.

22. Rawls, "Kantian Constructivism in Moral Theory," 519.

23. On the differences between Smith's and Hume's moral theories engendered by the former's more complex and capacious category of sympathy, see Raphael and Macfie's introduction to Smith, *Theory*, 13.

24. On the difference between Smith's impartial spectator and Roderick Firth's ideal observer, see, for example, T. D. Campbell, *Adam Smith's Science of Morals* (London: Allen & Unwin, 1971), 33.

25. Smith's argument that the capacity for self-review is a development of sociability anticipates, in some respects, Freud's account of the superego as well as Michel Foucault's account of the modern subject's constitution through disciplinary power. These parallels need, however, to be treated with caution. Hence Freud's superego is a development of forces over which individuals exercise no control, whereas Smith's impartial standpoint is at once a product of societal

dynamics and self-consciously cultivated. Likewise, Foucault's account of the subject's constitution at the hands—or, rather, through the gaze—of systemic Power posits a unidirectional influence that Smith would contest. The panoptical paradigm is unable to account for the perspectivism introduced by more reciprocal modes of intersubjective exchange (Foucault's modern individual or "prisoner" is unable to communicate with his or her fellow prisoners). For a reading linking Smith and Freud, see D. D. Raphael, *The Impartial Spectator: Adam Smith's Moral Philosophy* (Oxford: Oxford University Press, 2007). On Smith and Foucault, see Fonna Forman-Barzilai, *Adam Smith and the Circles of Sympathy: Cosmopolitanism and Moral Theory* (Cambridge: Cambridge University Press, 2010), especially ch. 3.

26. Editors' introduction to Smith, *Theory*, 16–17.

27. Kant writes: "Two things fill the mind with ever new and increasing admiration and awe, the more often and steadily we reflect upon them: the starry heavens above me and the moral law within me." See Immanuel Kant, *Critique of Practical Reason*, ed. and trans. Mary Gregor (Cambridge: Cambridge University Press, 1997), 133.

28. Immanuel Kant, *Critique of the Power of Judgment*, ed. Paul Guyer, trans. Paul Guyer and Eric Matthews (Cambridge: Cambridge University Press, 2000), 66.

29. Crediting Kant with being the philosopher who had discovered the faculty of judgment in his aesthetics, Arendt lamented that he "did not recognize the political and moral implications of his discovery." See Hannah Arendt, "Truth and Politics," in *Between Past and Future: Eight Exercises in Political Thought* (Harmondsworth, U.K.: Penguin, 1978), 241.

30. See Nazar, *Enlightened Sentiments*, ch. 2.

31. Hannah Arendt, "The Crisis in Culture," in *Between Past and Future*, 221.

32. Hannah Arendt, *Lectures on Kant's Political Philosophy*, ed. Ronald Beiner (Chicago: University of Chicago Press, 1992), 43.

33. Seyla Benhabib, *Situating the Self: Gender, Community, and Postmodernism in Contemporary Ethics* (New York: Routledge, 1992), 134.

34. Benhabib, *Situating the Self*, 24.

35. See, for example, Jennifer Nedelsky, "Judgment, Diversity, and Relational Autonomy," in *Judgment, Imagination, and Politics: Themes from Kant and Arendt*, ed. Ronald Beiner and Jennifer Nedelsky (Oxford: Rowman and Littlefield, 2001), 103–20.

36. It is beyond the scope of this essay to engage the feminist scholarship I cite here in any substantive way. Nor do I mean to fold Smith's claims about moral independence into the "relational autonomy" paradigm theorized by Nedelsky, for example. My aim here is to suggest broad parallels, a fuller exploration of which will have to be taken up elsewhere.

37. Adam Smith, "A Letter to the Authors of the *Edinburgh Review*," in *Essays on Philosophical Subjects*, ed. W. P. D. Wightman and J. C. Bryce (Indianapolis: Liberty Fund, 1982), 242–54. Smith's letter is discussed at length by Rasmussen, *Problems and Promise*; Hanley, "Commerce and Corruption"; and Jeffrey Lomonaco, "Adam Smith's 'Letter to the Authors of the *Edinburgh Review*,'" *Journal of the History of Ideas* 63, no. 4 (2002): 659–76.

38. Ibid., 251.

39. Ibid.

40. Ibid., 250.

41. On Rousseau's distinction between public and private man, see especially Judith N. Shklar, *Men and Citizens: A Study of Rousseau's Social Theory* (Cambridge: Cambridge University Press, 1969).

42. Jean-Jacques Rousseau, *The Discourses and Other Early Political Writings*, ed. and trans. Victor Gourevitch (Cambridge: Cambridge University Press, 1997), 187.

43. On the role of Defoe's novel in Rousseau's pedagogical treatise, see, for example, Brian McGrath, "Rousseau's Crusoe: or, On Learning to Read as Not Myself," *Eighteenth-Century Fiction* 23, no. 1 (2010): 119–39; Christopher Kelly, *Rousseau as Author: Consecrating One's Life to the Truth* (Chicago: University of Chicago Press, 2003); Denise Schaeffer, "The Utility of Ink: Rousseau and Robinson Crusoe," *Review of Politics* 64, no. 1 (2002): 121–49; Todd R. Flanders, "Rousseau's Adventure with Robinson Crusoe," *Interpretation* 24, no. 3 (1997): 319–37; and Maximillian E. Novak, *Defoe and the Nature of Man* (New York: Oxford University Press, 1963).

44. Ryan Patrick Hanley, "Rousseau's Virtue Epistemology," *Journal of the History of Philosophy* 50, no. 2 (2012): 239–63, 243.

45. Ibid., 255.

46. Jonathan Marks, "Rousseau's Critique of Locke's Education for Liberty," *Journal of Politics* 74, no. 3 (2012): 694–706, 701.

47. Rousseau argues: "A rule prior to opinion exists for the whole human species. . . . This rule judges prejudice itself, and only insofar as the esteem of men accords with it ought this esteem to be authoritative for us" (382). The Savoyard vicar, Jean-Jacques's mentor on the subject of natural religion in *Emile*, reinforces this sentiment: "There is in the depths of souls . . . an innate principle of justice and virtue according to which, in spite of our own maxims, we judge our actions and those of others as good and bad. It is to this principle that I give the name of conscience" (289). Reason is a necessary supplement to conscience, the vicar elaborates, because "the acts of conscience are not judgments but sentiments" (290). In his reading of Rousseau's account of the interrelationship of reason and conscience, Hanley observes that for Rousseau, "conscience . . . is not a sentiment passively implanted in the heart of man but a latent faculty, the excellence of which requires epistemic training." Hanley, "Rousseau's Virtue Epistemology," 256.

48. I take the term "ocularphobia" from Martin Jay's wide-ranging study of the history of visual tropes, *Downcast Eyes: The Denigration of Vision in Twentieth-Century French Thought* (Berkeley: University of California Press, 1993).

49. Vivasvan Soni aptly characterizes Rousseau's attitude toward the imagination as an "attempt to eradicate the fictionality of judgment." See Vivasvan Soni, "Committing Freedom: The Cultivation of Judgment in Rousseau's *Emile* and Austen's *Pride and Prejudice*," *Eighteenth Century* 51, no. 3 (2010): 363–87, 364.

50. The precariousness of Emile's autonomy is further revealed in *Emile and Sophie; or, The Solitaries* (ca. 1762), Rousseau's unfinished sequel to *Emile*. A cautionary tale, addressed to those who put themselves in situations where duty conflicts with desire, the fragment shows Emile's household unraveling with

the tutor's departure. Sophie, who is grieving the deaths of her parents and her daughter, betrays Emile when the young couple moves to Paris. Emile leaves home and sets out to sea, where he is captured by pirates and sold as a slave. The narrative takes the form of an unfinished, retrospective letter to the tutor, "my dear master" (685), after the period of Emile's enslavement and while he is presumably stranded on a desert island. Emile asserts that his education has been a success since Sophie's treachery and other vicissitudes of fate have failed to corrupt his self-sufficiency: "I am alone, I have lost everything, but I have myself left" (685). What kind of self, we must ask, is this? Emile describes it as a self always content with itself, no matter the circumstances. He writes the tutor, "From childhood there is nothing that I learned so much from you as to be entirely where I am, never to do one thing and dream about another" (700). Without dreams, imaginings, or access to perspectives other than his own, Emile's appears to be a profoundly sad, if complete, self-sufficiency. See Jean-Jacques Rousseau, *Emile and Sophie, or, The Solitaries* in *The Collected Writings of Rousseau: Emile; or, On Education; includes Emile and Sophie, or, The Solitaries*, trans. and ed. Allan Bloom and Christopher Kelly, vol.13 (Hanover, N.H.: Dartmouth College Press, 2009).

51. Mary Wollstonecraft's *Vindication of the Rights of Woman* (1792) remains one of the best interpretations of Rousseau's treatment of the sexes. Mary Wollstonecraft, *A Vindication of the Rights of Woman*, in *A Vindication of the Rights of Men and A Vindication of the Rights of Woman*, ed. Sylvana Tomaselli (Cambridge: Cambridge University Press, 2005). See also the essays collected in Lynda Lange, ed., *Feminist Interpretations of Jean-Jacques Rousseau* (University Park: Penn State University Press, 2002); Elizabeth Rose Wingrove, *Rousseau's Republican Romance* (Princeton, N.J.: Princeton University Press, 2000); Carol Pateman, *The Sexual Contract* (Cambridge: Polity, 1988); Joel Schwartz, *The Sexual Politics of Jean-Jacques Rousseau* (Chicago: University of Chicago Press, 1985); Zillah Eisenstein, *The Radical Future of Liberal Feminism* (New York: Longman, 1981); and Susan Moller Okin, *Women in Western Political Thought* (London: Virago, 1980).

52. Arendt, *Lectures on Kant's Political Philosophy*, 63.

Part III

Politics/Community

When the topics of judgment and action are taken up by thinkers, it is usually from the perspective of deeds or cognitions pertaining to a single individual. It is the rare theorist who has addressed the problem of action or judgment in the context of community. In the twentieth century, Hannah Arendt changed the naive assumption about the individual as the origin of judgment and action when she argued that both of these concepts make sense only under the condition of plurality. Judgment and action, she claimed, necessarily involved a horizon of others who judge and act differently. A theory of judgment and action would have to begin with this observation instead of studying these concepts in isolated individuals first and then attempting to generalize from there. In other words, some notion of politics and community were built into the structure of these concepts and shaped them indelibly, rather than simply being an afterthought or superficial modification of a structure already present in the individual case. The three essays in this section all proceed from Arendt's insight that the intelligibility of judgment and action require us to attend to a community of others, but they develop this insight in new directions.

Like Hauerwas and Beckwith in the previous section, McGowan is concerned with the intelligibility of action, and with what distinguishes action from mere behavior and reaction. However, for him, this intelligibility is necessarily intersubjective, dependent on a horizon shared with others: "The inattention to collective action in most accounts of action . . . makes us blind to cooperative and coordinated practices as sources of tremendous satisfaction and meaning." Even more strongly, McGowan argues that "the constitution of the field of action, of the very terms by which an action can be undertaken and named, is collective and cooperative, dependent on a fundamental agreement of the sort that makes a language mutually comprehensible to all its users." Noting that "it is striking to realize how impoverished our conceptual vocabulary is when it comes to describing and explaining collective action," McGowan aims to remedy this situation by providing a multilayered description of the dimensions of collective action.

Yeomans tackles the same problem in a different way. Beginning with those theorists who have sought to account for plurality in the realm of human agency, particularly Arendt and Robert Kane, Yeomans observes that they often mean different things by plurality, making their perspectives difficult to reconcile. For Arendt, plurality concerns the multiplicity of agents, whereas for Kane, it has to do with the multiplicity of competing purposes. Arendt takes an objective point of view on the problem of action, whereas Kane's is subjective. Nevertheless, both accounts are concerned with irreducible plurality in the phenomena of human agency. Yeomans proposes that a Hegelian synthesis of the two positions can allow us to see them as compatible rather than irreconcilable. He explains how we might ultimately arrive at an account where Arendt and Kane can supplement each other, providing a fuller understanding of the different ways that plurality shapes human agency.

Although Arendt has been the most generative thinker for those who want to theorize judgment from the perspective of community and politics, her own discussion of judgment remains largely incomplete. Zerilli has been engaged in a rigorous and sympathetic reconstruction of the Arendtian account of judgment, and her essay here constitutes one significant piece of this project. For Zerilli as for Arendt, the "collapse of the common world . . . is the real problem of judgment today." This does not mean the vanishing of a shared ideology, but rather of a shared space in which objects might appear for judgment. The key question that guides Zerilli's analysis, then, is "how speakers and claims that are not already heard as political could come to count as such within any given sociopolitical context." She argues that Arendt's ability to answer this question turns on a strong interpretation of Kantian aesthetic judgments, which have the unusual property of being simultaneously subjective and yet universal. By reading aesthetic judgments "neither as wholly subjective or self-referential nor as wholly conceptualist or cognitivist," Arendt "thinks about judgment as making a normative claim on others that is also a claim about how the world is seen by a particular subject." It is thus that a common world can be constituted while still respecting plurality. With the turn to aesthetic judgment, Zerilli's essay foreshadows the concerns that will dominate the final section of this collection.

Action as Meaningful Behavior

John McGowan

The premise I want to explore in this essay is announced in my title. Bodies move, and they are engaged in a number of ongoing processes. Animals, including people, breathe, sweat, twitch, change location, as well as smell, hear, and see objects. These—and the multiple other things that bodies do—form the set of things we call "behavior." A subset of behavior also qualifies for the label "action."

This essay considers whether some ascription of "meaningfulness" can explain which behaviors, which bodily functions and motions, qualify as actions. Like Stanley Hauerwas and Thomas Pfau in this volume, I am interested in the "intelligibility" of action. Or, to be more precise, I am suggesting that the concept "action" is in play when some way of ascribing intelligibility, some way of assigning meaning, is available in an account offered for a bodily movement. I will describe three variants of intelligibility: subjective intelligibility, which addresses the question "why"; linguistic intelligibility, which answers the question "what"; and forensic intelligibility, which offers ways of identifying "who." Generally, I see the site of intelligibility as intersubjective, a focus on the enabling relations of humans to each other that distinguishes (it seems to me) my approach from that of Hauerwas and Pfau.

The "as" in my title is a nod to Wittgenstein's "seeing as."[1] My hypothesis is that action is behavior seen under a certain description, a description that assigns meaning to the behavior in question. I should warn you at the outset that this essay's attempt to "cash out" (William James's phrase) that hypothesis proves messy and inconclusive. I end up considering a number of different meaning-ascribing descriptions that people employ when talking about behaviors. These different descriptions are, to some extent, incompatible, while no one of them satisfactorily denotes the whole field of things that, in ordinary usage, get called "actions." I am not even sure we can dignify what I have to offer here as constituting a field of Wittgensteinian "family resemblances."[2] Certainly, I am not able to identify any "essential" feature that everything we ordinarily call an "action" shares. My essay's value rests, instead, on its describing a variety (hardly all) of the ways we think and talk about action—ways that rely, in one way or another, on the category of "meaningfulness" as the way in which intelligibility is conferred.

1. Subjective Intelligibility (Why)

I want to begin with William James, who devoted much of his psychic and intellectual efforts during his lifetime to carving out a space for action, to combat the specter of determinism.[3] James mobilizes the concept of "possibility" to do the job. "When you say a thing is possible, what difference does it make? It makes at least this difference that if any one calls it impossible, you can contradict him, if any one calls it actual you can contradict *him*, and if any one calls it necessary you can contradict him too."[4] James's primary goal here is to combat determinism by indicating that certain things *may* happen, but are not guaranteed to happen (i.e., are not *necessary*). But his taxonomy of possible, impossible, actual, and necessary has important implications for how we think about action, implications that James develops in various places, although never systematically and not even terribly explicitly.[5] So what follows is partly James and partly what I derive from the hints he provides.

If something is impossible, then nothing a person might do will make that thing come into existence. Action in such a case would be futile, pointless, frustrating. It might not be meaningless. There may be times when it is important to one's self-image or to one's relationship to others to attempt something that is doomed from the outset to fail. (For example, it can be important for a doctor to do everything she can to try to save a patient's life even though there is almost no chance of success.) But if all our actions were futile, if they all failed to produce any fruit, action (at least, and maybe life in its totality) would be threatened with meaninglessness. Thus, at first blush, an action's meaning is at least partially linked to its results. Insofar as many actions are motivated by a desire to influence a state of affairs, that action's being meaningful or not rests on some success in having such an influence. The requirement of meaning seems to entail, from the outset, some notion of "purpose," since an action's meaning is a function (to some extent) of its achievement of that purpose. Actions are motivated bodily movements. Meaning in the sense being explored here addresses the question "why." Why, toward what end, for what reason, was the action undertaken? And, having identified the purpose, we then judge of the action's effectiveness in attaining its aims. The impossible defeats action because it makes little sense (except in certain extraordinary circumstances) to attempt to achieve something beyond one's power to effect.

If something is necessary (and here we encounter the specter of determinism), then it will exist or occur whether I do anything or not. Action, in this case, is irrelevant. It can make no difference. What will be, will be. This is a somewhat different species of pointlessness, but (again) meaninglessness threatens because the action, the thing I do, does not change anything, does not bring anything into existence, does not make something happen. The something that happens does so of its own accord without my input, or the stasis that prevails continues to prevail despite my efforts to intervene.

Finally, there is the actual, what exists already in this present moment. The actual, in certain respects, is brute fact, that which humans act on, either to maintain it or to change it. The actual names the conditions within which humans find themselves, and to which they react or adapt. James has a very Darwinian picture of how humans are located within an environment to which they respond and within which they attempt to find a suitable accommodation. At the very least, James implies at times, humans necessarily react, since they always must find a way to sustain life within the given environment. The actual demands something of us; a purely passive being would not survive in James's understanding of the animal condition.

But the actual is also what humans have made, what we often designate with the word "culture," which includes laws, institutions, and practices. The actual is, to some extent, what previous actions have created. This category is mostly covered for James by what he calls "habits," but he (unlike John Dewey) neglects both the ways that the "environment" for humans largely consists of structures that humans have made and that habits are socially formed and reinforced.[6] This will become important in the next section of this essay. For now, let's continue to pursue James's individualistic path, where the actual stands over against the self, as something with which the self must contend. The actual spurs us to action, but that means action is about (for the most part) changing the actual. "Meliorism" is James's term for what he sees as the continual human effort to make oneself more comfortable within, better served by, the environment.[7] We strive to improve our lot.

So "possibility" gets associated first with an optimistic belief that something beside the current actual can exist, and, second, with the creative ability to imagine that something else, and, third, with the wherewithal to do various things that will make the imagined possible become the actual. "Really it is the problem of creation; for in the end the question is: How do I make them *be*? Real activities are those that really make things."[8] A belief in possibility underwrites "striving"—and there is no nobler human doing for James than "striving."

> It will seem as if the striving itself has drawn or pulled them into actuality out of the state of merely possible being in which they were. . . . Sustaining, persevering, striving, paying with effort as we go, hanging on, and finally achieving our intention—this *is* action, this *is* effectuation in the only shape in which . . . the whereabouts of it can anywhere be discussed. Here is creation in its first intention.[9]

Action, then, is connected to effort, to effectiveness, and to creation. It is, in short, heroic. Because "there is always a *pinch* between the ideal and the actual," the "deepest difference, practically, in the moral life of man is the difference between the easy-going and the strenuous mood."[10] For the easygoing person, "shrinking from present ill is [the] ruling consideration" (260). But the strenuous striver does not cede so much ground to the actual. "Every now and then, however, some one is born with the right to be original, and his revolutionary thought or action may bear prosperous fruit. He may replace old 'laws of nature' by better ones; he may, by breaking old moral rules in a certain place, bring in a total condition of things more ideal than would have followed had the rules been kept" (258). Here is the exceptional self that fascinated Kierkegaard and Nietzsche, but with the suspension of the ethical justified by the good it does for all. James is not quite ready to endorse individualism simply for the sake of that individual. But he clearly values very highly indeed individual efforts to overcome the actual by replacing what *is* with what is imagined, which is then actualized through action.

Action, whether strenuous or not, becomes tied to meaning in a very distinctive way in James's work, one we can recognize as an outgrowth of the persistent subjectivism of his psychology. As Gerald E. Meyers puts it, "For James . . . the self was the ultimate mystery."[11] Why or how human being gets parceled out into selves is a question James cannot answer, but he takes the individual self, in all its difference from other selves and from the nonhuman, as the site of analysis in all his psychological writings. And that self is the source of action, the agent who gives "activity" its "definite direction, [its] desire and sense of goal."[12] Selves undertake actions that are meaningful to them, that link up to their judgment of what is desirable.

> Our judgments concerning the worth of things, big or little, depend on the *feelings* the things arouse in us. Where we judge a thing to be precious in consequence of the *idea* we frame of it, this is only because the idea is itself associated already with a feeling. If we were radically feelingless, and if ideas were the only things our minds could entertain, we should lose all our likes and dislikes at a stroke, and be unable to point to any one situation or experience in life as more valuable or significant than any other.[13]

The world is invested with significance; our lives and what we strive to accomplish through action in that life become meaningful, of value, only insofar as our feelings are engaged. "The occasion and the experience, then, are nothing. It all depends on the capacity of the soul to be grasped, to have its life-currents absorbed by what is given."[14] This is the flip side of James's interest in (and own experience of) depression. "In certain forms of melancholic perversion of the sensibilities and reactive powers, nothing touches us intimately, rouses us or wakens natural feeling. The consequence is the complaint so often heard from melancholic patients, that nothing is believed in them as it used to be, and that all sense of reality is fled from life."[15] In depression, the world goes dead for the self, everything loses flavor, all is pointless and meaningless.

James is not utterly consistent in the ways that he describes this subjective investment of the world with meaning. Sometimes he talks as if "the occasion is nothing" and selves can make anything at all meaningful. When striking this chord, he is inclined to add to his acceptance that there is no accounting for taste the additional proviso that the self's tastes, its judgments about where to fasten its attention, its investments, and its strivings are fundamentally "a vital secret, for sympathy with which we vainly look to others. . . . How insensible, each of us, to all that makes life significant for the other!"[16] James quotes Robert Louis Stevenson: "It is just this that makes life so hard to value, and the delight of each so incommunicable."[17] Each of us has our own idiosyncratic ways of being in the world, of finding delight and meaning in the occasions it offers, and there is no way to communicate those significance-bestowing feelings or to understand the feelings the other relies on. Where the self locates meaning determines where the self will direct its energies, undertake its strivings. But there is nothing more that can be said about the reasons or causes that underwrite the self's choices in this matter. And it is possible, in the state of depression, for the self to lose the ability to make any choice, to find anything of interest or of value.

In other places, though, James's way of describing the self's positioning in a world that affords opportunities for meaning does not suggest such a complete subjectivism.

> Wherever a process of life communicates an eagerness to him who lives it, there the life becomes genuinely significant. Sometimes the eagerness is more knit up with motor activities, sometimes with the perceptions, sometimes with the imagination, sometimes with reflective thought. But, wherever it is found, there is the zest, the tingle, the excitement of reality; and there *is* "importance" in the only real and positive sense in which importance ever anywhere can be.[18]

Here reality breaks in upon the fortress of the self by "communicating an eagerness." But, even more important, there is the need, the desire, for the real, for something nonsubjective about the "importance" to which the self attaches itself, that motivates its investments and actions.

In her meditation on these matters, Susan Wolf argues against any pure subjectivism in determining "meaning in life" by stating that almost every self has a stake in devoting his or her life to activities that are not trivial. And even selves who are indifferent to the charge of triviality, who happily give their whole life over to collecting bottle caps, are subject to the judgment of others. There are, Wolf insists, nonsubjective value judgments that can, if not absolutely at least comparatively, identify some strivings as more meaningful, more significant, than others.[19] Wolf does not engage James directly in her work, but what I am suggesting is that James, while deeply attracted to a purely subjectivist view of meaning, evidences at times a discomfort with subjectivism, a worry that subjectivism opens the door to an all-embracing tolerance that deprives the onlooker of any ability to judge one self's choices as more admirable or valuable than another self's choices. And James, at times, seems aware that selves themselves are going to have their moments of doubt, their moments when they will take the position of the spectator and judge their own choices.[20]

Let me sum up what I think my discussion of James has established to this point. It seems indisputably true to me that meaning has an irreducibly subjective element. The field of possibilities is very large, perhaps infinite. Which ones get taken up, which ones' selves try to actualize, depends largely on what selves find interesting and desirable. An obvious example is careers. There are many things that one can choose to pursue for a livelihood. But which one any given self undertakes is a decision that self has to make for itself in relation to its aptitudes and interests. That hardly seems controversial. Yet that same choice is, surely, going to be influenced by what others value, as well as by what the self finds meaningful. If the world deems the career choice of the self trivial, despicable, or a waste of her talents, those judgments are almost inevitably going to influence the self's sense of that pursuit's value. In short, actions (especially, because they are visible) are always subject to judgments of meaning, of whether they are significant or valuable, and the self's own judgments about that meaning (which, presumably, play a role in motivating the action in the first place) are complexly related to what others judge to be meaningful or valuable. The self is vulnerable to the other's question: *Why* are you doing *that*?

All of this seems obvious enough, but has two important consequences for the ways we think about action. The first entails classic worries about autonomy as contrasted to heteronomy. There is an in-built subjectivism to every account of action that values autonomy, that aims to establish the capacity of selves to decide on and execute an action without being subject to undue external influence. If there is an irreducible subjectivism to accounts of desire, motive, and action, I am suggesting that a commitment to autonomy (as a good to be protected and, wherever possible, achieved) goes hand in hand with, perhaps even generates, that subjectivism. Accounts of action persistently strive to banish heteronomy, which entails creating walls between the self and the nonself, even at the cost of "incommunicability" and "a certain blindness in human beings."

The second consequence is that, if some kind of subjectivism is achieved in the account offered of meaning and action, a bridge back out of the self to the world and to others must almost inevitably be built. Subjectivism is glorious in its freedom, and terrifying in its isolation, its lack of connection to anything else, to what often gets called (as James calls it) either "the world" or "reality." James is well aware that his picture of action and significance might simply portray manic striving, endless activity for the sake of activity but with no purchase outside the self, no purpose other than to express the self's vital energies. This worrying possibility is refuted by James's complicated theism. Put most simplistically, James uses God to ensure that action is not futile, that what the self does is effective in transforming the world the self encounters, and transforming that world in the directions that the self intends. The self's purposes, which then drive the self's actions, can be realized. "If this life be not a real fight, in which something is eternally gained for the universe by success, it is no better than a game of private theatricals from which one may withdraw at will. But it *feels* like a real fight—as if there were something really wild in the universe which we, with all our idealities and faithfulness, are needed to redeem."[21] There are no guarantees in James's faith, which posits an "unfinished" world that humans are given to improve, to redeem.[22] But, as he argued in his notorious essay "The Will to Believe," it saves us from despair if we act *as if* our actions will not be futile, if we (as James put it in a letter to his wife) "trust outward things to perform their part so as to make it a full harmony."[23] That trust may be misplaced, but James argues that we will lose all will and sink into do-nothing, feel-nothing depression if we do not maintain that trust.

The question of religious faith aside, the psychological point seems to me well taken. If action is predicated on an apprehension of possibility, then continued reliance on action is dependent on some experience of success. Only if an agent sometimes does manage to bring into existence (more or less) that which she intended to actualize will subsequent actions be undertaken. Utter futility would render action meaningless, superfluous. Whether we need a beneficent deity to have a world in which some actions are successful is a moot point. As James himself suggests, we may only need a "view of 'reality,' as something resisting, yet malleable," as something which human action can transform in desired directions, even if its resistances also mean actions often have unexpected and even undesirable outcomes.[24] "Harmony" between human desires and what reality affords is more than we need to have the conditions for actions to be successful sometimes. We only need malleability, some space of possibility in the domains of a "resisting" world. Action means something if it makes a difference in the world, if it brings something into being. Our strivings must bear fruit if they are to have meaning.

2. Linguistic Intelligibility (What)

Thus far, I have been talking about "meaning" in the admittedly vague way we use that term to mark that an activity is significant or valuable. As Susan Wolf puts it: "When the word 'meaningful' is used in characterizing a life (or in characterizing what is missing from a life), it calls *something* to mind, but it is not clear what, nor is it clear that it calls or is meant to call the same thing to mind in all contexts." Wolf attempts to combat this fuzziness by telling us that meaningfulness is "a category or dimension of value . . . which we have a serious reason to want for ourselves and for those we care about, and which is neither subsumable under nor reducible to either happiness or morality." And she proposes the following way to understand this "category":

> Essentially, the idea is that a person's life can be meaningful only if she cares fairly deeply about some thing or things, only if she is gripped, excited, interested, engaged, or as I earlier put it, if she loves something—as opposed to being bored by or alienated from most or all that she does. Even a person who is so engaged, however, will not live a meaningful life if the object or activities with which she is so occupied are worthless.

Thus "the category of value I have in mind . . . involves subjective and objective elements, suitably and inextricably linked."[25] As I have already suggested, "meaning" in this sense is about "why" an action was undertaken, about why some agent judged that course of action worth pursuing. I have, however, added that this subjective motive may not be enough to guarantee meaningfulness if the action undertaken is futile.

Wolf recognizes the pluralism that James stresses, the fact that another finds meaning in something that leaves me cold, but she struggles to avoid the pure subjectivism to which James is drawn. At the very least, her account does allow us to recognize the absence of other people in James's account. He imagines a self pitted against the world, or if not *against* at least *within* a natural environment, and action is directed toward shaping that natural setting to better suit the self's needs and desires. In James, the impetus for action comes from the self, and the thrill of it, its meaning, comes from the striving generated by the resistance of the outer world to being molded. But Wolf suggests that, in fact, when selves act they often have at least one eye on others, and they are also influenced by how those others will judge their actions. It takes a peculiarly stubborn or self-sufficient individual to persist in acting in ways his neighbors deem frivolous or meaningless. Choices about what to do are partly motivated by what others deem worthwhile pursuits.

To take this insight into the role others play in the self's actions in a Wittgensteinian direction is also to move from the exalted, but vague, notion of "meaningful" that I have pursued to this point to the more exact notion of "meaning" that pertains to linguistic significance. A word is meaningful insofar as it communicates something when used by a subject who is saying or writing that something to another user of the same language. In this framework, an action is meaningful only insofar as it can be named, that is, only to the extent that it can be apprehended and "told" as a meaningful element within the given language. The "objective" element for which Wolf is reaching would then be understood not as some psychological fact about how humans desire the "recognition" (or admiration) of other humans, but instead as the very ability to designate some bodily motion as an "action" at all. Here an account of "meaning" would not address the question "why," but would consider instead "what" an action is, that is, specify the conditions that allow speakers of a language to identify, to name, an action as an action of that particular type.

The primary thrust of Wittgenstein's argument against the possibility of a "private language" is, in my reading of it, that the self could not register its own subjective states or subjective actions without the suprasubjective terms provided by language and the fixity those terms acquire by virtue of their constant use by many selves in acts of communication.[26] In other words, not every bodily motion is understood as an action. Blinking one's eyes and breathing are not, under normal conditions, actions. And there are other bodily motions for which we don't even possess descriptions and which, for that reason, almost always go unnoticed. The motions that are apprehended as actions are ones for which we (and it must be "we," not an "I") have established terms—and those terms are not subjectively generated (for the most part). The field of possible actions, then, is constituted prior to the choices and actions of any particular self. The ability to "pick out" some bodily movement as an action—and to describe it as such to oneself and to others—depends on the prior existence of an intersubjectively generated and shared language. What Wittgenstein's discussion of private language denies is that a self could "give meaning to 'S' independently of any public language," and that includes giving meaning to the self's own experiences, even experiences as intimate as having a headache.[27]

Not surprisingly, it is the sociologists who have been most energetic in pursuing an account of action that places selves firmly within preestablished, intersubjectively constituted "conditions" of a quasi-Kantian character. We might think here of Anthony Giddens's influential account of action as occurring within "structure" or of Pierre Bourdieu's location of "practice" within the context of "habitus."[28] In both cases, something that transcends the self provides the very grounds that make action possible. In Wittgenstein, the term "grammar" seems to play the role that "structure" and "habitus" play in Giddens and Bourdieu, respectively.[29] And it is to John Searle's account of social facts that I want to turn now, because that account sticks more closely to using the term "meaning" to designate linguistic intelligibility as contrasted to the more vague concept of "meaningfulness" mobilized by William James and Susan Wolf.

Searle points us toward a subset of actions that can be best understood by appealing to the following description: bodily movement B counts as action A under conditions C.[30] I have altered Searle's formula a bit. Here is how he puts it:

> Anthropology texts routinely remark on the human capacity for tool using. But the truly radical break with other forms of life comes when humans, through collective intentionality, impose functions on phenomena where the function cannot be achieved solely in virtue of physics and chemistry but requires continued human cooperation in the specific forms of recognition, acceptance, and acknowledgment of a new *status* to which a *function* is assigned. This is the beginning of

> all institutional forms of human culture, and it must always have the structure X counts as Y in C.[31]

Searle focuses, partly, on "social facts" like money. A certain piece of paper (X) can only count (function) as money (Y) under certain conditions (C).

But the same structure applies to a range of bodily movements that acquire their significance, their designation, within the context of socially constituted conditions. The most obvious examples come from games. I step across a line carrying a football. The bodily movement is the stepping across the line. That movement counts as the action of "scoring a touchdown" if and only if a set of conditions are satisfied. Those conditions are rather elaborate. A game has to be in progress; I have to be a player who is eligible to carry the ball across the line; the play has to have been started properly and conducted properly (no one offside, no holding penalties, etc.). Searle's point is that the very naming of an action, the designation of that bodily movement as "scoring a touchdown," is dependent on a whole set of conditions that have been established prior to the movement taking place. And those conditions must not only be activated in order for the action to unfold, but also must be subscribed to by all the humans—both participants and spectators—who partake in or witness the action. Even though it is just football we are talking about, we are getting rather close here to what Wittgenstein calls "a form of life."[32] An action only has meaning, only acquires a name, within an overarching social "form" that also, to a very large extent, gives the action its point. Only because there is a game called football that gives me the motive of winning the game do I pick up a ball and hurtle myself against people who are trying to stop me from crossing a line drawn on a field. So linguistic meaning—the word "touchdown" used to designate this action—and the vaguer notion of meaning as a purpose or aim I strongly desire to attain merge. The game provides the conditions for the attainment of both kinds of meaning.

Searle's account has a number of interesting consequences that I will now take some time to explore. Let me begin by shifting the example from "scoring a touchdown" to "giving a lecture." Only under certain conditions does standing up and speaking at length about a given topic "count" as "giving a lecture." The enabling conditions here include a whole set of expectations about what a lecture is, as well as a suitable venue and a recognition of the speaker's status as someone qualified to talk on the designated subject. In short, there are "criteria" (another key Wittgensteinian term) for what counts as a lecture and what does not. One consequence of this account is that everything is explicit. The occasion is labeled as a "lecture," just as everyone at the football game knows that they are attending or participating in a football game. If you go to a lecture expecting a cocktail party, you will be either very confused or very disappointed. Thus even though Wittgenstein, like Giddens and Bourdieu, is very interested in how much social actors take for granted in various situations, how much the criteria are not a matter of conscious articulation, there is no assumption that the type of situation in which one is engaged is unknown or unconscious. Just the opposite. The agent can only perform the action, and the spectators register his actions as a true example of that specific type of action, if they are all clear that this is the type of action he is attempting to perform and clear about what the criteria are for something to count as an example of that kind of action. In other words, an agent can always answer the question "What are you doing?"[33]

Thinking about language use may make this difficult point clearer, although the example of language also introduces new perplexities. Two people speaking to one another in English know that they are speaking to one another in English. They may not (in fact, probably do not) know all the "rules" of proper English usage, and they take for granted the semantic and syntactical consistencies that underwrite successful communication in the language. But despite everything they do not know explicitly, the two speakers are fully competent to judge if one or the other of them is not speaking English. Similarly, without being able to fully articulate all the "criteria" for "giving a lecture," most people would be able to judge if something was a lecture or not once what was being done was given the name "lecture."

This whole way of understanding "meaning" depends on what can seem a very implausible amount of agreement among social actors. But Searle insists that when it comes to "social facts," only "human agreement" can "constitute" (and maintain) that fact.[34] Again, language offers a good example. Unless speakers of English agree that the sound represented by the letters "dog" be understood to designate a certain kind of furry animal, the action of referring to dogs in English conversation would not be possible. Unless we all agreed on the general lineaments of what it means to give a lecture, it would not be possible for lectures to be given. So we need to be explicit in saying this occasion is a lecture and have an implicit shared understanding about what a lecture is.

The nature of this agreement and how it could ever have come into existence has given twentieth-century philosophy fits. Either an attempt is made to tell an origin story even though such stories must be posited fictions, or we shrug our shoulders and tell ourselves that language was "always already" there as a fundamental feature of the human condition. Newton Garver tells us that Wittgenstein takes this second route. Wittgenstein accepts

> language-games as *given*. They do not *have* to exist, there is no necessity about them; but they *do* exist. They are there as features of human life. . . . Wittgenstein undoubtedly has this givenness of language-games in mind in the famous passage near the end of PI [*Philosophical Investigations*], p. xi: "What has to be accepted, the given, is—so one could say—*forms of life*." Wittgenstein is a naturalist in that he takes for granted that we have a complicated form of life whose features are accessible to observation and description but are susceptible neither to explanation nor skepticism.[35]

Humans find themselves within language, just as they find themselves in a natural environment, and philosophy can tell us nothing about why these are the enabling conditions of human existence. All philosophy can do is describe those conditions and ponder better and worse ways of acting within those conditions.

Such philosophical modesty is not very satisfactory. We are told that language and other enabling social institutions rest on a fundamental agreement whose origins are lost in the mists of time and whose continuance is a byproduct of our reliance on those institutions in our daily intercourse with one another. The fragility of such agreements, their susceptibility to collapse and disappearance as a result of human conflict, seems obvious. Certainly, we can identify various ritual practices and various strategies of sacralization that aim to reinforce foundational agreements, to activate them through constant reenactment. Such collective actions mimic the founding moment as if only its repetition could keep the agreement in force. And, of course, societies not only rely on ritual repetition, but also on formally stated codes and laws, along with formally established institutions, to maintain the possibilities for coordination and cooperation among selves that undergirds social existence. The "naturalistic" explanation for these elaborate social forms is the insistence that human life is not sustainable outside social relations, that only collective action gives the individual any chance to survive. But it is striking to realize how impoverished our conceptual vocabulary is when it comes to describing and explaining collective action, especially collective actions that establish the conditions for individual action.

Searle tries to say more than Wittgenstein does about the collective actions that create founding agreements. Searle argues that social facts or social institutions (the products of agreements) are secondary, that they can only be constituted by action. He activates the Kantian distinction between constitutive and regulative rules in order to focus on the constitutive. A constitutive rule (in football, for example) establishes what a "touchdown" is, what actions counts as a "touchdown." Contrasted to the "what" of the constitutive rule is the "how" of a regulative rule: "How" can that action of scoring a touchdown be performed? What ways of doing it are permitted, what ways forbidden? Thus a touchdown scored as a result of an "illegal lateral" is not permitted.[36]

What actions could bring "conditions C" into existence, could constitute the social field? Searle warns us against being fooled by nouns, which can lead us to think that the product comes before the process.[37] The criteria (i.e., the conditions C that lead to behavior B counting as action A) for "giving a lecture" did not exist prior to the first lecture. Rather, those criteria evolved as activities that came to be recognized as similar coalesced into something that became established (constituted) as a "lecture." Again, think about language or about the emergence of a game like football. People start by communicating or by playing a game. The activity itself begins to generate certain regularities and/or rules that only become more explicit or codified as time goes on.[38] And there does not need to be a full understanding of the rules to engage in the activity. Rules are ex post facto. The notion that our language has a "grammar" emerges long after the fact of that language's existence as a successful means of communication. The codification of English grammar is, in some ways, a panicked response to the perceived fragility of the agreements that keep the language functioning successfully. And that codification is, to a certain extent, a futile effort. The rules of grammar will always be behind the actual practice of speakers of the language. An English teacher can try to use those rules to influence practice, but it is much more common that changes (corrections?) in practice are made by practitioners within the activity itself, not by an appeal to the rules or to an external arbiter. In order to successfully "go on" (another Wittgensteinian term), agents adjust their behavior to one another. Our languages and our social institutions (and/or practices) are more dynamic than any model that portrays actions as rigid adherence to rules would allow. But that these dynamic practices do more or less work, do more or less enable us to "go on" in our communicative and cooperative interactions, attests to the existence of underlying agreements. Such agreements emerge from practice; they are not guaranteed or even underwritten by preexisting rules.

But disagreements emerge from practice as well. Because so oriented toward language, the Wittgensteinian line emphasizes the fundamental agreements that enable communication as existing below or prior to the various disagreements that characterize social life. But if we think about constitutive and regulative rules, agreement does not retain such absolute priority. Constitutive rules establish the social field, establish conditions C. In polities since the 1700s, a formal process of constitution has become the norm.[39] What counts as the legitimate processes of decision making and of enforcement of those decisions is hammered out through some kind of deliberative discussion followed by a procedure for ratification. The terms of the fundamental social agreement are thus established through an explicit process. Such a procedure would seem to undermine the claim that collective action comes first, out of which emerges agreement and formal codifications. Instead, the business of making a constitution seems to endorse the Hobbes-Locke notion that humans exist as isolated individuals first (in the "state of nature") and only form social relations to others through a secondary process that depends on separate individuals entering into a contract with one another. This fundamental question of the primacy of individual or of social modes of being to one side, it is important to recognize that even the constitutional (or contractual) effort to establish rules prior to practice cannot succeed in governing the field of social intercourse. Every constitutional regime has to be supplemented with a case law system that tries to reconcile the abstract nature of the written rules with the messy contingencies of actual on-the-ground practices. Constitutions also must be dynamic even if "originalists" strive to fetishize the constitution in ways analogous to someone obsessed with "proper usage" of a living language.

I don't wish to be detained here by the many puzzles the contract account of social origins generates, although I do believe that the formation of a constitution inevitably relies on a prior nonformal sense that a certain group of people already belong together and to one another. But I do want to suggest that explicit constitutions exist where the right to disagreement is prized, even while it is feared. The constitution is needed because the possibility of chaos, of civil war, looms large, but there is a balancing recognition that overly rigid agreements (an insistence on uniformity in practice and beliefs) are a major source of the feared conflicts. A modern (i.e., liberal) constitution attempts to establish a legal and institutional order that gives individuals leeway for acting out individual differences while also providing for regularities of conduct. Critics of liberalism from the start have objected to its individualistic focus, its neglect of the ways in which participation in collective actions is often the most significant part of an individual's life. If our vocabulary for describing collective actions is impoverished, that poverty goes hand in hand with our blindness to the extent to which many people find subsuming the self into supraindividual activities the most meaningful actions they can undertake. Participation in the collective practices that establish (constitute) a social realm is what some people find meaningful—and a critic like Hannah Arendt argues that it is exactly such participation that is impossible within modern liberal polities. For Arendt, constitution of the terms of social existence is one hallmark of political action, but that action is taken off the table by formal processes of constitution making.[40]

The inattention to collective action in most accounts of action not only makes us blind to cooperative and coordinated practices as sources of tremendous satisfaction and meaning, but also leads to the neglect of training and rehearsals ("practice" in a different use of that term) as aspects of many successful actions. Collective actions—think of an orchestra or a football team or most workplaces—depend on the coordination of individual performances within the larger enterprise. Humans devote significant time and energy to processes of preparing for ("practicing for") the moment of actual performance of a planned collective deed. Agreement and coordination under such circumstances is a considerable achievement, one won at the cost of much time and effort, and with a mostly explicit understanding of the desired end. Our individualistic accounts of action scant these processes, even as they underestimate the extent to which meaning is found in participation in these collective endeavors.

Prevailing accounts of action tend to worry much more about the threat of conformity. The Wittgensteinian account, because it emphasizes the collective and leans strongly toward cooperative social enterprises as contrasted to competitive ones, has been criticized as "conservative." His philosophy, as he himself says, would "leave everything as it is."[41] Such an attitude is anathema to those who value novelty and change just about over everything else. The sociological view that I am offering as a way of understanding Wittgenstein (but which I think you could also derive from Bourdieu's accounts of "practice") indicates that, yes, I play the game of football to win over my opponent, but unless my opponent and I agree that we are playing football and will abide by its rules, we don't get to play at all. No competition without an undergirding cooperation. (This maxim is fully tested by the counterexample of modern warfare, where there is full-bore competition with the absence of any rules.) The constitution of the field of action, of the very terms by which an action can be undertaken and named, is collective and cooperative, dependent on a fundamental agreement of the sort that makes a language mutually comprehensible to all its users.

But this collectively constituted field does provide space for individual differences, what we might call "style." Within the broad understanding of what it means to "give a lecture," there is room for idiosyncratic ways of approaching that task. And since the rules follow from the practice, there is also a way for the common understanding of what "giving a lecture" means to change over time. We are familiar with this dynamic especially in the arts, where since 1900 (at least) much artistic practice is aimed fairly explicitly at changing our definition of what an artistic object or practice is. When Duchamp offers the world his readymades, he is dramatically calling attention to the "conditions" part of the formula "B counts as A under conditions C." The action of making an artwork is shifted by Duchamp from the craft of rendering something in a specific medium to the linguistic act of shifting the term used to designate an object. And that linguistic act can only be successful if the broader conditions for the application of names to objects are manipulated successfully by Duchamp.

In other words, I can successfully (or felicitously, to use J. L. Austin's term) give a lecture by abiding within the accepted protocols of lecture giving. Or I can attempt to shift the prevailing understanding of what it means to give a lecture. (I don't want to make this an absolute either/or. Style mostly consists in "nudges," in trying to inflect the received understandings with a flavor of my subjectivity, in trying to occupy a social role in a way that also expresses what I deem to be my distinctive individuality.) Success in transforming the prevailing understanding depends heavily on "uptake" (another Austin term). Since the criteria for designation are always, in the final analysis, dependent on collective endorsement, the self cannot by fiat change meanings that are, fundamentally, social. This thought brings me all the way back around to Wittgenstein on private language. Wittgenstein's point is that the self could not persist for very long in holding on to meanings that no collective took up and endorsed. And his argument is not one about social pressure or desires for approbation; rather, he says a self could not hold idiosyncratic meanings in his head, that such meanings would evaporate because there was no external check or standard to keep them from a destabilizing indeterminacy.

The problem of novelty (which has bedeviled philosophers almost as much as the problem of the origin of our foundational social agreements) can be characterized as follows: when does what I do under the name of "giving a lecture" depart so far from received understandings of "lectures" that my performance is unrecognizable, uncategorizable? How do our categories stretch to incorporate the novel, as contrasted to the cases where those categories refuse to stretch to include the newcomer? One traditional answer to this question has invoked metaphor. We understand—and label—novelties through analogies to more standard cases. And at least from Aristotle's time, the ability to generate novelties, to push language and practice beyond its current boundaries, has been associated with a "genius" that is unaccountable and cannot be taught.[42] Novelties challenge the whole notion of linguistic meaning as the basis of "what counts as action A" because novelties refuse to abide by the "conditions C" of those acts of naming. In the case of felicitous novelties, ones that enjoy "uptake," individual actions can also (like collective actions do) change the terms of our underlying social agreements. In the modern world, we seem to cherish especially these acts of individual transformation, although it is worth remembering that Aristotle celebrates them as well. In aesthetics, such issues tend to cluster around the term "genre." Genres are aesthetic "kinds," terms for categorization, but are fluid, with fuzzy boundaries, and open to revision. Is Truman Capote's *In Cold Blood* a "novel," or does it require a new genre classification, "creative nonfiction"? And is there a "right" answer to that question?

The two notions of meaningfulness (of intelligibility) considered thus far come together here. An individual's actions ("what" she has done) can only have a meaning in the sense of being able to be named in language, a naming that rests on that action operating within a recognizable field of human endeavor. Actions have constituted those fields and can re-form them, but the fields have been collectively created and maintained in the course of social interactions—and, crucially, the fields now preexist any individual. So my ability to know that I am doing an action is predicated on the available terms I have for naming actions (even in cases where I am stretching received meanings fairly radically by employment of some species of metaphor). Meaning, I would venture to say, is always a matter of a relation between at least two terms, in this case the bodily movement and the name attached to it. The action is linguistically meaningful only insofar as it can be named. But that ascription of linguistic meaning also opens up the possibility of the wider, vaguer meaningfulness (the "why") that concerns James and Wolf. The name I use to designate my action indicates the significance I attach to it, the subjective value it holds for me. Others may very well contest my naming. What I call giving a lecture they may call incoherent ramblings. "Uptake" matters greatly here. My subjective aspirations to be understood as doing a certain thing will, Wittgenstein suggests, be very hard to maintain if others deny my action the name I want to label it with. Even if James is right that there is an irreducibly subjective element in what selves address their energies toward doing, it will be rare indeed for a self to persist in an activity that others deny deserves the name that encapsulates the self's understanding of that action's import.

Searle's argument leads him to insist on a firm distinction between social facts and natural facts and, by implication, between actions aimed toward altering the self's relation to others and actions aimed toward altering the self's relation to the world. One way of illustrating Searle's point here would be to return to James's notion of "possibility."[43] "Growing tomatoes" is a fundamentally different kind of action than "giving a lecture" because growing something means attending to and contending with natural conditions. The possibilities when growing or eating a tomato are not structured by social conditions or expectations. There are no distinguishing conditions C under which something counts as growing or eating a tomato whereas similar bodily movements do not count. When the self is encountering or doing something that involves its relationship to natural facts, the conditions for ascription (or description) are minimal (little beyond the existence of language itself). Thus, to "pick fruit off a tree" is a "natural" activity insofar as its description does not entail any social facts. But once we add the social fact of "property," the same action might be described as "robbing fruit" if condition C (the fruit does not belong to the one who picked it) is met. James's account of action is impoverished because he almost always thinks of action as something undertaken by the self in a natural setting. Searle gives us a good way to demonstrate why James's account is inadequate. But Searle also argues that James does accurately portray some actions; James is just insufficiently aware that actions within the social field have a very different structure.

We might characterize this difference by saying that an action can be primarily oriented toward altering the agent's relation to the world or to altering the agent's relation to other human beings. (Of course, some actions aim to do both.) At issue is whether there are significant differences in either the strategies employed or the ways we would describe the two types of action. If I rob the apple off the tree because I am starving, I am still, to some extent, making the rhetorical point that natural need should trump social categories of ownership. But if I grow tomatoes, am I addressing in any way at all the social conditions C that lead to us calling that activity "growing tomatoes"? The social element appears to drop out almost entirely. It is just a matter of my attempting to make something happen in the world. The meaning of the action resides in my (natural) need for food and my desire for tomatoes. The success of the action rests on my ability to get the tomatoes to grow and to ripen. A socially oriented action, by way of contrast, is an attempt to intervene in the order of meanings. What is deemed malleable, open to the possibility of transformation, in this second case are the conditions by which we understand who a person is and what she does. Giving a lecture is about either providing an audience with information that the lecturer thinks will alter their understanding of some topic or making hopefully persuasive arguments about why the audience should think of some topic differently. In both cases (I guess)—growing tomatoes and giving a lecture—the agent could also be oriented toward securing the admiration of others for her virtuosity, but such would have to be a by-product of doing the main thing well. I cannot solicit your admiration directly (or, if I do, I am very unlikely to win it). I must do the action itself, which also implicitly entails the understanding that both my audience and I think it an action worth doing and worth doing well.

Searle's insistence that there are (at least) two very different kinds of actions is in line with the Wittgensteinian pluralism that sees philosophy as led astray when it tries to identify one essence, one shared feature, for everything grouped under a single name. Why should we believe that everything designated in ordinary language as "action" can be adequately characterized within a "theoretical" account that will show what every action holds in common? Yet I will admit that Searle's insistence on a very hard line between natural facts (or natural reality) and social facts (or social reality) makes me uneasy. I am influenced enough by social constructivist arguments to want to resist the notion that "apple" designates a natural object to which I stand in a very different relation than I do to "property," which is a social object. Since both "apple" and "property" are picked out by language, which is certainly a social fact, it would seem they cannot be all that different from one another. Yet Searle is persuasive when he says that calling something an "apple" does not seem to rely on a complicated social apparatus standing behind that naming, whereas the term "property" is incomprehensible without that elaborate social (legal and institutional) framework.

Perhaps, however, the weight should be put not on the terms "natural" and social," but rather on "individual" and "collective." What Searle delineates are two classes of action. Constitutive actions are those that compose or construct a field, a set of conditions, within which (and only within which) specific actions are possible to be performed and able to be identified (linguistically designated). Constitutive actions must be collective if we accept the logic of Wittgenstein's private language argument, even while individual actions, like individual utterances, are rendered possible by the conditions the constitutive action establishes. "Natural," then, is a term applied to enabling conditions that are not (at least in any direct or obvious way) created by collective human action. That some trees bear apples does not seem the result of a collective human agreement, although the fact that English speakers call the fruit "apple" rather than "pomme" is a matter of such an agreement. Individual actions still need to be considered as taking place within certain conditions, but only some conditions are created by collective actions. Other conditions are experienced as "natural," a term that indicates that those conditions are amenable to direct physical actions that aim to alter them, rather than amenable to renegotiation of their terms through some kind of collective decision/bargaining process. Acting to pick an apple off a tree is a different kind of action from trying to persuade my collective to redefine its notions of property, although both actions can be taken individually or in cooperation with others. But the action of redefining the understanding of property can succeed only if it secures collective endorsement.

3. Forensic Intelligibility (Who)

I want now to turn to a third set of ways in which actions are deemed meaningful. I have considered thus far in my discussion of meaning or significance the relation between the acting self and the external world her action tries to alter, while also placing a lot of emphasis on why that attempt at alteration seems worth doing to the agent. Futility (a fairly constant inability to effect the alterations aimed for) and depression (an inability to find any action worth the effort of even undertaking) can both (from different directions as it were) generate the experience of "meaninglessness." The operative relations for the ascription of meaning here focus on the relation between the self and something external to it, since, even when considering the feeling of being invested, most selves will describe that feeling in terms of the "significance" ("value") of the external thing or person that is the object of the feeling, or the importance of what the action aims to accomplish. In linguistic meaning, the operative relation is between a bodily movement and the term used to describe it, what that movement is understood to be within the relevant collective (society) that has established the conditions for the movement's recognition and naming. But the third kind of meaning I want to explore rests on an imputed relationship between the action and some internal state of the agent.

There are multiple ways to approach this third way of finding bodily movements meaningful, and most of these ways lead to all kinds of puzzles, which is why I have left this one for last. Traditional psychology (i.e., faculties psychology, as contrasted to more recent forms of neuropsychology or chemical psychology) has devised a whole set of terms—the "will," "motives," "intention," "deliberation"—by which to designate the internal states or movements that are then described as, in some way or other, generating actions. Something happens inside the agent first, some intention is formed, some deliberation takes place that results in a decision, some movement of the will allows for the passage from an idea to an actual bodily movement. Only after some version of this internal machinery getting into gear has been accomplished can the visible action itself take place. And the meaning of the action is then understood by mapping the visible movement back to the invisible internal states that precipitated that movement. This mapping is forensic; it attempts to establish "who" did the action, locating intelligibility in the successful attribution of the act to its agent, while also attempting to say something about that agent's "character" or "motives."

The difficulties attending these efforts to identify the relevant internal states are notorious. I am not going to give an account that makes those difficulties disappear. Rather, my position is that the uncertainties afflicting any such efforts are inevitable, yet inescapable. The very concept of "action" has proved so relentlessly problematic for philosophers since at least Aristotle precisely because the concept entails ambiguities and uncertainties that cannot be overcome. Insofar as the understanding of action is tied to our interpreting it to tell us something about the "character" of the agent, there will always be a space of undecidability that constitutes, for that very reason, a space of contestation.

I will try to make this last claim persuasive by discussing two particular ways actions are interpreted in relation to the agent's internal origination of the action. The first way involves issues of "responsibility," the second issues of "character." (There are multiple other ways this connection can be made, utilizing terms like "intention" or "choice" or "motive." I will only discuss the two I have chosen here.) As might be expected by my Wittgensteinian leanings, I am persuaded by Barry Barnes's understanding of responsibility.[44] For Barnes, the concept "action" is collectively established (in a Searle-like fashion) as a crucial component of the ability of humans to live together and to cooperate. The category "action" is social through and through, and its primary social function is to establish "responsibility." Only if individuals are held accountable (or, more radically, it is only if something understood as the individual self is socially created with "responsibility" as one of that self's most significant distinguishing features) can the cooperative, coordinated activities that make human life possible be undertaken. In other words, despite all the difficulties of determining responsibility in specific cases, social life requires the notion of responsibility if social functions (from the production of necessities to the reproduction of social life through acculturation) are to even take place. We are bound to the others with whom we participate in those social functions through their recognition of us as individuals. And a crucial part of that recognition of an individual is ascribing to the individual an ability to act, where the ability to act is directly tied to the notion of being responsible for, of being the owner and originator of, the actions seen as emanating from that specific self. In this account, then, whether selves can (in some existential sense) actually be responsible for their actions is irrelevant. We would not have a notion of selves at all if we didn't also have a notion of responsible action, and we wouldn't be able to have the coordinated social actions that make life on this planet possible for humans unless society had a means of holding selves accountable. Selves (with the entailed concept of responsibility) are a secondary product of social processes. The very self that can stand as the answer to the question "Who?" is constituted by the process of asking and answering that question.

Barnes is not particularly interested in the consequences of what we might call the peculiar institution of responsibility. Here we have to turn to the brilliant essay by J. L. Austin titled "A Plea for Excuses."[45] What Austin unveils for us is the way ascriptions of responsibility call forth a number of language games and even more substantial institutions, most notably courts of law. Whether I was responsible for this or that action can always be a matter of negotiation or dispute. As Austin sees it, I have two lines of defense when I am accused of doing something reprehensible: I can either deny having done the deed in question, or I can make excuses. In many cases, denial is simply a nonstarter. So I have to fall back on explaining the various extenuating circumstances that mitigate my responsibility for the deed. Austin stresses that it is mitigation, not full exoneration, that is at stake here. "It always has to be remembered that few excuses get us out of it *completely*: the average excuse, in a poor situation, gets us only out of the fire into the frying pan—but still, of course, any frying pan in a fire. If I have broken your dish or your romance, maybe the best defence I can find will be clumsiness."[46] Ignorance, unexpected consequences, contingencies beyond my control, effects other than those I intended, the actions of others, or absent-mindedness are all possible ways to lessen my responsibility. Austin is interested, once again, in "uptake"—in which excuses under which circumstances are more likely to prove persuasive. But he also makes two larger points: one, that social relations would probably prove unsustainable if we didn't, at least some of the time, accept others' excuses; and two, that every time I use an excuse I diminish the strength (or maybe we should say "autonomy") of my self. To the extent that I am invested in being an individual, every excuse diminishes that individuality. So we might say that excuses, while absolutely necessary to the maintenance of social life, should be used sparingly because they come with a cost. I am less of an individual, less of an owner of my actions, every time I make an excuse. Extending this point even further would lead me to this formulation: to act responsibly means to be a self. The facts of responsibility are less important than the ascription of responsibility. The facts will in many, if not all, cases be contestable. There is usually room to make excuses. But while I have a stake at times in evading others' attempts to hold me responsible, I also have a vital stake in being seen, at least some of the time, as the responsible origin of actions that deserve to be called "mine." To cede all claims to being a self on these terms, to embrace complete irresponsibility, is to accept being a child forever in the way that our society (at least) has established the terms of selfhood. Thus the meaningful tying of an action back to an agent who willed it is not only a way of ascribing praise or blame, but also a way of establishing the agent as a recognized individual.

This way of thinking about responsibility makes it clear why the distinctions between voluntary/involuntary, autonomy/heteronomy, and chosen/compelled are so crucial in many accounts of action.[47] What I am suggesting is that for any given action, there are always going to be plausible competing accounts that differ on the question of just how voluntary the action was, how autonomous the agent, and the degree of compulsion (by circumstances, by others, by lack of resources or alternatives) under which the action was undertaken. And what the agent might gain in escaping blame, he might lose in his ability to claim the status of responsible adult self.

More generally, actions can be interpreted as indices of character. Hannah Arendt offers a particularly dramatic version of this way of understanding the meaning of action.

> In acting and speaking, men show who they are, reveal actively their unique personal identities and thus make their appearance in the human world, while their physical identities appear without any activity of their own in the unique shape of the body and sound of the voice. This disclosure of "who" in contradistinction to "what" somebody is—his qualities, gifts, talents, and short-comings, which he may display or hide—is implicit in everything somebody says and does. . . . This revelatory quality of speech and action comes to the fore where people are *with* others and neither for nor against them—that is, in sheer human togetherness. Although nobody knows whom he reveals when he discloses himself in deed or word, he must be willing to risk the disclosure.[48]

Arendt was fiercely committed to a distinction between behavior and action, where behavior designates what is "conditioned" and lawlike, of that which is "standard for all regions of life" (45). Action, on the other hand, is what is distinctive and unique; it is "revelatory" both because tied to "the miracle" of "natality" (of the eruption of something new into the world) and because it makes manifest (to actor and spectator alike) the unique identity of the one who acts.[49] For Arendt, I do not know "who" I am until, under the pressure of circumstances, as I relate to the world and to others through my words and deeds, I disclose to myself and to those others my character.

One result of this persistent tendency to "read" actions as indicators of identity is the development of what we might call a second-order discourse about actions. Arendt figures this discourse as "storytelling." The peculiarities of her account of such stories need not detain us here. What I want to draw from her work is the notion that stories are the form our desire to "make sense" of others' takes. The actions of others are woven into stories that "reveal an agent" (184). "*Who* somebody is or was we can only know by knowing the story of which he is himself the hero—his biography, in other words" (186). For Arendt, identity (finally) is coherent and singular. We can, if only after the life is complete, tell a story about someone that adds up, that gives us an adequate account of her character, or, at least, the fullest understanding we will ever achieve. And she insists on privileging this narrative account over any work a person may have produced. As contrasted to his biography,

> everything else we know of him, including the work he may have produced and left behind, tells us only *what* he is or was. Thus although we know much less of Socrates, who did not write a single line and left no work behind, than of Plato and Aristotle, we know much better and more intimately who he was, because we know his story, than we know who Aristotle was, about whose opinions we are so much better informed. (186)

Arendt appears committed to the Sophoclean view that we cannot know the story of a person's life until after her death, that only the complete biography can be revelatory. Arendt neglects first-person storytelling. Only the spectator, after the event, can tell the story in such a way that its meaning is fully captured. This notion follows from her, to me, implausible belief in selves possessing a single and coherent identity (knowable only after the self's death). I am more interested in first-person narratives, the retrospective accounts that an agent provides for her actions, accounts produced both for the benefits of oneself as well as for others. Because we live in intersubjective settings in which we will not only be held responsible for actions that are deemed to belong to us, but also in which those actions will be interpreted as privileged clues as to our identity, each self will be called on, at various times, to give an account of itself.

As Austin has called to our attention, the meanings of our actions, as located in the ways those actions are mapped to the agent who performs, define a hotly contested interactional domain. One way to participate in those contests is to make excuses. But Austin is clear that excuses are only one species in a larger field we can call "giving reasons."[50] In this language game, the meaning of my action is to be designated by the reasons I offer for its inception and execution. True, some excuses attend to the mishaps that afflicted the execution, not to the reasons that led me to undertake the action in the first place. But there are also plenty of excuses that pertain to the reasons, not the execution. I was trying to praise you, but it came out wrong and you were insulted. We come here to the "why" question again, but in a much more intersubjective setting. The "why" isn't the personal belief or feeling that led me to act, but (instead) the reasons I can offer to myself and others that will pass muster while also attesting to the worthiness of my character. The meaning of the action is created in this retrospective account of it, an account that leans heavily on there being auditors I want to accept those reasons' validity. I don't think we can maintain absolutely hard and fast distinctions here, but (roughly) we can see the difference between answering the question *what* are you doing by saying "Giving a lecture," and answering the question *why* are you doing it by saying "I want to argue for a Wittgensteinian understanding of action," and answering the question *how* are you doing it by saying "I am reading my essay to an audience at Duke." Only the answer to the *why* question points to interior states and offers reasons for my action. And given our forensic propensities when it comes to action, the audience at the lecture is going to reach conclusions about "who" I am (what in Aristotle's *Rhetoric* is called the "ethos" of the speaker) based on my performance and, perhaps, on my statements about my purposes.

Such accounts and the reasons they mobilize are always subject to being understood as "rationalizations." That's because, in the vast majority of cases, reasons are offered after the fact. And even where reasons are offered before acting, there is still special pleading involved. The agent, in these first-person accounts, is trying to justify the action, is trying to persuade others that the action was, if not the right or only thing to do, at least understandable. This giving of reasons straddles the line between explanation and justification, the factual and the normative. I am saying: "Here is the thought process that explains why I did what I did." I am telling an origin story. But I am also saying that these reasons are good ones, they should make you accept that I did a (if not "the") right thing. Standing before the bar of others' judgment, the language game of "giving reasons" is my only recourse. Precisely because so much is at stake, my performance is viewed skeptically, but there is not some other kind of performance to which I can resort, one that would guarantee my audience's assent to my self-presentation.

As with responsibility, all parties to the game of "giving reasons" have reasons not to abandon the game altogether, no matter how skeptical they might be of its validity in any single instance. The very meaningfulness of action is in question here. If a third-person causal account of actions, an account that erases "reasons" entirely from the picture, prevails, then we only have behavior (in Arendt's sense) and not action. This threat of determinism surfaces, for example, in Freud's *Psychopathology of Everyday Life*. In one way, Freud's approach takes the forensic approach to action to its furthest extreme. Every bodily motion, every twitch or inadvertent slip of the tongue, is meaningful. It can be "read" as an indicator of what lurks within the self. But the arationality of these motions, their disconnection from any plausible first-person account of their reasons (no matter if before or after the fact), makes them the sole province of the third-person narrator, with his scientific, causal account of their genesis. Character exists in Freud, but the self is the passive recipient of the character that has been lodged in him. As distinct from the Aristotelian account of action creating character, here character determines behavior.[51] And we might describe Freudian therapy as the attempt to provide to the patient an ability to act, an ability to tell a first-person story about his or her life. Unless I can own my actions by giving reasons for them, by tying them to intentions, desires, beliefs, values, and all the other paraphernalia of traditional psychology, I am going to find it awfully hard to experience those actions as meaningful. And I am going to find it equally hard to think of myself as being a self at all.

Activating this distinction between first- and third-person accounts of action suggests that action, from the point of view of the agent, can be expressive. It can be the way I have of manifesting who I am, of making my mark in the world. I can have a tremendous stake in seeing that the fact of my existence makes a difference, that my distinctive being (or my distinctive contribution) be recognized. The arts since 1750 (at least) have been very oriented toward aesthetic actions as expressive of the self who performs them. The third-person perspective is not expressive, but better characterized as diagnostic. Action seen from the outside is read as a symptom of an invisible state, a latency that lurks beneath what is manifest. This interpretive strategy depends, nonetheless, on the notion that action is expressive, that there is that link between what is seen and what is not seen. The path from the visible to the invisible may be very complex (hence justifying elaborate interpretive procedures), but a commitment to the idea that the invisible generates the visible (hence the invisible has priority over the visible in every sense of the word "priority") underwrites both an expressivist understanding of action and a diagnostic interpretation of action. We cannot distinguish between first- and third-person accounts on the basis of their commitment to distinctiveness. Depending on the circumstances, the first-person speaker may have a large stake in claiming that his action is typical, not unusual or markedly personal in any way. Selves don't always want to stand out. Still, third-person accounts will tend toward the impersonal, the aggregate, the general, while first-person accounts will highlight the individuality of the "I" who speaks.

Third-person accounts can be diagnostic in another way, one captured by Wittgenstein's notion of "a perspicuous representation."[52] A third-person account can also move from interpreting this action as an indicator of the agent's character to taking the action as representative of something true of human beings more generally. This tendency toward allegory, toward taking a specific action or a specific story as revealing a more general truth, seems especially baked into our ways of understanding literature. But we can perform the same operation in interpreting actual actions and agents. In such cases, we might say that the direction of interpretation shifts from going from the action to its invisible springs (in motive or desire or character) to moving from the action outward (instead of inward) toward the positing of a general fact about the human condition. It is worth stressing that such general facts are every bit as invisible as an agent's interiority, although it is an invisibility with a different ontological status, not existing as the inner "truth" (or "identity") of a person, but in whatever realm is set aside for generalizing propositions.

It is also worth noting that Wittgenstein, pluralist that he is, appeals to "perspicuous representations" precisely to combat overhasty and too broad generalizations. He wants "intermediate cases," not the "universals" that Aristotle lauds literature for providing.[53] The prestige of examples in philosophy (since at least Kant's *Critique of Judgment*) rests on this desire to find some kind of middle ground between pure singularity and all-encompassing universals. One way of finding meaning in actions is to see those actions as indicative of something true about some human beings, albeit not all. Actions interpreted this way are saved from the potential insignificance of the purely idiosyncratic while protected from the obvious error of thinking all humans alike. This kind of third-person interpretation, moreover, is more sympathetic to, more aligned with, a first-person account that stresses reasons than is the more diagnostic third-person approach. To explain how some action can be understood as a "perspicuous representation" is not to discredit the first-person account of that action, nor to substitute a causal (or symptomatic) reading of its origins for an account that relies on internal decision procedures. Instead, the interpretive strategy of the example is an effort to find the common ground that coexists within the landscape of difference, which seems like a good way of describing Wittgenstein's whole philosophical enterprise.

I feel that, in certain ways, I have come full circle. To the third-person observer, to Freud or to the neuroscientist or to the social scientist, actions might be meaningful insofar as they can be made sense of by a causal account that identifies the "who." But William James's insistence on some kind of privilege for the first person continues to trouble any totally objectivist account. James's position gets unexpected support from more intersubjective accounts like those of Wittgenstein, Searle, Austin, and Barnes. Written into our collective understandings of action are notions like "responsibility" and "choice" and "reasons" that tie the meaning of action to various kinds of relationships between the first-person agent and the action. Still, while a totally objectivist account won't do, a totally subjectivist one also seems a nonstarter. Accepting an irreducibly subjective component within a more broadly intersubjective understanding is the path I have pursued here, while also pushing on the ways we ascribe "meaning" to action in order to distinguish it from behavior.

To recapitulate: we ascribe meaning to action (render it intelligible) in a wide variety of ways, not all of which are compatible with one another. Actions are meaningful to an agent because they incorporate what she finds important and valuable; actions are meaningful insofar as they make a difference, are effective, manage to circumvent futility. Many actions only make sense within a set of socially established conditions, and agents' motives for, and even apprehensions of, action are deeply influenced (but not absolutely determined) by the social fields they occupy. In various cases, highly meaningful action is directly tied to participating in, contributing to, collective enterprises. Yet there also seem to be actions—eating a peach, washing one's hands—that appear completely "natural," not (necessarily) depending on a set of social conditions for their significance or their desirability. But actions are also meaningful as means of expression for selves, even as they are interpreted (by the agent and by others) as a means toward understanding interior states and "character." Furthermore, ascriptions of responsibility rely on this connection of action to interior reasons, motives, and will, thus providing the grounds for rendering selves accountable to others. Contestation over what actions mean is thus a very prominent language game and generates both first- and third-person accounts of an action's meaning. Finally, actions can also be read as not only telling us something about the individual agent, but something about human beings more generally. And I am confident that I have not exhausted the ways actions are described as meaningful with this list.

These results seem to me messy, but I think (and hope) that messiness reflects what people and societies need the concept of "action" to do on different occasions, needs that trump any conceptual clarity or rigor. My approach to this whole topic is driven by the conviction that no inquiry is going to uncover what action "is." Rather, it is more fruitful, even if more inconclusive, to consider where the notion of "action" is deployed, and what meanings are ascribed to that notion in the various situations of its deployment.

Notes

1. Ludwig Wittgenstein, *Philosophical Investigations*, 3rd ed. (1953; rpt., New York: Macmillan, 1968), 193–99. "I contemplate a face, and then suddenly notice its likeness to another. I *see* that it has not changed; and yet I see it differently. I call this experience 'noticing an aspect'" (193). We see something "now as one thing now as another.—So we interpret it, and *see* it as we *interpret* it" (193). This essay notices the aspect of "meaningfulness" and considers how noticing that aspect leads us to interpret behavior *as* action.

2. Ibid., 31–38 (pars. 65–80). "Instead of producing something common to all that we call language, I am saying that these phenomena have no one thing in common which makes us use the same word for all,—but that they are *related* to one another in many different ways. . . . I can think of no better expression to characterize these similarities than 'family resemblances'" (31–32 [pars. 65, 67]).

3. See Robert D. Richardson, *William James: In the Maelstrom of American Modernism* (Boston: Houghton Mifflin, 2007), 119–22, for a superb account of James's depression in his early years and of his famous decision to shake off the inertia inspired by the idea that all is determined, by declaring, "My first act of free will shall be to believe in free will" (120).

4. William James, *Pragmatism: A New Name for Some Old Ways of Thinking* (1907), in *Pragmatism and Other Writings* (New York: Penguin, 2000), 123–24.

5. Ibid., 219–41, 267–304. The essays "Is Life Worth Living?," "On a Certain Blindness in Human Beings," and "What Makes a Life Significant" are the first places to consult to see how James links the idea of possibility to the idea of action.

6. James's psychology is fundamentally individualistic. Social customs and/or institutions play very little role in his account of how people think and act. By way of contrast, John Dewey increasingly adopts a viewpoint best described under the term "social psychology," while George Herbert Mead provides the fullest version of a "pragmatist" philosophy wedded to a full-blown sociology.

7. "Meliorism treats salvation as neither necessary nor impossible. It treats it as a possibility, which becomes more and more of a probability the more numerous

the actual conditions of salvation become. It is clear that pragmatism must incline toward meliorism. Some conditions of the world's salvation are actually extant, and she cannot possibly close her eyes to this fact: and should the residual conditions come, salvation would become an accomplished reality. Naturally the terms I use here are exceedingly summary. You may interpret the word 'salvation' in any way you like. . . . What now are the complementary conditions? They are first such a mixture of things as will in the fullness of time give us a chance, a gap that we can spring into, and finally, *our act*. Does our act then *create* the world's salvation so far as it makes room for itself, so far as it leaps into the gap? Does it create, not the whole world's salvation of course, but just so much of this as itself covers of the world's extent?" (*Pragmatism*, 125).

8. "The Experience of Activity," appendix B of *A Pluralistic Universe*, in William James, *Writings 1902–1910* (New York: Library of America, 1987), 808.

9. Ibid., 808–9.

10. James, "The Moral Philosopher and the Moral Life," in *Pragmatism and Other Writings*, 254, 260. Subsequent page references are provided parenthetically in the text of my essay.

11. Gerald E. Meyers, *William James: His Life and Thought* (New Haven, Conn.: Yale University Press, 1986), 369.

12. James, "The Experience of Activity," 799.

13. James, "On a Certain Blindness in Human Beings," in *Pragmatism and Other Writings*, 267.

14. Ibid., 281.

15. James, "The Psychology of Belief," in *Writings 1878–1899* (New York: Library of America, 1992), 1035.

16. James, "On a Certain Blindness," 267.

17. Ibid., 271.

18. Ibid., 269.

19. Susan Wolf, *Meaning in Life and Why It Matters* (Princeton, N.J.: Princeton University Press, 2010).

20. I trust my reader can hear the echoes of Kant's description of judgment in my statement here. Judgment entails a kind of stepping away from the self to view it and the world from an "enlarged" or "broadened" perspective. It is only judgments that are derived from some such process that can proceed to solicit the agreement of the other. The nonsubjectivism of the process is what underwrites the claim to more than subjective validity.

21. William James, "Is Life Worth Living," in *Pragmatism and Other Writings*, 240.

22. "On the pragmatist side we have only one edition of the universe, unfinished, growing in all sorts of places, especially in places where thinking beings are at work" (*Pragmatism* in James, *Pragmatism and Other Writings*, 113).

23. Quoted from Richardson, *William James*, 181. For Gerald Meyers, James's subjectivism "is justifiable because there is a presumed harmony between our subjective interests and the objective world" (*William James*, 455). Without such a harmony, James's focus on the workings of subjective psychology would have no scientific value, no ability to tell us anything about the way things are. But James has no way, beyond an assertion of faith, to demonstrate the existence of that harmony.

24. James, *Pragmatism and Other Writings*, 113.

25. Quotations in this paragraph are from Wolf, *Meaning in Life*, 8–9.

26. The so-called "private language argument" is found in Wittgenstein, *Philosophical Investigations*, 88–104 (pars. 243–315). My understanding of this complex argument is highly influenced by Meredith Williams's interpretation of it in her *Wittgenstein, Mind and Meaning: Toward a Social Conception of Mind* (London: Routledge, 1999), esp. chs. 1 and 2. Richard M. Gale, "The Deconstruction of Traditional Philosophy in William James's Pragmatism," in *100 Years of Pragmatism: William James's Revolutionary Philosophy*, ed. John J. Stuhr (Bloomington: Indiana University Press, 2010), 108–23, notes James's "commitment to an in-principle private language that made James the major whipping boy of the later Wittgenstein" (111).

27. The quoted words in this sentence come from Hans-Johann Glock, *A Wittgenstein Dictionary* (Oxford: Blackwell, 1996), 311.

28. See Anthony Giddens, *Central Problems in Social Theory: Action, Structure, and Contradiction in Social Analysis* (Berkeley: University of California Press, 1979), and Pierre Bourdieu, *Outline of a Theory of Practice* (Cambridge: Cambridge University Press, 1977).

29. The concept of "grammar" is among the most difficult terms to grasp in Wittgenstein's work. I have found Newton Garver's essay, "Philosophy as Grammar," in *The Cambridge Companion to Wittgenstein* (Cambridge: Cambridge University Press, 1996), 139–70, an extremely useful guide to the issues here. Garver discusses the ways in which "grammar" in Wittgenstein plays a role similar to Kant's "transcendental conditions," as well as the ways in which Wittgenstein's view differs from Kant's. For my purposes, the important point is that "grammar" is a name for "conditions" that transcend the self and provide the grounds for the meaningfulness of individual actions; more radically, "grammar" indicates the conditions required to apprehend something as an action in the first place.

30. John Searle, *The Construction of Social Reality* (New York: Penguin, 1995). Searle is more directly influenced by J. L. Austin than by Wittgenstein. In particular, Searle's understanding of "social reality" is derived from Austin's work on performatives, and, more specifically, on Austin's meditations on the social conventions and institutions that underwrite the effectiveness of a performative utterance. To use one of Austin's favorite examples: to utter "I do" succeeds in enacting a marriage contract only when said in front of the requisite witnesses and before an official with the power to "pronounce" the two parties married. J. L. Austin, *How to Do Things with Words*, 2nd ed. (1962; rpt., Cambridge, Mass.: Harvard University Press, 1975). Austin outlines the conditions for a "felicitous" performance of a speech act on pp. 14–15.

31. Searle, *Construction of Social Reality*, 40.

32. "To imagine a language means to imagine a form of life. . . . The *speaking* of language is part of an activity, or of a form of life." Wittgenstein, *Philosophical Investigations*, 8, 11 (pars. 19 and 23).

33. Just how far such explicit awareness extends was a subject of debate at our conference on action. Even when I can answer the question "What are you doing?" by saying "I am playing tennis," I might very well be stumped by the question "How did you hit that backhand?," since I acted habitually in ways

established by years of practice. Generally, I am inclined to a Peircean and Wittgensteinian approach that would align consciousness with an ability to articulate something (no thoughts except through signs, to use Peirce's words), thus avoiding any notion of consciousness as a mental state that must accompany action or any substantive idea of an "unconscious" residing within the self. So the interesting question, for me, is the extent to which the agent is conscious of (i.e., can name) what she is doing, even though she is hardly conscious (in a mental state sense) at every moment when she is acting. I will only add here that I have not fully worked out how strong a claim about the consciousness of agents I think I can make, while fully admitting that certain habitual practices do resist articulation.

34. See Searle, *Construction of Social Reality*, 43–46.

35. Garver, "Philosophy as Grammar," 156.

36. As the example makes clear, the distinction between constitutive and regulative rules can be fuzzy. We can multiply the constitutive conditions so that actions which violate the regulations "don't count" as "touchdowns." In that case, all rules could come to look like constitutive rules. But think of minimum wage regulations. It is not that you have not hired someone to work for you if you pay them less than minimum wage. "What" action you are performing is still clear, but "how" you are performing that action (hiring someone) now violates society's regulation of how that action is to be performed.

37. Searle, *Construction of Social Reality*, 36.

38. Meredith Williams, in *Wittgenstein, Mind and Meaning*, captures this primacy of action in Wittgenstein when she writes: "Meaning is not passively given and then acted upon. Meaning is manifested in the acting itself. Meaning is shown in what is done. . . . Wittgenstein locates meaningfulness in its primary sense in the doing within a structured context. We may reflectively describe the meaning; but we do not thereby confer meaning on what was done. The meaning of what we do does not lie wholly within the individual's power to determine; indeed it mostly lies outside the individual's power. This is a consequence of the primacy of action. What we do in the circumstances carries a significance that cannot reflectively be altered" (56–57). This formulation carries a hint of the circularity that can drive readers of Wittgenstein crazy. But for my purposes in this essay, what Williams suggests is that we convey the term "action" precisely on those bodily movements that are meaningful. Actions create or manifest meaning; they are noteworthy, are attended to, are singled out as significant, because they are meaningful. And it is the names that we confer on an action that indicates the specific meaning we understand that action to carry.

39. Constitutions—and any kind of formal legal code—raise the fascinating issue of written versus unwritten rules. Written rules usually entail formal processes (and institutions) of enforcement, but unwritten rules are hardy unenforced, while the ways in which one learns unwritten rules can differ, but not necessarily so, from the way one learns written rules. For example, most baseball players have never read the rule book; learning the game involves both learning the written rules (the ones enforced by an umpire in a formal game) and the unwritten rules (which can be rules of thumb like never make the second out at third base or rules of etiquette like never try to steal a base when your team is winning by ten runs).

40. Hannah Arendt, *The Human Condition*, 2nd ed. (Chicago: University of Chicago Press, 1998), 198–99. Even in Arendt, the collective action (what she calls "acting in concert") that establishes the "space of appearances" that is the *polis* takes a back seat to the individualistic action that the space of appearances enables. But in her meditations on the "lost treasure" of the revolutionary tradition, she does provide a fuller account of the joys—and meaning—to be found in collective action. See *On Revolution* (1963; rpt., New York: Pelican, 1977), 215–82.

41. "Philosophy may in no way interfere with the actual use of language; it can in the end only describe it. For it cannot give it any foundation either. It leaves everything as it is." Wittgenstein, *Philosophical Investigations*, 49 (par. 124). For a discussion of the standard arguments for Wittgenstein's conservatism, along with an alternative way of reading him, see Bernard Williams, "Pluralism, Community and Left Wittgensteinianism," in *In the Beginning Was the Deed: Realism and Moralism in Political Argument* (Princeton, N.J.: Princeton University Press, 2005), 29–39.

42. Aristotle in the *Poetics* calls "metaphorical" namings "the most important by far," and goes on to tell us that skill in deploying metaphors "cannot be acquired from someone else, and is an indication of genius. For to make metaphors well is to observe what is like [something else]." Quoted from Vincent Leitch et al., eds., *Norton Anthology of Theory and Criticism*, 2nd ed. (New York: W. W. Norton, 2010), 108. Kant also describes "genius" as "an inborn disposition" that must be considered "natural," since it is "not a . . . skill that can be learned in accordance with some rule. . . . The author of a product that he owes to his genius does not know himself how the ideas for it come to him, and also does not have it in his power to think up such things at will or according to a plan, and to communicate to others precepts that would put them in a position to produce similar products." *Critique of the Power of Judgment*, section 46, quoted from Leitch et al., *Norton Anthology of Theory and Criticism*, 445–46. The source of novelty, then, is mysterious, something that demonstrably does happen, but cannot be accounted for and stretches the capacity of language to communicate, describe, or name it.

43. Giddens, *Central Problems in Social Theory*, defines action as "a stream of actual or contemplated causal interventions of corporal beings in the ongoing process of events-in-the-world" (55), which entails the notion of possibility insofar as action involves "'intervention' in a potentially malleable object-world" (56). Searle's point is that intervention in the natural world is very different from intervention in the social world because natural facts and social facts are differently constituted.

44. See Barry Barnes, *Understanding Agency: Social Theory and Responsible Action* (London: Sage, 2000).

45. J. L. Austin, "A Plea for Excuses," in *Philosophical Papers*, 175–204.

46. Ibid., 177.

47. Aristotle, *Nicomachean Ethics*, ed. and trans. Martin Ostwald (Upper Saddle River, N.J.: Prentice Hall, 1999), esp. book 3, provides one starting point for the ongoing philosophical engagement with the issue of voluntary (freely chosen) actions as contrasted to involuntary (compelled) actions.

48. Arendt, *Human Condition*, 179–80. Subsequent page references are provided parenthetically in the text of my essay.

49. Ibid., 257. "The miracle that saves the world, the realm of human affairs, from its normal, 'natural' ruin is ultimately the fact of natality, in which the faculty of action is ontologically rooted." I would argue that the grandiosity of this sentence, with its retreat to the ontological, evidences the thin ice on which Arendt's argument here rests. She has no better way of explaining novelty than Aristotle or Kant had to offer. She must assert novelty as a fact because she has no way to demonstrate it is so.

50. See "A Plea for Excuses," 175–77, for Austin's efforts to identify a full range of ways that one could give reasons for one's action.

51. Admittedly, the relation of action to character in Aristotle is problematic. Character (*hexis*) must be trained through the repetition of actions that lay a foundation of good habits. Once in place, character then (in most cases) will generate the right kinds of actions. William James adopts a similar approach in the famous chapter on habit in his *Psychology*. In Freud, however, character is a product of instinctual drives and early life experiences, not anything the self has done. Martin Ostwald captures the Aristotelean picture in his definition of the term *hexis* in the edition of *Nicomachean Ethics* I am using: "*hexis*: Characteristic, also Trained Ability, Characteristic Condition, Characteristic Attitude. A noun related to the verb *echein*, 'to have,' 'hold,' 'hold as a possession,' 'be in a certain condition,' designating a firmly fixed possession of the mind, established by repeated and habitual action. Once attained, it is ever present, at least in a potential form. The Latin interpreters of Greek philosophy rendered the term by *habitus*. . . . Hence, 'habit' has often been used as an English equivalent" (308–9). As we have seen, Bourdieu inflects the term "habitus" in a collective direction, whereas "habit" in James is fundamentally individualistic.

52. "A main source of our failure to understand is that we do not *command a clear view* of our use of words.—Our grammar is lacking in this sort of perspicuity. A perspicuous representation produces just this understanding which consists in 'seeing connexions.' Hence the importance of finding and inventing *intermediate cases*. The concept of a perspicuous representation is of fundamental significance to us." Wittgenstein, *Philosophical Investigations*, 49 (par. 122).

53. Aristotle, *Poetics*, 95. "For the historian and the poet do not differ according to whether they write in verse or without verse—the writings of Herodotus could be put into verse, but they would be no less a sort of history in verse than they are without verse. But the difference is that the former relates things that have happened, the latter things that may happen. For this reason, poetry is a more philosophical and serious thing than history; poetry tends to speak of universals, history of particulars." Quoted from Leitch et al., *Norton Anthology of Theory and Criticism*, 95.

The One and the Many in the Philosophy of Action

Christopher Yeomans

Most philosophers of action generally assume that there is a single phenomenon under discussion and a single (proper) conceptualization of notions such as agency, responsibility, and free will. But a strong minority tradition deserves recognition, one that emphasizes the essential role of plurality in the phenomena of agency. This tradition collects together philosophers as diverse as G. W. F. Hegel, Bernard Williams, Gary Watson, Hannah Arendt, and Robert Kane. In fact, one could even include Aristotle on this list, since he distinguishes between virtues of character and virtues of thought on the basis of which parts of the soul are involved, and further between virtue and continence as forms of successful agency. After an inquiry into the qualitative significance of this quantitative difference in the work of Kane, Arendt, and Hegel, we will end up with an appreciation of the value of a generalized form of what Wilfrid Sellars called the stereoscopic vision.

1. Robert Kane and the Plurality of Self-Conceptions

I want to begin with Robert Kane, who argues that the existence of multiple and competing purposes is a necessary condition for the kind of free will that libertarians hold is in turn necessary to validate our understanding of ourselves as sole and individual authors of our lives. Let's move backward, beginning at the end with Kane's structural conception of the process of free will and then asking why the striking pluralism of that conception is required. For our purposes, a consideration of Kane's view can state the theme of the one and the many, given the clarity with which he has developed both the specific shape of the many and its connection to the one.

Kane believes that sprinkled in among all of the actions for which we are responsible are some essential ones from which our deep responsibility for the others flows. He calls these Self-Forming Actions (SFAs), or, more precisely, Self-Forming Willings (SFWs), which he characterizes as the effort by which agents create and sustain their own ends or purposes. But it is essential to Kane's view that these Self-Forming Willings are cases in which we *struggle* to set the end that we want to set, and specifically because we also *want* to set some competing end, we *could* also set that competing end, and we have good *reasons* to do so. So as Kane sees it, these Self-Forming Willings are plural in three senses: they are plural voluntary, plural controlled, and plural rational. These track the three sense of willing itself, that is, that the will is desiderative, striving, and rational.[1]

In Kane's central example, a businesswoman who walks by a mugging on her way to a crucial sales meeting confronts a conflict between two internal perspectives, one urging her to establish or sustain the purpose of advancing her career and one urging her to establish or sustain the purpose of helping the victim.[2] The self-forming aspect of her decision is grounded in the fact that she could set either end (though it would take an effort either way), she wants to set each end (i.e., she has strong motivations both to advance her career and to help the mugging victim), and she has good reasons to set each end (since both the career and the assistance to the victim are objectively valuable pursuits).

But why is such plurality necessary? Here is Kane's answer with respect to two of the three kinds of plurality, namely plural rationality and plural voluntariness:

> To say that *these* self-forming acts could not be such that the agent's predominant motives and will were set one way when they were performed is to say that SFAs must be more-than-one-way rational or motivated. Moreover, we know that SFAs must also be plural voluntary from the R[esponsibility] condition of UR [Ultimate Responsibility], which requires that "something the agent voluntarily did, and for which the agent could have voluntarily done otherwise" made a difference in the agent's current motives and dispositions.[3]

But why plural (rational) control? Usually, the most that even libertarians think we need in the way of alternate possibilities for free will is a kind of two-way power to do or not to do something, in this case to set or not to set one of the purposes. Furthermore, the issue is not just coming up with a justification for leaving Ockham's razor unused in this instance. Rather, there is a real cost deriving from this plural control and the indeterminism it entails: "Paradoxical as it may seem, in order to have *ultimate* control over their destinies, possessors of free will must relinquish another kind of control at pivotal points in their life histories, namely, an antecedent determining control that would guarantee how things will turn out in advance."[4] So why pay this price?

As with the first two forms of plurality, that is, plural rationality and plural voluntariness, Kane's argument for the necessity of plural control is grounded in what he calls "Ultimate Responsibility." But then, of course, we need to ask why ultimate responsibility is worth wanting in the first place, and Kane's answer is that it is necessary for us to be individuals in the most robust sense of the term:

> In conclusion, then, why do we want free will? We want it because we want ultimate responsibility. And why do we want that? For the reason that children and adults take delight in their accomplishment from the earliest moments of their awakening as persons, whether these accomplishments are making a fist or walking upright or composing a symphony. This delight is no arbitrary feature of what we are. It is related to the fact that we first distinguish ourselves *as selves* distinct from the world by virtue of our ability to control some things by our wills, as the baby did her fist. Thereafter, we associate being a self in the full sense with imagining ourselves doing things—making, producing, creating, bringing about—as effecting changes in the world by our wills. . . . That is to say, creatures of higher consciousness such as we are have an unquenchable thirst for individuality and personhood (which I think are inextricably linked).[5]

Finally, Kane is almost unique in the contemporary literature on free will in drawing substantive moral and political conclusions from this view of free will: plural rationality requires a real value pluralism, and plural voluntariness requires that the political and social spheres make the plurality of values cognitively and affectively accessible to agents.

Well, so much for our forced march through Kane's very sophisticated and subtle theory, much of which has necessarily remained out of view; at this point I just want to get some different types of plurality on the table and use the justificatory structure provided by Kane to get a sense of their significance and connection. First, there is a plurality of aspects or axes of the will itself: the will is desiderative, rational, and striving. Second, there is plurality along each of these axes: SFWs are plural voluntary, plural rational, and plural (voluntary) controlled. Finally, there is a plurality of the objects of the will—of the ends that are desired, justified, and set and maintained through effort. And this last plurality is just as much objective as subjective on Kane's view, as one can see from his value pluralism. But the need for all of this plurality is grounded in a kind of singularity, that is, in the need to be somebody who matters as an individual as distinct from both other agents and the rest of the world. If we were not desiderative, rational, and striving creatures, we would not be identifiable sources of activity at all; and if we did not have the ability to set one particular end from among the many that we desire, that we find justified, and toward which we could strive, we would not be *ultimate* sources of activity. Finally, if there were not multiple objectively legitimate and incompatible ends and projects, the inner conflict that made such sourcehood possible would only be a matter of confusion, the proper object of therapy rather than respect.

I have long been struck by the similarity of the conceptual moves made by critical theorists and philosophers of action, despite the philosophical and social disdain with which each group regards the other. In what is probably only a continuation of my history of failure to successfully explain each to the other, here is another attempt. The basic form of this attempt will be to focus our attention on the similarities between Kane's and Arendt's interests in individuality. Since we've got structure in front of us, let's begin with some rough structural parallels:

> (1) for both, individuality is understood as a kind of sourcehood, and for both the grounding of the significance of that sourcehood in early childhood is more than a metaphor—rather a kind of metaphysics;
>
> (2) for both, there is a kind of indeterminacy or unpredictability that is necessary for true or ultimate sourcehood rather than just proximate sourcehood as a link in a longer causal or teleological chain;
>
> (3) for both, this conception of sourcehood is connected with the notion of public standing, of the need to "be somebody" irreplaceable in the shared world of appearance;
>
> (4) for both, it is in the very nature of (free) actions that they can be only a small minority of human activities.

But, of course, there are some essential differences on precisely these points:

> (1′) for Arendt, our natality means that sourcehood has to be distinguished from control—it is a kind of beginning without a goal to orient subsequent events; so whereas for Kane we are the source of *purposes*, for Arendt we are the sources of *new processes*;
>
> (2′) whereas Kane contrasts this indeterminacy with *antecedent* determining control, the contrast in Arendt is with *subsequent* determining control;
>
> (3′) whereas Kane thinks that one can "be somebody" in a number of different spheres and ways, Arendt thinks that such public standing can only be obtained in very specific circumstances; thus
>
> (4′) whereas Kane holds that true free action is a possibility available to most persons in modern society, Arendt despairs of its availability to any moderns, and precisely not in *society* as such.

Thus for each point there is a difference in conception that is related to a difference in justification. For the purposes of discussion we can group together the first two around the question of sourcehood and the second two around the question of the public shape of action. The first issue is thus predominantly conceptual and metaphysical, the second aesthetic and political. And in each issue there is a Hegelian intervention to be made to help us see how the two perspectives offer compatible insights into the nature of agency.

2. Sourcehood and Control

The issue of control has a long history in the debates about free will that we will not consider in any detail here. But most generally it has been associated with the kind of authorship needed to connect free will to individuality via the notion of *self*-determination. Here is where Arendt is at her most radical, since precisely because she wants to connect action to individuality in the strongest possible terms she denies that we can ever be authors of our actions in the relevant sense. Indeed, she goes as far as to say that action is essentially anonymous, and she sees no direct interpersonal mitigation of this unsettling aspect of action. At best one's action can be picked up by a fabricator of stories that take their place within a community of remembrance, but that is quite unlike the way that promising mitigates the unpredictability of action and forgiveness mitigates its permanence, which are the other two essential and unsettling features of action identified by Arendt. But the agent and the author of the story about the agent are engaged in two fundamentally different kinds of activity. The latter is one in which there is, in fact, no reflection of the author in the finished product, and so authorship is the wrong model for agency:

> The disclosure of the "who" through speech, and the setting of a new beginning through action, always fall into an already existing web where their immediate consequences can be felt. . . . It is because of this already existing web of human relationships, with its innumerable, conflicting wills and intentions, that action almost never achieves its purpose; but it is also because of this medium, in which action alone is real, that it "produces" stories with or without intention as naturally as fabrication produces tangible things. . . . Although everybody started his life by inserting himself into the human world through action and speech, nobody is the author or producer of his own life story. In other words, the stories, the results of action and speech, reveal an agent, but this agent is not an author or producer. Somebody began it and is its subject in the twofold sense of the word, namely its actor and sufferer, but nobody is its author.[6]

Stories are naturally produced by action precisely because the medium in which action takes place is the plurality of other agents and their perspectives; the space in which they appear is thus an interpretive space. That plurality then serves as both the condition for the possibility of being the main character in one's life story and yet the condition for the impossibility of having control over that story. Thus the significance of action cannot lie in purposes that are rarely, if ever achieved; instead, the significance of action lies precisely in its novelty, which is deeply connected to the kind of irreplaceable individuality Arendt sees as being embodied in true action. So, to take one recent political example, the U.S. ban on horse slaughter on the basis of animal welfare considerations has been found to result in poorer conditions for domestic horses, without a reduction in the overall number of horses slaughtered (who are simply shipped to Canada and Mexico for that purpose). One might then, from an Arendtian point of view, see the significance of the original slaughter ban in its reaction to the prior regime of domestic slaughterhouses, rather than in its subsequent effects.

But the radical nature of Arendt's view here should not blind us to the fact that Arendt and Kane have common cause against the notion of agency as self-mastery or absolute sovereignty—we already saw this in Kane's view that plural voluntary control was not just compatible with but in fact required the absence of antecedent determining control. The difference is in what they take to be the predominant form of disruption of that mastery and its temporal orientation. To begin with Arendt, the paradoxical thing about novelty is that it is essentially backward-looking; something is new with respect to what came before it rather than what comes after it.[7] On Arendt's description, the agent turns their glance away from a future they do not control and back to a past with respect to which they can at least control their difference. This is also true in the specifically political dimension of action as well, where Arendt emphasizes the priority of the retrospective legitimation of action by reference to prior agreement (i.e., true politics) as opposed to prospective justification of action by reference to a goal (i.e., administration or bureaucracy).[8] On Kane's description the agent looks forward to purposes that have to be set against the background of a plurality of psychic investments that undermines past control; on Arendt's description the agent looks back toward the past from which she differentiates herself against the foreground of a plurality of external perspectives that places the outcome of the processes she initiates outside her control.

As so often in philosophy, our guiding parable here ought to be the blind men and the elephant. There is every reason to believe that both sources of disruption and both temporal orientations are essential to agency. Here is where Hegel comes in, since he provides the conceptual structure to wed the two perspectives together, just as Kane and Arendt provide the phenomenology to articulate the significance of that structure. And to return to our opening question, the crucial point is that it is precisely the pluralism of each view that makes this possible.

One way of getting at this point is to pick up on Arendt's own self-understanding of the difference between her view and those in the free will debate as one between her own object-oriented perspective focused on public acts and their subject-oriented perspective focused on the will as an internal capacity. The dominance of this latter orientation in modern philosophy is part of the explanation for why it cannot see the distinction between labor and work (which is obvious, Arendt thinks, if one looks at the differences between the physical and social conditions and products of the two activities rather than attending only to the subjective intentional stances involved). These two poles—the object-oriented and the subject-oriented—are the two poles of what Hegel calls "reflection," which I have argued elsewhere is another name for the logical phenomenon of expression.[9] And what Hegel gives us is a framework for seeing the two orientations as two processes that are locked in a kind of recursive and reciprocal interaction.

There is no space to go into the details of Hegel's conception here, but some terminology may be helpful: expression ("reflection") involves two different sides: creation ("positing") and interpretation ("reflection-into-self"). They exist in a kind of dynamic feedback loop: first, an inchoate idea or content is posited in an articulated form that is differentiated both from its own simple content and from other articulated forms to which it stands in relation; then it is reflected into itself when aspects of this differentiated form are built back into the original idea, making it a more determinate basis for further creation.[10] But the crucial thing for Hegel is that any expression involves these two processes working in tandem, since he denies that one can make sense of expression as a simple disclosure or translation of an already given content. So whereas Maurizio Passerin d'Entrèves wants to distinguish between expressive and communicative aspects of agency in Arendt's thought, the Hegelian idea would be that the notion of communication just brings out the aspect of interpretation that was already implicit in the notion of expression.[11] Arendt sometimes writes as if the political actor were completely lacking in self-awareness—a mere condition for the construction of meaning by storytellers in their audience. But given the tight connection between action and speech and the paradigmatic status of Pericles's funeral oration, that cannot be her considered view.

There are clearly real advantages to Arendt's rigorously object-oriented perspective here, and enough similarities with Hegel's treatments of stoicism and Kantian moral psychology to suggest a deep political and aesthetic affinity that we will take up in the next section. In my view, *The Human Condition* in particular is remarkably effective at bringing into relief the different constellations of relations between agents' talents and interests, the public world and our collective projects in it; and also very good at illuminating the way that those different elements change their significance when their relations change: for example, the way the meaning of the public world of fabricated objects changes when those objects are primarily related to our talent for and interest in consumption rather than permanence or self-disclosure. But I will not be the first reader of Arendt to point out distortions in plain view as well. Of particular relevance to our theme is that she apportions the two sides of expression to two different intersubjective positions or, even more problematically, to two different kinds of people. There is the actor who creates and discloses, and the author or spectator who interprets. This gives us the strain in Arendt's thought that is sometimes characterized as elitist (Canovan) or heroic (Parekh), and her hyperbolic denials of the possibility of action in (mass) society as such in which all behavior has been regularized.

We have already seen in more detail the structural clarity enabled by Kane's rigorously subject-oriented perspective (i.e., his emphasis on free will rather than free action). The distortion thus introduced by Kane is the loss of the sense in which the projects or purposes set by the will are also relations to other persons or ways of life. Thus despite his cogent and (for a libertarian) unexpected attack on the conception of agency as self-mastery and his drawing of substantive moral and political conclusions, his conception remains atomistic, even if only by default. This comes out in his left-libertarian politics. But this seems to undermine his own acknowledgment of the need to be somebody in the public sphere, that is, the need for recognition or *Anerkennung* in the Hegelian sense. This distortion here is the cut between the plurality of motivational investments within the agent and the plurality of forms of activities and human relations present and possible in any given society. Thus the *qualitative* significance of the plurality of those investments tends to get lost in Kane's thought. Arendt's diagnosis of this general failing in modern philosophy of action traces it exactly back to the subjective perspective, arguing that it thus represents theorizing about action under conditions where it has effectively become impossible as a recognizable phenomenon in the public world.

Neither distortion is a complete obscuring, though they sometimes come close. Arendt acknowledges that actions have purposes—they just appear to play no role in their deepest significance on her view—and Kane acknowledges that the recognition of multiple ends as legitimate by other agents is a necessary condition for the internal plurality of ends.

But here is the thing about Arendt's view: she has rather little to say about how action and speech generate or constitute the kind of plurality that serves as their own condition of possibility. That plurality instead appears in her work as a kind of brute historical given with respect to the individual agent, and this is part of what leads her to a paradoxical conception of action that is simultaneously narrowly political and yet completely divorced from the content of politics. In fact, it is quite difficult to see what the content of action is, on Arendt's view. That the Hegelian diagnosis here goes under the name of "external reflection" should not be surprising given Arendt's object-oriented approach. Hegel thinks that we rather easily forget that interpretation itself is an activity, or, more broadly, that activity partially constitutes its own conditions.[12] Arendt is sometimes so taken with the radical novelty of action that she doesn't see that any action is only novel in some particular respect, which respect actually constitutes the sense in which the old hangs together as one thing from which the new differentiates itself. So the realm of nondifferentiation is taken to be objectively given (i.e., labor and work), rather than distinctively constituted by new action.

This will lead us on to the topic of the next section—the places and ways in which free action is possible—but before we go in that direction I want to point out a fundamental result: this distortion introduced by Arendt's view can be compensated by appeal to Kane's view. Once one can see the plurality of ends that serve as the basis of the effort of self-determination as itself a product of the agent's interpretations of the actions of other individuals in the public sphere, then one begins to see the way in which those other actions provide the content for the disclosure of the agent's individuality along Arendt's lines. Because Arendt doesn't have the structurally sophisticated metaphysics that Kane has, she has a kind of allergy to the notion that others' actions could provide that content, even when her own analysis of Greek political life shows otherwise. But Kane's view gives us the internal structure to show how these other projects and actions could serve as the input, as it were, for a robust process of self-determination. It would be a source of inner disruption, to be sure, but Kane has the rationale for precisely why such inner disruption is necessary for robust self-determination.

And the distortion introduced by Kane's view can then be compensated by Arendt's view, since the multiplicity of ends that make free will possible can itself be seen as a multiplicity of actual and potential relations to other agents. Thus the value experiments are less atomistic projects and more contributions to types or spheres of actions in which one can be somebody in the public world—but again this leads us to the topic of the following section, so we will leave off here. To conclude *this* section let us return to the question we posed at the outset of the essay, namely the qualitative significance of quantitative plurality.

More particularly the question is, What role is plurality playing here, and how it is playing it? The fundamental role that we have just seen is to displace the inner/outer distinction from its centrality in thinking about agency. Once we use the Hegelian logical scaffolding to join Kane's and Arendt's views together, we get a sense of the dynamic way in which the inner can take on the significance of the outer and vice versa. In terms of how plurality is playing this role, I believe that the kind of plurality that matters is a kind of mean. If we have no plurality—for example, if there is only one goal (on Kane's view) or only one way of behaving (on Arendt's)—we have no individuality at all and thus no true agency or action. And for the same reason: on that hypothesis, there is no beginning or even (on Kane's view) sustaining something begun against temptations or other motivations, therefore there is no sourcehood. But if we have too many goals or behaviors their differences run away into insignificance and thus we similarly lack the robust, contrastive identification with ends or courses of action that is required for sourcehood. This is something that post-Kantians such as Jacobi saw in Kant's moral psychology: action is either motivated by the moral law, or by natural inclinations that are just physical events like any other; in either case, it is essentially anonymous. Or, to use Hegel's logical jargon, individuality cannot be grounded exclusively in either universality or particularity.

Thus Kane's left-libertarianism seems an unsatisfying political response to his own theory of free will for reasons Arendt is well positioned to diagnose: that is, all of these different experiments in living have to be thought in relation to each other somehow, and so they are made commensurable by the one value of utility, which then has to be flattened out further into a mere concern for happiness that evacuates any remaining sense of contrastive significance of the experiments themselves. So, interestingly, both Kane and Arendt hold that truly free action is impossible under conditions of totalitarianism, but they differ in their political diagnosis of how widespread totalitarianism is in the contemporary world: Arendt thinks that it is the basic form of modern political life, whereas Kane sees it as an isolated phenomenon. And unless one has this tractable number of projects, ends, political factions, and ideals, the internal side of agency runs away into a blooming, buzzing confusion of mental states as on empiricist descriptions, and thus no meaningful map or translation can be offered between the inner options and outer differences that confront the agent.

And here is something important about the way in which Hegel's notion of reflection connects these two views: it is not so much a circuit as a continual development—a spiral, if you like, rather than a circle. Because expression never completes a circuit and comes back to exactly the point at which it started, it is always a matter of interpretation (in the technical sense above of "reflection-into-self") whether it has succeeded.

But once one has a plurality within this mean, one has a tractable number of contrasts, and the very significance of those contrasts works to break down the absoluteness of the individual subject as a unit of analysis. Kane's agent *works* to identify herself with one of the particular versions of the self that is pressing itself forward for consideration. Arendt's Greek politician *works* to display his own excellence in part by identifying with a particular faction.

3. The Public Shape of Action

In this section we want to pick up on the following similarities and differences from above:

> (3) for both Arendt and Kane, their conception of sourcehood is connected with the notion of public standing, of the need to "be somebody" irreplaceable in the shared world of appearance; but whereas Kane thinks that one can "be somebody" in a number of different spheres and ways, Arendt thinks that such public standing can only be obtained in very specific circumstances; and

(4) for both, it is in the very nature of (free) actions that they can be only a small minority of human activities; but whereas Kane holds that true free action is a possibility available to most persons in modern society, Arendt despairs of its availability to any moderns, and precisely not in *society* as such.

Here I want to pick up on a few themes that go to the points about plurality just made: that is, at the object level it displaces the inner/outer contrast, and at the theoretical level it allows for a kind of compatibilism.

The first point requires us to return to perhaps the most basic pluralism in Kane's view, which is the idea that the will is rational, desiderative, and striving. Part of the pleasure of reading *The Significance of Free Will* lies in the counterpoint between these three senses and their different forms of plurality. As it turns out, Hegel is up to something similar in distinguishing between three constitutive projects of self-determination: self-appropriation, specification of content, and effectiveness. That is, in action we are trying to take possession of ourselves, to distinguish the signal from the noise of our lives, and to actually do what we want to do.[13] There are rough structural parallels here with Kane—rationality is essential to self-appropriation, desires (in the broad sense) to the content of our wills, and striving is the effort to be effective—but what interests me most here is the tension between the three. What Hegel slowly comes to see is that these three projects are both mutually necessary and yet impossible to jointly carry out to their fullest extent. The very activities that allow for maximal specification of content, for example, tend to minimize our ability to appropriate that content or to play a fundamental role in realizing it in the external world. For example, the very wholehearted identification with one perspective can make it difficult to grasp other perspectives and thus to offer good reasons to others in defense of one's own perspective (self-appropriation) or to account for those other perspectives in carrying out plans defined by one's own (effectiveness).

The point I want to take away from this is that it leaves agency as a kind of problem that has multiple solutions, each of which has certain advantages and disadvantages compared to the others. This then generates an explicit connecting tissue between the inner and the outer, as a shared inner problem can be solved in at least three basic ways which are then embodied externally by different kinds of lives. For Hegel wonks in the audience, these basic ways are the three forms of accountability identified by Hegel in the Morality section of the *Philosophy of Right* as the rights of knowledge, intention, and insight into the good. And the embodiment goes under a name—"*die Stände*"—that is almost impossible to translate into English but is nowadays usually rendered as "the estates": farmers and soldiers, workers and managers, public servants and merchants.

Perhaps the most interesting and unexpected thing is the way that Hegel's social theory of agency maps onto Arendt's philosophical anthropology and yet offers importantly different interpretations of modern social life. So, to expand on the example above, Hegel associates the first form of accountability with success at specification of content, and thus with wholeheartedness, contentment, and enjoyment at the expense of long-term planning, principled justification, and efficacy over a wide range of conditions. This is the life of farmers and soldiers and, in his way of seeing things, women (due to their exclusive orientation to domestic life). There are, of course, many similarities between this description and what Arendt calls labor as opposed to work and action—similarities in the social location, orientation, and advantages and disadvantages of this way of life. But what Hegel's deeper pluralism about the structure of agency allows him to see is that there is real individual self-determination and thus action here, because there is at least minimal self-appropriation and effectiveness and great success at the other, third project of specification of content. Hegel is willing to meet Arendt halfway here in agreeing that those leading this way of life have difficulty recognizing their individuality—but precisely because of their tie to the particular features of geography and family that bound their lives, there is a uniqueness and specificity to their character that is appropriated largely in affective terms through enjoyment and trust. While we cannot address the point in detail here, there are similarly interesting connections between work and Hegel's second form of accountability, and action and the third.[14]

Instead, I want to focus on the shared problems of Arendt's and Hegel's view, or rather two different problems that stem from the same source, namely the apportioning of different forms of agency to different persons leading different ways of life in different spheres. For Arendt this apportioning is occasional, and it is problematic because of her steeply hierarchical account of the different activities. For Hegel the apportioning is fundamental, and it is problematic largely because the society to which they are apportioned bears so little resemblance to our own.

But we can radicalize Hegel's view of the three forms of agency even further by subjecting it to his own theory of reflection, and thereby at the same time maintain some of the phenomenological power of Arendt's description while rejecting her disdain for bourgeois life. As we have already seen, Hegel sees true self-determination in all three forms of agency, but agrees with Arendt that it is difficult to express the individuality of that self-determination both in what Arendt calls life and in bureaucratic administration. But I believe that the best analysis of the possibilities of agency in our own contemporary society requires combining the occasionalism, if I may, of Arendt's view with the more developed reflective or expressive structure of Kane's and Hegel's view. What I mean by the former is Arendt's recognition that all human lives involve labor, work, and action (even if any particular agent may be oriented *primarily* toward one of the three); what I mean by the latter is implicit in Kane and explicit in Hegel's notion that action partially constitutes its own conditions of possibility and significance (i.e., its presuppositions).

If we add to this conceptual idea a key component of Hegel's understanding of (civil) society—namely that it contains precisely the mixture of equality and distinctiveness that Arendt associates only with the political realm—I think we get something like the following picture: the three forms of activity are not fixed in terms of their ability to express individuality, but precisely by expressing individuality in a particular way each constitutes a background of conformity against which that individuality stands out. So, for example, one might express one's individuality through a deep investment in one's family, but at the cost of constituting one's career as "just a job" or even leaving the career to a spouse. Or one might dedicate oneself to public service, but at the expense of thinning out one's family relations to institutionally required performances or even not starting one's own nuclear family at all. We have, of course, common exemplars who represent the extremes of such choices—homemaking mothers would be an example of the first, celibate priests of the second—so there is always a complex and politically problematic relation between inner and outer here: between choices and roles, as it were. The temptations of strictly apportioning such roles to *kinds* or *types* of people, even on the basis of choice (as for men in Hegel), must be resisted. Nonetheless, the external visibility of the trade-offs entailed by precisely this radical power of action to constitute its own presuppositions is crucial in order to bring into relief the internal stakes of action, and thus to make individual self-determination possible.

4. Conclusions

Well, what do we get out of this big game of compare-and-contrast? The two fundamental theoretical benefits conferred by pluralism are that it displaces the inner/outer contrast at the object level and allows for a kind of compatibilism at the theoretical level. But it should be clear that these are just two sides of the same coin, or two different ways of seeing the same theoretical function. The very object-level plurality (whether of the aspects of the will in Kane and Hegel or the types of activity in Hegel and Arendt) provides multiple standpoints from which to formulate theories about action as a whole, each of which naturally emphasizes or clarifies some of its features while de-emphasizing or distorting others. There is, to generalize a term from Wilfrid Sellars, a kind of stereoscopic vision.[15] And to push the metaphor a bit further, in human beings what stereoscopic vision gives us is a sense of distance and thus what Sellars calls our knowing our way around a landscape.

Or, to use a related metaphor, the pluralism at issue is a bit like the topological notion of an atlas of maps. When a three-dimensional space such as a sphere (e.g., roughly, the earth) is projected onto two-dimensional maps, a non-Euclidean space is represented by a Euclidean space. This allows better comprehension of the topological characteristics of the space but at the cost of some distortion. What topologists call the maximal atlas is the collection of all such map projections and the additional transition map that allows points on one map to be transformed into points on the other map, and this atlas defines a non-Euclidean manifold in Euclidean terms. The forms of plurality we have considered are like the different map projections of the atlas: moderately distorted yet truth-revealing. But two natural tendencies must be resisted: on the one hand, the tendency to think that there is some further, single perspective from which every point immediately appears in undistorted relation to every other point; and, on the other hand, the tendency to think the ineliminability of distortion entails that we can have no firm grasp of truth and must therefore lapse into skeptical antirealism or a Heideggerian mysticism of unconcealment. To pick up particularly on the difference between Arendt and Kane, there is no third pure or absolute form of expression or reflection that would be both object-oriented and subject-oriented at the exact same time, but there are Hegelian conceptual ways of understanding how the distortions introduced by one orientation are compensated by accuracies introduced by the other orientation, and vice versa. Pluralism is what makes these reciprocal compensations possible.

Notes

1. Strictly speaking, this isn't quite right, since (a) voluntariness involves not merely desiring but desiring more than any other alternatives (and thus the plurality of voluntariness involves not merely desiring different things but the possibility that different things could be most desired); and (b) voluntariness also requires lack of coercion. See Robert Kane, *The Significance of Free Will* (New York: Oxford University Press, 1998), 30. But for our purposes in stating the theme, we will accept this minor distortion as the price to be paid for the structural clarity at which we aim.

2. Kane sees this as a conflict between moral and prudential reasons, but that interpretation isn't essential to the example, even on Kane's own view, since such moral choices are only the sharpest example of the incommensurability between purposes that necessitates the effort to set the will.

3. Kane, *The Significance of Free Will*, 114.

4. Ibid., 144.

5. Ibid., 100–101.

6. Hannah Arendt, *The Human Condition*, 2nd ed. (Chicago: University of Chicago Press, 1998), 184.

7. The notion of a beginning—also important for Arendt—just combines that novelty with the subsequent causal or teleological chain, and so shares this predominantly retrospective character.

8. See, e.g., Arendt, *Crises of the Republic: Lying in Politics; Civil Disobedience; On Violence; Thoughts on Politics and Revolution* (New York: Mariner Books, 1972), 151.

9. Christopher Yeomans, *Freedom and Reflection: Hegel and the Logic of Agency* (New York: Oxford University Press, 2011).

10. In schematic form this is actually quite close to Sellars's understanding of the "dialectical interplay" between the manifest image (which limits itself to correlations between perceptible events) and the scientific image (which posits imperceptible objects to explain those correlations). See "Philosophy and the Scientific Image of Man," in Wilfrid Sellars, *Science, Perception, and Reality* (London: Routledge & Kegan Paul, 1963), 1–40, at 19–20.

11. Maurizio Passerin d'Entrèves, *The Political Philosophy of Hannah Arendt* (London: Routledge, 1993), ch. 2. For a characterization of Arendt on expression quite close to the one of Hegel offered here, see John McGowan, *Hannah Arendt: An Introduction* (Minneapolis: University of Minnesota Press, 1997), 64.

12. There is every reason to think that Arendt should have seen this, given her views about how historical events do the same thing (and thus cannot be said to be caused in the strict sense), but again her object-oriented approach continually blurs this feature of individual human agency—it is there, but out of focus and therefore prone to being forgotten or minimized. This is a nice example of Sellars's point that in the stereoscopic vision each perspective is present in the image of the other perspective, but distorted ("Philosophy and the Scientific Image of Man," 8). See Arendt, *Essays in Understanding, 1930–1954*, ed. Jerome Kohn (New York: Harcourt Brace, 1994), 319, and the discussion in McGowan, *Hannah Arendt*, 55–56.

13. See Hegel, *Hegel's Philosophy of Right*, trans. T. M. Knox (London: Oxford University Press, 1967), §§25–26. A fuller argument for the interpretation briefly summarized here can be found in my *Expansion of Autonomy: Hegel's Pluralistic Philosophy of Action* (New York: Oxford University Press, 2015).

14. Briefly, in each case Hegel roughly agrees with Arendt on the division of phenomenal features between the forms of agency—and roughly their social location as well—but his more detailed pluralism allows him to see agency where Arendt denies it and to problematize it where she sees it. Work is the province of the estate of producers and managers and turns primarily on the power of self-appropriation via the products, skills, and teamwork involved. For action, however, there is a more fundamental contrast. Hegel sees politics (outside of the monarch) as largely the province of civil servants and others who put their shoulders to the wheel for the common good and thus tend to become anonymous. Whereas Arendt's typology of activity is intended to build up to the one pure form of action that delivers individuality, Hegel's is intended to reveal the success, failures, and pathologies of individuation that attend to each form of activity.

15. And perhaps it is not much of a generalization, since it is easy to see Kane as emphasizing the scientific image of human beings and Arendt as trying to trace the manifest image back to the original image of which it is the "sophistication and refinement" ("Philosophy and the Scientific Image of Man," 18). Furthermore, the suggestion of a mediating tissue of types or social groups is crucial to Sellars's own suggestion for the way to make the stereoscopic vision come into focus and is, at least at one point in the essay, associated with Hegel's distinctive contribution to the problem (ibid., 16, 39–40).

Toward a Democratic Theory of Judgment

Linda M. G. Zerilli

What would it mean to foreground the capacity to judge critically and reflectively as a central feature of modern democratic citizenship? This question, raised poignantly albeit not systematically in the work of Hannah Arendt, is of crucial importance for political theory today. For Arendt, the problem of judgment arises in the wake of the collapse of inherited criteria for judgment, or what she called the final break in tradition brought about by the political catastrophes of the twentieth century.[1] For contemporary theorists the problem of how to judge in the absence of these criteria remains an important one. But our focus must be different. The problem is not only the collapse of traditional standards but also how to take account of the plurality of standards that characterize multiethnic and multiracial societies such as the United States and, increasingly, Western Europe.

In light of political events and the "clash of civilizations" declared by neoconservatives such as Samuel Huntington, we find ourselves increasingly called on to make judgments about practices and cultures not always our own, judgments that require, among other things, an ability to imagine how the world looks to people whose standpoints we do not necessarily share. As Huntington's work suggests, the temptation here is to employ our own concepts as rules with which to judge other practices and cultures. But then the question arises as to whether we have engaged in the act of critical judging—or have we, rather, applied the concepts of "our" culture to the particulars of "theirs," all the better to confirm what we already know and claim to be? With this question arises a related temptation: if we reject such a rule-governed practice of judgment as, say, uncritical and ethnocentric, then perhaps we have little choice but to adopt the position of the proverbial relativist. As radically divergent views can be equally valid depending on one's standpoint and membership in a particular culture, so this relativist holds, it is best not to judge at all. Who are we—outsiders—to judge?[2]

The presuppositions about judging that inform the aforementioned positions have been criticized in a rich philosophical literature on the possibility of understanding another culture. Whereas the first assumes that to judge tout court is to subsume particulars under concepts already given in one's society, the second assumes that we cannot comprehend, let alone judge, what is foreign or unknown to us at all. As Ludwig Wittgenstein, Peter Winch, Charles Taylor, John McDowell, and Donald Davidson show us, there are good reasons for questioning these related pictures of judging, beginning with the idea that to judge is to organize experience according to a "conceptual scheme," which can be radically incommensurable across cultures.[3] Such an idea misconstrues language as a prison house of sorts, which greatly inhibits or renders fully impossible communication between members of different linguistic communities.

This philosophical debate, though invaluable, does not address another—and in my view more troubling—feature of these twin views of judging. The idea that judgment is a wholly rule-governed practice whose inherent conceptual dogmatism can be avoided only through the infinite deferral of judging itself is not only philosophically incoherent but also politically untenable. We, citizens of Western democracies, need to make judgments about cultures and practices not always our own and, where appropriate, lend or refuse them our political support. In fact, we already make such judgments: we make them when we vote for our political representatives on the basis of their public judgments (e.g., where to give foreign aid or to intervene militarily, whether English should be the official language of the United States, or whether to allow Sharia law in the settling of disputes among American Muslims, to take obvious examples); and we make them in everyday life (e.g., when we decide what products to buy or to boycott, what causes to support or to fight, what neighborhood to live in or to avoid). The question, then, is not whether we make judgments but what making them entails. "Ultimately," to speak with Vivasvan Soni, "it is not judgment itself that can be avoided, only responsibility for the judgment and recognition of the process of judgment."[4]

The Problem of Judgment

In contemporary political theory there are several ways in which judgments are formed and yet the problem of judgment is occluded. The first concerns the tendency in the work of neo-Kantian democratic thinkers such as John Rawls, Jürgen Habermas, and Seyla Benhabib to define the problem of judgment wholly as a problem of adjudicating value conflicts in the absence of universal criteria and a transcendent conception of the good. It is not that these theorists mourn the loss of a common standard according to which such conflicts could be rationally adjudicated, nor do they lament the empirical fact of value pluralism itself; on the contrary, they celebrate both as the achievement of liberal democratic societies. Nevertheless, this celebratory spirit is also deeply cautious and tempered by a persistent worry about widespread value differences run amuck, as it were, with no way of deciding in favor of liberal democratic values, save by means of a groundless will.[5] To forestall such decisionism, neo-Kantians advance the idea of public reason, with which they seek ever more neutral grounds "to separate by argumentation generalizable interests from those that are and remain particular," as Habermas puts it.[6]

The problem with the neo-Kantian ideal of public reason is not so much that it seeks to restrict certain kinds of speech, as many critics before me have held, but that it becomes hard to see how speakers and claims that are not already heard as political could come to count as such within any given sociopolitical context. If a central problem of judgment today, as Arendt suggests, is how to judge without falling back on concepts that render the unfamiliar the already known, then we should ask whether adherence to the rules of public reason, which works to sort particular from generalizable claims, might not hinder rather than facilitate the ability to judge critically and reflectively, that is, in the absence of a rule. Haunting the neo-Kantian deliberative approach is what Arendt called "the problem of the new," that is, how to take account of the inaugural character of phenomena at all.[7]

But there is another problem. Deliberative approaches to intercultural value conflicts assume that disputes can be resolved by discursive argumentation.[8] The ability of conceptual, discursive rationality to settle stark differences of opinion on public issues tends to presuppose the very shared sensibility that neo-Kantians deny as having any real relevance to political life. It is not difficult to see how I might reach agreement with someone who already shares my sense of what Rawls calls "reasonableness," itself rooted in basic values, cultural background, or worldview. In that case, the proper application of concepts to the particulars of political life may well strike me as having "the unforced force of the better argument," to speak with Habermas. But are those the conflicts that really concern us today?

These two tendencies in neo-Kantian democratic theory—the tendency of public reason to foreclose the inaugural power of speech and action, on the one hand, and the reliance on conceptual, discursive rationality as the means for settling value conflicts, on the other—may well lie behind what I see as a second way in which the problem of judgment is occluded in contemporary political theory. I am speaking about the ontological turn to affect (and, in some cases, cognitive neuroscience) that characterizes the work of an ever-growing group of scholars, including William Connolly, Leslie Thiele, Jane Bennett, Davide Panagia, John Protevi, and Jennifer Nedelsky.[9] The efforts of these theorists to uncover and foreground the noncognitive processes tracked in affect theory and cognitive neuroscience can be understood as recoiling from the rationalism that shapes neo-Kantian deliberative models of democracy.[10] More specifically, they recoil from the highly conceptualist interpretation of the Copernican turn, according to which, as Wilfrid Sellars puts it, "to have the ability to notice a sort of thing is already to have the concept of that sort of thing."[11] On the face of it, this strictly conceptualist way of thinking about our relation to the world, as these thinkers suggest, makes it hard to see how we could discern anything new in it at all.

As someone who has been critical of the overly cognitivist models of political thinking, action, and judgment that inform neo-Kantian approaches, I understand and in certain respects appreciate this development in political theory. I recognize as important the challenge to conceptions of politics that rely on exaggerated ideas of human autonomy and reason and that remain in the grip of what Stanley Cavell has called the epistemological quest. The general ascendancy of an ontological register in political theory, of which the turn to affect is part, recognizes the dependence of propositional intentionality on a background of practical attunements to situated environments. In this sense, the turn to affect takes place on the larger terrain carved out by postfoundational thinkers such as Heidegger, Wittgenstein, Taylor, and Gadamer, each of whom conceives of propositional knowledge ("knowing-that") as connected to a vast, ungrounded background of preconceptual ways of being in the world ("knowing-how"). But there is also a crucial departure from this hermeneutic strand of philosophy. Affect is presented as a distinct layer of experience that is both prior to and beneath intentional consciousness. When the postfoundationalist avowal of embodied "knowing-how" is interpreted in terms of so-called "layer-cake" ontologies of practice, as it is in affect theory, there is a tendency "to simply assert the conceptual priority of previously denigrated terms—affect over reason, practice over representation," observes Clive Barnett. "This model of conceptual priority puts in place a view of practical attunement as a stratum that is autonomous of propositional intentionality. It is treated as a layer that, Robert Brandom writes, 'could be in place before, or otherwise in the absence of the particular linguistic practices that permit anything to show up or be represented as merely *there*.'"[12]

The problem with the turn to affect is not the critique of excessively cognitivist models of action and judgment, nor the attempt to account for the neglected embodied dispositions of subjects when thinking about ethical and political agency. The problem, as Barnett clarifies, is that affect theory "reduces embodied knowing to the dimension of mute attunement and coping with environments. This elides the aspect of embodied knowing that involves the capacity to take part in 'games of giving and asking for reasons.'"[13] Though it is surely right to question the starkly conceptualist approach of the neo-Kantians when we think about such language games, it is hard to see how the layer-cake model of human practice, which posits a level of experience that is already there *independently* of language, avoids the very problems associated with naturalism and empiricism to which this approach was originally a response. When understood as preconscious, precognitive forces, completely free of meaning, signification, or association to their triggering source, affects figure a mind-world relation in which there is a passive reception by the senses that occurs prior to and independently of autonomous, normative processes of rational thought—and that is what Sellars, himself taking up the Kantian legacy, famously called "the Myth of the Given."[14]

Whatever their differences, affect theorists share with neo-Kantians the view that the capacity to judge—insofar as it operates within what Sellars called "the space of reasons," the rational and normative structure that governs the use of concepts—must be the wholly rule-governed practice of subsuming particulars under concepts.[15] Failing that, judgments are little more than the effects of already primed dispositions that lie beyond the reach of consciousness and meaning. Concepts function here as determining in advance how the world can appear to us. To employ Kantian language, it seems as if sensible intuitions are always already conceptually determined, and in such a way that nothing can arise from experience for which we do not have a concept ready to hand. It is easy to see how affect could then be cast as fully outside the conceptual and as properly reacting to the world in all its diversity and novelty, albeit at the expense of remaining inarticulable. And it is also easy to see why the affective turn to the preconceptual would raise worries among those political thinkers concerned not to lose rational criteria for critically evaluating competing claims to truth.

Thinking about concepts as bounded and fixed, then, almost inevitably leads to the position that there is something in our experience that escapes or exceeds language and that finds its expression in our affective responses. It seems impossible to account not only for what is new in our experience but also for what is singular. As Joseph Tinguely notes, "If, following Kant, concepts are general or universal, and intuitions or appearances are always singular or particular, how could it ever be possible that we could conceptualize individual items as individuals rather than as mere instantiations of a general kind?"[16] Any plausible answer to this question needs to take into consideration Kant's own attempt to respond to the problem of the particular in the third *Critique*, especially his account of aesthetic judgments of taste. In what appears to be a retreat from the heavily conceptualist interpretation of the Copernican turn advanced by Sellars and John McDowell, writes Tinguely,

> Kant's aesthetics appears to be based on an intentional encounter with an object which we can behold and attend to but for which we have no concept. This "aesthetic Kant" [of the *Critique of Judgment*] seems a far cry from the "epistemological Kant" [of the *Critique of Pure Reason*] who declared intuitions without concepts to be blind. Moreover, perhaps even more devastating to the heavily conceptualist reading . . . , the central theme of the entire third critique—namely, reflective judgment—is premised on an operation of the mind where [Kant writes] "only the particular is given and judgment has to find the universal for it." (5:179)[17]

This picture of the "two Kants" has given us the familiar binaries (e.g., determinate versus reflective judgment, empirical [cognitive] judgment versus aesthetic [noncognitive] judgment, reason versus feeling) within which the voluminous secondary literature on Kant's theory of judgment unfolds. It is also a picture that has held the political theory debate on judgment captive, to paraphrase Wittgenstein, insofar as it presents an impossible choice: judgments are either based on concepts and can therefore be assessed according to accepted truth criteria, or are based on feeling and can therefore make no such normative claim. Crucial to this picture of the two Kants is once again a view of concepts as bounded and fixed. If the reflective judging examined by the "aesthetic Kant" must eschew concepts entirely, so this portrait suggests, it is because the conceptual determination examined by the "epistemological Kant" brings the activity of reflection to a grinding halt: the universal has been found, the particular has served its function to demonstrate the validity of a general kind.

We can loosen the hold this picture has on us by rethinking the understanding of concepts as bounded and fixed. If one has a more flexible view of concepts—as Kant, Arendt, and Wittgenstein in their different ways do—one can insist, with Sellars and McDowell, that consciousness is conceptual all the way down, without yielding to the highly cognitivist conception of judging that characterizes neo-Kantian political theory. One can also give due place to affective responses as irreducibly internal to human conceptual capacities without becoming mired in the politically troubling radical noncognitivism of affect theory. Rationalist cognitivism *or* visceral precognitivism need not be our only choices when thinking about judgment and politics.

Arendt's Kantian Alternative

In the pages that follow, I argue that Arendt's Kant is an alternative both to the highly conceptualist neo-Kantian interpretation of the Copernican turn, on the one hand, and to the radical noncognitivism of affect theory, on the other hand. It may seem strange to present Arendt's Kant as an alternative to noncognitivism, since it is precisely noncognitivism of which her reliance on Kant's third *Critique* stands accused in neo-Kantians receptions of her work. This debate turns on Arendt's insistence that politics involves the exchange of opinions that seek to persuade others, not truths that compel their agreement. Like aesthetic judgments on Kant's account, political judgments cannot be treated as truth claims, for they are not based on concepts or the giving of proofs. Arendt's turn to the third *Critique*, argues Habermas, is symptomatic of her refusal to provide a "cognitive foundation" for politics and public debate.[18] As Ronald Beiner, editor of Arendt's Kant Lectures, explains:

> It is not clear how we could make sense of opinions that did not involve *any* cognitive claim (and therefore by implication truth claims that are potentially corrigible) or why we should be expected

> to take seriously opinions that assert no claims to truth (or do not at least claim *more* truth than that claimed by available alternative opinions). It would seem that *all* human judgments, including aesthetic (and certainly political) judgments, incorporate a necessary cognitive dimension.[19]

In Beiner's influential interpretation, noncognitivism is just where the problems begin. Not only does Arendt reject cognition as relevant to political judgment, she seems to reject the very idea that there is something we could so much as call *political* judgment. Indeed, in her later work, what Arendt comes to seek in Kant, writes Beiner,

> is no longer a theory of political judgment, for, as she now conceives the matter, there is only *one* faculty of judgment, unitary and indivisible, which is present in various circumstances—in the verdict of an aesthetic critic, the verdict of a historical observer, the tragic verdict of a storyteller or poet—and the variety of circumstance does not relevantly affect the character of the faculty thus instantiated. Hence there can be no distinct faculty that we might identify, characteristically, as *political* judgment; there is only the ordinary capacity of judgment, now addressing itself to political events (or as Arendt would say, political appearances).[20]

In Beiner's view, this shift from political judgment to judgment as such reveals the gap between Arendt's earlier and more political account of judgment, where judging was linked up to "representative thinking" and acting, and what emerges as her "definitive formulation," in which judging withdraws from the *vita activa* into the life of the mind.[21]

The idea that Arendt's later work on judgment represents a withdrawal from politics, then, is rooted in more than the charge of noncognitivism, which I have critically addressed in previous work.[22] It is also rooted in the accusing observation that she is no longer interested in *political* judgment as a distinct species of judgment at all, but only in the faculty of judging as such. This observation turns on the idea that political judgment is political because it takes as its object political things. What would count as a political thing in Arendt's work is notoriously hard to pin down. But let's take as an ordinary example the election of political representatives. So a judgment about, say, who should be the next mayor of Chicago would be a political judgment because the office of mayor is a political matter.

But there is another way of thinking about what makes a judgment political, and that is when we say that "political" characterizes the means or process by which the judgment proceeds. (To see the contrast here, think about the phrase "diplomatic policy": "In the first case," to speak with Joseph Tinguely, "it can describe policies about diplomatic matters . . . [that] need not themselves be arrived at by any diplomatic procedures; in the second case, it can be understood to mean a policy that is arrived at diplomatically.")[23] Thus the mere notion of "political judgment" can itself be understood in two quite distinct senses. In the former case the "political" is that about which a judgment is made, that is, about an external and prior object that is independent of the judgment itself (e.g., the office of mayor); in the second case the "political" arises as something internal to the very process of judging itself. The key interpretive question in reading Arendt is whether the term "political" refers to a particular mode (form) of judgment or only to a particular kind of object (referent) judgments can have. I shall argue that it is the former, and I will be basing my case on a parallel argument made by Joseph Tinguely about how to understand Kantian aesthetic judgments.[24]

Even to ask what Arendt means by "political judgment" is deceptive: throughout her writings, Arendt rarely uses the term "political judgment," preferring to speak of "the capacity to judge as a specifically political ability."[25] For her, judgment is not political because it is about political things that are prior, independent, and external to it; it is political because it is a judgment that is arrived at politically—that is, with Arendt's Kant, by "think[ing] in the place of everyone else."[26] This form of thinking from the perspectives of other people, which Kant calls an enlarged way of thinking (*eine erweiterte Denkungsart*) and Arendt redescribes as "representative thinking,"[27] is a crucial part of judging in her view.[28] The objects one considers from these perspectives are not external objects in the way that, say, the office of mayor is. They emerge into view *as* "objects" in need of our judgment, the judgment of citizens, only as part of the very process of judging and of a broader process of orienting oneself in what Arendt calls "the common world." Writes Arendt: "The capacity to judge is a specifically political ability in exactly the sense denoted by Kant, namely, the ability to see things not only from one's own point of view but in the perspective of all who happen to be present."[29] Arendt's formulations will waver somewhat on the scope of the people whose perspectives need to be taken into account. But she never wavers on speaking about judging as political because of the means or process by which it proceeds, not because it deals with objects whose political character is already given prior to judging itself.

If one thinks, with Beiner and the neo-Kantian critics, that the proper meaning of political judgment is judgment of objects that are prior and external to the operation of judging itself, then it must indeed seem puzzling to exclude the cognitive dimension of judgment. What else would the faculty of judgment be judging if not the status of these objects? But if one thinks about what is political in judgment as a *mode* of judging rather than as a particular kind of *object* (referent) judgment can have, as Arendt does, then cognition is only one way in which judgment might proceed. Arendt's point was never to exclude cognition from judgments about the common world; it was to question the view of judging as the mere adjudication of truth claims. On this view, the objects of judgment are already given to us, and judging itself is a cognitive practice of subsuming an object under a concept. As we have seen, this is the position advanced by the neo-Kantians, for whom the whole problem of judgment in multicultural democracies is how to decide among competing truth claims about *existing* objects of judgment in the absence of universally shared criteria. For Arendt, by contrast, the problem is rather how it is that citizens get certain objects into view as objects of judgment at all. It is a problem of creating and sustaining "the common world," as we shall see. Rather than, as critics claim, embracing a politically naive noncognitivism, Arendt's turn to the third *Critique* advances a form of interpretive understanding focused on the common world and how it is that new objects of judgment come into view for us.

We can now grasp why Arendt's turn to Kantian aesthetics to talk about her ostensible topic of political judgment would strike critics as deeply puzzling, for they have a very different understanding of the judging faculty. This difference concerns more than the mode versus referent models of judging just described. The critique of Arendt's noncognitivism also turns on her critics' fairly strict division between aesthetic and empirical judging, between the reflective judgments of taste, discussed in the third *Critique*, and the determinative judgments of objects discussed in the first, the *Critique of Pure Reason*. But this strict division does not hold in Arendt's interpretation of Kant, any more than it holds in Kant's own work. The point is not to exclude the relevance of cognition to politics; it is to emphasize the reflective character of all judging, aesthetic and empirical.[30]

There is a reflective moment implicit in determinative judging, only this moment tends to get occluded in the highly conceptualist interpretation of the Copernican turn advanced in neo-Kantian political theory and, indeed, in certain formulations of Kant himself. Reflection—the process of *searching* for a concept under which to subsume a particular—becomes explicit in Kant's treatment of aesthetic experience. When the imagination and understanding are in "free play," as they are in aesthetic judging, we find the imagination's dialectical play of apprehension and exhibition, which is also at work in empirical judging, far more clearly thematized than it is in the first *Critique*.[31] For Arendt, this reflective character of judging is an irreducible element of its political character: the ability to see things from different points of view.

Judgments of taste foreground the reflective character of judging, but they also bring with them another set of problems. For such judgments are affective: they express the subject's pleasure, but appear to tell us nothing about the empirical world.[32] As Kant himself puts it, a judgment of taste expresses the subject's feeling of pleasure; it "has no bearing at all on the object" and "it brings to our attention no quality of the object." This rose is beautiful because it is *judged* to be beautiful. "Beauty is not a property of the flower itself" (*CJ* §32, p. 145). And yet judgments of taste, though they make no use of objective concepts, are not merely subjective, as are claims about the agreeable (e.g., "I like canary wine"). It would be "ridiculous" to say that this rose "is beautiful *for me*," argues Kant, for a judgment of beauty takes for granted that everyone else *ought* to agree (*CJ* §7, p. 55). But even if we accept the idea of "subjective universality" as Kant's way of describing the strange normativity of aesthetic judgments, we are still left wondering how a claim about the universal communicability of a feeling (pleasure) that makes no reference to worldly objects but only to the subject's mental state could possibly be the model for judging politically. Once the shared object of judgment drops from view, it would appear that all that is left is the self-referentiality of the subject's pleasure in taste: "The pleasure of taste is nothing other than the subject's explicit, conscious awareness of the validity [that is, the universalizability] of an implicit self-referential judgment."[33]

There are many different interpretations of Kant on this point, which turn mostly on the question of whether he holds a theory of pleasure that is internal (identical) to judgment rather than prior and external to it. "While there is a growing consensus in recent scholarship that Kant understood the pleasure of taste not as the object but (somehow) the form of judgment," writes Tinguely, "there has been remarkably little agreement as to what . . . the proper object of such a judgment is. If pleasure is itself a judgment, what is it judging?"[34] As explained previously, the most widely accepted view holds "that the pleasure of taste is a judgment 'about' oneself, that is, the 'object' of the judgment of taste is some special state or capacity of the judging subject."[35] In the view of Hannah Ginsborg, for example, the "free-play" of the faculties that Kant describes as part of aesthetic judging is a purely self-referential activity by which the judging subject reflects upon its mental state to see if the pleasure it feels is merely private or whether it is universally valid, that is, can with right be imputed to other judging subjects. A judgment of taste, then, is a claim not about the object but about the validity of the subject's pleasure.[36]

Accounts of the self-referential structure of aesthetic judgment leave us wondering how judgment connects with objects of empirical experience and, further, how any object becomes a candidate for aesthetic judging in the first place.[37] "As Ralf Meerbote has argued," comments Tinguely,

> if the only constraint that the empirical object can have on a judgment of beauty is that it provides the mere occasion for a judging subject's cognitive faculties of the imagination and understanding to come into a self-relation in a way that is normative for all other judging subjects then, in fact, "every object is beautiful." . . . In other words, if the deduction of beauty is grounded only in the subjective relation of the mental faculties, rather than in any feature of the object, then any object could be judged beautiful if taken up in the right mental stance.[38]

As it turns out, this is not a position that Kant himself finally held. In *CJ* §23 Kant writes: "The attunement of the cognitive powers [imagination and understanding] varies in its proportion, depending on what difference there is among the objects that are given." What Kant suggests here, explains Tinguely, is that "even the subjective self-relation of the faculties of judgment depends, somehow, upon actual 'differences among objects.' The question is whether it is possible to accommodate the differences among objects in judgments of beauty without breaching the insistence [on the part of many interpreters of the third *Critique* but also often enough of Kant himself] that aesthetic reflective judging is wholly subjective."[39]

The question of the place of the object in aesthetic judging invites us to critically interrogate accounts of the stark difference between aesthetic and empirical judging and to pursue the entanglement of aesthetics in any claim to knowledge.[40] For the most part, theorists who would save the aesthetic from the charge of subjectivism attempt to show that aesthetics has cognitive content (e.g., Aesthetic Cognitivism), whereas the more promising task would be to show that cognition has aesthetic content. Kirk Pillow, Rudolf Makreel, and Joseph Tinguely, among other Kant scholars, have argued that there is a way to bring together Kant's conception of cognition as the recognition of objects under concepts and a more nuanced conception of understanding, which is inclusive of both cognitive and aesthetic dimensions.[41] Pillow explains:

> What is distinctive about aesthetic experience is not the utter absence of concepts in our reflection on an object; such a complete absence is unintelligible in any case. Instead, aesthetic experience is distinguished from cognition narrowly construed by the fact that our response to the object is not to subsume it under a conceptual rule. Our aesthetic response instead plays at multiple ways of appreciating a form and, in the case of works of art, at multiple ways of construing meanings, rather than settling on any reductive conceptual determination. To be interpretive, our response to aesthetic ideas must draw on concepts, and this is consistent with that response being noncognitive in the narrow sense, because interpreting aesthetic ideas entails more than subsuming properties of objects under predicates of concepts. Interpretive understanding is not governed by determinative conceptual rules, but it does employ conceptual resources while working to make sense of its object.[42]

It is not only Kant's account of aesthetic ideas that invites us to think beyond the dualism of empirical versus aesthetic judging. Taking up Kant's account of the "reflective specification" of concepts in the "First Introduction" to the *Critique of Judgment*, Makreel has argued that Kant regards the concept "as a content to be formed instead of as a form that is fixed."[43] As Tinguely likewise remarks, "Kant himself seems to allow that it is not just that exhibition of general concepts guide apprehension of particular objects, but rather apprehension of actual objects itself plays a role in specifying or determining the form or the meaning of the general concept."[44] A concrete example, then, does not simply give specificity to the general concept but actually expands it.[45] The imaginative presentation of aesthetic ideas "expands the concept itself in an unlimited way" (*CJ*, §49, pp. 182–83), writes Kant, but so too does the work of apprehending imagination, guiding exhibiting imagination in empirical judgments. And "it is not just the exhibiting imagination that is itself flexible," comments Tinguely, "but rather it is in the nature of *concepts* themselves to be 'expansive.' "[46] Concepts are employed in relation to intuitions and reshaped to take account of the vast variety of empirical experience that could be counted as falling under a concept. "If it is concepts themselves . . . which are expansive or elastic, then the apprehension would not just identify new instances of a concept whose meaning one already possessed, rather, the apprehension would deepen or enrich one's understanding of the term," Tinguely rightly concludes.[47]

Already in Kant, then, we find an account of concepts not as fixed but elastic, which thinkers such as Wittgenstein would later make explicit. One need not go beneath consciousness and language to uncover precognitive processes that—it is claimed—alone can take account of the novelty and richness of empirical experience, as the affect theorists hold. Nor need we think about judging as a form of conceptual determination that is free of any aesthetic character, as the neo-Kantians maintain. Instead we can recognize that concepts are always already involved in any experiential uptake without losing their responsiveness to the world as it actually is. For my purposes, however, this elasticity of concepts is more than a philosophical point. It needs to be considered in relation to Arendt and the problem of politics in multicultural democracies. After all, whether we treat concepts as elastic or fixed is not decided by the philosophical character of concepts themselves but is rather a matter of what we do with concepts, how we employ them in any particular practice, including that of democratic politics.

Judging as a World-Building Practice

Allow me to resituate the philosophical debate about the elasticity of concepts and the status of the aesthetic object in a political register. I have already suggested that what Arendt takes from Kant's notion of aesthetic judging is the idea that the term "aesthetic" refers to a particular mode (form) of judging rather than to a particular kind of object (referent) judgments can have. I then attempted to transpose this insight into the debate about what Arendt means when she speaks of judging as a political ability, arguing that such judging is political because it involves the ability to see from perspectives other than one's own, not because it reflects on a specific class of objects that are external and prior to it (e.g., the office of mayor). We can now see how this argument must answer to the question of the self-referential character of judging. If aesthetic judgment has a purely self-referential structure, it would be difficult to understand how such judgment connects with the things of this world, which surely must be of concern for anyone interested in politics and therefore for Hannah Arendt. We might well wonder, then, whether Arendt, who saw in the radical subjectivism of modernity a failure of basic orientation or lack of relation to people and place that she called "worldlessness," would embrace the idea of judgments as wholly self-referential. What could the judging subject's (pleasurable) reflection on the universal validity of its own pleasure possibly have to do with politics? The neo-Kantians would have us explain Arendt's turn to Kantian aesthetics as an unfortunate error that is hard to square with her critique of subjectivism and explicitly normative commitments to democratic world-building.

In my view, there is no error. Arendt's reading of the third *Critique* conceptualizes judgment neither as wholly subjective or self-referential nor as wholly conceptualist or cognitivist. Instead, she thinks about judgment as making a normative claim on others that is also a claim about how the world is seen by a particular subject, that is to say, his or her opinion. Embracing opinion in its original Greek sense as how the world "appears to me," Arendt does not adopt the broadly empiricist approach according to which perceptual content is immediately available to the senses prior to the activation of any conceptual categories.[48] In this she follows the fundamental Kantian insight that conceptual categories are already drawn on in receptivity.[49] Thus any claim about how the world appears to me, any opinion, is for her not merely subjective but always normative. But on what is this normativity based?

Arendt explicitly rejects the "abstraction requirement" of the traditional conception of objectivity.[50] An irreducible epistemological demand that has been fundamental to metaphysical accounts of meaning, this requirement is premised on the view that our subjective endowments have a tendency to distort our grasp of how things really stand in the world. As Alice Crary explains, objectivity on this view requires that "the regularities constitutive of a sound conceptual practice must transcend the practice in the sense of being discernable independently of any subjective responses characteristic of us as participants in it."[51] The more objective our judgments, the less they rely on any human subjective properties. Although Arendt rejects this understanding of objectivity, she does not (*pace* her critics) dismiss the question of validity. What she does, rather, is to ask: what kind of validity is proper to the realm of politics, where we are concerned with the problem of human freedom (how to affirm rather than deny it) and with sustaining the condition of freedom; namely, plurality?[52] Objectivity requires not simply that one "be in agreement with one's own self [logic's principle of noncontradiction], but . . .

consist[s] of being able to 'think in the place of everybody else.'"[53] That is what it means "to truly *see* topics from various sides—that is, politically," as Arendt puts it.[54]

Arendt's critics too reject the abstraction requirement. We have seen, however, that the fear of relativism leads them to insist that an otherwise "impenetrable pluralism" of opinions be managed by public reason, which would "separate by argumentation generalizable interests from those that remain particular."[55] Without such means, argues Beiner, we would be left with little more than the subjectivizing language of preferences, namely the language of values that characterizes liberalism. This "intrinsically subjectivizing language," he writes,

> suggests . . . that value originates not in what is admirable or worthy of being cherished in the world, but in the idiosyncrasies of our own inner life. . . . It has the effect of canceling out the claims to real validity anchored in the world. . . . Talk of values implies that we do not find goodness in the good things there in the world, but confer value from our own subjectivity.[56]

I agree with Beiner that values are not subjective projections onto the otherwise value-free things of the world and also with his critique of liberalism on that score. But I disagree that to avoid the subjectivizing idiom of values we must treat political judgments as wholly cognitive validity claims.

Arendt's turn to the third *Critique* is not an unfortunate embrace of values understood as subjective preferences. It is an effort to navigate between the Scylla of the conception of validity put forward in the traditional conception of objectivity (in which our subjective endowments and affective life can play no role) and the Charybdis of subjective preferences (in which an aesthetic claim based on the judging subject's feeling has no normative standing). The claim "*This* painting is beautiful" is neither objective nor merely subjective, argues Kant—and Arendt agrees. If our appreciation of beauty is not part of a cognitively based discourse ethics, as Beiner following Habermas wants it to be, that is because such appreciation outstrips the limits of our discursive, claim-making abilities. There is no rational decision procedure, no deductive or inferential claim, by which one could prove to another judging subject that *this* painting is beautiful, argues Kant. The claim to beauty can never prove itself as valid based on the "unforced force of the better argument," to cite Habermas again. And yet this claim is not mere preference or an expression of "the idiosyncrasies of our own inner life." That is because such judgments make a normative claim on the feelings of others: others too *ought* to find this painting beautiful. Whether others do in fact so find it is an entirely different (empirical) question in both Kant's and Arendt's view. Nevertheless, a judgment of beauty would not be possible were it restricted to the "ridiculous" claim "It is beautiful *for me*" (*CJ* §7, p. 55).[57]

The problem that Beiner has identified in modern liberalism is one with which Arendt would surely agree. But the reductive language of subjective preferences requires a more nuanced understanding of the normativity of aesthetic judgments, not a flight back into the language game of criticizable validity claims or the rules of public reason.

Kant himself gives us a way to think about judgments that are normative and yet not based on concepts or, better, are not conceptual in the way that Arendt's critics think they must be. This is the distinction, mentioned previously, that Kant draws between persuasion (*Überredung*) and conviction (*Überzeugung*). As Tinguely explains, the distinction between persuasion and conviction is more than semantic.

> Because the German word "*reden*" refers to speech or discourse, persuasion as *Überredung* literally carries the sense of being "talked-over" or cajoled through speech to a position one is unable to refute. This emphasis on the manipulative potential of discourse exposes a worry that modeling knowledge on the order of discursive concepts and the inferential connections between them leaves one vulnerable to a kind of fast-talking sophistry and the suspicion that "persuasion is mere illusion." . . . Unlike persuasion, conviction is not merely a position which I cannot refuse but one which I recognize as my own, one for which I take responsibility. Put otherwise, a conviction is not a position foisted on me from the outside, as it were, heteronomously but one which I issue from within, autonomously.[58]

The distinction between persuasion and conviction in the first *Critique* can be connected with Kant's claim in the third *Critique*, continues Tinguely,

> that some forms of knowledge or truth require more than discursive or inferential articulation: "all proofs must . . . not [merely] persuade, but convince" (5:461). Kant is thus repeatedly concerned to point out a gap between the actual "holding something to be true" (A820/B848) of personal conviction and the mere seeming to be (or sounding) true of conceptually valid, honey-tongued persuasion. In other words, rationalistic decision procedures by which one logically infers from one concept or position to another seem to come up short, not just of experiences of beauty, but of any standard of knowledge that we could recognize as our own. (*Orientation*, 4)

I point to Kant's reservations about the limits of our discursive, claim-making abilities to suggest that the proper application of concepts does not settle the problem of normativity in the way the neo-Kantians assume it should. We are still left with the question of what it means to be convinced rather than merely persuaded by an argument, and this issue cannot be settled by means of proofs. The third *Critique* gives examples of the poet who is convinced that his judgment of beauty is right, who "refuse[s] to listen to reasons and arguments" (*CJ* §33, p. 148), who will accept no proofs that his judgment is wrong. He feels, in the deep sense that Kant reserves for conviction, that his judgment is right—the relevant experts be damned. This raises the question of feeling, not below the level of language and consciousness, where the affect theorists would place it, but within the space of reasons, that is, as normative. Indeed, comments Tinguely, "the aim of Kant's aesthetics is to bring affectivity within the domain of normativity; in quarreling about taste, we place demands on the feelings of others."[59]

In the *Critique of Judgment* Kant explains this normativity in terms of sensus communis, "a subjective principle, which determines only by feeling rather than concepts, though nonetheless with universal validity, what is liked or disliked" (§20). Sensus communis is the condition of possibility for the communicability of feelings, representations, which makes (or ought to make) possible the capacity to think in the place of other subjects—what Kant calls an enlarged way of thinking (*eine erweitete Denkungsart*).[60] It was just this manner of thinking from standpoints not one's own that Arendt found crucial to developing her own political account of judging, a manner of thinking that left the narrow conception of cognition behind in favor of a conception of aesthetic normativity for which "truth" is hardly the highest value.

I argued earlier that judging is political, not because it is about political objects that are prior and external to it, but because it proceeds by taking into account the perspectives of others. What we count as "political" arises in, is internal to, the very process of judging itself. Understood in this way, judging is constitutive of the space in which the objects of judgment can appear. Rather than think of judgment with the neo-Kantians as a problem of reaching agreement, as the adjudication of value conflicts in the absence of a transcendent idea of the good, Arendt focuses our attention on what we might call the prior question of what it means to have a world in common, a world in which value differences present themselves not as preferences but as politically relevant objects for judgment in the first place. To speak with Arendt, the problem of judgment is not simply how to judge in the absence of universal rules but rather how to recognize objects as candidates for our judgment. The corrosive effect of the radical subjectivism that characterizes modernity in Arendt's view is to destroy the common world in which these objects can so much as appear.

The world we have in common is not something we cognize in the narrow sense of cognition that I have been questioning. Indeed, the more nuanced conception of the aesthetic discussed previously may well be what Arendt had in mind when, turning to Kant's idea of enlarged thinking, she developed her own political conception of "representative thinking" as a practice of building the common world. We can think representatively not because we eschew concepts but because we are called on to see an object or event in something other than *narrowly* cognitive terms. Space is made, in other words, for considering the opinions of others on things, for opinions call on us to do something more than redeem them as validity claims. Consequently, the exchange of opinions involves more than the proper application of concepts. But that does not mean that opinions make no reference to concepts at all, only that they are not restricted to the narrow act of deciding which conceptual rules apply.

If what makes such judgment political is not the intrinsically political nature of an object but thinking about it from different points of view, perhaps we can say that this kind of thinking enables us to see previously unseen—that is, uncounted—objects as politically relevant, as part of the common world. Judging is the most political of our mental abilities, in Arendt's view, because—in the proper sense of the term—judging itself cannot begin without taking account of the viewpoints of others. The irreducible ground of judging is plurality—not just the empirical existence of other people, but the active taking into account of their points of view. Only in this way is the elasticity of concepts discussed earlier of *political* significance. If we can respond to the variety and richness of empirical experience (without taking flight in the preconceptual register of affect), such responsiveness must go beyond our life with language (as a purely philosophical account might lead us to believe); it is something we, democratic citizens, need to do—to acknowledge or count unfamiliar utterances and events as potentially significant for the world we have in common.

We can now better understand that what makes a judgment aesthetic (Kant) or political (Arendt) is not the relation to the judged object, which is external and prior to the judging practice, but the mode by which the judgment proceeds. Judging is neither the mere reaction of the subject to an external object nor to its own inner life. The judging subject's relation to the object is never direct in the sense of an effect (pleasure) to its cause (beauty) but rather is mediated through the standpoints of other subjects. It is not, then, that the object is nothing, as the argument for aesthetic judgment's self-referential character would suggest. It is rather that things come into view for us as objects of judgment in the first place by means of their mediation through the standpoints of others.

This mediated relation to objects makes judging a world-building practice. Only a practice that takes account of the viewpoints of others can grasp the inaugural character of judging and its distinctively political character. As Arendt explicitly states in her Kant lectures, it is the judgment of the spectators that creates the space in which the objects of the common world can appear, not the other way around.[61] To have a "common world" in Arendt's sense is *not* to share a worldview. On the contrary, this common world exists only where there is a plurality of worldviews. Our sense of what is common, "the sameness of the object," as Arendt puts it, can appear only when it is seen from different perspectives. "The end of the common world has come when it is seen only under one aspect and is permitted to present itself in only one perspective," she writes.[62] Consequently, the loss of competing perspectives or views results not in a world that is shared but in a loss of what we have common. It is this collapse of the common world, and not (as the neo-Kantians hold) the adjudication of value differences, that is the real problem of judgment today.

Notes

1. Whereas her contemporaries (e.g., Eric Voegelin and Leo Strauss) tended to see in the ruin of inherited standards a crisis of judgment, Arendt saw a problem but also an opportunity to practice judgment anew. Judgment is a crisis only if we think about it as the subsumption of particulars under known rules. The real problem, in her view, was not the loss of standards but the tendency to cling to rules like so many "banisters" for judging, long after they had lost their ability to speak to actual experiences. The problem was not relativism, as it was for Strauss and Voegelin, but dogmatic certainty about criteria of judgment that had lost their meaning in the postwar reality. See Hannah Arendt, *Lectures on Kant's Political Philosophy*, ed. Ronald Beiner (Chicago: University of Chicago Press, 1982); Hannah Arendt, "The Crisis in Culture," in *Between Past and Future: Eight Essays in Political Thought* (New York: Penguin, 2006), 194–222. I discuss Arendt's account of judgment as a response to totalitarianism in Linda M. G. Zerilli, "'We Feel Our Freedom': Imagination and Judgment in the Thought of Hannah Arendt," *Political Theory* 33, no. 2 (2005): 158–88.

2. Arendt confronted similar questions in her report on the Eichmann trial and, more generally, as she struggled to respond to the political catastrophes of the twentieth century. In her view, there is a tendency to think that firsthand experience is the condition of all judging. Thus those individuals who did not live through the Nazi terror are in no position to judge those who did experience it, whatever their role might have been. Eichmann was merely following orders in a context where to do otherwise would have been tantamount to signing one's own death warrant, the defense argued; would not each of us have done the same? Arendt not only refuted the idea that Eichmann was a monster who did not feel himself bound by moral law but also that he was an ordinary person whose actions we, outsiders, were in no position to judge.

3. See Donald Davidson, "On the Very Idea of a Conceptual Scheme," *Proceedings and Addresses of the American Philosophical Association* 47 (1973–74): 5–20; John McDowell, *Mind and World* (Cambridge, Mass.: Harvard University Press, 1996); Peter Winch, "Understanding a Primitive Society," *American Philosophical Quarterly* 1, no. 4 (1964): 307–24; Charles Taylor, "Foundationalism and the Inner-Outer Distinction," in *Reading McDowell: On Mind and World*, ed. Nicholas Smith (New York: Routledge, 2002), 106–20; Ludwig Wittgenstein, *Philosophical Investigations*, ed. Joachim Schulte and P. M. S. Hacker, trans. G. E. M. Anscombe, 4th ed. (Oxford: Wiley-Blackwell, 2009).

4. Vivasvan Soni, "Introduction: The Crisis of Judgment," *Eighteenth Century* 51, no. 3 (2010): 261–88, at 263.

5. On this point see Linda M. G. Zerilli, "Value Pluralism and the Problem of Judgment: Farewell to Public Reason," *Political Theory* 40, no. 1 (2012): 6–32.

6. Capturing this sense of urgency, Habermas writes: "The limits of a decisionistic treatment of practical questions are overcome as soon as argumentation is expected to treat the generaliz*ability* of interests, instead of being resigned to an impenetrable pluralism of apparently ultimate value orientations (or belief-acts or attitudes). It is not the fact of this pluralism that is here disputed, but the assertion that it is impossible to separate by argumentation generalizable interests from those that are and remain particular." Jürgen Habermas, *Legitimation Crisis*, trans. Thomas McCarthy (Boston: Beacon, 1975), 108.

7. Hannah Arendt, *Willing*, vol. 2 of *The Life of the Mind*, 1-vol. ed. (New York: Harcourt Brace, 1978), 28–34.

8. Although there is no single idea of the good that can or ought to be defended in the neo-Kantian view, there can and ought to be agreement about the ground rules for debate. In the case of Rawls, we can agree to disagree and leave the most divisive topics off the public table. What we do agree to debate can in principle be discussed rationally through the use of shared concepts (justice as fairness) and norms (e.g., reasonableness). Habermas, by contrast, believes that all topics can in principle be on the table if subjected to certain procedural norms of argumentation, for implicit in all human communication, regardless of cultural particularity, is an orientation toward rational legitimation. Universality in public matters is thus based on agreement or rational consensus achieved at the end of a "discourse of reasons" (or public debate) to which various individuals take part. Implicit in our discursive practices is an assurance that the claims we make are capable of being validated with respect to the truth of what they assert, their appropriateness to the situation, and our sincerity in uttering them.

9. See William Connolly, *Neuropolitics: Thinking, Culture, Speed* (Minneapolis: University of Minnesota Press, 2002); Jane Bennett, *Vibrant Matter: A Political Ecology of Things* (Durham, N.C.: Duke University Press, 2010); Davide Panagia, *The Political Life of Sensation* (Durham, N.C.: Duke University Press, 2009); Leslie Paul Thiele, *The Heart of Judgment: Practical Wisdom, Neuroscience, and Narrative* (Cambridge: Cambridge University Press, 2006); Jennifer Nedelsky, "Receptivity and Judgment," *Ethics and Global Politics* 4, no. 4 (2011): 231–54; John Protevi, *Political Affect: Connecting the Social and the Somatic* (Minneapolis: University of Minnesota Press, 2009). For a good critique of Connolly, see Alexander Livingston, "Avoiding Deliberative Democracy? Micropolitics, Manipulation, and the Public Sphere," *Philosophy and Rhetoric* 45, no. 3 (2012): 269–94. For an excellent critique of the turn to cognitive neuroscience and affect in political theory, see John G. Gunnell, "Unpacking Emotional Baggage in Political Inquiry," in *Essays on Neuroscience and Political Theory: Thinking the Body Politic*, ed. Frank Vander Valk (New York: Routledge, 2012), 91–116; John G. Gunnell, "Are We Losing Our Minds? Cognitive Science and the Study of Politics," *Political Theory* 35, no. 6 (2007): 704–32.

10. My critique is not directed at scholars who take up the important question of affect in the ordinary sense of the term. It is directed rather at those thinkers (e.g., the new materialists, the vitalists, the new materialist vitalists) for

whom affect is not a synonym for feeling, emotion, or sentiment, expressions of which are semiotically mediated and at once public and personal. As Eric Shouse explains, "Affect is not a personal feeling. Feelings are personal and biographical, emotions are social, . . . and affects are pre-personal. . . . An affect is a non-conscious experience of intensity; it is a moment of unformed and unstructured potential. . . . Affect cannot be fully realized in language . . . because affect is always prior to and/or outside consciousness. . . . The body has a grammar of its own that cannot be fully captured in language." Eric Shouse, "Feeling, Emotion, Affect," *M/C Journal* 8 (December 2005), 2, 3; journal.media-culture.org.au/0512/03-shouses.php. On a similar point see Brian Massumi, *Parables for the Virtual: Movement, Affect, Sensation* (Durham, N.C.: Duke University Press, 2002), 27. For a comprehensive critique of affect theory, see Ruth Leys, "The Turn to Affect: A Critique," *Critical Inquiry* 37, no. 3 (2011): 434–72. Leys finds a striking compatibility between Spinozist and Deleuzian-inspired affect theorists and affective neuroscientists at the level of their "shared anti-intentionalism." "What the new affect theorists and the neuroscientists share is a commitment to the idea that there is a [temporal] gap between the subject's affect and its cognition or appraisal of the affective situation or object, such that cognition or thinking comes 'too late' for reasons, intentions, beliefs, and meanings to play a role in action usually accorded to them" (443). This is what makes affect so politically potent. In that small space of time the media, corporations, politicians, and other malicious figures experiment with the background conditions of bare life. Though feeling is surely important when accounting for the tenacity of oppressive social and political forms, the theory of affects as radically outside meaning and signification and free of their triggering source leaves us with no way to link an affect to an object and, consequently, no way to subject such manipulation to critical judgment. I discuss these and other problems with affect theory in Linda M. G. Zerilli, "The Turn to Affect and the Problem of Judgment," *New Literary History* 6, no. 2 (Summer 2015): 261–86.

11. Wilfrid Sellars, *Empiricism and the Philosophy of Mind* (Cambridge, Mass.: Harvard University Press, 1997), 87. According to Sellars's famous interpretation of Kant, experience is always already conceptual. This argument is developed a decade later by John McDowell, who insists that all receptivity is always already rational and normative. There can be no "experiential intake" (what Kant calls intuition) without the use of concepts: "The relevant conceptual capacities are drawn on in receptivity. . . . It is not that they are exercised on an extra-conceptual deliverance of receptivity," writes McDowell (*Mind and World*, 9). As sympathetic as I am to this conceptualist account of intentionality as a critique of empirical naturalism, it more or less summarily excludes any significant role for affect in cognition, thereby leaving us once again with the impossible choice of affect *or* reason.

12. Clive Barnett, "Political Affects in Public Space: Normative Blind Spots in Non-Representational Ontologies," *Transactions of the Institute of British Geographers* 33 (2008): 186–200, at 188. The Brandom quote is from Robert Brandom, *Tales of the Mighty Dead* (Cambridge, Mass.: Harvard University Press, 2002), 332. The layer-cake model involves a crucial departure from the thought of philosophers such as Wittgenstein, who shows not only that propositional intentionality is entangled in and unthinkable apart from a more basic

level of preconceptual, practical intentionality, but also that there is no sharp line between unarticulated know-how and explicit knowledge. The lack of stark demarcation between "knowing-how" and "knowing-that" allows the language game of doubting to rely on an unquestioning acceptance of many things without turning the sedimented certainties at what Wittgenstein calls "bedrock" into permanently unquestionable assumptions. Critical judgment on what stands fast for us remains an open possibility and with it our openness to the inaugural character of phenomena that Arendt called "the problem of the new." I discuss Wittgenstein's account in "Doing without Knowing: Feminism's Politics of the Ordinary," *Political Theory* 24, no. 4 (1998): 435–58.

13. Barnett, "Political Affects in Public Space," 187.

14. Sellars, *Empiricism and the Philosophy of Mind*, 33. Whereas Sellars was questioning the idea, core to traditional epistemology, that there must be some fundamental cognitive states in direct contact with reality on which all our (inferential) knowledge lies, the new materialists treat their "given," namely matter or sensation, as that which undercuts rather than supports claims to knowledge. Though their aims are antiepistemological in the extreme, the new materialists accept—indeed, celebrate—the ontological idea of the subject's direct contact with a reality that is "merely *there*," to cite Brandom again, outside language. This prediscursive reality then works in mysterious ways behind the subject's back, so to speak, in the form of visceral forces and intensities that govern its being but of which it can know nothing.

15. Sellars, *Empiricism and the Philosophy of Mind*, 76.

16. Joseph Tinguely, "Reflective Judgment and the Myth of the Given" (unpublished paper, The New School for Social Research), 1–10, at 4.

17. Ibid., 2.

18. Jürgen Habermas, "Hannah Arendt's Communications Concept of Power," in *Hannah Arendt, Critical Essays*, ed. Lewis Hinchman and Sandra Hinchman (Albany: State University of New York Press, 1994), 211–30, at 225. For a similar criticism see Albrecht Wellmer, "Hannah Arendt on Judgment: The Unwritten Doctrine of Reason," in *Judgment, Imagination, and Politics: Themes from Kant and Arendt*, ed. Ronald Beiner and Jennifer Nedlesky (Boston: Rowman & Littlefield, 2001), 165–81, esp. 169. Seyla Benhabib finds in Arendt's "disturbing" turn to Kant's third *Critique* further evidence of the failure to provide a normative foundation for politics from which it would be possible to assess competing validity claims (*The Reluctant Modernism of Hannah Arendt* [Thousand Oaks, Calif.: Sage, 1996], 193–94).

19. Ronald Beiner, "Hannah Arendt on Judging," in Hannah Arendt, *Lectures on Kant's Political Philosophy*, 89–156, at 137. In Beiner's view, "the problem with this exclusion of knowledge from political judgment is that it renders one incapable of speaking of 'uninformed' judgment and of distinguishing differential capacities for knowledge so that some persons may be recognized as more qualified and some as less qualified to judge" (ibid., 136). But this is just the kind of qualification that Arendt, following Kant's insights on the peculiar nature of aesthetic judging, would have us question. In her strikingly original view, the capacity to judge should be expected from each and every citizen. Although Arendt turned to Homeric impartiality, Aristotelian phronesis, and Kantian enlarged thinking in working through her ideas on judgment, it is not Homer or Aristotle or for that

matter Kant to whom we can attribute her account. Rather, it is Hannah Arendt herself who first discovers judgment as a *political* capacity of ordinary democratic citizens, not elites or individuals with special knowledge or abilities. This discovery is at least equal to her conception of action, which is normally taken to be the central feature of her political thought.

20. Ibid., 138.

21. Ibid.

22. See Zerilli, "'We Feel Our Freedom.'" In this essay I argue that Arendt holds to the distinction between opinion and truth insofar as her interest in judgment is focused not on the neo-Kantian problem of how to adjudicate competing validity claims but on how to sustain political freedom.

23. I borrow this example from Joseph Tinguely, whose excellent dissertation on Kant I discuss below. "Orientation: Kant and the Aesthetic Content of Cognition" (Ph.D. diss., New School for Social Research, 2011), 99 (hereafter cited in text and notes as "Orientation").

24. Tinguely's reading argues that for Kant "feeling itself is a kind of judgmental capacity." His broader aim is to force "the question not primarily whether aesthetics has cognitive content [as various brands of Aesthetic Cognitivism try to do] but, more fundamentally, whether cognition has aesthetic content" ("Orientation," 1). What we see in the third *Critique* is "the emergence, out of the void between discursive normativity and total nonsense, of a new terrain of rational persuasion—one which draws on and places claims on our affective sensibilities" (ibid., 51). Kantian aesthetic judging is a kind of "knowing by feeling or in feeling," to speak with Stanley Cavell (quoted in ibid., 52). This feeling is not the radical noncognitivism of the affects, which remain (on the view described in this essay) inaccessible to consciousness and thus judgment, but the normativity of sensus communis that animates the anticipated universal agreement behind every judgment of taste.

25. A survey of Arendt's entire corpus shows that she speaks of "political judgment" only six times. The real issue is not how many times she actually mentions *political* judgment but what the adjective "political" means: does it signify the object which is being judged or does it signify the mode by which judgment proceeds?

26. Arendt, "The Crisis in Culture," 217.

27. Arendt translates Kant's phrase as "an enlarged mentality" ("The Crisis in Culture," 217). For Arendt's remarks on "representative thinking," see Hannah Arendt, "Truth and Politics," in *Between Past and Future: Eight Essays in Political Thought* (New York: Penguin, 2006), 223–59, at 237.

28. Arendt writes: "The power of judgment rests on a potential agreement with others, and the thinking process which is active in judging something is not, like the thought process of pure reasoning, a dialogue between me and myself, but finds itself always and primarily, even if I am quite alone in making up my mind, in an anticipated communication with others with whom I know I must finally come to some agreement" (Arendt, "The Crisis in Culture," 217).

29. Ibid., 221.

30. For an excellent account of the reflective dimension of Kantian judgment, see Béatrice Longuenesse, *Kant and the Capacity to Judge: Sensibility and Discursivity in the Transcendental Aesthetic of the Critique of Pure Reason*, trans. Catherine Porter (Princeton, N.J.: Princeton University Press, 1998).

31. I discuss these points in Linda M. G. Zerilli, *A Democratic Theory of Judgment* (Chicago: University of Chicago Press, 2016).

32. The pleasure obtained in the act of judging is subjective. It is based on a priori principles and entails the agreement or harmony of the faculties (understanding and imagination) in the absence of a concept, for reflective judgment fails to produce any conceptual determination. That is why Kant speaks of aesthetic and teleological judgments as merely reflective judgments (*nur reflektierende, bloß reflektierende*). Immanuel Kant, *Critique of Judgment*, trans. Werner S. Pluhar (Indianapolis: Hackett, 1987), 399, 412; see also 396 (hereafter cited in text and notes as *CJ*).

33. Tinguely, "Orientation," 117.

34. Ibid., 112. The interpretations at issue here are responses to Paul Guyer's claim that Kantian aesthetic judging consists of "two acts": the first act involves the encounter with an aesthetic object that gives rise to a feeling of pleasure, and the second act judges the validity of this pleasure. Paul Guyer, *Kant and the Claims of Taste*, 2nd ed. (Cambridge: Cambridge University Press), 99. This two-act view treats pleasure not as the means by which we judge but as entirely prior to and independent of the judgment itself. What one judges is one's pleasurable reaction to an object, that is, whether one can demand that others too feel this pleasure. Furthermore, Guyer advances a causal theory of pleasure, according to which such feeling is caused by the free play of the faculties (i.e., of imagination and understanding). This suggests that there is nothing normative in the feeling itself. "It follows on the causal theory," writes Tinguely,

> that neither the feeling of pleasure nor the harmonious play of the faculties can be considered as an accomplishment for which we can take credit—a rational mode of engaging or discerning an object for which we are responsible or for which we could criticize others—rather it is something that merely *happens* to one under the right conditions by virtue of what Robert Pippin decries as a "peculiar psychological quirk" which happens to be shared by all humans. . . . Just as it is a physical quirk that some people laugh when tickled, so too is it a psychological quirk—albeit one universally shared by all humans—that we feel pleasure when apprehension and exhibition reinforce each other in harmonious play. In neither case is there anything anyone can *do* about it, except perhaps cultivate an awareness or sensitivity in recognizing what is causing the experience of pleasure; because feelings, like sensations, are causal and thus not rational, it would be ridiculous to praise or blame someone for their good sense of taste as it would be to praise or blame them for being ticklish. ("Orientation," 107)

In *A Democratic Theory of Judgment* I argue against this two-act theory, for it deprives aesthetic (and, by extension, Arendtian political) judgments of their normativity and also makes it impossible to think about them as being at once rational and affective. This would leave us with the impossible choice of reason *or* affect that is presented, respectively, in the work of neo-Kantians and affect theorists.

35. Tinguely, "Orientation," 112. This is the view of Hannah Ginsborg, who argues against Guyer that pleasure is internal to judgment, not prior and external

to it. Pleasure consists in the awareness that one's pleasure is universally valid, that is, normative. This self-referential act of judgment makes a claim on the feelings of others, "demanding that all perceivers of the object in question should judge it as I do," writes Ginsborg. "But this demand, being universal, applies just as much to myself as to any other perceiver of the object." Ginsborg, "On the Key to Kant's Critique of Taste," *Pacific Philosophical Quarterly* 72 (1991): 290–313, at 302. There is, in other words, every reason to remain in this subjective state, leaving the judging subject in a kind of endless self-referential circle. Ginsborg agrees with Guyer that the object of a judgment of taste is not the aesthetic object but one's subjective mental state. As Tinguely explains, the only difference is that "for Guyer taste is a judgment *about* a (external) pleasure; for Ginsborg taste judges *by means of* a (internal) pleasure" ("Orientation," 115). See also Hannah Ginsborg, "Aesthetic Judging and the Intentionality of Pleasure," *Inquiry* 46, no. 2 (2003): 164–81.

36. See especially Ginsborg, "On the Key to Kant's Critique of Taste."

37. In the view of Vivasvan Soni, for example, the self-reflexive character of aesthetic judgment leaves the object stranded. "The retreat into self-reflexivity is the privileged strategy for evading judgment about the object itself" ("The Crisis of Judgment," 278). I agree that there are real dangers associated with the indefinite suspension of judgment, and that these arise in certain interpretations of Kant (though I would disagree that the interpretations get Kant right on this score). In the case of Arendt, however, whom Soni finds equally guilty of this subjectivizing move, the point is not to suspend judgment but rather to create the space in which objects can so much as appear as requiring our judgment. Arendt does not endorse suspension of judgment as an alternative to a rule-governed determination of judgment because she does not take for granted that we already know which objects we need to judge. The problem of judgment is not simply how to judge in the absence of universal rules but also how to recognize objects as candidates for our judgment in the first place.

38. Tinguely, "Orientation," 40. See also Ralf Meerbote, "Reflections on Beauty," in *Essays on Kant's Aesthetics*, ed. Ted Cohen and Paul Guyer (Chicago: University of Chicago Press), 55–86, at 81. Karl Ameriks argues that Kant does not provide sound reasons for rejecting the objectivity of beauty. "How to Save Kant's Deduction of Taste as Objective," in Karl Ameriks, *Interpreting Kant's Critiques* (Oxford: Oxford University Press, 2003), 284–305. Taking up Ameriks's argument about the objectivism of beauty, Hannah Ginsborg holds that he cannot explain autonomy as a crucial condition of aesthetic judgments. The Kantian judgment of beauty rests on the idea of beauty as self-referential awareness. Hannah Ginsborg, "Kant on the Subjectivity of Taste," in *Kants Ästhetik/Kant's Aesthetics/L'esthétique de Kant*, ed. H. Parret (Berlin: Walter de Gruyter, 1998). See also Hannah Ginsborg, *The Role of Taste in Kant's Theory of Cognition* (New York: Garland, 1989), esp. 463–65. For a good discussion of this debate see Katalin Makkai, "Kant on Recognizing Beauty," *European Journal of Philosophy* 18, no. 3 (2010): 385–413.

39. Tinguely, "Orientation," 40–41. Space does not permit an extended account of the debate over the self-referential character of aesthetic judgments in Kant. I am persuaded by the critique of this reading offered by both Robert Pippin and Joseph Tinguely. It would be strange for Kant to conclude an inquiry into the

validity of our response to objects with a wholly self-referential theory about the pleasure we take in validating our own experience of pleasure. Although the status of the object is exceedingly complex in his account, it seems misguided to fully eliminate it in the structure of aesthetic judgment. See Robert Pippin, "The Significance of Taste: Kant, Aesthetic and Reflective Judgment," *Journal of the History of Philosophy* 34, no. 4 (1996): 549–69; Tinguely, "Orientation," 119–25.

40. In a marvelous reading of Kant's 1786 essay, "What Does It Mean to Orient Oneself in Thinking?," Tinguely endeavors to relate the status of Kantian orientational judgments to aesthetic ones. Taking up an insight of Heidegger's, he shows that no subjective feeling—be it that of left and right in the case of orientational judgments or pleasure in the case of aesthetic judgments—is possible without an actual engagement with objects and states of affairs. Feeling itself is a kind of judgmental capacity in Kant. Tinguely's broader aim is to force "the question not primarily whether aesthetics has cognitive content [as various brands of Aesthetic Cognitivism try to do] but, more fundamentally, whether cognition has aesthetic content" ("Orientation," 1). This involves a radical rethinking of the relationship between aesthetic and empirical judging.

41. In his account of the aesthetic idea, Kant points the way toward recognizing understanding as an interpretive practice that is not devoid of cognition but also not reducible to the subsumption of particulars under rules. While it is true that for Kant "no rule for conceptual subsumption can determine an aesthetic idea because the content of such an idea is not a collection of predicates characterizing the properties of some set of objects," writes Kirk Pillow, it is also true that "the 'indeterminacy' of an aesthetic idea does not render it an incoherent train of associations." Kirk Pillow, "Understanding Aestheticized," in *Aesthetics and Cognition in Kant's Critical Philosophy*, ed. Rebecca Kukla (Cambridge: Cambridge University Press, 2010), 245–65, at 252. In other words, the aesthetic idea is not that which is incomprehensible but "is an interpretive supplement to conceptual understanding. It supplements conceptual cognition because it goes beyond the categorization of objects to (try to) comprehend complex conceptual meanings" (253). Kant's own example of the lightning in the claws of Jupiter's eagle, for example, takes for granted that we can see the lightning as lightning. The genuine achievement of genius, remarks Pillow, is not so much at odds with cognition as it is "the capacity to communicate a broad and deep understanding of something" (254). This capacity, however, is visible only on the condition that we broaden "our conception of understanding to encompass narrowly cognitive and widely creative means" (255).

42. Ibid., 256.

43. Rudolf Makreel, *Imagination and Interpretation in Kant: The Hermeneutical Import of the "Critique of Judgment"* (Chicago: University of Chicago Press, 1990), 58.

44. Tinguely, "Orientation," 79.

45. Fred Rush has made a similar argument in relation to the exhibition or schematizing of empirical concepts. "Schemata do not merely register or mark in intuition some summed general image or model of what could count as an instance of a particular concept, whose content is limited to prior experience of that type. Rather, a schema must be able to countenance instances of the concept that may vary in novel ways from past experiences and this requires an ability to

produce a rule for the application of a concept to the sensible manifold that can chart (that is, imagine) a range of completely new instances that might fall into the range of the concept sought to be applied." Fred Rush, "The Harmony of the Faculties," *Kant-Studien* 92 (2001): 38–61, at 46. Citing Rush, Tinguely observes: "It is concepts themselves, and not merely their schemata, which are expansive or elastic" ("Orientation," 80).

46. Tinguely, "Orientation," 80.

47. Ibid.

48. Hannah Arendt, "The Concept of History," in *Between Past and Future: Eight Essays in Political Thought* (New York: Penguin, 2006), 41–90, at 51.

49. The most explicit articulation of this Kantian legacy is given in the work of Wilfred Sellars and John McDowell. See note 11 above.

50. Alice Crary, *Beyond Moral Judgment* (Cambridge, Mass.: Harvard University Press, 2009), 21.

51. Ibid., 21.

52. I discuss Arendt's distinctive political approach to the problem of validity in Zerilli, *A Democratic Theory of Judgment*, ch. 4, and in "Truth and Politics," in *Truth and Democracy*, ed. Jeremy Elkin and Andrew Norris (University Park: Pennsylvania State University Press, 2012), 54–75.

53. "As logic, to be sound, depends on the presence of the self, so judgment, to be valid, depends on the presence of others," writes Arendt. "The principle of agreement with oneself is very old; it was actually discovered by Socrates, whose central tenet, as formulated by Plato, is contained in the sentence: 'Since I am one, it is better for me to disagree with the whole world than to be in disagreement with myself.' From this sentence both Occidental ethics, with its stress upon being in agreement with one's own conscience, and Occidental logic, with its emphasis upon the axiom of contradiction, took their starting point" (Arendt, "The Crisis in Culture," 217, 216–17).

54. Hannah Arendt, "Introduction into Politics," in *The Promise of Politics*, ed. Jerome Kohn (New York: Schocken, 2005), 167. Arendt finds this conception of objectivity exemplified in Homeric poetry. "This Homeric impartiality . . . is still the highest type of objectivity we know. Not only does it leave behind the common interest in one's side and one's own people which, up to our own days, characterizes almost all national historiography, but it also discards the alternative of victory or defeat, which moderns have felt expresses the 'objective' judgment of history itself" (Arendt, "The Concept of History," 51). The modern conception of objectivity, in contrast, is premised on the idea that standpoints, intrinsically deceptive, should be eliminated, based as they are on subjective sense experience. Objectivity is a clean relation to the facts; it requires "abstention" from judgment (ibid., 49).

55. Habermas, *Legitimation Crisis*, 108.

56. Ronald Beiner, *What's the Matter with Liberalism?* (Berkeley: University of California Press, 1992), 40–41.

57. I discuss the problem of judgment as subjective preference in relation to political and moral debates around emotivism in Zerilli, *A Democratic Theory of Judgment*, ch. 1.

58. Tinguely, "Orientation," 3.

59. Ibid., 59.

60. Sensus communis is the condition of possibility for the communicability of feelings, representations, which makes (or ought to make) possible the capacity to think in the place of other subjects—what Kant called an enlarged way of thinking. Sensus communis "is not a matter of social consensus, and even less one obtained by a ballot," observes Jean-François Lyotard. "The beautiful does not get elected like Miss World." Lyotard, "Sensus Communis," in Andrew Benjamin, ed., *Judging Lyotard* (London: Routledge, 1992), 1–25, at 11. It is neither empirical nor objective, neither anthropological nor historical. It is a transcendental a priori principle, something we have to presuppose if we are to make sense of judgments of taste. Notwithstanding warnings in the third *Critique* against what Kant calls "empirical realism," argues Lyotard, sensus communis is often interpreted in overly unifying anthropological and sociological terms, terms that Kant himself invites and Arendt employs. See Jean-François Lyotard, *Lessons on the Analytic of the Sublime*, trans. Elizabeth Rottenberg (Stanford, Calif.: Stanford University Press, 1994), 220. But that idea of sensus communis, I argue, is not what Arendt seeks in Kant. She has no need to reduce it to some kind of communal unity because the anticipated agreement with others that animates the practice of judging rests on seeing the same object from *multiple* perspectives.

61. I discuss this point in Zerilli, "'We Feel Our Freedom.'"

62. Hannah Arendt, *The Human Condition*, 2nd ed. (Chicago: University of Chicago Press, 1998), 58. I discuss Arendt's account of the common world in Zerilli, "Value Pluralism and the Problem of Judgment"; Zerilli, *A Democratic Theory of Judgment*, ch. 1.

Part IV

✦

Aesthetics/Image

Aesthetic experience would appear to be the natural site for reflection on judgment. Not only is a refined and discriminating taste necessary for the adequate appreciation of aesthetic objects, but one would also think of the work of judging, assessing, and evaluating as the very source of aesthetic pleasure. The text usually credited with inaugurating modern aesthetics is called *The Critique of Judgment*, where "critique" is understood not as criticism but as establishing the conditions of possibility for judgment. Yet nowhere is the modern allergy to judgment more visible than when aesthetic judgment is frowned on or simply avoided in the name of appreciation. To want to judge art rather than understand it appears to be the height of philistinism. And in a museumgoing culture where aesthetic contemplation is structured as passive, the relation of art to action appears even more attenuated. The essays in this final group address themselves directly to these paradoxes of modern aesthetics, offering rich new theorizations and detailed analyses of images, to show how rethinking our modes of aesthetic engagement might revitalize our capacity for judgment and action.

Menke argues that aesthetic judgments are unusual kinds of judgments, because they do not merely raise the usual questions about the criteria for aesthetic evaluation but instead ask more fundamental questions, such as "Why do we judge aesthetic objects—and why do we judge at all?" The self-reflexive and self-questioning nature of aesthetic judgments means that they are always incomplete, but it also means that they have a productive relation to the objects that they judge: "The aesthetic reconception of judgment consists in understanding the *act* of judging in aesthetic matters as being itself an aesthetic—a 'dark,' 'unconscious'—doing." Aesthetic judgment, on this view, becomes a way not simply of judging but of grappling with the paradoxes of judgment. Thus "aesthetic taste is reluctant taste . . . intolerable to itself," and "aesthetic judgment is reluctant or repugnant judgment: judgment that is conscious of the aporia that defines the aesthetic judgment of taste." Neo Rauch's painting *Amt* may be judged to be a bad painting, Menke argues, because it does not provoke this kind of complex aesthetic response.

Klinger approaches the uncertainty about aesthetic judgment through the paintings of Gerhard Richter. For him, the question that pervades Richter's aesthetic production is how the artist can be comfortable with programmatic claims and provoking us to judgment, while nevertheless maintaining an anti-essentialist view of art. The answer that Klinger proposes is that "Richter's artistic program takes as its goal to replace traditional essentialist models of artistic form by a pragmatic model." Like McGowan in an earlier section, it is through this pragmatic model that Klinger and Richter mean to reconceptualize the operation of judgment. This leads to a number of surprising conclusions, for example, that judgment is the "basic act of making a difference" and that that "which makes the relevant difference" is form; that "not representation but reaction is the goal; the painting does not attempt to disclose a 'true reality' of the event, but to transform it to a new level of shared availability"; and that "art is bound neither to a meaning or truth, nor to the promise of moral betterment; . . . it is the performative fact of the constitution of interaction as such."

Attending to the long history of Christian theological discourse on the image, Pfau arrives at nearly the opposite view of the hold that the image has on us, so that we end this collection with the debate about the nature of judgment and action very much alive. For Pfau, the phenomenological experience that has the most to teach us about how to conceive action as something other than reactive behavior is the act whereby we give our attention to an image. More than simply idle curiosity or taking an interest in visual data, giving attention to an image implies both generosity and commitment. It becomes, as Pfau describes it, a form of "spiritual action." These observations lead to a far-reaching reconceptualization of action away from "modernity's epistemological default position and its attendant concerns with procedural correctness," by way of Hopkins's notion of "inscape" and a scene from Tolstoy's *Anna Karenina*. Perhaps most importantly, we "assent to an image not as an object or proposition but as a reality and as a good." The significance of this claim for reconfiguring our understanding of action cannot be overstated: "Inasmuch as its source and telos originate in a *vision* of the good rather than in a *movement* prompted by subjective desire or aimed at formal correctness, action seeks to communicate that good as a *meaning* susceptible of communal uptake." In short, "*figura* at once affirms the historical, empirical reality of a given appearance as well as its narrative orientation toward a transcendent meaning." However, it is not only action but judgment too that is implicated in Pfau's discussion of the image: "The act of giving our attention, then, begins with a judgment or ethical appraisal." Thus, in Pfau's ambitious essay, all the themes of our collection are braided together: judgment and action, but also contemplation (attention), ethics (the orientation toward the good), community, and, of course, the aesthetics of the image.

Judging What Cannot Be Judged

The Aporia of Aesthetic Critique

Christoph Menke

When the question of aesthetic judgment is raised, it is quite often, in philosophy and in public debates, taken as a question about the *criteria* of aesthetic judgment. One then can ask questions like the following: are there specific criteria for aesthetic judgments? Can these criteria be defined in such a way that they are universally shared? Can we thus hope and strive for a criteria-based consensus on aesthetic judgments or are these judgments on the contrary merely expressions of personal ideals or even projections of private preferences? By asking questions like these, the discussion on aesthetic judgment starts too late. For such questions presuppose that one has already answered another set of questions—questions like: What is the role of judgment in the aesthetic field? How do we proceed in judging aesthetic objects? Why do we judge aesthetic objects—and why do we judge at all? The question of aesthetic judgment cannot take its object for granted. It cannot assume that there actually *is* a specific kind of judgment called "aesthetic judgment"—and then proceed to investigate its distinctive criteria. Rather, "aesthetic judgment" is the name of a problem, even a paradox. For in aesthetic judgment, the very possibility, and necessity, of judgment is at stake.

I will explore this problematic or paradoxical nature of "aesthetic judgment" by proceeding in four steps: I will initially (1) sketch the locus of the problem that arises in aesthetic judgment by setting it in relation to the dialectic of practical judgment: the problem of aesthetic judgment is the problem of *amenability* to judgment—whether and how there are objects that can be judged. I will then (2) sketch the central argument: namely, that "aesthetic critique" is the enactment *and* questioning of judgment at the same time. I will continue (3) by taking up the question of what it means for an artwork that it *can* be judged—that it is *possible* to judge it. Finally (4), I will try to draw some consequences for the practice, and community, of aesthetic critique.

1. "Judgment"

This is briefly what I understand, roughly following Hannah Arendt, in the following by "judgment": to judge means to draw a distinction—a distinction of a peculiar kind: a normative distinction, a distinction of value.[1] By judging we do not just distinguish between different kinds of things; by judging we draw a distinction that refers to the relation or attitude that we have toward something. Normative judgments say how things are in relation to us, to subjects. The most elementary way in which we do this is by "tasting" objects: by saying whether a certain object, or more precisely, our relation to a certain object, gives us pleasure or displeasure (or even excitement or lust or, conversely, repulsion or disgust). In a more reflective way, we judge objects by saying that they are good or bad, right or wrong, and so on, referring to certain standards or measures for which we might be able to claim general validity. In all these cases judgments operate with the opposition of negation and affirmation, of rejection and acceptance. And in all of those cases of judging, the opposition of rejection and acceptance refers as much to the actual attitude of a subject toward an object—as an attitude of either acceptance or rejection—as to the future engagement with that object: judgments are about present (or past) objects but they shape future actions. Judgments divide the field of future behavior into two different, even opposed, types: between those actions which one should or must avoid and those which one must choose or should prefer. One can also say that judgments *commit* us to perform certain actions and not to perform others. This hints at a third dimension of judgments: judgments are not just (1) about a *subject's* attitude toward an object and (2) determine future modes of *action*. Judgments also (3) address *others* by establishing orders of commitment: judgments have a social meaning—they define which behavior of others is appropriate and inappropriate. Judgments are not reports that a subject gives of its attitude toward an object. Judgments have a performative force: by judging I determine the public status of an object; I shape the future possibilities of acting, by myself and others, with respect to that object.

The aspects of judgment I have mentioned characterize it as constitutive in three respects. (a) Judgment constitutes *subjectivity*: subjects are entities that pass judgment, which distinguishes them from their objects—subjects are capable of judging. (b) Judgment constitutes *actions*: actions are consequences of judgments—to act means to implement a judgment. (c) Judgment constitutes social *communities*: communities express an agreement in judgment—judgments form the fabric of which the social is made. This tripartite characterization can be read backward as well as forward. Read backward, judgment is about the self-government of social communities; read forward, about the self-government of subjects. And both always take place at once; the self-government of subjects that, in passing judgment about objects, express their attitude regarding these objects and determine their conduct vis-à-vis them can take place only by their adopting, influencing, and revising the judgments that manifest the agreement of a social community: "I judge as a member of this community."[2] Yet the converse is also true: the social agreement in judgment that constitutes a social community cannot exist other than in, and by virtue of, the self-governing subjects' adopting and assimilating these judgments. The judging self-government of subjects and the judging agreement in communities take place as one: they are necessarily performed in one and the same act—there is neither merely private self-government of the subject nor social agreement in judgment without its efficacy in the self-conduct of subjects—but they are not therefore necessarily concordant. Their interrelation can always only take place via a difference.

The simultaneity in difference of subjective self-government and social agreement describes the *dialectic* of judgment: the concordant and discordant interplay between its social validity and its subjective implementation in which the relation between society and individual unfolds. This dialectic defines the field of the practical; practical judgments are as social as they are subjective, and practical judgment is the medium of socialization (of the individual) as much as of subjectivation (of the community).

The problem of *aesthetic* judgment must be clearly distinguished from this dialectic of practical judgment. The problem of the aesthetic comes *before* the dialectic that defines the practical: "aesthetic judgment" is the name of a problem that precedes and underlies the question—which arises in all practical judgment—of how the individual and the community can be mediated to each other in their discordance. The practical problem of judgment is this: how can a subject govern itself by virtue of its judgment and therein gain social recognition as an individual? Or, conversely, how can the agreement in judgment of a social community attain individual reality in the self-conduct of the subjects? Yet this practical problem of judgment presupposes that the aesthetic problem has already been solved, and indeed made to disappear. For what practical judgment presupposes as a given is experienced as fundamentally precarious and uncertain in aesthetic judgment: practical judgment presupposes that there *is* an object *on* which judgment can be passed.

In her reinterpretation of Kant's *Critique of Judgment*, Hannah Arendt has described this aesthetic presupposition of practical judgment by sketching the interrelation between "common sense" and "imagination." Common sense is the faculty enabling the subject not merely to pass private and individual judgment, but to judge in the name of the community: to realize, in its subjective judgment, social agreement. This realization builds on the achievement of the imagination, which Arendt understands as the object of judgment's being constituted by the subject's distancing itself. As long as I am "directly affected" by something, I cannot pass judgment on it. I need to take a step back, to break with direct affection:

> Imagination, that is, the faculty of having present what is absent, transforms an object into something I do not have to be directly confronted with but that I have in some sense internalized. . . . This is "the operation of reflection." Only what touches, affects, one in representation, when one can no longer be affected by immediate presence—when one is uninvolved, like the spectator who was uninvolved in the actual doings of the French Revolution—can be judged to be right or wrong, important or irrelevant, beautiful or ugly, or something in between. One then speaks of judgment and no longer of taste because, though it still affects one like a matter of taste, one now has, by means of representation, established the proper distance, the remoteness or uninvolvedness or disinterestedness, that is requisite for approbation and disapprobation, for evaluating something at its proper worth. By removing the object, one has established the conditions for impartiality.[3]

Practical judgment, with its dialectic of individual and society, is predicated on the removal of the object, on the disruption of affection effected by the subject's imagination, which engenders an object that can be judged. Because there cannot be judgment without something that can be judged, practical judgment (whose dialectic Arendt is exploring in this passage) must presuppose that this aesthetic constitution in the imagination has been concluded, and successfully so. Yet the *problem* of aesthetic judgment—the problem whose name is "aesthetic judgment," the problem that unfolds in judging in aesthetic matters—lies in the fact that this act of engendering what can be judged can never be conclusively successful. That renders the problem of aesthetic judgment paradoxical: it is a judgment that has no object—a judgment without something to be judged. But how should we judge, if there is no object that can be judged? How, if there is no such object because the subject that objectivates, that distances itself, that disrupts its affection, does not exist? How, if that is the case precisely because the force of imagination that is supposed to effect this objectivation in order to establish the possibility of judgment is in reality an aesthetic force: a force at play—and not a faculty of distancing? The paradox of aesthetic judgment is that, in its performance, as an aesthetic performance, it at once calls the amenability of its object to judgment, which it must presuppose, in question. If its object cannot be judged, if it eludes judgment, that is an effect of the judgment; it is the process of judging that renders the act of conclusive judgment impossible.

2. Aesthetic Critique

As the awareness of a paradox, our awareness of the impossibility of judgment founds neither a theory of skepticism concerning judgment nor a practice of abstention from judgment—although the "temporary suspension of the critical pendulum" is a crucial virtue (or strategy) of the critic, the judge; it helps "[lure] forth the soul of a thing."[4] Rather, the awareness of the impossibility of judging expresses a self-reflection of judgment that locates the resistance to its conclusion not out there, in the object it attends to, but in the performance of judgment itself.

This self-reflection of judgment has its theoretical place in the philosophical discipline of aesthetics; its practice is aesthetic critique. Both, aesthetics and critique, must be understood on the basis of their belonging to the "aesthetic regime" (Jacques Rancière). Outside the aesthetic regime of art, there is neither aesthetic theory nor aesthetic critique. That is not just a terminological nicety; it is a conceptual observation, and thus of immediate consequence to how judgment is understood in aesthetic critique. If by "aesthetic critique" we mean any description and argument leading to a judgment concerning the beautiful or ugly, the sublime or banal aspect of a piece of nature or the success or failure, the perfection or miscarriage of a piece of art, we ignore not only the difference—Rancière has interpreted it as historical—between the regimes of art, but also, crucially, the difference between (ancient) poetics and (modern) aesthetics.[5] By adopting this ostensibly neutral usage of the term "critique," we also commit the much more far-reaching error of basing our understanding of the judgment of aesthetic critique on its outcome, on the judgment it passes. Yet it is not judgment passed that is the essence of aesthetic critique, but rather its conception of the ground, and hence also the process, of judging; put another way, what matters is not the fact that aesthetic critique, too, judges, but *how* judging takes place in it: aesthetic critique judges in such a way that the how of judging calls the what of judgment into question. That is why aesthetic critique cannot be defined based on its ostensible result, the judgment it passes. The aesthetic judgment is not the purpose and end of aesthetic critique, it cannot serve as the basis of our conception of aesthetic critique, because the crucial insight of aesthetic critique is precisely that an unbridgeable chasm gapes between the ground of judgment and the act of judging, and hence also between the process of judging and the fact of judgment passed. The syntagma "the aesthetic critique of judgment" is grammatically ambiguous, because the genitive may be read as subjective as well as objective: aesthetic critique is that practice of judgment that is at once also a critique of judgment.

To understand why that is so, we need to recall a crucial trait of the aesthetic regime of art. In his description of the essential shortcoming of the aesthetic contemplation of art, Hegel delineated this trait as follows: "Just as it is essential for the statue to be the work of human hands, so is the actor essential to his mask—not as an external condition from which artistically considered we must abstract; or, so far as we do have to make abstraction from it, we admit just this, that Art does not yet contain in it the true and proper self."[6] The law of the aesthetic is the law of the "not yet": of not yet being the realm of the "true and proper self," the realm or practice of the self-conscious, rational subject. Art, *aesthetic* art, is an act, the act of representing, that does not yet fully comprehend itself, that is not yet in the full sense conscious of itself. Aesthetic art, as Adorno says taking up Hegel's definition, consists in making things that one does not know.

Hegel's definition of art under the sign of the "not-yet" describes art by virtue of an essential deficiency or lack: it does not yet "contain in it the true and proper self." This aesthetic deficiency—the deficiency that *is* the aesthetic—is a deficiency of self-knowledge or self-consciousness: art is an act of making that escapes the subject for it is an act that is incapable of "knowing" and "asserting" itself. Art essentially eludes itself: its act of making is not an object of its knowing or a content of its asserting. The law of the "not yet" (that is the law of the aesthetic) states the insuperable severance between doing and knowing in the arts. For the deficiency of knowledge characteristic of art is not exterior to its doing but rather defines the doing of art as an aesthetic doing. In overcoming this deficiency, that is to say, in gaining consciousness of its doing, art would thus precipitate its own disappearance. The *knowledge* of aesthetic doing would no longer be a knowledge of an *aesthetic* doing. The doing that we can know because it is a doing by force of "the true and proper self"—a doing that is an expression of knowledge (on the part of the doing self) and can thus become an object of knowledge (on the part of the observing self)—this knowable, because self-conscious, doing is not an aesthetic doing. The aesthetic doing is not a knowable doing because it is not a self-conscious doing. This is the positive formulation of Hegel's negative definition of aesthetic art: that art does not yet know itself means that the aesthetic doing is not an object of knowing because it is not grounded in knowing. Aesthetic doing eludes knowledge; it is a doing before and therefore beyond all knowledge—an act or doing that therefore philosophical aesthetics calls "dark" or "obscure" (Baumgarten).[7]

A further and more precise explanation of what defines a process of representation as an "aesthetic" one expresses: the aesthetic process of making a representation does not yet (and will not ever) contain a self-conscious subject, because the aesthetic process consists in the unfolding of "unconscious" forces (Herder). The logic of the unfolding of these aesthetic forces is the logic of play. That means that aesthetic forces unfold in an essentially paradoxical way. A force only exists by expressing itself—by producing something, as its effect; a force is effective. At the same time, a force in the play of its realization turns against its own products. Each force dissolves what it has produced; a force is as transgressive as it is effective. The idea of aesthetic force (or the idea of the aesthetic as the unfolding of forces) thus refers to an infinite process of producing and dissolving what it has produced. Art, aesthetically understood, unfolds the play of representation as a "process of gaining and simultaneously of playing down the gains. . . . This could be illuminated by a sentence from Borges: 'that imminence of a revelation that is not yet produced is, perhaps, the aesthetic reality.' "[8] The aesthetic process of the playful expression of force is thus not mere indetermination. The aesthetic process rather consists in producing determinations as momentary effects—determinations that cannot be established and safeguarded against their dissolution by the same force that had produced them but which precisely therefore gain momentarily, as long as they exist, a kind of evidence which promises a "revelation" (Borges).

This definition of the aesthetic making and doing at hand, we can return to the question of how aesthetic critique judges. Aesthetic critique is the judgment of aesthetic objects. But if aesthetic objects are not inert things but processes or performances, which cannot be understood as realizations of self-conscious subjectivity because they essentially include an aesthetic doing, as the playful expression of unconscious forces, then there cannot be a judgment of aesthetic objects that does not also partake of such doing—and is, in so partaking, *like* the aesthetic doing: to pass aesthetic judgment is to join the aesthetic play. The aesthetic judgment passed on the aesthetic object must likewise have been an aesthetic doing and, hence, a move in the aesthetic play. Or: the judgment passed on the doing or making in which the aesthetic object consists is, like that doing or making itself, "not yet" the doing or making of a self-conscious subject. Aesthetic judgment is not a completely self-conscious act and hence not an act of the application—let alone of the reflectively scrutinizing application—of general criteria to a particular case. The act of aesthetic judgment exceeds the control of self-conscious subjectivity. For this act is *expression*: an expression of the aesthetic force whose expression in the work of art this act, as an act of judgment, attends to.

The insight that judgment in aesthetic matters is itself aesthetic-expressive in nature constitutes the fundamental trait of "aesthetic critique"—the reconception of judgment in the aesthetic regime of art. This reconception, that is to say, does *not* consist in identifying a new and secure ground for judgment in the entity known as the "subject." Rather, the aesthetic reconception of judgment consists in understanding the *act* of judging in aesthetic matters as being itself an aesthetic—a "dark," "unconscious"—doing: the aesthetic judgment encounters its object as "devan[çant] tout examen," encounters it "avant aucune discussion"; the aesthetic "appréhension" is an "impression soudaine" or a "sentiment subit."[9]

The aesthetic character of the act of judging an aesthetic object is, on the one side, that the aesthetic act of judging is itself a move in the playful unfolding of a sensuous force that is not yet, and will never become, the subject's own deed. The other side is that in the moment of proclaiming a judgment the subject splits from the aesthetic play of unconscious force: by judging *about* the aesthetic process, turning it into an object, the subject breaks with (or steps out of) the aesthetic process. The act of judging is thus the act of the conscious, rational subject's self-constitution. In judging, the subject suspends the power of the aesthetic apprehension and asks for reasons. This is the moment, the space and time, of aesthetic critique. The aesthetic critique is the enactment of an infinite difference: between judgment as an expression of a sensible force and the reasons by which the subject tries to guarantee its validity—the difference between aesthetic sensuality and self-conscious rationality. Aesthetic critique of judgment does not abolish this difference, either by its reconciliation or by an act of decision for either side. The aesthetic critique of judgment rather unfolds this difference, it keeps the gap open between the judgment as an effect of aesthetic force and as the result of a rational procedure. The aesthetic critique both conceives of and carries out judgment in such a way that it is characterized by an irresolvable contradiction: the contradiction between the intuitive apprehension of an object *and* the methodological deduction of a judgment from transparent reasons; between the sudden sentiment *and* the endless unfolding of connections; between the sensible evidence of "thus it is" (*So ist es*, in Alex Düttmann's words)[10] and the rational reflection on preconditions and results. Judging aesthetically means unfolding this contradiction, not resolving it; to understand every judgment as both equally urgent and premature. The critique of judgment is thus a reciprocal operation: the critique of the aesthetic, sensual apprehension by rational reflection (for the sensual apprehension is always premature) and the critique of the rationally reflecting judgment by aesthetic apprehension (for rational reflection is always taking too long). The aesthetic critique of judgment unfolds this double movement of mutual critique: the aporia of judging.

This is different than to declare, or hope for, an aesthetic "ending" of judgment; the aim of the aesthetic critique of judgment is not (in Deleuze's formula) "To Have Done with Judgment."[11] For to hope for an end of judgment would presuppose a judgment about judgment: the "critical" judgment that judgment is bad and should, and can, be left behind. The aesthetic critique instead does not judge judgment, but exhibits its structural impossibility: the impossibility of ever overcoming its inner contradiction. Furthermore, the aesthetic critique shows that it is precisely, and only, this impossibility of judgment—of being able to either overcome the internal split of judgment or decide in favor of either side—that makes a different, alternative praxis of judgment possible. Aesthetic critique is a praxis of judgment that makes the aporia of judgment into its defining form.

3. How (Not) to Judge an Artwork: Neo Rauch, *Amt*

One consequence of the preceding argument is that the normativity of aesthetic critique is a normativity of second order. As any act of judgment, aesthetic critique claims an object to be bad or good, to be rejected or affirmed. However, first and foremost aesthetic critique claims the goodness of a certain *way* of judgment on whether an object is good or bad—namely a performance of judgment that unfolds its inner aporetic structure. But this poses a further question: the question of whether one actually *can* judge an object in this way. For it seems that this does not depend only on the judging subject; it's not a matter of that subject's arbitrary decision. Rather, it depends on the engagement of the subject with the object, and this too in turn depends on the object. This suggests a thesis that may sound either tautological or paradoxical: namely that the normativity of the second order that defines aesthetic critique—being about the goodness of the aporetic way of judgment—also establishes a second-order criteria for the goodness of aesthetic objects: any object that allows for aesthetic critique is thereby good. Or, the goodness of an aesthetic object consists in nothing else than making possible its aesthetic critique. The tautological version of this thesis reads: any aesthetic object is good; to be *aesthetic*, that is, an object of aesthetic critique, means to be aesthetically *good*. The paradoxical version of this thesis says: any object that can become the object of an aesthetical judgment about its being good *or* bad, *is* good. Let me briefly try to show this by reference to an example of a bad artwork, for which I take a painting by Neo Rauch.

In Rauch's painting *Amt* (2004), three different spaces are violently abutted against and built on top of one another.[12] In the upper portion of the painting, a rocky, snow-covered peak set almost in the middle, only slightly offset to the right, projects into a black sky crisscrossed with white lines. The bottom portion of the painting is dominated by a scene stretching from the rear on the left side toward the front on the right: hunched-over men in motion beneath two lamps looming upward are dragging something appearing amorphously organic out of a mine shaft. In the extreme foreground of the painting's lower edge, there is a still life consisting of four books, one of which is open, a bone-like thing that at one of its ends appears as a sort of tool, and an unidentifiable object to the right revealing a crystalline structure. A pronounced tension dominates between the wild dynamism of the sky (which can also be seen, as if through an optical illusion, as a nighttime sea with quietly lapping waves) up above or to the rear, the middle section with people and the organisms, and the dead things far below or in the foreground. Yet simultaneously, between the picture's three different spaces one can make out ambiguously decipherable figures and zones that seem to belong not only to one portion of the picture, but to another as well. This ambiguity makes them puzzling, transforming them into objects that can be viewed in a twofold, reversible manner: a man seems to be climbing out of the scene in front of the mine shaft directly onto the snow-covered mountain; another man is sitting in the mountain snow, yet seems to be keeping watch over the carriers; a house on the side of the mountain seems simultaneously to belong to the ensemble of buildings surrounding the shaft; upon a closer look, a fir tree on the opposite edge of the mountain resembles Caspar David Friedrich's sailboat stranded in the ice.

And there is a second, quite different level on which the painting is organized, a level at which its three fields and worlds are linked to one another: through the sparingly utilized, yet highly effective coloration of individual elements on this surface otherwise kept predominantly black and white: yellow for one of the books at the bottom, for the light in the middle, and for a spot on the mountain; red for the crystalline structure at the bottom right, for the shirt of the man kneeling in the middle, for the little red sailboat/fir tree; and, finally, violet for the pants of the man kneeling and the short coat of the man climbing onto the mountain. And then there are traces of green dully shining through here and there. As Gottfried Boehm has stressed, the colors in Rauch's paintings unfold a "complex and tension-filled play of exchange, which directs the entire structure of the image on a hidden level."[13]

And yet engaging all of this effort and refinement has left us in the cold. You see it and shrug your shoulders. Yes, yes, one can see that this is all supposed to be very puzzling. But the perturbation of the fantastic which first appears on the scene when one no longer knows if the world of the image—thus, the world itself—makes sense, does not come out at all. Rauch's paintings are as distressing as postcards of Roger Corman film stills; nothing about his picture puzzles puts one in a state of unrest, haunts one's dreams. And maybe they do not even want to do that; perhaps it was not at all Rauch's intention to challenge and anguish us. Mysteriousness can only unsettle whoever still, or already, attempts to understand. In contrast, Rauch's paintings seem to just pass on their receptivity to the incomprehensible: a miracle, not a problem; amazement, wonder as the end, not the beginning, of thinking.

And the colors? That is perhaps the most surprising (and least satisfying) aspect of this painting: the play of colors does not change anything, it merely confirms and reinforces the indifference called forth by Rauch's mystification. The coloration of this picture set in black and white does not manage to create a second level, and different kind, of interrelations in tension with the first level, the level of the things, figures, and scenes depicted. This second level appears merely on the side. Even in this most basic relation of the painting, the relation that defines it as a painting, the relation between the what and the how of the painting, between its object and its appearance, the logic of mere indifference dominates; hence the avoidance, the cessation of conflict. The arrangement of colors does not manage to create any distance between the world in the painting. The colors are lacking in precisely that crucial aspect whose attainment was the greatest concern for modernist painting: Rauch's colors lack *force*.

In an interview with Holger Liebs for the *Süddeutsche Zeitung*, Rauch says of his painting: "Unenlightened zones are necessary, because otherwise the painting dries out since it's totally disinfected. I have to continually decide at which stage of pushing forward with the painting I will impose this rupture and posit the regions of disturbance. That always happens when the feeling arises that the parts which are spelled out are overly weighty."[14] Thus it sounds as if Rauch had taken Wolfgang Iser's theory of the "gap," an empty space in which Iser saw the aesthetic potential of literary texts, a little too literally, as the mandate to distribute a few empty spaces throughout the painting. Rauch understands the aesthetic gap of indeterminacy spatially: as something aside or between spaces of fullness, of determinacy (those spaces in which one can recognize something), thus also as something that he can just decide to add, from outside, to whatever he has already painted in a figural way. Yet Iser intended an emptiness, a *negativity* whose aesthetic quality consists in hollowing out all determinacy from the inside.

Since Rauch's work does not allow this very hollowing out all determinacy from inside to emerge, one thing never happens when looking at his (objectively considered) ludicrous figural arrangements; in fact, it never happens at all when viewing his paintings: one never laughs; a manifest meaning is never replaced by a latent one lurking, springing forth in a lightning flash. And for this same reason also the very impression of what his paintings seem calculated to be will never emerge: the impression of a secret. Just as one has nothing to laugh about in front of his paintings, one also has nothing to ask about, to wonder and think about. *This is it*, the opposite of *thus it is*, seems to be all that they want to say to us.

4. Aesthetic Taste Is Reluctant Taste: Two Conclusions

In *Minima Moralia*, Adorno wrote about taste, the faculty of aesthetic judgment: "Taste is the most accurate seismograph of historical experience. Unlike almost all other faculties, it is even able to register its own behavior. Reacting against itself, it recognizes its own lack of taste. . . . It is precisely the nerves most highly developed aesthetically that now find self-righteous aestheticism intolerable."[15] Taste is the faculty of aesthetic judgment—or, taste is an aesthetic faculty—in that it "reacts against itself." It is intolerable to itself: the aesthetic faculty of judgment does not tolerate its own judgment. For all judgment is "self-righteous." To judge in matters of right and wrong, correct and incorrect, means to believe—it means to know one believes—that one is in the right. There is no judgment without the self-righteousness of this belief in one's own rightness. It is against this belief, and thus against itself as the faculty of judging, that taste reacts. In other words, it reacts against itself not out of consideration or tolerance for the other, the object of its judgment, but rather out of intolerance against itself. Aesthetic taste cannot stand itself. In the self-righteousness of its judging, it gets on its own nerves: it is "the nerves most highly developed aesthetically" that "find self-righteous aestheticism intolerable."

In her explication of Adorno's figure of aesthetic taste's reaction against itself, Silvia Bovenschen has used the concept of idiosyncrasy to explain this crucial thought: "By performing this idiosyncratic reaction against itself, taste can become a sort of aesthetic conscience. If taste guides the idiosyncrasies, the latter are conversely constitutive of taste; they are—in a process of infinite one-upmanship—the other side of taste, ensuring that it does not degenerate into rule or diktat."[16] The turn of taste against itself is an act of "aesthetic conscience" because it flows from taste's knowledge of itself; conscience is knowledge of self, is conscious awareness of what taste is in reality (or: conscience is "honesty" [*Redlichkeit*], in the sense Nietzsche gave to the term). Taste turns against itself, against the self-righteousness of its judgment, because it knows of itself that it is, as an aesthetic faculty, not a faculty of autonomous subjectivity: not a faculty, that is to say, that could vouch for the success of its acts of judging. Aesthetic taste is essentially a reaction of the nerves. *That* is why the nerves of taste turn against the self-righteousness of its judgment: because its judging, in the self-righteousness with which it grounds itself in the faculty of autonomous subjectivity, represses the regard in which it is itself a reaction of the nerves, the expression of a sensation, a passion (*pathos*) or energy. The turn of taste against the self-righteousness of its judgment expresses the aesthetic reluctance to embrace subjectivity, the "repugnance [*Widerwillen*] for all aesthetic subjectivism"[17]—the repugnance for taste as a faculty that puts criteria and procedures at the subject's disposal that vouch for the correctness of its judgment. Aesthetic judgment is reluctant or repugnant judgment: judgment that is conscious of the aporia that defines the aesthetic judgment of taste.

This allows me to say, first, what the description of Neo Rauch's *Amt* I just sketched can teach us about the problem of aesthetic judgment in general. The rejection of this picture, the negative judgment its description has implied, is based not on the picture's failure to satisfy one or another aesthetic criterion of judgment, but rather on the fact that it is not amenable to aesthetic judgment at all. The repugnance for the picture is based precisely on its inability to engender the repugnance of the one who judges for himself, for his own judging or his own taste. That means—always presupposing that the description I have sketched is correct—that this picture is "bad": it is not an aesthetic object at all, since to be "aesthetic" means precisely not to be a thing, an object for a perceiving or judging subject; it means, instead, to be the counterpart, and indeed the opposite, of the subject that is capable of triggering the subject's repugnance for its "subjectivism." Rauch's picture is bad because it lacks the strength to render the judging subject intolerable to itself.

I have described the picture and, in so doing, judged it; I have offered my description to justify my (negative) judgment. There is no distinction between the two, the judgment and the description. The description did not lead us beyond the judgment. That means nothing other than that the description of the picture does not articulate an aesthetic experience. The experience of the picture was not an aesthetic one, as it did not have the strength to make the subject's "nerves" react against that subject, against the self-righteousness of its judgment. The picture, that is to say, is bad only because the judgment of it—the judgment that it is bad—is true: because this picture *can* be judged; because it is merely an object that calls for judgment, and not for an aesthetic critique (of the judgment). The aesthetically bad is the mere object—that in which the subject can find itself reflected, in its negative *or* positive judgment. (As a consequence, the object of a positive judgment would likewise be aesthetically bad.) The aesthetically bad is the object of the judgment concerning good or bad that, as a mere object, does not have the strength to make the subject react against itself. The aesthetically bad leaves the subject in agreement with itself.

A second conclusion leads us back to the question of community, to the form of the social the judgment founds or expresses. In a recent contribution to *Texte zur Kunst* (his opening statement at the conference celebrating the twentieth anniversary of that magazine), Diedrich Diederichsen described the situation of aesthetic critique—as practiced in *Texte*—as defined by the tension between two attitudes: "Between the antisocial joys of unfriendly exclusion by means of definitive last words on an issue and a social inclusion that, in a self-reflective examination of its language and its literal social reality, strives to be friendly."[18] The two attitudes of aesthetic critique Diederichsen outlines with gentle mockery are vigorous or energetic judgment and reflective judgment, a contrast he aligns with the opposition between asocial (or even "antisocial") and socially inclusive (or "pro-social"). And both attitudes, Diederichsen argues, are equally necessary, however much they conflict with each other. That is why he concludes his reflection with the call for a "positive synthesis of the antisocial energy of the aggressive statement with the pro-social caution of reflectivity."[19] How this synthesis is to be conceived (and whether it may be a "positive" synthesis) depends on how we understand the two attitudes of judgment in their relation to each other. And the answer to that question also determines the constitution of the community or society of the subjects of aesthetic judgment.

The first description of this relation sees it as dialectical. It understands the two attitudes as proceeding from two antagonistic aspects of judgment, which both sides agree in understanding as assertion (or "statement," to use Diederichsen's word). To make an assertion of judgment is, on the one hand, a joyful act that is "unfriendly" because it is directed against other, opposing judgments. In this regard, the judgment is "apodictic," Diederichsen writes, which is to say, it is conclusive, irrefutable: it is the basis for what follows—for further judgments and actions. Yet the judgment that is to serve as the basis for something must itself be given a basis. That is the objection of the other, the reflective attitude of judgment: to the extent that the assertion of judgment proceeds from a basis, it is not an apodictic proposition that suddenly springs forth, but in fact a conclusion that gradually builds and whose validity is dependent not least importantly on the reflection of the subject of judgment: on our "compar[ing] our judgment not so much with the actual as rather with the merely possible judgments of others, and put[ting] ourselves in the position of everyone else, merely by abstracting from the limitations that happen to attach to our own judging."[20] The two attitudes of judgment, the energetic and the reflective one, each bring one of the two sides to bear that define the judgment as an assertion: its claim to truth (by which it declares everything else and all others that conflict with it to be wrong) and its need to be given a basis, to be justified, through procedures of reflection and self-reflection (which compel it to take the points of view of those others into consideration, since they might draw its attention to important aspects it may have failed to see).

The second description of the relation between the two attitudes of judgment, the "energetic" and the "reflective" one, sees it not as dialectical but as aporetic. That is the description offered by Adorno's figure of the repugnance of taste for itself. What the dialectical description sees as counterparts fall on the same side in this description: they are two aspects of one and the same view of judgment as a subjective act—two aspects of "subjectivism"—against which, according to Adorno, "the nerves most highly developed aesthetically" react. That, after all, is what it means to be a subject: to claim validity for an assertion against others—and to justify that claim for others (and with others). The aporia that defines the aesthetic judgment, however, concerns not the two sides of judgment as justified assertion, but the judgment as assertion *and* as nonassertion—as sensation, passion, pathos. The aporetic description of the relation between the two attitudes of judgment, the reflective and the energetic attitude, sees in them the expression of an irresolvable tension within the aesthetic judgment which belongs, on one side, to the order of proposition, of assertion and justification, and on the other side belongs to the nonorder of expression, of the aesthetic play of imagination and sensation. These two attitudes of what is therefore an aporetic judgment find their negative synthesis in the repugnance of aesthetic taste for its own asserting and justifying.

Taste that is repugnant to itself and thus aesthetic describes a new figure of community or society. Judgment as assertion, and as justification of that assertion, founds a community by reference to the content of judgment: we agree, that is to say, in *what* we assert in judging—or in the shared quest for such content as may withstand the pro and contra of the various aspects and arguments. The aesthetic-aporetic judgment, too, intends agreement and, by virtue of it, community. Yet this is an agreement not in the *what* but in the *how* of judging. The aesthetic community is a community of subjects who judge in the same way. This is the aesthetic way of judging, as the enactment of aesthetic taste. If (following Adorno) taste becomes aesthetic by reacting "against itself," then each act of judgment in order to be aesthetic must also internally be a reaction against judging itself. To enact judgment *and* to react against judgment at the same time: this is what defines the aesthetic form of judging. The aesthetic attitude of judging is the performance of judgment against the will to judge: to judge repugnantly (or reluctantly: *widerwillig*).

This attitude is the only determination which the participants of the aesthetic community share. It is their sensus communis: they share the attitude of judging repugnantly.

Notes

This chapter was translated by Gerrit Jackson. It is the revised and amended version of an argument that I have published in Daniel Birnbaum and Isabelle Graw, eds., *The Power of Judgment: A Debate on Aesthetic Critique* (Berlin: Sternberg, 2010), 9–29; and Cátedra Jorge Oteiza, ed., *Juzgar el arte contemporáneo—Judging Contemporary Art* (Pamplona: Universidad Pública de Navarra, 2012), 79–104, 217–42.

1. For this definition, see Hannah Arendt, *Lectures on Kant's Political Philosophy*, ed. Ronald Beiner (Chicago: University of Chicago Press, 1982), lectures 11–13.

2. Ibid., 67.

3. Ibid., 66–67. Concerning the interrelation of the two planes I here call "practical" and "aesthetic" in Kant's reflective theory of judgment, see Christoph Menke, "Aesthetic Reflection and Its Ethical Significance: A Critique of the Kantian Solution," *Philosophy and Social Criticism* 34, nos. 1–2 (2008): 51–63.

4. Friedrich Nietzsche, *Human, All Too Human: A Book for Free Spirits*, trans. R. J. Hollingdale (Cambridge: Cambridge University Press, 1986), 1.621, p. 196.

5. Jacques Rancière, *Le partage du sensible: Esthétique et politique* (Paris: La Fabrique-éditions, 2000), 28ff.; translated into English as *The Politics of Aesthetics*, trans. Gabriel Rockhill (New York: Continuum, 2004), 21ff.

6. Georg Wilhelm Friedrich Hegel, *Phenomenology of Spirit*, ed. J. N. Findlay, trans. A. V. Miller (Oxford: Oxford University Press, 1977), 444. The following two paragraphs summarize an argument I have laid out more fully in Christoph Menke, "Not Yet: The Philosophical Significance of Aesthetics," *Nordic Journal of Aesthetics*, no. 39 (2010): 34–47.

7. On the following see my *Force: A Fundamental Concept of Aesthetic Anthropology* (New York: Fordham University Press, 2012).

8. Wolfgang Iser, *Das Fiktive und das Imaginäre: Perspektiven literarischer Anthropologie* (Frankfurt am Main: Suhrkamp, 1991), 409; the passage is absent from the existing English translation, *The Fictive and the Imaginary: Charting Literary Anthropology* (Baltimore: Johns Hopkins University Press, 1993). For the quotation from Borges, see J. L. Borges, "The Wall and the Books" (1950), in *Other Inquisitions: 1937–1952*, trans. Ruth Simms (New York: Simon and Schuster, 1965), 3–9, at 5.

9. Jean-Baptiste Dubos, *Réflexions critiques sur la poésie et sur la peinture* (Genève: Slatkine, 1967), vol. 2, sect. 22, 343–44. Dubos is only one example; similar arguments against the possibility of, as well as the need for, a methodization of ("sensual") apperception and judgment have been made by Pascal, Leibniz, and Vico; see Menke, *Force*, chs. 1 and 2.

10. Alexander García Düttmann, *So ist es: Ein philosophischer Kommentar zu Adornos "Minima Moralia"* (Frankfurt am Main: Suhrkamp, 2004).

11. Gilles Deleuze, "To Have Done with Judgment," in *Deleuze: Essays Critical and Clinical* (Minneapolis: University of Minnesota Press, 1997), 126–35.

12. Oil on paper, 268 by 200 cm, Kaufmann Collection, Berlin.

13. Gottfried Boehm, "Plötzlich, diese Übersicht. Farbe und Imagination bei Neo Rauch," in *Neo Rauch: Neue Rollen. Bilder 1993–2006* (Cologne: Catalogue Wolfsburg, 2006), 35–39, at 35.

14. Holger Liebs, "Im Interview: Maler Neo Rauch—'Mir ist nichts mehr peinlich,'" *Süddeutsche Zeitung*, May 17, 2010; available at http://www.sueddeutsche.de.

15. Theodor W. Adorno, *Minima Moralia: Reflexionen aus dem beschädigten Leben* (Frankfurt am Main: Suhrkamp, 1978), 191; English translation, *Minima Moralia: Reflections on a Damaged Life*, trans. E. F. N. Jephcott (London: Verso, 2005), 145; translation modified.

16. Silvia Bovenschen, *Über-Empfindlichkeit: Spielformen der Idiosynkrasie* (Frankfurt am Main: Suhrkamp, 2000), 89.

17. Adorno, *Minima Moralia*, 191.

18. Diedrich Diederichsen, "Introduction," *Texte zur Kunst* 21, no. 81 (2011): 45–49.

19. Ibid., 49.

20. Immanuel Kant, *Critique of Judgment*, trans. Werner S. Pluhar (Indianapolis and Cambridge: Hackett, 1987), §40, p. 294.

To Make That Judgment

The Pragmatism of Gerhard Richter

Florian Klinger

1. Today's Situation

In fall 2009, the journal *October* published a questionnaire on the theme of contemporary art. It addressed art critics and curators in the United States and Europe, asking them to respond to the following diagnosis formulated by Hal Foster:

> The category of "contemporary art" is not a new one. What is new is the sense that, in its very heterogeneity, much present practice seems to float free of historical determination, conceptual definition, and critical judgment. Such paradigms as "the neo-avant-garde" and "postmodernism," which once oriented some art and theory, have run into the sand, and, arguably, no models of much explanatory reach or intellectual force have risen in their stead.[1]

Overall, the responses confirm that Foster indeed articulates a minimal level of consensus, beyond which, however, there is little agreement—a fact that, taken by itself, further confirms the consensus. According to this diagnosis, our present is determined by nondetermination, by the fact that so far its paradigmatic orientation has not arrived.

While modernism can be described as a sequence of essential determinations of art that overrule one another, postmodernism and neo-avant-garde in turn are all about questioning the possibility of such determinations. The modernist tendency involves a *dogmatism* or *essentialism* geared toward stating what art *is*, and tries to define it on principle; it is methodical, theoretical, and ideological. Concentrating on "the essential norms and conventions" of art, writes Clement Greenberg, "Modernism has found that these limits can be pushed back indefinitely . . . ; but it has also found that the further back these limits are pushed the more explicitly they have to be observed and indicated."[2] The postmodernist tendency, in turn, reflects a *skepticism* or *antiessentialism* that denies the very possibility of such definitions, and at its extreme—at times with joy, at times with horror—arrives at the conclusion that *anything goes*. In a polemical formulation by Andy Warhol: "How can you say any style is better than another? You ought to be able to be an Abstract Expressionist next week, or a Pop artist, or a realist, without feeling you've given up something."[3] In their dialectical interdependence, however, both tendencies form two sides of the same modernist-postmodernist paradigm concerned with negotiating the essence of art. This paradigm, if we follow Foster and the respondents to the questionnaire, appears exhausted today and confronts us with an impasse: we content ourselves neither with categorical definitions of art, nor with categorical pronouncements of the impossibility of such definitions. While there has never before been this much art and interest in art, it is, perhaps for the first time, quite unclear how to make art or to talk about it.

Yet not only has the old paradigm run out of plausibility, but the very thought of a succession of paradigms itself appears as a part of the old paradigm—and *as such* out of date. "Artists"—writes the curator Mark Godfrey in his response to the questionnaire—"no longer see their practice as a development from, or argument with, art of the past twenty years, or as a brand-new moment in a neat line of 'movements' or 'paradigms,' in the way that (for instance) Conceptual artists in the early 1970s positioned themselves against Minimalism and Abstract Expressionism."[4] Here it is important not to toss out the baby with the bathwater. If we declare, together with a majority of the respondents, the teleological sequencing of movements or paradigms obsolete, we cannot conclude from this, together with a majority of that majority, that the category of paradigm is *as such* to be dismissed, and a new, aparadigmatic condition must instead be accepted. "With this situation," Godfrey continues, "who would presume to name a new paradigm? A new name would assume a totalizing explanatory power and be akin to a hubristic, neo-colonialist move."[5] This position that forms a largely unchallenged commonplace among contemporary intellectuals, brushes aside the fact that Foster's diagnosis does not concern a bagatelle, but a manifest problem and an impasse: if there are no paradigmatic conditions that indicate whether something counts as art, art becomes arbitrary; in a very basic sense, we don't know what we are talking about. Now whether the commonplace position can be refuted and a new paradigm can be conceived depends on the concept of paradigm one has. According to Thomas Kuhn, whose notion of scientific paradigm ("disciplinary matrix") I take the liberty to expand here, a paradigm consists of the pretheoretical framework of any practice. While rules and principles, where they exist, grow out of the paradigm, the paradigm can in turn guarantee the functioning of the practice in the absence of rules.[6] On this premise, the idea of a succession of states ruled by principle and connected by teleological necessity does not belong to the concept of paradigm as such, but specifically to the modernist-postmodernist paradigm.

Thus it is *possible* to conceive a paradigm for our present that would (1) not perpetuate the past paradigm by means of its attempted reversal, critique, deconstruction, and so on; and that would (2) nevertheless effectively address the modernist-postmodernist impasse by providing a model that renders art a determined practice, yet without therefore taking recourse to principle.[7]

With this question I now turn to the work of Gerhard Richter. Richter appears relevant here because, while a contemporary of postmodernism and neo-avant-garde, he has never accepted these movements as paradigms for his production—and the same holds for his relationship to modernism. This is not because Richter did not have an idea of what was going on, but, on the contrary, his avoidance of the dominant paradigmatic constraints shows a quasi-programmatic insistence. What makes Richter's works instructive in our present situation is the fact that he, in a kind of imperturbable anachronism, seems to have always worked from its condition. From the beginning of his work that counts today, his production finds itself put in a field defined by the impasse of essentialism and skepticism, which appears to him as a false alternative between the randomness of that which is predetermined and the other randomness of that which is undetermined. From the beginning it is clear that none of these options will work for him.

In brief, my thesis is that Richter's artistic program takes as its goal *to replace traditional essentialist models of artistic form by a pragmatic model.*[8] The latter is virtually indistinguishable from a pragmatist account of *judgment*—the basic act of making a difference that Richter also characterizes as *distinction*, *reaction*, *decision*, or *formulation.* By such a model, as I will show, the modernist-postmodernist paradigm gets neither affirmed, nor perpetuated in the mode of its reversal, critique, or deconstruction, but replaced by something else that forms an effective reaction to the situation precisely as it cannot be derived from it. Which explains, for example, why Richter's work does not programmatically exclude modernist or postmodernist influences, but takes the liberty to make use of the whole available repertoire, according to what is required by the circumstance. A pragmatic model of art does not imply that everything must be done in a fundamentally different way, but on the contrary seeks its distinction in abstaining from fundamental assumptions about what art is supposed to be.

Here lies the possibility of the unusual heterogeneity of Richter's production, which in the spread of its themes, styles, materials, procedures, or objectives is comparable to few others. Next to classical oil painting there are sculptures and installations, drawings, overpainted photographs, windows and mirrors, collages, books (with photographs, texts, prints), film, and computer graphics; next to abstract paintings there are paintings from photographs; next to portraits there are still lifes, nudes, monochromes, history paintings, landscapes, and paintings of cities and animals (see www.gerhard-richter.com). Art according to the pragmatic model does not render a particular style for easy identification; unlike pop art, minimal art, or conceptual art in the 1960s, it offers nothing that signals its belonging to a "movement" or "direction."

There is no indication here that art reinvents itself yet another time, or that a historical sequence gets carried forward once more—not even in the inverse mode of the postmodernist denial of Grand Narratives. But the very matrix on which such a refusal of historical sequencing was equally possible as its affirmation, the matrix on which the whole modernist-postmodernist alternative rested—this matrix itself now appears suspended. Instead, Richter takes as his starting point that "there isn't a dominant trend at present. . . . There's just work."[9] The manifest lack of orientation in no way precludes the making, but, on the contrary, it opens up a new freedom.

Is Richter alone in this? Certainly not; in this context, there is much to say about Duchamp, Cage, or Warhol, and if one thinks of contemporary artists such as Bruce Naumann, Rosemarie Trockel, or even Julie Mehretu, there appears to be plenty of material offering itself for parallels. However, no matter how such parallels turn out, they will discredit neither the specificity nor the relevance of Richter's program; rather, they will confirm both by showing that this program forms a reaction to a more pervasive problem that concerns others as well. Which is why my discussion of Richter has *exemplary* status—a claim that I will explain at the end of this essay.

In what follows, I will first draw on a selection from Richter's works and writings that help to unfold my thesis of a replacement of traditional conceptions of artistic form by a pragmatic conception. Second, I will outline why I think that such a model successfully reacts to the impasse of our situation and indeed suggests itself as a new paradigm.

2. Richter's Pragmatist Conception of Form

[artistic program] It seems clear in what direction this must go: if a generalized orientation of art is as much to be avoided as a generalized lack of orientation is, all that remains is orientation each time. For this purpose, any kind of principle or general prescription is in the way. Such prescriptions concern mainly: (1) The technical side of artmaking, its poetics: in the process of painting, Richter seeks to remain unpredictable and refuses guidance by methods or concepts. "I pursue no objectives, no system, no tendency; I have no programme, no style, no direction. . . . I steer clear of definitions. I don't know what I want . . . ; I like the indefinite, the boundless; I like continual uncertainty."[10] *There is certainty in freedom from principle.* (2) What art is about: Richter opposes all claims of art to immanent signification, meaning, or sense, which includes art's alignment with specific purposes, and its ties to representation in a broad sense. "Pictures which are interpretable, and which contain a meaning, are bad pictures,"[11] the goal being "pictures that wouldn't be subject to ideological interpretation."[12] "Art can be truly relevant only when it isn't directly employed to do a job."[13] *There is a relevance that is not ideological.* (3) The question of innovation: Richter bans the *topos* of creativity, of having ideas, of invention from the artistic process. "Letting a thing come, rather than creating it"[14] is the goal. "Art takes shape . . . always unexpectedly; art is never feasible."[15] *There is innovation without creation.* These three aspects indicate that for Richter a suspension of principles is not only not detrimental to artmaking, but that, on the contrary, the latter has its possibility *only* in such suspension.

[distinction] The critical strategic move by which Richter achieves this suspension is his choice of the *act* as the relevant unit of the painterly process—the *single distinction* and difference, judgment at its most basic, or, as Richter mostly says, *form*. His entire poetics can be condensed to the observation that "in painting one form is a response to another, and so on."[16] Here we must extend and revise our everyday understanding of "form" as outline, *Gestalt*, figure, and the like. From William James's postulate that "every difference must *make* a difference"[17] all the way to the more recent accounts by George Spencer Brown and Niklas Luhmann, a differential conception of form takes as form that which bears functional distinction, that is, which makes the relevant difference: this brushstroke, this Gestalt, this surface structure, this blue shade, this painting in its entirety, or this constellation of paintings—what counts as the singular act depends entirely on the context. Functional distinction means that the form has no inherent qualities, but what it *is* gets determined by what it *does* (compare Wittgenstein's sentence "The meaning of a word is its use in the language"). But it also means that the form, in order to articulate itself, is always in need of a medium, even as it remains indifferent to its specific medium (as well as changes of media). It bears the same indifference to theme, motif, genre, manufacturing process, or purpose of the work. To be sure, art relies on all these distinctions in order to articulate itself in specific ways, but it nevertheless remains independent of them in that none of them constitutes art's distinction *as* art.[18]

[primacy of the act] A demonstration of what it means to conceive a painting as form is given by Richter's opus 1, the painting *Table* (1962). The figurative image of a table is painted over by a dark swirl, so that the represented space that holds the table, and the space of representation formed by the surface of the painting, strive apart in maximum disintegration. The table, one wants to say, is "in" the painting, while the swirl is "on" the painting.

Already a second look reveals the painting to function as a quasi-didactic instruction for seeing that thematizes the differentiation of the two spheres. Every brushstroke contributing to the table is equally "on" the painting, just as every stroke of the swirl has to be understood as equally being "in" it. Since one then has to take table and swirl as *one* form, the limit between the representational and the nonrepresentational is questioned, just as is the limit between the "flat" space of the surface and the "deep" space of the figure. What here appears showcased, then, is the traditional problem

Tisch, 1962 (CR 1). Oil on canvas, 90 × 113 cm. © 2016 Gerhard Richter.

of image-representation—the tension between surface and depth, materiality and illusionism, self-reference and world-reference (or whatever other formulation one chooses to employ).

But the instruction does not stop here, for the expressive dynamics of the swirl also says something else: the swirl is painted later than the table, the table is overpainted or overswirled; it is painted explicitly as an act, implying, as it were, the sweep of the brushstroke—and thus presents itself as a kinetic signature of performance itself. The problem of representation, then, is being exhibited by way of a tension of equal components (surface/depth)—only in order to be overturned by the performance of the painting, by which something entirely different shifts into the focus: the pragmatic dimension. What counts now is not what the painting represents, expresses or means, but what it *does*. The meta-painting *Table* by which Richter inaugurates his official work declares performatively the primacy of the act. It shows what it takes to conceive the painting as form: to conceive it *as act*—a basic intuition shared with Action Painting or Fluxus.[19]

[performance] The idea that form is one with its execution is not necessarily easy to entertain. To give it some plausibility, let us take a closer look at

James's formula *to make a difference*—a phrase that, by merging at least two distinct meanings of *making*, appears to capture the pragmatist project in a nutshell. First, to be sure, the formula says that the difference is operative, effective. But, second, it also says that the difference is being *made*, that it is not already there but there for the first time. Third, the fact that it is the difference itself that makes the difference—that the difference being made is the making of the difference—unites observations one and two by saying that difference here is neither just the product or effect, nor just the fabrication or making, but that both, effect and making, are one and the same thing. From which, fourth, springs the pragmatic notion of act and activity as that which is a becoming and an effect at once—one may therefore also say it is that which *works*—that is to say, in the distinction of which form and formation (morphogenesis) are indistinguishable.[20] For Richter this means, for instance, "that you can't represent reality [*Wirklichkeit*] at all, that what you make represents nothing but itself, and therefore is itself reality."[21] Richter's term *Wirklichkeit* (Latin *actualitas*, ancient Greek *enérgeia*)[22] refers to what is real and actual, approximated in the English "reality" if "reality" gets imbued with a strong connotation of activity. The term means performance as that which is effective, at work (*im Wirken*). What for representational logics remains distributed across the three positions—of that which effects, the act of effecting, and the resulting effect (in semiotic terminology: signifier, act of signification, and signified)—in the order of performance appears contracted to a *unity* in which these positions become indistinguishable. Painting, as Richter says, is "reality . . . creating itself," an intricate formulation that seeks to account for the fact that the genesis of painting cannot be told apart from its work or its effect.[23]

[reaction] In order to conceive such unity, Richter employs the model of *reaction*. The reality of form, then, is the reaction to a reality that precedes it—of an object, a photograph, another form in the painterly process, or whatever it may be. The point of reaction is that while the new reality relates to the old one, it does so not as its doubling, reflection, signification, meaning, or other derivative, but as a new reality in its own right.[24] Reaction is never secondary, but the structural beginning of interaction: "The origin and primitive form of the language game is a *reaction*," notes Wittgenstein, and "only from this can more complicated forms develop. Language—I want to say—is a refinement, 'in the beginning was the deed.'"[25] This is the same Goethe quote that Richter employs in support of his claim that form can neither be understood as a signifier of a reality outside the painting, nor as a derivative of an idea that logically precedes it. "The idea as a point of departure for the picture: that's illustration. Conversely, *acting and reacting* in the absence of an idea leads to form"[26]—ideas can be triggered by form, but form cannot in turn be founded through ideas. Conceived this way, the painterly process is a reacting of form to form, of a primary thing to a primary thing, without a secondary thing (a mediation by thinking, or language, or reference) ever coming into play. "Painting has nothing to do with thinking, because in painting thinking is painting. . . . Einstein did not think when he was calculating: he calculated—producing the next equation in *reaction* to the one that went before—just as in painting one form is a response to another, and so on."[27] On this account, essential commensurability (in the relationship between the painting and the painted object or an idea) gets replaced by contextual commensurability (in the relationship between the forms within a work, between works, between practices), for all that counts now is that the form functionally connects to the previous form and in turn makes itself connectable to other forms. The form is not determined by correspondence to a reality that precedes it but by coherence with the full context of forms reacting to one another. Representation, to be sure, does not disappear; paintings still depict "content" and still carry meaning—yet both are subject to the primacy of reaction, so that representation has the status of a reality in its own right.[28]

[chance] If Richter refuses to work from prescriptions and previously developed conceptions, he equally disapproves of letting himself be guided by spontaneous ideas, excluding the whole topos of "creativity" and "invention" from its relevance to painting. Having thus stripped the artistic process of conception, method, and invention, for it to be able to nevertheless bring about actualization of possibilities and transgression of the status quo, Richter resorts to the category of *chance*. Chance emergence instead of creation and invention[29]—a strategy informed by the improvisational structure of Fluxus events and the aleatoric compositions of John Cage, in which the artist figures less as the agent of innovation than as its enabler.[30] The results, as Richter emphasizes, surpass by far what he could create intentionally. "I'm often astonished to find how much better chance is than I am":[31] "Letting a thing come, rather than creating it . . . in order to gain access to all that is genuine, richer, more alive: to what is beyond my understanding. . . . The abstract pictures: more and more clearly, a method of not having and planning the 'motif' but evolving it, letting it come."[32] We may think here of the extensive and uncontrollable application of paint in the large abstract paintings (more about this in short); of the copying of photographs springing from the wish "not having to invent anything any more,"[33] or *Atlas*, the archive of templates conceived for the same purpose; of the unconscious sweeps of *Inpainting*, or the aleatorics of the color charts of *4900 Colours* or of *Cathedral Windows, Cologne*, the specific arrangements of which are determined by a random generator.[34]

[decision] Because chance alone renders nothing but randomness, the form is in need of a second component: the *decision* that has to determine which elements of chance are allowed to persist. This is Richter's understanding of form according to decision: a form is produced wherever we make a distinction, that is, where we decide between alternative possibilities. It is an evaluative operation.[35] For this reason Richter holds on to a criterion of commensurability, a "rightness [*Richtigkeit*] or better bindingness or commensurability [*Verbindlichkeit*] of painting":[36] a meta-criterion or formal criterion that has no defined content but in each case determines anew what it is that counts as right *this time*—so that it turns out always differently and can by definition not be predicted. Only what is right bears commensurability, communicates itself and can be connected to, and such connectivity does not come with any additional guarantees, because as an ultimate criterion, rightness cannot in turn be backed by further criteria (it forms a *primitive* in the sense of Davidson). It is in this context that Richter most frequently identifies form as *judgment*, the name he appears to regard as its fullest description. The act previously described as *distinction* and *reaction* now undergoes further development to *decision* and includes the element of rightness. Qua rightness, form as judgment combines underivability (it is not informed by principle) with commensurability (it can be connected to), thus constituting the operation by which the modernist-postmodernist impasse can structurally be left behind.[37]

This happens with every act: to continue the figure in this or that way, to draw the line till here or till there, to cover the field with a red or a blue tone, and so on—from the decision for a certain format and technique all the way to the microstructure of the surface there is nothing in a painting that is not determined by decisions of this kind. Decision is distinction, and where there has been no decision there is nothing to see. That is why for Richter, the artistic act proper is not the technical procedure of working the paint, but the performance of the decision: "The artist's productive act" has "nothing to do with the talent of 'making by hand,' only with the capacity to see and to decide *what* is to be made visible. *How* that then gets fabricated has nothing to do with art or with artistic abilities."[38] It is this split between the centrality of the decision performed in the act of seeing and the marginality of its technical-medial articulation on which the conception of differential form is built. For Richter, the split is epitomized in the readymade, the production of which consists entirely in the act that identifies a found object as art, the act of *taking* or *seeing* something *as* something—by which it is being transformed without physical alteration. "That's why Duchamp is so important: his readymade is nothing but an act that exposes the basic skill at the heart of the matter: to be able to see something."[39]

Perhaps best described by Wittgenstein, seeing-as is the structure of the simple distinction in which something is seen *as* something and not something else. Take, for example, the famous drawing that can be seen either as showing the head of a duck or the head of a rabbit (or perhaps something else). Unlike simple seeing (seeing something), seeing-as (seeing something as something), requires an alternative with at least two *aspects*—distinct ways of looking at the drawing, noninterdependent options. "The head seen like *this*," Wittgenstein notes, does not show "the slightest similarity to the head seen like *this*—although they are congruent."[40] This alternativity indicates that the distinction of form has the character of choice and decision—the basic structure of judgment (something as something). If we consider the drawing a form in Richter's sense, its aspects appear as ways of connecting to it each in a certain respect; it can be seen as *something* only insofar as it is being *taken* in this specific perspective. Just as the drawing *in itself* contains no information as to what it represents, the readymade performs the elimination of essence (inherent determination) from the work, the artistic distinction of which can then only be determined pragmatically.[41] What lacks function has no phenomenal distinction either—it can literally not be perceived. Wittgenstein describes the change of aspect thus: "Where there were branches before, now there is a human shape."[42] Or, in a more organizing function: "When the aspect changes, parts of the picture go together that before did not."[43]

[unity of the act] But how do chance and decision intersect, how do they perform the reaction? Because chance can be taken as *this* or *that*, presenting an open or equivocal situation that is to be decided toward rightness and unequivocality, form seems a two-part procedure: first random production, second critical selection. The first—transgressive—component is aleatorics; the second—commensurating—component is decision, which filters chance according to useful and nonuseful elements. For *4900 Colours*, the random generator creates a wealth of combinations from which Richter then chooses; in the large abstract paintings, the aleatoric part is rendered by specific techniques of applying the paint, whereas selection is executed by painting over parts of the picture (more on this soon). This details the structure of reaction: that which appears right (the "selected" elements) is spared, that which appears arbitrary (the "deselected" elements) is painted over and replaced by a new unleashing of chance. Reaction, then, is not a positive creation of new articulation, but just the sparing of that which happens to fit; the actual transgression of the status quo is left to chance.

Each form generates and decides chance, but the chance it decides is not the chance it generates: the act takes the *previous* act as the matter to be decided—the given, the case, *casus* or *chance*—and *in* this reaction it produces the matter for the connecting act.[44] Now whether judgment proper consists in the distinction between the "selected" and the "deselected" material, or in the act of erasure that effectively adds the spared material to the formal buildup of the work—for this question, Richter's pragmatic conception offers no theoretical horizon. Separating both options would mean to think of the act of distinction as the premise and direction of its painterly execution—and it is precisely such direction against which Richter devises form as a unity of that which effects, the act of effecting, and the resulting effect. The functional commitment of the act leaves no room for a separation into the components of "decision" and "execution." It is only *one* act that reacts to the situation—the decisive act of sparing and erasure. While every act is the answer to, as well as the decision and determination of, the previous act, it is at the same time the case, question, and challenge for the act to follow.[45]

[evolution] The process makes do with a simple binary code: "Picture-making consists of a multitude of Yes/No decisions, with a Yes to end it all."[46] Richter's more detailed description depicts the process as a funnel-shaped reduction of contingency, with almost complete contingency at the beginning, followed by a scale of discrete steps—the singular acts of decision—toward decreasing contingency of the overall form of the painting, which gradually gains stability in itself.[47] While this can aptly be described as formal closure, the end of the process is not marked by an act of "conclusion," but it is reached simply where there is nothing left to correct, at the point where the painting has ceased to be a situation (that is, for production; it continues to be a situation for viewing). Here is Richter's most recent description of the process in an interview with Benjamin Buchloh:

> RICHTER: When I first approach a canvas, . . . I can smear anything I want on it. Then there is a condition I must react to, by changing it or destroying it—for there is no concept. It's not like a figurative painting with a template. Something happens spontaneously. Not by itself, but without plan or reason. . . .
>
> BUCHLOH: You paint without a plan, but you know exactly when it's right. So what's the correlation between planlessness and making the judgment: "Now it's a painting"?
>
> RICHTER: Each step forward is more difficult and I feel less and less free until I conclude there's nothing left to do. When, according to my standard, nothing is wrong anymore, then I stop. Then it's good.
>
> BUCHLOH: And what's right and wrong? The wrong consciousness, material, or process?
>
> RICHTER: It just doesn't look good. Then it's wrong.
>
> BUCHLOH: Can we dig deeper than looking good or bad?
>
> RICHTER: It's extremely difficult. We're all completely equal here. The producer and consumer, artist and observer, both must have one quality: to be able to see if it's good or not. To make that judgment.[48]

[*Cage 4*] This process is documented for a number of Richter's works—and with special thoroughness for the series of abstract oil paintings entitled *Cage*. The six canvases, each approximately 3 by 3 meters, were painted in 2006 and are on permanent exhibition at the Tate Modern. As a whole, the constellation forms a suite in six movements that each operate as a reaction

Cage 1–6, 2006 (CR 897-1 to 897-6). Oil on canvas, in six parts, 290 × 290 cm and 300 × 300 cm. © 2016 Gerhard Richter. Private collection, on loan to the Tate Modern, London.

to the others in thc specified sense (here displayed in the order 4-5-6, 1-2-3): like most of Richter's large abstract works of recent decades, *Cage* is painted with a squeegee, a long blade made of Plexiglas that gets dragged across the canvas. While direction, speed, pressure, and angle of application are variable, the technology allows only for a comparatively small amount of control and thus provides the source of chance production Richter seeks, layers of color being cluttered, scraped off, smoothened, compressed, smeared into each other, or lacerated, creating fissures and abrasions of all kinds.[49]

Thanks to a book by Robert Storr (*Cage: 6 Paintings by Gerhard Richter*), a series of photographs that document the making of each of the *Cage* paintings in nine or ten dated pre-stages has been made publicly available.[50] These photographs, on which I will draw in the following, can be used by the analysis as discrete acts of form or judgment, as well as, at the same time, the scenarios of chance that trigger the ensuing act. Of course the photos provide

no exhaustive documentation of the series of reactions in the painting process, but they form contingently chosen snapshots from it, while the process could actually be broken down into any number of such stages.[51] I want to now take a closer look at the stages that lead to *Cage 4*, the following reproduction showing eight stages and the final version.

[interactive context] Strikingly, the stages don't build on one another in a constructive way. According to the structure of reaction, the way each stage relates to the previous stage is neither reinforcing nor dialectical, neither are articulations subject to development (by the elaboration of an outline, the carrying on of a color value or movement), nor balanced out or met with their contrary (by the contrasting of light and dark, the reversing of a proportion). Every stage functions as the "destruction" of the previous one,[52] forming a series of structural privations or revocations, "until the picture

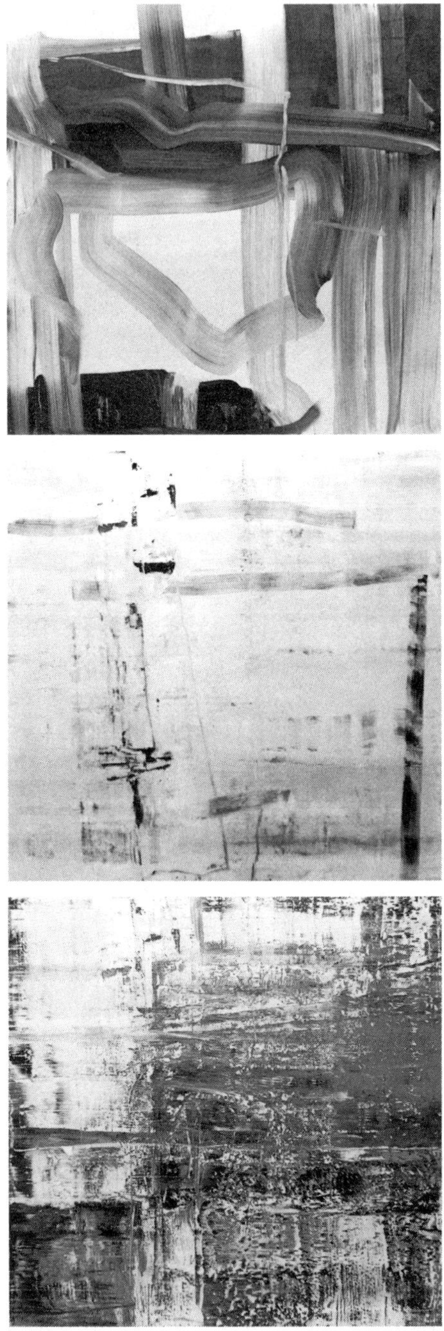

The making of *Cage 4*. Photographs by Hubert Becker.

is finished and has nothing left but openness."[53] The new stage abrades and scratches off, cuts and crushes, covers and blurs, fragments and scatters the formal inventory of the previous one. It *takes* or *decides* it in such a way that it appears under a new *aspect*: while the "deselected" material gets painted over, the "selected" material undergoes a functional reemployment. A line that in context A produces a certain proportion reappears in context B as part of a grid; a blue dominating the foreground becomes the shading of the background, and so on. What is achieved hereby: on the one hand, every stage appears under the aspects of all the following stages, resolved into a series of connecting acts; on the other hand and at the same time, all aspects are available at once since every stage remains present enough to allow the painting to display the full interactive context.

Because each of the stages insists on its own formal value, their layering exhibits an overall roughness of integration, a dissonance with each other that renders a formal spectrum of considerable depth. In *Cage 4*, for example, the red of stage 6 sharply cuts through the covering gray of the final stage without in the least radiating off into it; the diagonal scratches of stages 2 and 5 run against the vertical-horizontal grid established in phase 3; or the extreme gestural reduction and all-over structure of stage 2 contrasts with the expressionist and centralizing gesture of stage 1. One sees how Richter prefers dissonance over indifference. In an anamnesis of the whole process, the final version displays all its incommensurable aspects *at once*—a composition dominated by red and a composition dominated by gray, a surface organized by diagonals and a surface organized by a horizontal-vertical grid, a distribution of elements that is even and bears no relation to a frame, and a distribution that is centered and reinforces the boundaries of the canvas.[54] Neither can one derive any of the stages from the previous one, nor the overall development from the beginning or the end; the beginning is not the seed that contains and programs the whole series, and the series does not strive toward fulfillment in a final stage.

[change of aspect] The painting thus consisting of discrete acts or stages offers itself to connecting acts in such a way that to each act corresponds a perspective from which it can be taken. What Richter calls "openness" is nothing but the *enhanced connectibility* that comes with the enrichment by aspects (in the context of the figurative paintings he says that the blurred image is "more open," since it can be taken in more different ways). The painting is open insofar as it opens up possibilities for seeing; the ways it can be seen appear less and less limited, freer from the standardizing constraints of stylistic, interpretive, or ideological prescriptions. The series of revocations in which formal closure (reduction of contingency, increase of commensurability) directly correlates with contextual openness (freedom from limiting prescriptions) comes with a rise in pragmatic power of the communication.

In offering itself to be taken in *this* or *that* way, *Cage* does not cater to a steadiness of aspect, a simple *seeing*, but it requires a *change* of aspect, a *seeing-as* that multiplies its possibilities in the layering of the stages.[55] Because the layering joins disparate and incompatible perspectives, Richter can say that it "presents itself as the Unmanageable, the Illogical, the Meaningless. It demonstrates the endless multiplicity of aspects [*die Zahllosigkeit der Aspekte*]."[56] Due to this logical heterogeneity rooted in the conception of aspect, formal complexity is not a mere additive consequence of the layering, but reciprocal amplification, if not exponentiation, of the layers. Indeed, the formal happening of the *Cage* paintings is so highly resolved that many aspects can acquire their distinction only fleetingly, in passing. Because each layer includes the formal substance of all previous ones, the painting works as a compressor in which the stages or forms cut or converge, contract or condense to the effect of a certain graying—an effect quite dominant in the *Cage* series as a whole. However, we are not looking at a "dead" gray as the mean of formal indifference, but at a fabric of allusions, nuances, and reflections the pragmatic resolution of which exceeds, as it were, the resolution by color or line. Its aspects achieve no stability anywhere but take the viewer on an indefinite detour through shifting resonances. All in all, Richter's poetics comes down to this pragmatics of change: as often as possible and as unpredictable as possible—a maximizing of activity that Richter interprets as a *boost in reality* (*Wirklichkeit*).

[artistic reality] With this, artistic reality is established as a reality of its own kind. First, its *quantitative* distinction lies in the fact that its specific density or intensity surpasses the density of most other interactive contexts. Second, this quantitative dimension rests on a *qualitative* or functional distinction: in contrast to nonartistic formal production, art is all about the change of aspect *as such*—a claim first made by Wittgenstein and since taken up by Richard Rorty, by myself, or, just recently, by Michael Lüthy.[57] Unlike any other interaction, artistic interaction does not decide between the aspects, but is concerned with their change. Artistic form distinguishes itself by the aspect change bearing functional value as such. The form is not to appear as a rabbit *or* a duck, but first as a rabbit *and then* as a duck, across a caesura that requires a realignment of the entire context. Richter is not interested in smoothening out the process of making or viewing, but in the "innumerability of aspects" disclosed in frequent change. Ultimately, however, if one looks at the work as a whole, this change stabilizes itself in a heterogeneous *simultaneity* of aspects—a present-day update of the operations of *enérgeia* or *ékphrasis* from ancient rhetoric.

About this surpassing of nonartistic reality Richter notes that painted images "sensually disclose a reality that we can neither see nor describe,"[58] for it is impossible to see aspect change proper because it belongs to the order of the act, of seeing-as and not seeing, of morphogenesis itself which we can access only by *performing* the change. This is what the specific reality of art ultimately does: it opens access to the order of the act as such. In nonartistic practices, this order usually remains unnoticed, the focus being on *what* the interaction is about. Here, in contrast, activity itself is at stake, the factuality or *thatness* of interaction that itself becomes the aim of interaction, so that we may say the practice happens for the sake of its own happening.

[community] What is the point of this, why Richter's strong interest in the factuality of performance? Here I want to recall that the interaction of forms in the work carries on into the interaction of forms of the work with its viewers (or connecting forms). Because of the painting's extraordinary ability to make itself available to connection, which means, as it were, that it communicates through multiple frequencies at once, it is able to connect its viewers even in cases where their perspectives are so unrelated that they would otherwise never enter communication.[59] If, in looking at the drawing, I always and exclusively see a rabbit head, whereas you always and exclusively see a duck head, there is no way for us to come together given that the drawing itself contains nothing that might make one challenge or abandon one's own aspect. That we both connect to the same drawing is not sufficient for coming together, for the aspects don't relate and the form conducts us past each other. (This way, we can live in the same world without ever having to do with one another.) Only once the drawing starts to function as a duck-rabbit head—that is, once it starts working like the artistic form in which seeing becomes seeing-as and aspect *change* is performed—there is a possibility for us to come together. We now both connect to the same form in such a way that your perspective, in its unmitigated incompatibility with my own, appears to me *as well*. It does so not as something I can choose to see, but as something I am forced to take into account as an option and possibility. In achieving this, the form does not resolve tensions and problems between incompatible perspectives, but it creates the very conditions under which tensions and problems can articulate themselves (between separate aspects there is no relation and no comparability). It is a beginning of our relating—from this point on we are dealing with one another. "Art," as Richter says, "serves to establish community" (*Kunst dient der Vergemeinschaftung*).[60]

Which is not to say that art is for this or that communication or community, but it has the purpose of setting us up with each other and enabling us to enter a shared context in the first place. The community it creates is strictly performative; we belong to it not based on common qualities, purposes, or identifications, but only by taking part in the interaction. Not the "vertical" reference to a shared idea, essence, or culture makes us belong, but the "horizontal" activity of relating and participating. It is not necessary for the functioning of form that we connect it to a joint purpose, attach a common relevance to it, or value the aspects in the same way. Agreement, explicit or implicit, is not required. All that matters is *that* we are dealing with the form, that we are dealing with the form *at all*. This is also not about the positive sharing in the perspectives, stakes, or commitments of others by means of empathy or reflection; the shared world emerges not from understanding or reenactment, but from shared action alone—the bare fact of reacting to one another.

This of course is reminiscent of Kant's theory of common sense (*Gemeinsinn*) according to which aesthetic judgment performs the structural grounds of communication in general (*Mitteilbarkeit überhaupt*, "communicability as such") while the object remains indeterminate.[61] But one is also reminded of Luhmann's theory of symbolically generalized communication media, where art forms an answer to the problem of "how to communicate effectively in situations where this would otherwise appear improbable"[62] and works to the effect of "normalizing improbable societal structures." To both approaches, however, Richter's model relates only on the condition of a pragmatist qualification: to be sure, the form aims at communicability as such (*überhaupt*), but unlike for Kant, this "as such" does not involve an a priori universality (the categories of the understanding), but it is a performative generated in the respective act. And while the form is indeed instrumental in enabling improbable communication, it involves not "symbolic generalization"[63] but a generalization (see below) only through the fact of sharedness, the relating at the origin of interaction that is structurally a first and thus only for *this* time, *this* situation.

[formulation] The form structurally departs from a situation that we don't sufficiently have in common or don't have in common at all, and that therefore possesses a deficient reality (*Wirklichkeit*), and it transforms this situation to a higher level of sharedness which is also a higher level of reality. Which is not to say form has no *aboutness*, as happens to be the case with the abstract paintings; it can well exhibit/represent *something*, which means that this something (I apologize for the abbreviated account) cannot be taken from only one isolated perspective (as Richter claims about the photograph),[64] but from multiple perspectives at once. The chair in the photograph is not the same thing as the chair painted by Richter; the latter is more visible and has a higher degree of reality. As Richter repeatedly says, it has received its "formulation" (*Formulierung*)[65] and thus appears resolved into an interactive context of discrete decisions or aspects: "Formulating something is a great start. I trust form."[66] By virtue of its higher perspectival dissolution, the painting has more visibility and more generality,[67] for in the reality of form, its phenomenal and its pragmatic distinction—that is, its visibility and its connectivity—are indistinguishable. "What counts is that the pictures then become universal. They are there and show themselves. . . . That's why form is so important," says Richter, and then adds a much stronger claim: "because without form, communication stops."[68] Which gets even further extended by the assertion "that it is only form that renders a matter communicable and thus is able to constitute community."[69] Without form, we are not only dealing with a deficient reality, but we cannot *ever* be certain that we share any reality at all.

This, for Richter, is the basic problem art has to respond to. The reality deficit consisting of the pragmatic one-dimensionality of nonartistic reality constitutes a general condition: "the dilemma that our seeing [the normal seeing in contrast to seeing-as] lets us discern things [it presents them under a certain aspect], but that at the same time, it restricts and partly precludes our apprehension of reality [the seeing of a multiplicity of aspects]."[70] It should be clear that this is not a perpetuation of the troubles inherited from the past paradigm, but a wholly different concern that comes with the conception of a nonmetaphysical world. Appropriating a term coined by Heidegger, we might describe such a deficit of world as *poorness in world* (*Weltarmut*). Heidegger's complementary concept of *worldmaking* or *world formation* (*Weltbildung*) would then correspond to what Richter calls "formulation"—emphasizing the latter's global necessity:[71] "We must always, no matter what it is we encounter, give it a form, in order to be able to deal with it in any way at all."[72] The necessity concerns by no means only instances where the deficiency appears explicit—involving, for example, terror, pain, or despair—but all situations in general, even the most quotidian and harmless ones; they all demand "to be coped with in this way."[73] But the challenge such coping faces becomes greater when we are confronted with the bombing of Dresden, the terror of the Red Army Faction, or the 9/11 attacks. The more overwhelming the event, the more numerous, dispersed, and incompatible the perspectives from which it shows itself—and the more challenging the constitution of its reality. As Richter notes in his treatment of the Iraq War in the book *War Cut*, "in this case the factual is so overpowering that we need to undertake many more attempts at formulation than elsewhere. Because here the content is so important, the form is of greater importance as well. We simply need it more to come to terms with it."[74]

If the painting *September* from 2005 claims to give a form to the events of 9/11, the aim is not to comprise the entire imaginary of the event in an image (as a symbolic representation might attempt), but to bring us together *at all*, to achieve relating *in this case*, to produce a single image that fulfills its purpose in being shared. Not representation but reaction is the goal; the painting does not attempt to disclose a "true reality"[75] of the event, but to transform it to a new level of shared availability. *Taken* in the right way, it becomes more visible and more real. To judge, for Richter, means not only to distinguish, to react, or to decide, but also, and perhaps most importantly, to "formulate": to make visible, real, common. Describing in detail how this happens—how in "formulating" a specific event, the aboutness of form relates to the bare factuality of participation—would require engaging Richter's conception of mimesis, a task I have undertaken elsewhere.[76] For my present purposes, the

September, 2005 (CR 891-5). Oil on canvas, 52 × 72 cm. © 2016 Gerhard Richter.

brief look at *September* is supposed to show how artistic "formulation" figures as both the center and the outer experimental rim of sharedness, the structural beginning of worldmaking and its ultimate resource.

3. Pragmatist Form as the New Paradigm?

[form as paradigm] What has been achieved? As judgment, form positions itself in a number of different ways. Qua *distinction* it rids itself of inherent qualification and allows determination only through what it *does*. Qua *reaction* it gains freedom from both its traditional ties to representation, as well as methodological and ideological prescriptions. Qua *aleatorics* form suspends the dogma of "creativity" and leaves the transgressive component in innovation entirely to chance. Qua *decision* (taking-as) it turns chance into distinction, acquiring commensurability without recourse to rule or principle. Finally, qua *formulation* and the constitution of a performative community, the form seals its indifference to the ideological fixations of the modernist-postmodernist paradigm. Conceived in this way, art is bound neither to a meaning or truth, nor to the promise of moral betterment; it does not serve as a political intervention, nor does it promote beauty or creativity for their own sake—nor is it, finally, the reversal, critique, or deconstruction of any of these goals. It cannot be contained in a specific proposition, action, or experience, but it is the performative fact of the constitution of interaction as such.

All of this suggests that Richter's pragmatic conception of form indeed reacts to the past paradigm in a way that (1) shows sufficient structural indifference toward it to not appear as its perpetuation and that (2) effectively addresses the modernist-postmodernist impasse by virtue of a positive model of art that joins its uncompromised determination with its independence from principle. The conception provides a vocabulary that enables us to talk about art present and future, even and especially if it looks utterly different from and operates from radically different historic, thematic, stylistic, or medial premises than Richter's own, or anything we can imagine here and now. But does this already mean that pragmatic form offers itself as a new paradigm—refuting the commonplace position that, with Godfrey, accuses any such attempt of presuming a "totalizing explanatory power"?

[example and paradigm] The concept of paradigm does not pose a problem here. According to Kuhn, the paradigm is not grounded in principle but forms the pretheoretical pragmatic framework that can generate principles and rules, without in turn depending on them. This means that there can be a paradigm of unprincipledness, one that not only makes do without principles, but that consists of there being no principles—including a principle that prohibits principles. Now does Richter subscribe to such unprincipled unprincipledness, or is he entrapping himself in the self-contradiction of a principled prohibition of principle?[77]

While it seems obvious that Richter's artistic program is really a program and includes explicit bans of principle, it seems equally obvious that this program concerns his own production and makes no demand for universal implementation. He does not position his work by appeal to universal relevance, leaving its relevance entirely to *exemplarity*. By showing itself, Richter's painted and written work proposes the conditions under which the making of form is possible today: true to its poetological premises, it claims to be only *one* among an indefinite number of possibilities; at the same time, though, it gives reality to the very formal preconditions without which there can be no such indefinite number of possibilities.

Whether this counts as evading the trap of self-contradiction depends on the concept of exemplarity one employs. According to a metaphysical interpretation that takes the example to be the demonstration or representation of a universal, exemplification is always and inevitably a universalization. In this tradition, Giorgio Agamben calls the example an "exclusion by inclusion" because, precisely in exhibiting itself as an exemplar, it transgresses its status of exemplar; its particularity is fundamentally—from the origin—corrupted.[78] If Richter's work were to offer itself as an example in this way, it would stand in opposition to its own program, since its explicit denunciations of principle would appear universalized, even though it contains no claim for universalization.

This interpretation, however, contrasts sharply with a pragmatist account of exemplarity. While Richter does not formulate such an account himself, it is what best fits the premises of his work. Here the example does not constitute itself by universalization, but by connection. In taking Richter as an example, I make him the example of something that emerges only in my taking. Without taking there can be no example, because only the taking of something *as something* determines for what it is an example. The universal—the respect in which Richter and I are comparable—is not a preexisting entity, but gets constituted in the act of taking; it is needed, but secondary to the act. It is in this sense that Aristotle defines the example as neither the move from the particular to the universal (induction), nor the move of the universal to the particular (deduction), but as the move from the particular to the particular—in the way that "one is better known than the other."[79] Both relate qua analogy through a *genus* or *tertium* that forms the respect in which they are comparable; yet the "vertical" relationship found in deduction and induction appears shifted to a "horizontal" relationship, where the *genus* does not rule the comparison but gets constituted in its very act.

It can now be explained how we get from the example to the paradigm: by "horizontal" connections. Every time we take something as an example, we confirm its exemplarity and therefore increase its paradigmatic validity—it gets, with Aristotle's expression, to be "better known." The new paradigm constitutes itself by others following the example—according to Kant's distinction between "imitation" (*Nachahmung*) and "succession" (*Nachfolge*): I contribute to the formation of the paradigm not by painting or talking like the example, but only by reacting to it and carrying it forth through my acts (rejection contributing to the formation of the paradigm as well).[80] Kuhn's own divergent usages of the concept, at times referring to "example," at times to "disciplinary matrix,"[81] confirm a structural continuity according to which the example is the paradigm, the consensus of a disciplinary matrix growing out of and ultimately becoming indistinguishable from agreement on paradigms-as-exemplars.[82] A continuity that involves only movements from the particular to the particular, for which universalization is operative but not constitutive. If Richter is a paradigmatic artist, he is such in the way that he presents something that, if taken up in multiple ways, can become a paradigm. Far from exhibiting its own universality and thus avoiding the trap of self-contradiction, his example then would be paradigmatic in the sense of a specific *possibility*.

What does this possibility look like? That something is "better known" indicates its increased visibility; the better known is the more powerful and influential, it offers itself for connection and in the chorus of forms to be taken, it occupies, as it were, a place in the foreground. To what extent it gets *in fact* taken remains contingent—or else it would be a universal—but it has a relatively higher chance of being taken, suggesting itself by an amplified connectivity, relevance, reality. To the extent to which Richter's work achieves this, it can count as paradigmatic. And it can claim this ambition without undermining its own premises.

Notes

1. Hal Foster, "Questionnaire on 'The Contemporary,'" *October* 130 (2009): 3–124, at 3. For a broader diagnosis, see Jörg Heiser, "Torture and Remedy: The End of -isms and the Beginning Hegemony of the Impure," *e-flux* 11 (2009): 81, 83–84: "There is no clearly distinguishable movement in sight that would lead out of this apparent deadlock. . . . The seeming disappearance of clearly distinguishable movements is not at all exclusive to visual art, as similar developments can be discerned in other realms such as music, philosophy, and politics. In other words, a more fundamental sea change seems to be at work."

2. Clement Greenberg, "Modernist Painting," in Greenberg, *The Collected Essays and Criticism*, vol. 4: *Modernism with a Vengeance, 1957–69* (Chicago: University of Chicago Press, 1993), 89–90.

3. Andy Warhol in Gene R. Swenson, "What Is Pop Art? Answers from 8 Painters, Part I," *Art News* 62, no. 7 (1963): 24–27, 59–64, at 26. Compare Arthur Danto, *After the End of Art: Contemporary Art and the Pale of History* (Princeton, N.J.: Princeton University Press, 1997), 47, 44: "It became apparent that there were no . . . constraints. There is no special way works of art have to be . . . : one thing is, so to say, as good as another."

4. Mark Godfrey in Foster, "Questionnaire," 31.

5. Ibid., 30.

6. Thomas Kuhn, *The Structure of Scientific Revolutions* (Chicago: University of Chicago Press, 1962), 42. For the complex reception of Kuhn's notion of paradigm by art historians, see Caroline Jones, "The Modernist Paradigm: The Artworld and Thomas Kuhn," *Critical Inquiry* 26, no. 3 (2000): 488–528. Jones discusses and dismisses the possibility of using the incommensurability of paradigms to give legitimacy to postmodern pluralism. Claiming that paradigm means something larger, and unified, she terms it (especially in its interpretation by Michael Fried) a category structurally tied to modernism and its teleology. What Jones fails to see is that paradigmatic sequence by no necessity includes teleology (see following note), and she therefore disregards what I am considering here: the possibility of a large paradigm shift that takes us beyond modernism/postmodernism or metaphysics/antimetaphysics.

7. The relevant distinction, if one wants to continue historical narration without continuing historical teleology, runs between a meta-narratio grounded in the *paradigmatic* and a meta-narratio grounded in a *pragmatic* continuity that affords narrative coherence. This equals the work *within* a paradigm vs. the work *across* a paradigm shift. Or, as Dewey says: "Intellectual advance occurs in two ways. At times increase of knowledge is organized about old conceptions, while these are expanded, elaborated and refined, but not seriously revised, much less abandoned. At other times, the increase of knowledge demands . . . alteration, not

addition. Men's minds grow cold to their former intellectual concerns; ideas that were burning fade; interests that were urgent seem remote. Men face in another direction; their older perplexities are unreal; considerations passed over as negligible loom up. Former problems may not have been solved, but they no longer press for solution." John Dewey, "The Need for a Recovery of Philosophy," in *The Essential Dewey*, vol. 1 (Bloomington: Indiana University Press, 1998), 46.

8. As I argue in Florian Klinger, *Theorie der Form: Gerhard Richter und die Kunst des pragmatischen Zeitalters* (Munich: Carl Hanser Verlag, 2013). The present essay reframes the main thesis of the book in order to explore a paradigm shift *as a possibility*—an undertaking that relies on the *pragmatist notion of exemplarity* I develop toward the end.

9. Gerhard Richter, *Writings 1961–2007*, ed. Dietmar Elger and Hans Ulrich Obrist (New York: Distributed Art Publishers, 2009), 104. References to the German edition: Gerhard Richter, *Text 1961 bis 2007: Schriften, Interviews, Briefe*, ed. Dietmar Elger and Hans Ulrich Obrist (Cologne: Verlag der Buchhandlung Walther König, 2008).

10. Richter, *Writings*, 46.

11. Ibid., 32.

12. Ibid., 63.

13. Ibid., 66.

14. Ibid., 140.

15. Ibid., 248.

16. Ibid., 15.

17. William James, *The Varieties of Religious Experience*, in *Writings 1902–1910* (New York: Library of America, 1987), 398.

18. Pragmatic articulation cannot be demonstrated by example—which is why Wittgenstein insists that his philosophy does not change the world but instead changes how we see it. See Jonathan Lear, "Leaving the World Alone," *Journal of Philosophy* 79, no. 7 (1982): 382–403.

19. Harold Rosenberg, "The American Action Painters," *Art News* 51, no. 8 (1952): 22–23, 48–50: "At a certain moment the canvas began to appear . . . as an arena in which to act—rather than as a space in which to reproduce, redesign, analyze or 'express' an object, actual or imagined. What was to go on the canvas was not a picture but an event. The painter no longer approached his easel with an image in his mind; he went up to it with material in his hand to do something to that other piece of material in front of him. The image would be the result of this encounter."

20. William James, *A Pluralistic Universe*, in James, *Writings 1902–1910*, 751: "What really exists is not things made but things in the making." Or p. 808: "If we take an activity-situation at its face-value, it seems as if we caught *in flagrante delicto* the very power that makes facts come and be. . . . Real activities are those that really make things be, without which the things are not, and with which they are there."

21. Richter, *Writings*, 59.

22. See Aristotle, *Metaphysics*, book 9; *Art of Rhetoric*, 3.11.

23. Richter, *Writings*, 247.

24. Rosenberg, "American Action Painters": "The innovation of Action Painting was to dispense with the representation of the [artist's psychic] state in favor

of enacting it in physical movement. The action on the canvas became its own representation."

25. Ludwig Wittgenstein, *Culture and Value*, ed. G. H. von Wright, trans. P. Winch (Oxford: Blackwell, 1980), 31, emphasis added.

26. Richter, *Writings*, 159, translation modified, emphasis added.

27. Ibid., 15, emphasis added.

28. For an attempt at founding a correspondence model in a coherence model, see Donald Davidson, "A Coherence Theory of Truth and Knowledge," in Davidson, *Subjective, Intersubjective, Objective* (Oxford: Clarendon, 2001).

29. Richter, *Writings*, 142.

30. Ibid., 214, 461, 531–32.

31. Ibid., 182.

32. Ibid., 141–42.

33. Ibid., 31.

34. Birgit Pelzer, "Der Zufall als Partner: Gerhard Richters Farbfelder 2007"; Pelzer, "Die Asymptote des Zufalls: '4900 Farben' von Gerhard Richter—'Version II'—in der Serpentine Gallery in London," both in *Gerhard Richter: Texte zu "4900 Farben,"* ed. Dietmar Elger et al. (Ostfildern-Ruit: Hatje Cantz Verlag, 2009).

35. Richter, *Writings*, 15.

36. Ibid., 92, translation modified; compare p. 181, where the same *Verbindlichkeit* appears as "coherence that is the utter opposite of randomness." On rightness as a philosophical category, see Nelson Goodman, *Ways of Worldmaking* (Indianapolis: Hackett, 1978), 132, 138–40; Nelson Goodman and Catherine Z. Elgin, "A Reconception of Philosophy," in Goodman and Elgin, *Reconceptions in Philosophy and Other Arts and Sciences* (London: Routledge, 1988).

37. Klinger, *Urteilen* (Zürich: Diaphanes Verlag, 2011), introduction.

38. Richter, *Writings*, 169.

39. Ibid., 476, translation modified.

40. Ludwig Wittgenstein, *Philosophical Investigations*, trans. G. E. M. Anscombe (Oxford: Blackwell, 1953), 167.

41. Compare Goodman, *Ways of Worldmaking*, 66–67: "A thing may function as a work of art at some times and not at others. . . . The real question is not 'What objects are (permanently) works of art?' but 'When is an object a work of art?'" According to Thierry de Duve, the readymade demonstrates that art belongs to the realm of judgment—in Duchamp's own words: "*To make is to choose and always to choose.*" De Duve, *Kant after Duchamp* (Cambridge, Mass.: MIT Press, 1996), 394.

42. Wittgenstein, *Philosophical Investigations*, 167.

43. Ibid., 177.

44. Compare the description of form according to a marked and an unmarked side in George Spencer Brown, *Laws of Form* (London: Allen and Unwin, 1969), and Niklas Luhmann, *Art as a Social System*, trans. Eva M. Knodt (Stanford, Calif.: Stanford University Press, 2000).

45. Compare Rosenberg, "American Action Painters": "Each stroke had to be a decision and was answered by a new question. By its very nature, action painting is painting in the medium of difficulties." A footnote continues: "Action Painting has extracted the element of decision inherent in all art in that the work

is not finished at its beginning but has to be carried forward by an accumulation of 'right' gestures."

46. Richter, *Writings*, 247. Compare Luhmann, *Art as a Social System*, 193: "Every operation—whether the artist's or the beholder's—must decide whether a given form does or does not fit, whether it can be integrated into the emerging work (or into the work one is about to inspect) in ways that secure connectivity. Every observation places the detail it indicates into the recursive network of further distinctions and, from this viewpoint, makes a judgment about the success or failure of this detail. . . . This is how a binary code works."

47. Richter here anticipates Luhmann's account of the "small-scale evolution of the single work" which operates via the two stage process of random production and critical selection: "The first distinction, the one from which the artist starts out, . . . can only occur spontaneously—even though it implies a decision concerning the work's type (whether it is to be a poem, a fugue, or a glass window) and perhaps an idea in the artist's mind. Any further decision tightens the work, orienting itself toward what is already there, specifying the unoccupied sides of already established forms and restricting the freedom of further decisions. Once the distinctions begin to . . . relate to one another recursively, what occurs is precisely what we expect from evolution: the artwork finds stability within itself." Luhmann, *Art as a Social System*, 215–16 (translation modified).

48. Text and translation taken from Corinna Belz's documentary *Gerhard Richter Painting* (Berlin: Zero One Film with Terz Film, 2011), DVD.

49. Robert Storr, *Cage: 6 Paintings by Gerhard Richter* (London: Tate, 2009), 69.

50. Ibid. Some of the pre-stages are also in Ulrich Wilmes, *Gerhard Richter: Zur Entstehung der Abstrakten Bilder* (Dresden: Gerhard Richter Archiv, Staatliche Kunstsammlungen Dresden; Cologne: Verlag der Buchhandlung W. König, 2009).

51. In Mark Godfrey, Nicholas Serota, and Achim Burchardt-Hume, eds., *Gerhard Richter: Panorama, a Retrospective* (London: Tate, 2011), 131, Richter says: "A picture like this is painted in different layers, separated by intervals of time."

52. Richter, *Writings*, 67.

53. Ibid., 183 (translation modified).

54. Storr, *Cage*, 84.

55. Camille Morineau, "The Blow-Up, Primary Colours and Duplications," in Godfrey et al., *Gerhard Richter: Panorama*, 131: "A succession of freeze-frames or multiple points of view—on a common pictorial or mental 'object.'"

56. Richter, *Writings*, 32–33.

57. Wittgenstein, *Last Writings on the Philosophy of Psychology*, vol. 1: *Preliminary Studies for Part II of "The Philosophical Investigations,"* ed. G. H. von Wright and Heikki Nyman, trans. C. E. Luckhardt and Maximilien A. E. Aue (Chicago: University of Chicago Press, 1982), 81: "But the application [of the aspect], after all, is completely different in aesthetics and descriptive geometry. In aesthetics isn't it essential that a picture or a piece of music, etc., can change its aspect for me?—And, of course, this is not essential for that topological demonstration." See also Richard Rorty, *Contingency, Irony, and Solidarity* (Cambridge: Cambridge University Press, 1989), 78; Klinger, *Urteilen*, ch. 7, and *Theorie der Form*, 141–42; Michael Lüthy, "Das Medium der ästhetischen Erfahrung: Wittgensteins Aspektbegriff, exemplifiziert an Pollocks Malerei," in *Imaginäre*

Medialität—Immaterielle Medien, ed. Gertrud Koch, Kirsten Maar, and Fiona McGovern (Munich: Fink, 2012), 125–42.

58. Richter, *Writings*, 121 (translation modified).

59. Ibid., 14: "The first impulse towards painting, or towards art in general, stems from the need to communicate" that Richter describes as "our deepest desire, not to be private. To be public, open to the world" (392).

60. Ibid., 15.

61. Immanuel Kant, *Critique of the Power of Judgment* (New York: Cambridge University Press, 2000), part 1.

62. Niklas Luhmann, *Love as Passion: The Codification of Intimacy*, trans. Jeremy Gaines and Doris L. Jones (Cambridge, Mass.: Harvard University Press, 1986), 8–9.

63. "Symbolically generalized" means "that social agreement can be attained only if the underlying commonalities last for more than a single situation" (Niklas Luhmann, *Theory of Society*, trans. Rhodes Barrett, vol.1 [Stanford, Calif.: Stanford University Press, 2012], 191). This, in Richter, is clearly not the case, since such lasting, while it may get enabled by the form, is not part of its operation.

64. Richter, *Writings*, 278: "Photography has almost no reality. . . . And painting always has reality." Or p. 284: "[The painted picture] has more reality than a photograph [to which it reacts, or the cup shown by both]. . . . That gives it a reality of its own, which then as it were substitutes for the reality of the cup."

65. Ibid., 461–62. The passage containing the first occurrence of *Formulierung*, p. 470 in the German edition, is missing in the English translation.

66. Ibid., 461.

67. On effects of painterly "generalization" in Richter's landscape paintings, see Dietmar Elger, "Landscape as a Model," in *Gerhard Richter: Landscapes*, ed. Elger (Ostfildern-Ruit: Cantz, 2011), 26.

68. Richter, *Writings*, 239, emphasis added.

69. Ibid., 506, translation modified.

70. Ibid., 57.

71. While for Heidegger, these terms serve the purpose of distinguishing man from animal, the underlying concern, I think, relates to the pragmatist worry that world is subject to a more or less. Martin Heidegger, *The Fundamental Concepts of Metaphysics: World, Finitude, Solitude*, trans. William McNeil and Nicholas Walker (Bloomington: Indiana University Press, 1995), part 2.

72. Richter, *Writings*, 461, translation modified.

73. Ibid., 31, translation modified.

74. Ibid., 462, translation modified and expanded. Again, the English does not render the text in full.

75. Ibid., 109, translation modified.

76. Klinger, *Theorie der Form*, chs. 2 and 4.

77. It deserves to be noted that the possibility of a paradigm of pragmatic form does not depend on Richter himself being consistent, but only on such consistency being a possibility.

78. Giorgio Agamben, "What Is a Paradigm?," lecture at European Graduate School, August 2002. Recordings of the lecture are available at https://www.youtube.com/playlist?list=PL080808CE58864A27.

79. Aristotle, *Art of Rhetoric*, 1357b; *Prior Analytics*, 69a17.

80. Kant, *Critique of the Power of Judgment*, §47, 49, translation modified.

81. Thomas Kuhn, "Second Thoughts on Paradigms," in Kuhn, *The Essential Tension: Selected Studies in Scientific Tradition and Change* (Chicago: University of Chicago Press, 1977), 293–319.

82. Kuhn himself applies "the notion of a paradigm as a concrete achievement, an exemplar" to the arts (*Structure*, 208–9), implying a shift from vertical determination by principle to horizontal determination by example (operating through connecting acts): "Some of the notorious difficulties . . . may vanish if paintings can be seen to be modeled on one another rather than produced in conformity to some abstracted canons of style."

Varieties of Nonpropositional Knowledge

Image—Attention—Action

Thomas Pfau

> Action flows not from inferences, but from impressions.
>
> —John Henry Newman

Ever since Hobbes framed human agency in terms of efficient causation and the mechanist logic of modern physics, ordinary language has tended to employ the concept of action as a variant of efficient force. Action came to be construed as the implementation of a subjective resolution, the imposition of a will (Hobbes's "last appetite"), and hence as the moment when the curtain has fallen on the drama of thought and its attendant vagaries of introspection. In the wake of Hobbes, action appears intrinsically noncognitive, a focused discharge of "power" within a social space, single-minded, unhesitating, and often violent.[1] Its sole measure of success is the attainment of an interest, the implementation of an objective whose success can be readily ascertained by empirical perception. Inasmuch as the criterion of effective action here is one of perceptually verifiable change, the antonym of action is less some notion of passivity than the (in origin Platonic) idea of spiritual contemplation that a number of patristic writers developed between the third and sixth centuries. For what is occluded by the modern, quintessentially Hobbesian, view of action as efficient force is nothing less than the realm of ideation and transformative meaning, of previously untapped potentialities in the agent, and of a suprapersonal good for the sake of which action is deliberatively pursued, and in which it allows the agent to participate.

Fundamentally opposed to the Hobbesian account, then, is a concept of action understood as the "realization" (Hegel's *Verwirklichung*) of meanings whose scope and significance will also leave the agent changed. The distinction at issue basically correlates with that drawn by Aquinas between "action that goes forth into exterior matter" and another type that "is the perfection of the agent."[2] What follows is an attempt to restore a rich semantic dimension to the concept of action by approaching it as a noninstrumental form of knowing, a way of participating in meanings that at once transcends the conceptual reach of finite cognition yet at the same time solicits our attentive and undesigning engagement. On this model, action is an integral part of a narrative movement that begins with the apprehension of a conceptually inexhaustible fullness (*pleroma*) such as gives itself in images—particularly of a nonartificial (*acheiropoietic*) kind. A first step here involves briefly tracing the struggle of patristic writers over the ontological distinctness and theological legitimacy of the image, one whose presence is not derived from ordinary object perception. The result of this prolonged debate, reaffirmed by the outcome of the iconoclast controversies in eighth- and ninth-century Byzantium, is that the theological and philosophical dignity of the image (*eikon*) can neither be secured nor gainsaid on the grounds of its material referent. Instead, it pivots on a distinct, nonproprietary mode of vision to which the icon gives rise.

Hence part 2 of this essay will scrutinize the concept of *attention* as the main phenomenological correlate of the concept of the image. When understood as a nonproprietary mode of participating in the visual world, attention amounts less to a contingent, subjective "state" than to a distinctive "act" whereby the beholder acknowledges (and gives him- or herself over to) the fullness of what is seen—not as a source of subjective pleasure but as the condition for transcending the idolatrous bondage of subjectivity itself. In its forensic verbal tracing of the act and experience of visual attention, a poem such as Hopkins's "Hurrahing in Harvest" not only eschews the technical lure of ekphrasis and its underlying aesthetic of illusion and simulation; it also avoids confining the fullness of what is visually disclosed to a merely symbolic statement, thereby effectively subordinating the phenomenal to the noumenal. Informing this essay's conceptual and hermeneutic investments is also another, more fundamental objective: to contest the commonplace opposition between the "real" world of empirical and pragmatic action and an imaginary realm of art capable, at best, of an "imitation of an action" whose beholder is conceived as but the passive consumer of virtual and spuriously enticing forms.[3] A first step toward dislodging this antinomy (and the only one this essay can take) is to recover the dual function of the image, namely, as an *imago* inviting us to attend to its incontrovertibly rich presence and, concurrently, as *figura* anticipating our participation in a noumenal reality consubstantialized in the abundant givenness of the image.

1. Image

The aim of this section is to inquire into the phenomenology of the image and how images may bring about nonpropositional forms of knowing, albeit not of a mystical or intuitionist kind but arising from and remaining grounded in what Jean-Luc Marion calls "saturated phenomena." So as to hint at the stakes and challenges of such a project, I will begin by sketching, ever so briefly, patristic theology's vexed outlook on the realms of the visible, material world and on the image in particular. Doing so should help identify some of the stakes and background vis-à-vis which my two principal examples (Hopkins and Tolstoy) acquire particular relevance. Crudely put, my premise is that under certain circumstances images will give rise to a knowledge that transcends the matrix for cognition established by modern epistemology: such knowledge cannot be paraphrased; it cannot be methodologically predicted or contained; it cannot be quarantined as some affective or intellectual, subjective experience (*Erlebnis*); and it cannot be resisted any more than a gift can be resisted: for even where we reject a gift, we can only reject what has already announced itself and has already been given *as a gift*; rejection cannot turn it into something less and, hence, always comes too late. To reject the *donum* of, say, an image, is never a subjective, value-neutral preference but, inevitably, a moment of spiritual failure.[4] For the givenness of the image proves anterior to modern epistemology's preemptive, skeptical restriction of human cognition to conceptual and methodological warrants of our own devising.

Yet as this first description suggests, our understanding of images is thereby both simplified and complicated. It is simplified in that modernity's epistemological default position and its attendant concerns with procedural correctness appear to have been suspended, for the image will do its work only if it is not subjected to the methodological regimen of distance, detachment, doubt, and intersubjective verification—all attributes of what Charles Taylor has dubbed modernity's "buffered self." Yet the matter is also complicated in that, in the absence of these established methodological procedures, any responsible and searching engagement with images demands that we develop new conceptual techniques and warrants such as allow for a rigorous and unsentimental accounting of our essential involvement with images, how we participate in them, are subtly transformed by them, and how it is possible for us to assent to an image not as an object or proposition but as a reality and as a good.

To a considerable extent, such an alternative framework—descriptive rather than determinative—has been elaborated by modern phenomenology, from Husserl's 1905 lectures on "image-consciousness" (*Bildbewusstsein*) via Heidegger, Gadamer, Merleau-Ponty, all the way to Jean-Luc Marion. Without acknowledging my countless debts to these voices in every instance, then, let me proceed by drawing an entirely preliminary distinction between ordinary perception and our response to images. As the anthropologist Arnold Gehlen notes, it is in the nature of a perception to call for an explanation, to demand a causal account and, by this supplement only, to achieve any legitimacy whatsoever.[5] Quotidian perception thus owes its significance and, indeed, reality to the conceptual resourcefulness with which we assimilate it to (putatively) equivalent sensations and, having thus contained it, integrate a given perception into our constantly shifting finite and practical concerns. In its initial presentation as sheer *appearance*, that is, any perception is deemed incomplete and underdetermined. It invites, indeed compels doubt insofar as the structure of its appearance has not as yet disclosed to the perceiver the underlying causal mechanism whereby it was brought forth. Whatever epistemological legitimacy a perception may claim it thus seems to owe to an extraneous network of cross-references within which the perceiver has situated it. Following Hobbes's and Locke's accounts of empirical perception, the affect and ethos shaping modern epistemology is one of anxiety and control, respectively.

Something nearly obverse appears to characterize the image. Here the principal quality is one of fullness, indeed abundance, rather than incompleteness. The insistent, Cartesian suspicion of ephemeral and deceptive appearances orchestrated by a *dieu trompeur* is replaced by the image's indubitable, charismatic presence. The beholder will not greet the image with prevarication and doubt but, on the contrary, will unreservedly and attentively participate in it. Where the image engages us in all its fullness, we have left behind the realm of propositional and discursive reasoning. The dominant ethos and affect here is one of surprise, unselfish attention, and quiet gratitude. We neither wish nor feel compelled to authenticate an image by taking recourse to some a priori method of verification, let alone assign it some extraneous function. Instead, the advent of the image—what Marion calls "the happening phenomenon"—commands our assent insofar as here the *sujet* that has been captured both *in* and *as* a specific image seems more real, more true, more present in virtue of its iconic *Gestalt*. Crediting the image with an ontologically distinct "mode of being" (*Seinsweise*), Hans-Georg Gadamer remarks on how the image brings about "an increase in Being" (*ein Zuwachs an Sein*) in that *of* which it is the image.[6]

If nothing else, this preliminary sketch tells us that conceptualizing the image exceeds the purview of both modern epistemology and aesthetics. Thus beginning with Locke, epistemology disputes the ontological distinctness of the image by treating it as a derivative of a perception, whereas, beginning with Shaftesbury, modern aesthetics seeks to quarantine the image in either affective or formalist categories, thereby eclipsing the question concerning its truth value.[7] Simply put, with the exception of phenomenology, modern verificationist or formalist approaches to the image will either dispute its ontological standing or restrict themselves to tabulating its formal and cultural characteristics. To extricate the image from the blind spot of modern, method-based inquiry, we need to return to the historical moment when the revelatory power of the image—and indeed the metaphysical dignity of the material world *of* which it is the image—was being contested by Neoplatonic and pre-Nicaean thought. Indeed, whatever insights into the unique power and efficacy of the image we may claim are in large measure the dialectical fruit of its prolonged struggle for theological and philosophical legitimacy, an intricate history about which both modern epistemology and aesthetics have proven culpably uncurious. That history may well be said to culminate in the writings of Byzantine monastics and clerics (St. John Damascene, St. Theodore of Stoudios, Nikephoros, Photius) struggling to defend the spiritual integrity of the *eikon* against political interference and appropriation by imperial and episcopal power in eighth- and ninth-century Byzantium and, in the process, evolving a highly sophisticated theory of the image as a legitimate and indispensable type of intercession.[8]

Yet the story does not begin here. Rather, as detailed and compelling analyses by Florovsky, Ladner, and Schönborn have shown, the theological legitimacy of the material world and the image is crucially shaped by the problematic reception of Platonic thought in the theology of Origen (ca. 185–254 CE), possibly mediated by Philo, and influentially extended in the writings of Eusebius, pseudo-Dionysius, and John Scotus Eriugena.[9] Questioning the spiritual and epistemological legitimacy of material, visible reality, Origen's stridently spiritualist approach (further exaggerated by his descendants, as Hans-Urs von Balthasar has argued) appeared to reinforce the Platonic disjunction of spirit and matter also pursued by his near-contemporary, Plotinus. At times, Origen's theology appears uncomfortably close to the Gnostic view of matter (*hylē*) as not merely deficient as such but, by its very existence, betraying the "fullness" (*plēroma*) of the creator-god (*demiourgos*). Where the "highest aim is image-less, purely spiritual contemplation," the image tends to be conflated with its material scaffolding, a point subsequently echoed by the iconoclasts' alternately mocking or vituperative references to the worship of wooden boards.[10] As is also evident in some of its modern, radically spiritualist offshoots—for example, in Joachim Fiore's and William Blake's apocalypticism, or in seventeenth-century radical Puritanism or early eighteenth-century German Pietism—an exclusively spiritual framework risks evolving into a theology of despair rather than hope.[11]

Beginning with Athanasius (ca. 296–373 CE), for whom "seeing was a critical *means* of knowing, not a metaphor for it," a separate genealogy of Christian thought thus pushes back, insisting (as Irenaeus of Lyon had put it) that in the very plenitude and remarkable diversity of creation "God [is] manifested and . . . shows forth."[12] Unlike Gnosticism's absentee demiurge—faintly echoed in the deism of seventeenth- and eighteenth-century natural theologians such as John Ray or William Paley—God here is understood as abidingly "present with His Handiwork."[13] As Erich Auerbach notes, Tertullian was among the first to criticize Origen's one-sided reliance on "figural interpretation to invalidate the literal and historical authority of the Old Testament."[14] A fuller exploration of the conjunctions between *figura* and *imago* (Greek: *typos* and *eikon*) still remains to be pursued but cannot be offered here; suffice it to say that the emergence of *figura*, which precedes the iconoclast debates that unfold in eighth- and ninth-century Byzantium, helped prepare the ground for two crucial interlocking claims by the iconodules: first, that *figura* at once affirms the historical, empirical reality of a given appearance as well as its narrative orientation toward a transcendent meaning. Even as that meaning remains unfulfilled from the viewpoint of the finite, historically contingent beholder, the distinctive, charismatic presence of the visible already attests to the possibility of its eventual fulfillment. As Tertullian puts it, "There could have been no figure, unless it had been a veritable body" (*figura autem non fuisset, nisi veritatis esset corpus*).[15] Similarly, Jerome criticizes Origen's habit "of fleeing the truth of history" (*historiae fugiens veritatem*). Second, even as Origen's critics understand *imago* and, by extension, *figura* to be grounded in the reality of an appearance, they also insist on the capacity of what is empirically present to the beholder to initiate a narrative progression. For Lactantius, *figura* names the capacity of "small and unimportant things . . . to foreshadow great things" (*saepe diximus minora et exigua magnorum figures et praemonstrationes esse*). In its very being, visible, mundane reality appears imbued with "a deeper meaning that suggests something in the future."[16]

For Origen's theological critics, divine transcendence is not the categorical *other* of history but, instead, pivots on our alertness to spiritually significant, narrative potentialities within the realm of empirically given appearance. Such a stance credits appearance with reality rather than peremptorily stigmatizing the phenomenal world as the deficient or deceptive antagonist of divine transcendence. Instead, the divine is seen to manifest itself precisely in the sheer presence and fecundity of appearance as such. Not coincidentally, Irenaeus is the first Christian theologian to maintain, very much against Origen, that "salvation is accomplished *in* rather than *beyond* history."[17] Similarly, Gregory Nazianzen recognizes that an apophatic framework still requires forms of mediation, such that "reason . . . leads us up to God through visible things" and that (referencing 1 Cor. 13.12) "all knowledge takes its stand upon little images of the truth."[18] Much of the tangled development of post-Nicaean theology thus can be traced back to this question: to what extent is a fully articulated incarnational theology commensurable with its distant Platonic sources? The question becomes more pressing as the original *imago dei*, Christ, and direct apostolic testimony of his presence fades away. By the third century, that is, the search for new forms of representation or intercession naturally acquires increasing urgency; and where better to locate divine plenitude—understood not as a symbolic proxy but as real presence—than in the charismatic fullness of the created world, taken not as the material substratum of perception but as an image not fashioned by human hands (*acheiropoiēsis*). Notably, both Hopkins and Tolstoy focus on this type of image, rather than on the overtly artifactual *eikon*, a decision whose implications we will yet have to consider.

The attempt of Irenaeus—and, following him, Gregory of Nyssa and Basil the Great—at reintegrating the natural world into a comprehensive divine economy finds a particularly fulsome expression in the writings of Maximus the Confessor (580–663 CE). Here we first encounter the argument—central much later to G. M. Hopkins's rehabilitation of image and "inscape"—that the material world not only is not merely the correlate of mundane perception but, in fact, is never even properly realized in that contingent modality. For quotidian perception proceeds by subsuming that which gives itself to be seen under some abstract scheme of classification or other; in so foreclosing on the radical particularity and singularity of what is seen, perception not only drains the phenomenon of its charismatic presence but also prevents the beholder from becoming aware of his or her profound relatedness to the visible world. The dominant ethos here is one of prevarication, distance, and containment. Maximus resists (neo)Platonism's and Origenism's peremptory suspicion of the material world's multifarious and dynamic appearance, a suspicion that, in its very attempt at safeguarding God's transcendent purity, effectively "overleaps the reality of His creation."[19] As he strives to rethink the relation between the visible and the invisible, Maximus conceives of that relation as neither one of strict antithesis nor some undifferentiated amalgamation. Instead, he envisions a "mutual ontological presence (*perichoresis*) [that] not only preserves the being particular to each element, to the divine and the human natures, but also brings each of them to its perfection in their very difference."[20] "Being" (*ousia*) and "Person" (*hypostasis*)—that is, what is subject to *perception* and to *recognition*, respectively—should be understood in generative, productive relation with one another. Von Balthasar speaks of a "tension within the world between the intellectual and phenomenal realms, the world of thought and the world of sense" (*die innerweltliche Spannung zwischen geistig-intelligibler und sinnlich-phänomenaler Welt*), and of a "twofold, incomprehensible, and irreversible self-opening [*Teilgabe*] of this unity to both the world as a whole and the world in all its particulars."[21] As Maximus puts it:

> The whole spiritual world seems mystically imprinted on the whole sensible world in symbolic forms, for those who are capable of seeing this. . . . And again, "The invisible realities [ἀόρατα] from the creation of the world have been perceived [καθορᾶται] and are recognized through things he has made," says the divine Apostle [Paul, Rom. 1:20]. And if we perceive what does not appear by means of what does, as the Scripture has it, then much more will visible things be understood by means of invisible by those who advance in spiritual contemplation. Indeed, the contemplation of intelligible things by means of visible realities is spiritual knowledge and understanding of visible things through the visible.[22]

To Maximus, the pivotal passage from Paul implies at least two things: first, that there is an indelible nexus between what is phenomenally given and its transcendent source, between *visibilia* and *invisibilia*. Second, this very nexus itself is not the fruit of unbridled enthusiasm or esoteric theological speculation. Rather, it arises from a specific form of visual attention of which humans are uniquely capable. In the *Ambigua* (ca. 632 CE), Maximus specifically insists that the operation of the "senses [be] informed by reason," thereby "allowing no room for sensation to operate independently of the reins of reason, nor allowing reason itself to range beyond the simplicity of the intellect." In sharp contrast to modernity's fundamentally disjunctive account of sensory and intellectual functions, Maximus's integrative vision is premised on—and conducive to our apprehension of—a cosmic order, such that "the mediating power of reason conducts the forms and figures perceived by the senses toward their manifold inner principles [*logoi*], and concentrates the manifold diversity of the principles that are in beings . . . into a uniform, simple, and undifferentiated intuition." Whoever succeeds at that "has acquired a true impression (as much as is humanly possible) of their creator, sustainer, and originator."[23]

Maximus's commitment to negative (apophatic) theology is unwavering. Yet inasmuch as the task of theology is to "make manifest what is hidden by means of an apophatic negation," it must find a way of engaging the reality and presence of the visible, created world that does not confine it to a merely sensory *effect* of an absent, divine cause but attests to God as the "eternally active creator" (*energeian esti Demiourgos*).[24] Ordinary rhetorical and figurative speech, such as the intimation of a transcendent *plērōma* by symbolic means, will not do, since apophatic theology by its very nature is incommensurable with ordinary acts of referential or syllogistic predication—a view that Maximus takes from the Cappadocians (esp. Gregory Nazianzen) and Dionysius the Areopagite. Instead, "leaving aside every capacity to picture the truth by means of figures and signs," those engaged in contemplation are to be "lifted up in silence by the power of the Spirit from written words and visible things to the Word Himself. . . . For when the letter is desired only for itself, it tends to kill the indwelling Word, . . . just as the beauty of creatures, when not beheld for the glory of their Creator inevitably deprives beholders of their rational devotion to the Word."[25]

To the extent that it is relevant, indeed an integral component of Maximus's theology, the image (*eikon*) is not to be confused with a rhetorical or expressive technique such as is deployed for contingent, pragmatic reasons. Far from some artifice fashioned by a subject who enjoys independent spiritual standing, the image prima facie unveils and delineates the scope and direction of spiritual reflection. Where contemplation is concerned, only the *eikon* has agency, moving as it may the human being engaged in its contemplation: "From the same source whence we received our being, we should also long to receive being moved, like an image [*eikon*] that has ascended to its archetype, corresponding to it completely, in the way an impression corresponds to its stamp."[26] For Maximus, the image uniquely entwines the singular source (*logos*) of the cosmos and "the marvelous physical phenomena that we see, which are naturally interconnected, so that the harmonious web of the universe is contained within it like the various elements in a book." Thus God "leads us to a unitary idea of the truth, allowing Himself to be seen *by analogy* through visible things."[27] In its abundant and inexhaustible givenness as a focal point of visual attention, each and every created form functions simultaneously as an image (*eikon*) of the divine *logos* and as a figure (*typos*) of a fullness (*pleroma*) and rational order (*cosmos*) fleetingly indexed by our attentive contemplation of visible form. Paradoxically, then, Maximus insists that apophatic theology positively demands the visible and a distinctive kind of vision that is within reach of finite human beings: "Creation itself—stripped of the soiled preconceptions of those who till then believed they saw it clearly, but who in fact were deceived and bound to sense-perception alone—now appearing in the variety of different forms that constitute it, all declaring the power of the Creator Word, in the same way that a garment makes known the dignity of the one who wears it."[28]

"Those who are capable of seeing" not only take in what is phenomenally apparent; they also achieve the kind of sustained quality of "attention" (a word much later put to similar use by Simone Weil and Iris Murdoch) that allows them to apprehend the visible as *real* in an incarnational sense, that is, as far more than the sum of its mundane, discrete aspects. Such noetic seeing simultaneously constitutes a noematic act of understanding whereby the Real enters into a complex economy of meaning. Yet this meaning, for Maximus, can be of different kinds. To be sure, an appearance may prompt an observer to embed it within a frame of seemingly equivalent phenomena—a "taking of X as Y" such as is said to underlie Wittgenstein's language games. Yet Maximus also sees another possibility, one largely eclipsed by the strictly horizontal perspective of modern epistemology. As he puts the choice made by the beholder: "The mind which is settled in the contemplation of visible realities searches out either the natural reasons of things or those which are signified by them, or else it seeks the cause itself."[29] Beyond isolating "natural reasons" of finite, visible matter by laterally cross-referencing it with analogous phenomena, we may also engage the world as it comes into visibility. As von Balthasar notes, Maximus sees consciousness originate in

> a general, confused first impression of reality (*pragma*) and gradually grow clearer in content until [it reaches] the full knowledge of the individual object. What flashes upon us "in an undivided way" (*ameristos*) "in the first encounter" is not some empty general concept of being—a contradiction in terms!—but a revelation (*logos*) concerning the Monad (*peri monados*), the unity of that being that truly is one: a *logos* that instructs the thinking mind that God and the world are undivided and so makes possible all thought of things different from God.[30]

When approached not as a circumscribed object but as *manifestatio*, as the fullness of an image rather than a finite perception begging causal explanation, the visible unveils its underlying narrative logic as *figura*. It is real in the dual sense of materiality phenomenalized as "sight" (*visus*) and as "insight" (*visio*), as a finite, embodied thing absorbing the beholder with its eventual, typological fulfillment. In crediting "visible things" with giving real presence to "those which are signified by them," Maximus notably does *not* mean to convert them into symbols, let alone allegories of some inaccessible, transcendent order. Rather, *figura* impresses on the beholder/reader the coinherence of what is phenomenally given with its as yet unconsummated, spiritual significance. As Auerbach puts it in his eponymous essay on *figura*, referencing Dante's supreme realization of this model, "The literal meaning and historical reality of a character do not contradict that figure's deeper meaning. Rather, they figure it. Historical reality is not annulled by this deeper meaning."[31] The "future fulfillment or *veritas*" integral to *figura* must itself be real and phenomenally distinct; there is nothing notional or abstract about it.

With his nuanced retreat from the Platonism of pseudo-Dionysius and his careful avoidance of pantheist and emanationist tendencies that would subsequently flourish in John Scotus Eriugena, Maximus helped lay the groundwork for the Byzantine iconodules' defense of images by providing a rich theological rationale for the ultimate "inseparability of image (*eikōn*) and the idea (*ennoia*) in the eikon."[32] For he shows that to stigmatize the realm of created, particular, and visible being is to miss the distinction between a mundane perceptual and a revelatory image-consciousness—a distinction echoed much later by Husserl as the distinction between the truth of correctness and the truth of disclosure.[33] What's more, where that distinction between *visus* and *visio* has been lost, all talk of God gravitates toward the purely notional and the abstract; and where that development continues unchecked, it will become increasingly difficult to establish a compelling nexus between faith and action, by which I here mean a teleological (not transactional) process aimed at the realization of a substantive good rather than at the satisfaction of contingent, subjective desires or interests.

2. Attention

At this point, it should be noted that the earlier distinction between ordinary perceptual and a more focused type of "image-consciousness" (Husserl's *Bildbewusstsein*) only served a heuristic purpose; as Merleau-Ponty had put it, an "objective psychology" of perception only "represents a first phase of elimination rather than a means of total explanation." For ultimately, what Merleau-Ponty calls our "perceptual faith" involves a form of active, nonpropositional assent, "prior to every opinion, of inhabiting the world by our body, of inhabiting the truth by our whole selves, without there being need to choose nor even to distinguish between the assurance of seeing and the assurance of seeing the true," a prediscursive and preratiocinative state where "perceiving and imagining are now only two modes of *thinking*." In a formulation that could have come straight out of Newman's *Grammar of Assent*, Merleau-Ponty succinctly captures the essential secondariness and poverty of the Cartesian stance: "Doubt as a destruction of certitudes is not a doubt. It is no different when the doubt is made methodic."[34] The commonplace opposition between perceptual- and image-consciousness rests on the *proton pseudos* of a world exclusively attained and measured by acts of critical reflection. In a particularly eloquent passage, Merleau-Ponty delineates what he had earlier sketched as "another point of departure"—one that neither abides by nor merely rejects the critical-reflective take on the visible:

> The visible things about us rest in themselves, and their natural being is *so full* that it seems to envelop their perceived being, *as if our perception of them were formed within them*. But if I express this experience by saying that the things are in their place and that we fuse with them, I immediately make the experience itself impossible: for in the measure that the thing is approached, I cease to be; in the measure that I am, there is no thing, but only a double of it in my "camera obscura." The moment my perception is to become pure perception, thing, Being, it is extinguished; the moment it lights up, already I am no longer the thing. . . . It is mine only by *finding in some way a place in my present*, in making itself present anew. As we never have at the same time the thing and the consciousness of the thing.[35]

At its most elemental, our contact with the visible is altogether undesigning; there is nothing discretionary, let alone prevaricating, in the way that the reality of the visible finds "a place in my present"—becomes presence and fullness (*pleroma*). Before distance, objectivity, and doubt can insinuate themselves and attenuate the force and, perhaps, even the reality of perception, the visible envelops and temporarily suspends the incertitude attendant on conscious awareness. Here the only reality is that of the visible *qua* image, and its phenomenology is one of timeless attention. As the font of whatever discursive, critical, or "focal" awareness may yet eventuate, this anterior image consciousness thus arises from our uptake of a holistic *Gestalt* whose charismatic "fullness" and cohesion envelops the beholder, "as if our perception of [it] were formed within [it]." In its imponderable givenness and splendor, the visible may unpredictably acquire reality and presence by drawing us into its unique organization or, as Merleau-Ponty puts it, "by finding in some way a place in my present." For something to appear at all it must first and literally be *remarkable*. Our relation to a specific phenomenon thus cannot be one of passive recipiency or elective curiosity; rather, it involves an act of unpremeditated, real assent whereby we actively engage and participate in the phenomenon as it gives itself. I am thinking here of a more robust version of what John McDowell means by the "non-conceptual content" of a mind engaging the phenomenal world. As he acknowledges, "The understanding is already inextricably implicated in the deliverances of sensibility themselves," and the "impressions" that our senses mediate for us "already have conceptual content."[36]

Contrary to Hobbesian and Lockean empiricism (to say nothing of its skeptical offshoots from Hume to Nietzsche and beyond), our rational commerce with the world cannot unfold as the methodical cultivation of sheer receptivity and critical detachment vis-à-vis discrete data but, on the contrary, begins with our assenting to the reality and unconditional givenness of the phenomenon. Were it otherwise there would not even be anything for us to doubt or want to investigate further. As Michael Polanyi puts it so well, scientific knowledge begins as our attempt "to achieve a frame of mind in which I may hold firmly to what I believe to be true, even though I know that it might conceivably be false."[37] Cognition thus pivots on our concerted and sustained engagement of an appearance, rather than on the contingent perception of some "object." Husserl's blunt clarification that "phenomena don't appear; rather, they are experienced" hints at this dynamic, participatory nature of vision. All empirical perception or sight (*visus*) begins as an incontrovertible insight (*visio*) into the coherence of the given phenomenon as something in whose very reality and charismatic presence we actively participate; to see means prima facie to be involved in, not detached from, the world and, thereby, to grasp ourselves as capable and ethically responsible agents of whatever knowledge may yet eventuate.

In a world defined by unparalleled degrees of specialization, "expert-knowledge," and an ever-expanding inventory of technical terms, we may easily lose sight of ordinary language as a source of insight. Words such as action, judgment, goodness, or attention routinely surface in everyday speech even as we seem largely unaware of their conceptual richness and force. Indeed, it is only when we find ourselves or someone else to have failed to live up to the meaning of these words that we can glimpse their submerged complexity. Remaining for the most part outside our purview, the importance of a word such as attention will typically divulge itself only in moments of crisis or (less frequently, perhaps) wonder. An ideal honored more in the breach than the observance, attention seems all but inseparable from the particular situation that called for it but, often enough, did not receive it. On the face of it, then, there is very little about the idea of attention that can be stated in general terms. It concerns some particular object, issue, phenomenon, or person and appears exclusively defined by the specificity and richness of what we attend *to*. As Weil put it long ago, attention "consists of suspending our thought, leaving it detached, empty, and ready to be penetrated by the object . . . [or] in order to receive into itself the being it is looking at, just as he is."[38] A first and provisional conclusion, then, might be that attention appears to be an antonym of control.

Hence it cannot surprise that the concept of "attention" should no longer engage modern and, especially, contemporary philosophy. For since Descartes's *Discourse on Method* (1637), and reinforced by Hume's skepticism about *qualia* of any kind and Wittgenstein's agnosticism about "inner states," modern thought has been wary of mental phenomena that do not readily conform to its methodological protocols. What kind of "evidence," after all, could there ever be that someone is properly "attending" to something or someone, other than her verbal assurances that she is doing so? Yet in that case, the prototypical modern skeptic will be quick to insist on the difference between a verbal assurance ("I *am* paying attention") and the putative fact of attention itself. To *be* and to report oneself *as being* in a state of attention (or love, anger, remorse, etc.) are evidently two separate things. For the modern skeptic, the first order of business thus becomes disentangling something as specious as inner states, such as attention, from the propositional language employed by individuals *claiming* to inhabit some such state. For it would be an unpardonable blunder, as well as an affront to the philosopher's professional *amour propre*, to be caught mistaking a simple proposition for the state to which it ostensibly *refers*.

Naturally, once inner states are deemed to lack objective, measurable criteria for their verification, it is but a small step to deny them any reality and legitimacy as topics for philosophical inquiry. If the mental phenomenon of attention can command any respect whatsoever from modern thought, it is only as a type of *behavior* such as can be captured in the verbal and physical trappings of outward representation. To the philosopher committed to objective, quantifiable verification, attention thus becomes fused with looking or behaving *like* someone who is paying attention. As is the case with other inner states or *qualia*—such as sincerity, faith, love, or grief—the reality of attention is assimilated to one's making an effective rhetorical pitch for it, rather in the spirit of what John L. Austin calls a successful ("felicitous") performative utterance. Conversely, today's heir apparent of Humean skepticism, neuroscientific reductionism, seeks to dissolve *qualia* such as attention into a distinctive, measurable data-stream. Naturally, any explicit and putatively "conscious" assurance about one's inner state ("I am in love" or "I am paying attention") would be quarantined simply as a *separate* neural event. Now in either scenario, the major premise driving modern inquiry will be that attention, if it is anything at all, amounts to a distinctive *state* of mind, that is, some measurable and quantifiable spike in the computational acuity with which an individual's brain can be shown to process some specific data input. The skeptic and the reductionist thus tend to "solve" admittedly elusive and perplexing phenomena, such as that of "attention," either by confining them within a preestablished matrix of objective measurement and verification or, where such attempts fail, by disputing the reality of the phenomenon altogether.[39]

The picture changes considerably, however, if we replace the prevailing notion of attention as a "state of mind" and think of it instead as an *act* in the strong sense first established by Aquinas, who contends that the reality of a being is inseparable from the way in which it realizes itself *in actu*. In the realm of the human, action finds intellect and will fully entwined. For only where we engage the world for the sake of a good, however tentatively apprehended, can we speak of action. The rest, as Hannah Arendt has observed, is a mere *doing* "in order to" get something or somewhere, a manipulation of the ambient world that leaves the doer uninvolved save as the efficient cause of some change outside ourselves.[40] To close in on why this shift in perspective—from attention as a state to attention as *actus*—should matter, it helps to consider situations in which the idea of attention comes alive for us. Let us begin with the intersubjective scenario, so familiar to any parent enjoining a child to "pay attention." To ask our child to "pay attention" typically means more than, indeed prima facie something different from, a call for intensified concentration. It asks the person—say, a teenager whose glance keeps drifting away from an obscure biology textbook page about cell division to the bright screen of her cell phone—to focus on what truly matters at *this* moment, to be fully present in *this* situation, and to recognize why doing so is indeed the right thing to do. Put differently, to pay attention is not simply a matter of increasing, seemingly at will, one's computational prowess but, first and foremost, to recognize and assent to what deserves our attention and why.

The act of giving our attention, then, begins with a judgment or ethical appraisal whereby we recognize and acknowledge what we owe to the particular phenomenon or person in our purview. Where the domains of fact and value appear substantially entwined, what is *just and right*—to give our attention—can never be construed as a function of our sheer will. In her "Reflections on the Right Use of School Studies," Weil specifically rejects the widespread confusion of attention "with a kind of muscular effort. If one says to one's pupils: 'Now you must pay attention,' one sees them contracting their brows, holding their breath, stiffening their muscle. If after two minutes they are asked what they have been paying attention to, they cannot reply. They have been concentrating on nothing. They have not been paying attention. They have been contracting their muscles."[41] If it is a mistake to think of attention as issuing from a self exercising its will, it would also be wrong to think of it as entirely adventitious. More plausibly, attention belongs to a deep-structural pattern of action that Aquinas captures under the heading of *habitus* and regards as indispensable for an education into the virtues. On this model, to attend properly means to assent to an as yet unconsummated form of the good, one realized only if we unconditionally and habitually bestow our attention on what presents itself to us, and one lost if we don't. As a creative and an ethical act, attention allows itself to be filled by the reality of what we attend *to*.

Yet even as attention involves a self-emptying or *kenosis*, it is not to be confused with a passive, hedonistic stance such as would have the individual abide in mindless desire for the sheer novelty of some object "out there." Rather, attention constitutes an achievement, a habit of focused seeing and participating in what gives itself to us, for which reason Weil repeatedly likens it to prayer.[42] Similarly, for Coleridge "attention has for its object the order and connection of Thoughts and Images," and he finds it supremely realized in Wordsworth's *Lyrical Ballads* (1798), which succeeds in "awakening the mind's attention from the lethargy of custom, and . . . directing it to the loveliness and the wonders of the world before us." Elsewhere, Coleridge also stresses the strong link between attention and the visual, a process that finds "the eyes quietly and steadfastly dwelling on an object, not as if looking at it or as in any way exerting an act of sight upon it, but as if the whole attention were listening to *what the heart was feeling and saying about it*."[43] Our capacity for attention thus reveals much about the overall quality of our orientation toward the world, with "world" here being understood not as an inventory of impersonal objects and agendas but as a realm of as yet unrealized potentialities.

What rationality one may ascribe to the work of attention, then, surely belongs to the domain of practical, not theoretical, reason. Yet inasmuch as concepts of practical reason cannot be syllogistically demonstrated, a different approach is needed to illuminate the distinctive character of attention. One way to proceed is by engaging in what Samuel Taylor Coleridge calls "desynonymization," namely, by sifting how the meaning of attention differs from closely related concepts.[44] Rather than juxtaposing attention to its putative antonym, "distraction," we proceed by disentangling attention from "interest," a concept whose quasi-forensic and enduring intentionality would seem to place it in close proximity to attention. Yet the resemblance deceives. For where we are interested, we proceed on the basis of a priori notions or commitments that would have us prejudge the world or, more likely, some particular aspect of it. Interest, as Kant had put it, is by its very nature "determinative." Ordinary language offers some guidance here. Thus one is said to "take" an interest in something or other, whereas attention is something we can only "give." What prompts us to take an interest in something is, ordinarily, the prospect of an expected or at least highly probable "return." Our interest in X pivots on its supposed instrumental relation to something else to the attainment of which we are already committed. Interests can only be "realized" as a desire "fulfilled," an opportunity "seized," or an object "acquired." For precisely that reason, however, our interested take on the world can never fundamentally alter or transform who we are. Rather, we only take an interest in some fact or opportunity where doing so promises to let us consolidate knowledge of and control over an already familiar world, that is, to engage it solely on *our* terms.

By contrast, attention is solicited by our intuitive sense of meanings as yet undefined, unrealized, unfulfilled—such as will only disclose themselves in proportion to the attention we bestow on the phenomenon or person in question. Here the underlying ethos is one of generosity rather than some claim staked in conceptual or quantifiable form. It is here, too, that we begin to see why our interaction with works of art offers a particularly good case of how to understand attention. Before pursuing that connection further, however, one more caveat is in order. For if attention appears incommensurable with the acquisitive and controlling stance of "interest," we would be equally misguided in seeking to assimilate it to a notion of "disinterest" that Immanuel Kant had famously identified as a key feature of aesthetic judgment. Leaving aside that a merely negative definition will rarely afford us a full grasp of a concept, any affiliation of attention with disinterested pleasure would once again obscure what has already been urged as the fundamental characteristic of attention—namely, that it amounts to an *act* rather than a *state* of mind. In attending to a person, an image (natural or man-made), a work of literature or music, we assent to the reality and integrity of the particular phenomenon as it incontrovertibly presents itself. As Murdoch notes, where "I attend properly I will have no choices and this is the ultimate condition to be aimed at." The act of attention differs from other acts in that it can neither be reduced to a function of the will nor be construed as the very antonym of volition. Attention is not something conceived and resolved a priori and now merely "implemented." The reality to which attention, and it alone, grants us access cannot be known, predicted, or even desired. Yet neither can we remain strictly agnostic or gratuitously elective about the world to which attention opens access.

For to attend is to enter the realm of significant meaning, one whose possibility, once we glimpse it, cannot possibly be viewed with indifference. Attention, that is, belongs to what Edmund Husserl terms the "truth of disclosure" rather than that of mere formal-syllogistic "correctness."[45] Here, then, we have reached the point where we can see why attention is so profoundly realized in our encounter with works of art, perhaps only surpassed by our encounter with another person or what Levinas calls the infinity that is "the face of the other."[46] For a number of reasons, the art of photography encapsulates many of the distinctive features that characterize attention, indeed, where pursued with care may itself be understood as a specific type of attention. Far less dependent on expensive tools now than it was a hundred years ago, photography in its contemporary, mainly digital practice has to rank among the most affordable and democratic of arts. To be sure, that fact also allows for the proliferation of mindlessly acquisitive, gratuitous "snapshots" that neither reflect nor bring about a viewer's considerate and attentive engagement with her subject. Like morality, which Murdoch so sensibly characterizes as the capacity for "accurate vision," the art of photography hinges on the cultivation of the eye. Even so, or rather because of the tacit efficacy of visual habituation, some of the most powerful and iconic photographs seem to have been above all the fruit of an unpremeditated responsiveness to what gives itself to be seen. For Hans Belting, the "analogy of today's photography [with *acheiropoiesis*] seems appropriate. Priority was given not to art itself or to the artist's invention but to utmost verisimilitude. This attitude takes us to the heart of the early use of images. The beholder was in touch with the real presence in, and the healing power of, the image. These could be guaranteed, however, only by an exact match between likeness and original, the intervention of an artist being unwanted."[47] Like attention itself, of which it is a prima facie instance, photography at its most compelling originates not so much in an act of will as it is a fruit of habituated, undesigning attention. That the image *finds* the photographer, rather than the other way round, becomes especially apparent in documentary photography—for example, in the work of Robert Capa, W. Eugene Smith, Dorothea Lange, and Sebastião Salgado. At once ephemeral and poignant, the flicker of life captured in such photography impresses on us what, as Murdoch notes, "we are usually too selfish and too timid to recognize, the minute and absolute random detail of the world, and reveals it together with a sense of unity and form."[48]

In Sebastião Salgado's close-up of a worker at a Kuwaiti oil well, the act of attention and its photographic result convey above all the subject's stillness. Slumping forward, his facial expression a mix of exhaustion, resignation, and pensiveness, his body utterly caked over and glistening with the dark sheen of crude, the well worker's overall pose verges toward the art of sculpture. He also appears bereft of all perspective. There is no "scene" and hardly any "background" to offer us any orientation, an impression compounded by the absence of any distinct source of light. All we see is a blend of gray tones, of flesh and skin vanquished by the ubiquitous and alien texture of oil. As beholders of this nameless man, caught off-center against what is barely distinguishable as the massive, grimy wheel of a lorry, our viewpoint is just as confined as that of the subject in the picture. Indeed, it is just this fusion of the subject's and the beholder's perspective that prompts us to attend to what we see, to *see this* man, nameless yet real, rather than enjoying perspectival dominion over, and thus merely *looking at*, some generic worker in a generic desert landscape. And because as beholders of this image we find ourselves in such close proximity to the subject, our gaze gradually comes to rest on the man's face, itself oblivious to our attention. For it is here, if anywhere, that subject and beholder might yet achieve their humanity in an act of recognition. It is this incipient acknowledgment of the subject's reality and presence that constitutes the ethical vanishing point of the photograph. The moment of recognition has not occurred, to be sure, but it is what the photograph—understood not just as *eikon* but also as *typos*—asks us to anticipate or imagine as its ultimate fulfillment. Something of this dynamic appears to inform Murdoch's more general characterization of art as never "a diversion or a side-issue [but] the most educational of all human activities and a place in which the nature of morality can be *seen*."[49]

A strikingly similar instance of attention as spiritual action appears to have crystallized for Gerard Manley Hopkins already during his studies at Balliol College and long before his cursory readings in Duns Scotus's *Opus Oxoniense* allowed him to put the matter in more technical terms. My brief

Sebastião Salgado, *Worker at Rest, Oil Wells, Kuwait*, 1991. Copyright © Sebastião Salgado-Amazonas/Contact Press Images.

foray into Hopkins today mainly seeks to draw out his intriguing fusion of perceptual and spiritual cognition, both of which he takes to originate in our apprehension of the distinctive formal organization or "inscape" of a particular appearance (something he would later find echoed in Duns Scotus's notion of *formalitas*).[50] Two journal entries from 1869 and 1872 illustrate the way in which perceptual consciousness first crystallizes as the active participation in and transformation by a singular, cohesive *Gestalt*:

> On the 9th there was snow but not lying on the roads. On the grass it became a crust lifted on the heads of the blades. As we went down a field near Caesar's Camp I noticed it before me squalentem, coat below coat, sketched in intersecting edges bearing "idiom" all down the slope:—I have no other word yet for that *which takes the eye or*

> *mind in a bold hand or effective sketching or in marked features or again in graphic writing*, which not being beauty nor true inscape yet gives interest and makes ugliness even better than meaninglessness.
>
> Ground sheeted with taut tattered streaks of crisp gritty snow. Green-white tufts of long bleached grass like heads of hair or the crowns of heads of hair, each a whorl of slender curves, one tuft taking up another—however these I might have noticed any day. I *saw the inscape freshly, as if my eye were still growing*, though *with a companion the eye and the ear are for the most part shut and instress cannot come*. . . . All the world is full of inscape and chance left free to act falls into an order as well as purpose: looking out of my window I caught it in the random clods and broken heaps of snow made by the cast of a broom.[51]

What Hopkins as early as 1868 characterizes as our responsiveness to a thing's "inscape" first manifests itself, according to Maximus and, later, Duns Scotus, in a mental image (*phantasma*). It is here that we first encounter the mind's primal orientation toward the phenomenon insofar as it senses something commensurable within the latter: "The mind turns to it, not as to the object, nor as to anything representing the object, but so as to intensify its own likeness to the object."[52] I note the active and transformative nature of vision ("as if my eye were still growing"), which for Hopkins unfolds as a kind of sustained attention to meanings that can neither be purposely sought, yet whose reality can also not be disavowed once it has disclosed itself to the beholder. It is just this kind of active, albeit wholly unpremeditated *adaequatio* of mind and world, consciousness and phenomenon, which informs Hopkins's 1876 sonnet "Hurrahing in Harvest":

> Summer ends now; now, barbarous in beauty, the stooks rise
> Around; up above, what wind-walks! what lovely behaviour
> Of silk-sack clouds! has wilder, willful-wavier
> Meal-drift moulded ever and melted across skies?
>
> I wálk, I lift up, I líft úp heart, éyes,
> Down all that glory in the heavens to glean our Saviour;
> And, éyes, héart, what looks, what lips yet gáve you a
> Rapturous love's greeting of realer, of rounder replies?
>
> And the azurous hung hills are his world-wielding shoulder
> Majestic—as a stallion stalwart, very-violet-sweet!—
> These things, these things were here and but the beholder
> Wánting; whích two whén they ónce méet
> The heart rears wings bold and bolder
> And hurls for him, O half hurls earth for him off under his féet.[53]

One is reminded here of Murdoch's undesigning Platonism, such as in her passing observation that "we use our imagination not to escape the world but to join it."[54] The sonnet offers us a phenomenology of transcendently "charged" world that discloses itself as a distinctive, richly textured image. The sonnet's conventional iambic patterning has yielded to irregular, "sprung" rhythms designed to trace an unanticipated, "rapturous" amalgamation of perceptual, emotive, and reflexive values. We witness the unique convergence of mind and world that Husserl was to call "image-consciousness"—at once unpredictable, irresistible, and suffused with transcendent significance. Yet the motif of the harvest also ensures that image so evocatively unfolded in the sonnet's octet will not simply be consigned to the domain of the miraculous and ineffable. Rather, alluding to Christ's earthly presence, the speaker affirms that "these things were here." Inasmuch as the attentive beholder captures the timeless rhythms of agrarian life and work as both *eikon* and *typos* (*imago* and *figura*) they function as both the sheer appearance of the visible and as theophany—of what was "here" and is destined to return. Unlike Proust's unsought-for *mémoire involontaire*, triggered by our chance encounter with some miscellaneous object or sensation, Hopkins's visual epiphanies hinge on our receptivity to what is, unfailingly and incontrovertibly, given: "these things were here and but the beholder / Wánting."

It is above all the modern, verificationist model of perception and generically preestablished poetic conventions of taste (what Hopkins, in his devastating, early critique of Tennyson, calls "Parnassian") that will cause the beholder to appear "wánting"—that is, inadequate or altogether absent.[55] Poetry here is not to be confused with subjective, versified "expression" but "speech for the inscape's sake."[56] The sonnet's protomodernist, defamiliarizing imagery ("silk-sack clouds" / "meal drift") ensures that the total image, "barbarous in beauty," will not expire in polite and civil Englishness. Instead, Hopkins's sonnet completely fuses the event of beholding and the act of affirming the reality of what is so beheld. As Kevin Hart puts it, "The entire poem is set in the mode of *how*, not *that* or *what*."[57] The second quatrain's *accelerando* pattern and increasing frequency of stressed syllables highlights the speaker's real assent to the incontrovertible and absorbing reality of the visible scene ("I walk, I lift up, I líft up heart, éyes" and "And, éyes, héart, what looks, what lips yet gave you a / Rapturous love's greeting of realer, of rounder replies?"). Harvesting the scene as materially real and present evidence, as *figura*, demands that the language steers clear of all subjective affect. With good reason, Jean-Luc Marion thus insists that "the gaze would see absolutely nothing if evidence remained a mere subjective impression, an effect of consciousness, in short, an idolatrous mirror where the mind refers to itself an impression that impresses only it."[58] Implicitly, then, Hopkins's sonnet rejects as false the choice between romantic sublime transport and Ruskinian, dispassionate objectivism; the title's precise wording ("Hurrahing *in* Harvest," not *at*, *during*, or *after*) hints that the acheiropoietic image is neither apprehended as sublime, transcendent experience nor as a correlate of Darwinian, forensic naturalism. Instead, sonnets like "Hurrahing," "The Windhover," or "As Kingfishers Catch Fire" offer a phenomenological description of the beholder's attentive and active participation in the sheer givenness of the visible; only so can the visible register as both image and *figura*, rather than as some strictly intramundane perception. Indeed, the fulfillment of the visible *qua figura* is not to be sought in some unspecified beyond but unfolds precisely within the intricately constructed or "inscaped" domain of the sonnet. In sharp contrast to the Wordsworthian sublime or Keatsian, objective ekphrasis (e.g., "To Autumn"), "Hurrahing in Harvest" unfolds as an Ignatian, spiritual exercise.[59] The poem's meditative *operatio* centers on the speaker's quest for bearing articulate witness to his transformative encounter with the unconditional givenness of the Real *as* image. Hence it is the *world*, and not some mystical beyond, that (to quote another of Hopkins's epigrammatic openings) is "charged with the grandeur of God."

3. Action

If Hopkins's nature sonnets amount to a literary tour de force in the way they distill transcendent meanings from the sprung rhythms of visual experience, their insight proves notably unpredictable and remains confined to the solitary individual; as Hopkins remarks in his journals, "With a companion the eye and the ear are for the most part shut and instress cannot come."[60] To the extent that inscape is consummated by an act of vision as something unconditionally given, and "not imposed outwards from the mind," Hopkins's world ("charged with the grandeur of God") essentially belongs mainly to the order of *imago* rather than that of *figura*.[61] Another mode of seeing, more focused on the visible realm as prefiguring the beholder's flourishing in the mode of physical *cum* spiritual action, pivots on a more stable and settled temporality, a rhythmic pattern that can, for example, be mapped onto the cycle of the seasons. To close in on this alternate scenario, it bears recalling that an exclusively conceptual and propositional mode of framing the phenomenal world as the correlate of our "notional assent" cannot by itself move the subject to action. For by its very nature conceptual thought abstracts from and so attenuates the charisma of what is phenomenally given. Ratiocination aims to create a zone of safety by enabling the subject to know beforehand where it is tending; it is inherently risk-averse, intent on maintaining distance between the beholder and that which gives itself.

By contrast, action disrupts this "buffered self" by originating change and possibilities that cannot be mapped onto the strictly notional or experientially familiar. As Maurice Blondel puts it, "We do not act, if we do not draw from ourselves the principle of our action, if this principle does not surpass past experiences, if we do not sense in it something else, if we do not make of it a kind of transcendent reality. One is never interested in one's own acts unless they are mixed in with some passionate ideology. . . . We die, as we live, only for a belief."[62] Inasmuch as its source and telos originate in a *vision* of the good rather than in a *movement* prompted by subjective desire or aimed at formal correctness, action seeks to communicate that good as a *meaning* susceptible of communal uptake.[63] To comprehend the good, it must disclose itself, visibly or at least in some nonconceptual form. Wholly inaccessible to the precincts of the notional, the safely methodical, and the subjective-experiential, it is in the image as both presence and fulfillment, that *communio* and *actus* become fused. Unlike the romantic sublime, with its exceptionalist and symbolic underpinnings, the model of image-experience and its communal realization to which we now turn operates within an established, rhythmic conception of time and a liturgical model of action.

Part III of *Anna Karenina* (1876) opens with Konstantin Levin contemplating a scene of abundance at the

> turning point of summer, when the harvest of the current year is assured, . . . [when] the mowing is at hand, when the rye has all come into ear and its grey-green, unswollen, still light ears sway in the wind, when green oats, with clumps of yellow grass scattered among them, thrust themselves unevenly amidst the late-sown crops, when the early buckwheat is already bushing out, covering the ground, when the fallow fields are half ploughed . . . [and] awaiting the scythe, the intact meadows stand in an unbroken sea, with blackening piles of weeded sorrel stalks here and there. (240–41)[64]

It is a scene quite similar to those transmogrified in Hopkins's *Journals*—suffused with visual detail and tactile sensations that cumulatively trigger memories of our having been in such a place.[65] The precise timing of the passage further reinforces the Platonic motif of *anamnesis*. For unlike a routine description of so many discrete details—which is often taken to be the bread and butter of Tolstoyan "realism"—the narrative's visible particulars here coalesce into a complex image only because they happen to be encountered at "that time of year" and at a moment where no practical tasks interfere with Levin's attention.[66] Ever so obliquely, the scene's symbolic powers fade into view; vision merges with recognition, that is, with a heightened awareness of the meaning and significance of what is phenomenally given. An intuitive nexus is established between the presence of a form and the mandate for transformative action encoded in it. This pivot of visual apprehension toward spiritual action tends to have a strong ritual dimension. Already in classical Greek societies and well before its Eucharistic consolidation, Gadamer notes, the *symbolon* functioned principally as "a token of remembrance. The host presented his guest with the so-called *tessera hospitalis* by breaking some object in two. He kept one half for himself and gave the other half to his guest. If in thirty or fifty years time a descendant of the guest should ever enter his house, the two pieces could be fitted together again to form a whole in an act of recognition."[67]

Yet the dynamics of recollection are not confined to matters external to Levin; rather, the distinctive familiarity of the scene that beckons his active engagement also intimates his own potential completion and flourishing as a person. Gadamer's account of the symbol here maps rather precisely on Auerbach's account of *figura*. For in the case of the symbol, the "particular represents itself as a fragment of being that promises to complete and make whole whatever corresponds to it. Or, indeed, the symbol is that other fragment that has always been sought in order to complete and make whole our own fragmentary life."[68] Caught at the precise moment when cyclical, agrarian time lets the image stand forth and disclose itself in all its luminous fullness, Levin's vision is not descriptive but transformative. He encounters not "nature" but specific *things*—richly textured, profoundly familiar, and effortlessly merged into a single *Gestalt*, such as "the tall grass softly twined around the wheels and the horse's legs, leaving its seeds on the wet spokes and hubs" (241). Suffused with such sensuous qualities, the visible scene here is taken in not as the correlate of some detached perception but as an enveloping, acheiropoietic presence. Levin is literally *in the midst of it*, visually absorbing it rather than looking *at* it.

For Levin, who does "not like talking or hearing about the beauty of nature . . . [because] words took away the beauty of what he saw" (241), what makes this visible scene real is not its verifiable, empirical character but the epiphanic intensity with which it draws him in. The prevailing affect is not one of subjective pleasure (*hedonē*), disinterested or otherwise, such as a tradition of aesthetic thought extending from Shaftesbury to Kant had posited as the foundation of modern sociability (sensus communis).[69] Instead, the scene is one of active, if notably quiet contemplation whose precise timing ("when a short break comes in the farm work") allows Levin's "attention [to be] absorbed by the sight of a fallow field on a hillock, in some places yellow with grass, in others trodden down and cut criss-cross or dotted with heaps" (241). The precision with which the narrative here traces Levin's gaze, the astonishing depth of field (no pun intended) of his vision, so responsive to minute yet significant details, sharply contrasts with his verbal ineptitude during that "vexing" conversation with his brother, Sergej, the day before Levin resolves to join in the mowing of the fields. It is his "physical movement" (248) during those two days of vigorous, productive, and unalienated work that shows the image of as yet unharvested fields to embody the patristic conception of *figura*. Levin's immersion in the image qua work constitutes spiritual fulfillment of the acheiropoietic image.[70] Drawing on Arendt's careful distinction between labor and work (*ponos* and *ergon*), we thus should think of Levin's mowing of the fields as "work." As his contentious exchange with his brother (part III, chapter 3) makes clear, Levin is not concerned with labor as the source (or mechanical cause) of surplus or profit but with work as the completion of a natural and just order visibly realized in his familiar, agrarian world. Whereas labor merely ensures bare life (*zoē*), work is an integral factor in a person's spiritual flourishing—ensures life in the strong sense of *bios*.[71]

To be sure, in Tolstoy's "anthropic theology" there is no ecclesiastic or theological framework mediating Levin's experience of the initial natural image, let alone compelling his conclusion to join in the mowing.[72] Tolstoy's misgivings about the Russian Orthodox Church—already running deep in 1876 and culminating in his harsh indictment of the Church in his last novel, *Resurrection* (1899), followed by his excommunication two years later—ensure that Levin's epiphanies are couched in ostensibly nonreligious language.[73] Instead, the focus is placed on a Hopkinsian interplay of symmetries and irregularities in a landscape visibly transformed by the steady, recurrent motions of forty-two men moving across "the curved semicircle of the mowed space, grass and flower-heads bending down slowly and wavily about the blade of [the] scythe" (250–51). Far from a product of the myriad rules and regulations arduously debated and adopted at the *zemtsvo* meetings that Levin so abhors, community here is realized as the fulfillment of the initial image. Tolstoy's prose unfolds for us a liturgical process whose "strenuous rhythm" dramatizes "the passion of work" (251). Instantiating the logic of *figura*, Levin's empirical perceptions effortlessly coalesce into an image (*eikon*) wherein what is visibly given and the fulfillment of its transcendent import appear at once distinct and entwined. As in Dante, so in Tolstoy "the moral order is contained in the physical."[74]

Yet by "transcendence" Tolstoy understands less a personal God than a conception of human fulfillment and flourishing no longer circumscribed by notions of Western-style, economic "improvement" and its affective corollaries of subjective "pleasure" and private "contentment."[75] On the contrary, having unsuccessfully debated with Sergej the supposed virtues of agrarian modernization and Western political economy, Levin recovers the meanings so elusive in that discussion in the liturgical structure of embodied work in the fields. Rarely does Hannah Arendt's characterization of "life, *bios* as distinguished from mere *zoē*, . . . [as] 'somehow a kind of *praxis*'" come across with such epiphanic intensity as in the image of Levin mowing the field.[76] Chronometric time here appears suspended ("Levin lost all awareness of time" [251]), and the boundaries between self and other have all but faded away:

> A change now began to take place in his work which gave him enormous pleasure. In the midst of his work moments came to him when he forgot what he was doing and began to feel light, and in those moments his swaths came out as even and good as Titus's. . . . The

> longer Levin mowed, the more often he felt those moments of oblivion during which it was no longer his arms that swung the scythe, but the scythe itself that lent motion to his whole body, full of life and conscious of itself, and, as if by magic, without a thought of it, the work got rightly and neatly done on its own. (251–52)

There is nothing sentimental here as Tolstoy takes care to show Levin rejecting the false choice between either aestheticizing the world of peasant life (as does his detached, sight-seeing brother, Sergej) or naively identifying himself with the peasantry. Instead, action and contemplation here have merged in a nonpropositional form of knowledge, very much akin to what Maximus had called "knowledge embodied in practice" (*gnosis empraktos*).[77] Konstantin's labor in the fields intimates a kenotic dimension in "passion" all but occluded in Western modernity; very much alert to its presence in active contemplation, Maximus had spoken of such "passion" (*hedone*) as "an ecstatic power, elevating the passive recipient to the state of an active agent."[78] Perfectly mindful that he belongs to a different social class than the "muzhiks," Levin nonetheless understands himself to be very much part of the same community and the same life-world, one in which differences of education, wealth, and political authority need not harden into political antagonisms. In the event, the harvest scene winds up with a rapturous account of Levin atop a haywain enveloped in "a thundercloud of merriment" that is the sound of "some fifty different coarse, high, healthy voices" of women singing: "The whole meadow with the distant fields . . . started moving and heaving to the rhythm of this wild, rollicking song" (275).[79]

If, as Alasdair MacIntyre insists, the idea of "intelligible action is more fundamental than the concept of action as such," it is also the case that action as a movement of the will cannot arise strictly from a syllogism.[80] Rather than implementing some syllogistic and impersonal conclusion, action originates in a moment of incontrovertible presence, of intuitive certitude, or (to quote Newman) in an act of "real [rather than notional] assent" to a meaning, a value, a good.[81] Action does not gratuitously project transcendent (spiritual) meanings onto an ephemeral and corrupt here and now. On the contrary, it crystallizes when the phenomenally given world is visually apprehended as a unified and compelling image (*eikon*), rather than registering as a succession of discrete and mundane perceptions. As Maximus had argued long before, the cosmos as an infinitely variegated and richly structured presence cannot be reduced to an inventory of discrete and transient particularities. Rather, it discloses itself simultaneously as the reality of individual appearance and as *figura* of the right order (*logos*) to the realization of which the beholder is invited by the appearing phenomenon: "In applying itself to visible things the mind knows them in accordance with nature through the medium of the senses, so that neither is the mind evil, nor is natural knowledge, nor the things, nor the senses, for all these are all works of God."[82] What makes

Tolstoy's harvesting scene a spiritual *figura* is how the richly textured and deeply familiar landscape registers simultaneously as *visus* and *visio*, as empirical sight and as *eikon*. Levin's active participation in the image and in the quasi-liturgical rhythms of agrarian work constitutes both an instance of humility in the face of the image (*eikon*) and acknowledges its intrinsically narrative depth-structure as *figura*. To honor the charisma and abundance of the acheiropoietic image in the modality of communal work is to forgo the idolatrous preoccupation with subjective sentiment and autonomous doing in favor of spiritual and transformative action—one in which the potentialities of the visible realm and the beholder are reciprocally honored and fulfilled. For all their theological and intellectual differences, Hopkins and Tolstoy concur in viewing truth not as some transcendent other of the phenomenal world, but as intrinsic to the reality and sheer givenness of that world *qua* image—if only we learn to see it.

Notes

1. On Hobbes's conception of agency, volition, and action, see Pfau, *Minding the Modern: Human Agency, Intellectual Traditions, and Responsible Knowledge* (South Bend, Ind.: Notre Dame University Press, 2013), 185–205, and critical literature by Schneewind, Gillespie, Strauss, Oakeshott, Koselleck, and Skinner cited there.

2. See *Summa Theologiae* Ia, q. 18.3, ad 1; ibid. Ia, q. 54.1, ad 3; see also *Summa Contra Gentiles* 2.53, which specifically notes how in the latter kind of action the act "remains in the agent and is the perfection of the agent, such as seeing" (*una quae manet in agente et est perfectio suae, ut videre*) and goes on to note that God is only capable of this type of (immanent) action, "for his act is his substance" (*cum sua actio sit sua substantia*). *Summa Theologiae* (Scotts Valley, Calif.: Create Space, 2008); *Summa Contra Gentiles*, http://dhspriory.org/thomas/ContraGentiles.htm, accessed May 27, 2017. On action in Aquinas, see David Burrell, CSC, *Aquinas: God and Action* (Scranton, Pa.: University of Scranton Press, 2008), 133–66.

3. For a forceful (though in my view deeply flawed) critique of art and mimesis, see Emmanuel Levinas's "Reality and Its Shadow" (1948), in Levinas, *Collected Philosophical Papers*, trans. Alphonso Lingis (Dordrecht: Martinus Nijhoff, 1987), 1–13; the argument developed here is fundamentally at odds with Levinas's suggestion that representation, broadly speaking, and image and rhythm in particular, "marks a hold over us rather than our initiative, a fundamental passivity." Echoing the Byzantine iconoclasts, Levinas tends to conflate any image with the "idol [that] leads us to the ontological significance of its unreality . . . a semblance of existing" (2, 8).

4. See Jean-Luc Marion's critique of Derrida's attempt to contain the notion of the gift within a reciprocal and calculative economy of exchange: *Being Given: Toward a Phenomenology of Givenness*, trans. Jeffrey L. Kosky (Stanford, Calif.: Stanford University Press, 2002), 70–118.

5. Gehlen, *Urmensch und Spätkultur* (Frankfurt: Klostermann, 2004), 60–66.

6. Hans-Georg Gadamer, *Truth and Method*, trans. Donald Marshall and Joel Weinsheimer (New York: Continuum, 2004), 130–52; Gadamer's account is clearly indebted to Husserl's 1905 lectures on *Phantasy and Image-Consciousness*, esp. §§8–25.

7. I concur with James Simpson that eighteenth-century aesthetic formalism and "the Enlightenment treatment of the image . . . shares many of the iconoclast's aims." See Simpson, *Under the Hammer: Iconoclasm in the Anglo-American Tradition* (Oxford: Oxford University Press, 2010), 11; the argument is developed in the book's final chapter, 116–54.

8. On this debate, see David Freedberg, *The Power of Images: Studies in the History and Theory of Response* (Chicago: University of Chicago Press, 1989), 378–428; Alain Besançon, *The Forbidden Image: An Intellectual History of Iconoclasm*, trans. Marie Todd (Chicago: University of Chicago Press, 2009), 109–46; Hans Belting, *Likeness and Presence* (Chicago: University of Chicago Press, 1994), 102–83; on the philosophical theology of the icon, see Marie-José Mondzain, *Image, Icon, Economy: The Byzantine Origins of the Contemporary Imaginary* (Stanford, Calif.: Stanford University Press, 2005), 69–117; Christoph Schönborn, *God's Human Face: The Christ Icon*, trans. Lothar Kraut (San Francisco: Ignatius, 1994), 135–243; Emanuel Alloa, "Visual Studies in Byzantium: A Pictorial Turn *avant la lettre*," *Journal of Visual Culture* 12, no. 1 (2013): 3–29; on the prehistory of Byzantine iconoclasm in patristic thought, see Robin Jensen, *Face to Face: Portraits of the Divine in Early Christianity* (Minneapolis: Fortress, 2005), esp. 71–99. For a compelling historical account, see Peter Brown, "A Dark-Age Crisis: Aspects of the Iconoclastic Controversy," *English Historical Review* 88 (1973): 1–34, and the exhaustive cultural and political account of iconoclasm (though remarkably indifferent to the debate's theological stakes) by Leslie Brubaker and John Haldon, *Byzantium in the Iconoclast Era, c. 680–850* (Cambridge: Cambridge University Press, 2011).

9. See Gerhard B. Ladner, "The Concept of the Image in the Greek Fathers and the Byzantine Iconoclastic Controversy," *Dumbarton Oaks Papers* 7 (1953): 1–34; and George Florovsky, "Origen, Eusebius, and the Iconoclastic Controversy," *Church History* 19, no. 2 (1950): 77–96. Their arguments are further developed in Schönborn, *God's Human Face*, 47–133.

10. Schönborn, *God's Human Face*, 53.

11. Not without reason, the "beautiful soul" in book 6 of Goethe's *Wilhelm Meister's Apprenticeship* (1796) is reclaimed from Pietist orthodoxy by an uncle who teaches her how properly to look at and relate to paintings.

12. On Athanasius and his Cappadocian followers (esp. Gregory of Nyssa and Basil of Caesarea), see Jensen, *Face to Face*, 101–8; quote from 103.

13. Gesa Elsbeth Thiessen, *Theological Aesthetics: A Reader* (Grand Rapids, Mich.: Eerdmans, 2004), 17.

14. Erich Auerbach, *Time, History, and Literature: Selected Essays of Erich Auerbach*, ed. James I. Porter, trans. Jane O. Newman (Princeton, N.J.: Princeton University Press, 2014), 80.

15. Ibid.

16. Ibid., 83.

17. Besançon, *Forbidden Image*, 90.

18. Gregory Nazianzen, "Second Theological Oration," sect. 16 and 20, *Nicene and Post-Nicene Fathers*, 2nd ser., 14 vols. (Peabody, Mass.: Hendrickson, 2012), 7:293; see also his paean to the visible and superabundant natural world, ibid., 7:298.

19. Hans-Urs von Balthasar, *Cosmic Liturgy: The Universe according to Maximus the Confessor*, trans. Brian E. Daley, SJ (San Francisco: Ignatius, 2003), 48; the translation has been altered here to retain Balthasar's precise wording, viz., when characterizing Alexandrian theology as confined by antitheses of "ground and appearance, *Theos* and *Theophaneia*, a conception based strictly on categories of revelation that overleaps created reality" (*ein Denken in reinen Offenbarungskategorien unter Überspringung der kreatürlichen Wirklichkeit*). *Kosmische Liturgie: Das Weltbild Maximus des Bekenners* (Einsiedeln: Johannes Verlag, 1988), 39. On Maximus, see also Andrew Louth, *Maximus the Confessor* (London: Routledge, 1996), 3–77. It bears noting that in appealing to Plato as the source for their aniconic views, Origen and Eusebius may well have been caught up in a widespread misapprehension of Plato's arguments. As Lambert Wiesing has argued in fine detail, accounts of Plato on the question of images have persistently conflated "depiction" and "mimesis," thus occluding the presentational aspect of an image. Resemblance is not the same as a copy, just as twins are not copies of one another. Thus "imitations are artifacts deliberately produced for the sake of resemblance. An object becomes an imitation only if and when resemblance was intended in a process of production. . . . That is why we can say that in an image it is not something actual that resembles something else but something appears to a viewer to resemble something else. And this, precisely, is what is different in the case of the copy." Failing to recognize that "'mimesis' is a genus [that] corresponds to a wide concept of imitation," a long and regrettably effective history of Plato interpretations has failed to see that "Plato does not criticize the production of depictions but only that of bad copies." Wiesing, "Plato's Concept of Mimesis and Its Concealed Canon," in his *Artificial Presence: Philosophical Studies in Image Theory*, trans. Nils F. Schott (Stanford, Calif.: Stanford University Press, 2010), 102–21, at 106–9; perhaps the most probing discussion of Plato on images is found in Emmanuel Alloa, *Das durchscheinende Bild: Konturen einer medialen Phänomenologie* (Zurich: Diaphanes, 2011), 15–61; on Plato's deeply ambivalent conception of images, see also Horst Bredekamp, *Theorie des Bildakts* (Frankfurt: Suhrkamp, 2010), 36–43.

20. Von Balthasar, *Cosmic Liturgy*, 63–64.

21. Ibid., 84, 86.

22. Maximus, *The Church's Mystagogy*, ch. 2 in *Selected Writings*, trans. George C. Berthold (New York: Paulist, 1985); the point is echoed in Richard of St. Victor's third species of contemplation, viz., as a "grasping of the quality of invisible things by means of the similitude of visible things." Qtd. in Kevin Hart, "For the Life Was Manifested," in *Material Spirit: Religion and Literature Intranscendent* (New York: Fordham University Press, 2014), 73–93, at 83.

23. Maximus, *Ambigua*, 1:363 (Ambiguum no. 15, to John), in *On the Difficulties in the Church Fathers: The Ambigua*, 2 vols., trans. and ed. Nicholas Constas (Cambridge, Mass.: Harvard University Press, 2014).

24. Ibid., 1:101 (Ambiguum no. 7, to John); David Faberberg calls this the paradox of "apophasis and revelation" (229), an early version of which can be found in Gregory Nazianzen's description of the Godhead as "at once earthly and heavenly, tangible and intangible, comprehensible and incomprehensible" (Epistle 101 in *Pre-Nicene Fathers,* 7:439).

25. Ibid., 1:197–99 (Ambiguum no. 10, to John); in Ambiguum 7, Maximus elaborates on his commitment to apophatic reflection: "No argument will ever be able to demonstrate the simultaneous interdependence of being and what transcends being" or of "the diverse species or concepts (*logoi*) and the *logos*" (1:101). Early in the twentieth century, Pavel Florensky reaffirms Maximus's distinction as that between the image of ascent, an aesthetic technique or "mere mechanism constructed in accordance with the moment of its psychic genesis" and "the descending image [that] incarnates in real images the experience of the highest realm." Florensky, *Iconostasis*, trans. Donald Sheehan and Olga Andrejev (New York: St. Vladimir's, 1996), 45.

26. *Ambigua* 1:91 (no. 7, to John).

27. Ibid., 1:195 (no. 10, to John).

28. Ibid., 1:193.

29. *The Four Hundred Chapters on Love*, 1:98, in Maximus, *Selected Writings*, 46.

30. *Cosmic Liturgy*, 123; as von Balthasar summarizes the main point: "The idea of a thing is its 'truth'; this is just as much the case for particular things as for things in general" (ibid., 119).

31. Auerbach, "*Figura*," ch. 7 in *Time, History, and Literature*, at 111.

32. Jaroslav Pelikan, *Imago Dei: The Byzantine Apologia for Icons* (Princeton, N.J.: Princeton University Press, 2011), 3.

33. Husserl, *Formal and Transcendental Logic*, trans. Dorion Cairns (Dordrecht: Martinus Nijhoff, 1977), 120–27 (§§44–45).

34. Maurice Merleau-Ponty, *The Visible and the Invisible*, trans. Alphonso Lingis (Evanston, Ill.: Northwestern University Press, 1968), 24–25, 28–29, 106. In his incisive critique of a philosophy of reflection, Merleau-Ponty attacks modernity's habitual assumption of perceptual and propositional knowledge as wholly convertible. In fact, the (originally Cartesian) project of establishing the reality of the visible by way of a thoroughgoing critique of perception fails to acknowledge how the category of "illusion" or "semblance" hinges on the anterior reality of appearance: "There is no *Schein* without an *Erscheinung*." Failing to heed the reality and presence of the visible as ontologically anterior to its critical appraisal, "the philosophy of reflection replaces the 'world' with the 'being-thought' " (ibid., 41, 43). Husserl had offered a strikingly similar argument in his 1910/1911 lectures on *Basic Problems in Phenomenology* (§14); closer to Merleau-Ponty, a similar line of argument informs Michael Polanyi's insistence that "focal awareness" presupposes "subsidiary" or "background awareness" and the necessary "unspecifiability" by which epistemic agents "feel their way forward." See Polanyi, *Personal Knowledge: Towards a Post-Critical Philosophy* (Chicago: University of Chicago Press, 1958), 55–63.

35. Merleau-Ponty, *The Visible and the Invisible*, 43, 122 (italics mine).

36. McDowell, *Mind and World* (Cambridge, Mass.: Harvard University Press, 1996), 9.

37. Polanyi, *Personal Knowledge*, 214.

38. *The Simone Weil Reader*, ed. George A. Panichas (Wakefield, R.I.: Moyer Bell, 1999), 49.

39. Perhaps the most cogent and forceful critique of reductionist accounts of consciousness has been undertaken by David Bentley Hart; see *The Experience of God: Being, Consciousness, Bliss* (New Haven, Conn.: Yale University Press, 2013), esp. 152–237; see also Pfau, *Minding the Modern*, 581–90.

40. Hannah Arendt, *The Human Condition*, 2nd ed. (Chicago: University of Chicago Press, 1998), 154.

41. Weil, "Reflections on the Right Use of School Studies with a View to the Love of God," in *Simone Weil Reader*, 44–52, at 47–48.

42. Ibid., 46.

43. *The Notebooks of Samuel Taylor Coleridge*, ed. Kathleen Coburn (Princeton, N.J.: Princeton University Press, 1991), vol. 2, no. 3025 (February–May 1807).

44. Coleridge, *Biographia Literaria*, ed. James Engell and Walter Jackson Bate, 2 vols. (Princeton, N.J.: Princeton University Press, 1983), 1:82–84.

45. On this distinction, initially elaborated by Edmund Husserl, see Robert Sokolowski, *Introduction to Phenomenology* (Cambridge: Cambridge University Press, 2000), 157–59.

46. It is in the work of Blake and Coleridge in particular that the theological significance of the human face as the quintessential *imago dei* emerge with particular force, such as in Blake's "Cradle Song" ("While o'er thee thy mother weep / Sweet babe in thy face. / Holy image I can trace") and in Coleridge's oeuvre, extending from the early "Frost at Midnight" to a remarkable late passage describing how an infant will visually trace not merely the "shape" of the mother's face but, in it, the reality and goodness of God's presence (*Opus Maximum*, 131); on that passage, see Pfau, *Minding the Modern*, 565–66; on Coleridge's and Levinas's tellingly divergent account of "face" and "person" (ibid. 591–604); see also Roger Scruton, *The Face of God*, The Gifford Lectures (New York: Continuum, 2012), esp. 73–112.

47. Belting, *Likeness and Presence*, 53; similarly, David Freedberg remarks on the unique status of *acheiropoietai*, a "class of images [that] allows for no inaccuracy" and, as such, realizes what all other images aspire to: "the greatest possible verisimilitude. Then we will have not merely an image of Christ; we will have an image that so closely mirrors the miracle of the Incarnation that absence becomes presence and representation reality" (*Power of Images*, 212).

48. Iris Murdoch, *The Sovereignty of Good* (London: Routledge, 1970), 84.

49. Ibid., 85.

50. On Hopkins and Scotus, see Christopher Devlin, "The Image and the Word," *The Month* 2 (1950): 114–27, and 3 (1950): 191–202, as well as Phillip A. Ballinger, *The Poem as Sacrament* (Leuven: Peeters, 2000), 103–50, and Bernadette W. Ward, *World as Word: Philosophical Theology in Gerard Manley Hopkins* (Washington, D.C.: Catholic University of America Press, 2002), 158–97.

51. Gerard Manley Hopkins, *The Journals and Papers*, ed. Humphrey House (Oxford: Oxford University Press, 1959), 195, 228, 230; italics mine.

52. Duns Scotus, qtd. in Devlin, "The Image and the Word," 118; on the theological underpinnings of "inscape," see also Ward, *World as Word*, 158–97; Ballinger, *Poem as Sacrament*, 119–50.

53. Hopkins, *The Major Works*, ed. Catherine Phillips (Oxford: Oxford University Press, 1986), 137.

54. Murdoch, *Sovereignty*, 88.

55. Letter to Baillie, September 10–11, 1864, in Hopkins, *The Collected Works of Gerard Manley Hopkins*, vol. 1 (Correspondence 1852–1881), ed. R. K. R. Thornton and Catherine Phillips (Oxford: Oxford University Press, 2013), 67–73; both in Wordsworth and Tennyson, the evolution of a distinctive and recognizable style causes the infinite particularity and charisma of things to vanish under the poet's preestablished gaze or what Hopkins calls "too persistently his way of looking at things" (ibid., 71).

56. "Poetry and Verse," in *Journals and Papers*, 289; see also Hopkins's earlier draft (while at Balliol College) on "Poetic Diction," ibid., 84–85.

57. Hart, "For the Life Was Manifested," 81.

58. Marion, *Being Given*, 20.

59. On Hopkins's sonnets in relation to Ignatian, spiritual exercises, see Ballinger, *Poem as Sacrament*, 61–102; Hart, "For the Life Was Manifested."

60. *Journals and Papers*, 228; see also ibid., 182.

61. Ibid., 215.

62. Maurice Blondel, *Action: Essay on a Critique of Life and a Science of Practice* (1893), trans. Oliva Blanchette (South Bend, Ind.: University of Notre Dame Press, 1984), 114; elsewhere, Blondel speaks of action as an all-pervading "system of spontaneous or willed movements, a setting of the organism into motion, a determinate use of one's vital strengths, in view of some pleasure or interest, under the influence of a need, an idea or a dream" (ibid., 36).

63. As Murdoch puts it, "Any artist will readily understand [how] the idea of a patient, loving regard, directed upon a person, a thing, a situation presents the will not as unimpeded movement but as something much more like 'obedience' " (*Sovereignty*, 39).

64. Tolstoy, *Anna Karenina*, trans. Richard Pevear and Larissa Volokhonsky (Harmondsworth, U.K.: Penguin, 2000); page numbers are cited above.

65. That the precision of Tolstoy's passage is not merely the fruit of his literary exertion becomes clear in his letters; see his letter to A. A. Fet (May 16, 1865), which appraises the abundant and luscious fruits of agrarian work against the backdrop of famine elsewhere in the region: "We have pink radishes on our table, yellow butter, and soft, well-baked bread on a clean table cloth; . . . but elsewhere the evil devil famine is already at work, covering the fields with goose-foot, causing cracks to appear in the dried-up earth, chafing the calloused heels of the peasants and their women, cracking the hooves of the cattle." *Tolstoy's Letters*, 2 vols., trans. and ed. R. F. Christian (New York: Scribners, 1978), 1:195.

66. "Occasionally over the months some hours of leisure and silence occur, when little by little your own atmosphere is created around you, undisturbed, and in this atmosphere all the phenomena of life begin to occupy the place they

should have and do have for you, and you are conscious of yourself and your powers, . . . And at such moments you really want to work for yourself (not for others)" (to N. N. Strakhov, September 13, 1871, *Tolstoy's Letters*, 1:239).

67. Hans-Georg Gadamer, *On the Relevance of the Beautiful*, trans. Nicholas Walker (Cambridge: Cambridge University Press, 1986), 31.

68. Ibid., 32.

69. See Shaftesbury, "Sensus Communis" (taken up in Kant's *Critique of Judgment*, §§18–22), and the discussion of Shaftesbury in Pfau, *Minding the Modern*, 217–48. Like Hopkins, Tolstoy is deeply suspicious of aesthetics and art (including literature) as a specialized human endeavor; in *A Confession*, he notes how, having "enjoyed watching life through the mirror of art," he soon "began to feel the necessity of living," at which point "I found this mirror either unnecessary, superfluous and ridiculous, or tormenting." *A Confession and Other Religious Writings*, trans. Jane Kentish (London: Penguin, 1987), 33. Elsewhere, he remarks that "our literary language is spineless" (to N. N. Strakhov, March 22/25, 1872, *Tolstoy's Letters*, 1:244).

70. Tolstoy's acute fusion of image-consciousness and action here is echoed by Seamus Heaney; recalling his childhood on the family farm at Mossbawn in Northern Ireland, Heaney recalls frequently "following the mowing machine, lifting and tying the sheaves, stoking and hutting. I did those jobs routinely, with siblings and with neighbours. I actually enjoyed work in the hay. There was a terrific rightness and likeness about the forks and rakes, a wonderful sense of the hand and the tool being made for each other. I loved to dress a ruck, comb it down, give it a nice firm set." In Dennis O'Driscoll, *Stepping Stones: Interviews with Seamus Heaney* (New York: Farrar, Straus and Giroux, 2008), 56.

71. See Arendt, *Human Condition*, esp. 87–109 (on labor), 144–59 (on work). See also Blondel, *Action*, esp. 109–44; and Pfau, *Minding the Modern*, 87–97, 360–67.

72. I take the phrase from David Patterson, who sees Tolstoy trying to map a third way between orthodox Trinitarianism and modern Socinianism by "understand[ing] the union of Father and Son posited in the Gospel as a union of the inner divine essence of man with God, so that the phrase 'Son of God' is an expression of every human being's relation to God." "The Human Image Divine: Tolstoy's Anthropic Theology," *Christianity and Literature* 40, no. 1 (1990): 23–36, at 28. A fuller discussion of Tolstoy's extraordinarily rich and complex theological views would have to scrutinize Tolstoy's *A Confession* (esp. chs. 9–12) and later statements on the subject, most of which are gathered in Tolstoy, *What Is Religion and Other Writings* (Guildford, U.K.: White Crow Books, 2010).

73. On Tolstoy and religion, see A. N. Wilson, *Tolstoy: A Life* (New York: Norton, 1988), 295–339; Patterson, "Human Image Divine"; and the landmark study by Richard F. Gustafson, *Leo Tolstoy: Resident and Stranger* (Princeton, N.J.: Princeton University Press, 1986).

74. Auerbach, "The Three Traits of Dante's Poetry," in *Time, History, and Literature*, 192; what animates Auerbach's brilliant reading of Dante can also be predicated of Tolstoy's literary oeuvre: "The human world in all its breadth and depth is gathered into the structure of the hereafter and there it stands: complete, unfalsified, yet encompassed in an eternal order; the confusion of earthly affairs is not concealed or attenuated or immaterialized, but preserved in full evidence

and grounded in a plan which embraces it and raises it above all contingency." Auerbach, *Poet of the Secular World*, trans. Ralph Manheim (New York: NYRB, 2001), 133.

75. Gary Saul Morson sees the entire harvest episode as Tolstoy's way of distancing himself from the Western-liberal program of modernization and improvement that Peter the Great had first instituted, and that continues with undiminished (if also unfulfilled and likely unwarranted) enthusiasm during the *zemtsvo* movement of the 1860s; see Morson, *"Anna Karenina" in Our Time: Seeing More Wisely* (New Haven, Conn.: Yale University Press, 2007), esp. 143–67.

76. Arendt, *Human Condition*, 97.

77. *Ambigua* 1:3 ("Preface").

78. Ibid., 1:115 (no. 7, to John).

79. Yet it is here, too, that the limits of the scene emerge into view; Levin understands that he can never be part of the world of the muzhiks. Instead, the harvest image and its quasi-liturgical fulfillment in strenuous work makes palpable for Levin his own, impending "transition from the old life to the new" (276)—one wrought not magically from above but, rather, practically and from within. On the visible as theophany, see Andrew Louth, "Beauty Will Save the World: The Formation of Byzantine Spirituality," *Theology Today* 61 (2004): 67–77, esp. his discussion of Maximus the Confessor, 69–73.

80. MacIntyre, *After Virtue* (South Bend, Ind.: University of Notre Dame Press, 1981), 208–9.

81. On the transformative character of "action," in contradistinction to "behavior," see Blondel, *Action*, esp. 111–31; and Pfau, *Minding the Modern*, 315–18, 395–98; as Murdoch puts it, "Man is not a combination of an impersonal rational thinker and a personal will. He is a unified being who sees, and who desires in accordance with what he sees, and who has some continual slight control over the direction and focus of his vision" (*Sovereignty*, 39).

82. Maximus, *Four Hundred Chapters on Love*, 2:15, in *Selected Writings*, 48.

Appendix

✦

A Broken Vessel, or What It Means to Be an Agent

Stanley Hauerwas on Theology and Practical Reason

James Wetzel

What does theology—which for Hauerwas is an exercise of practical reason and a declaration of particular love—have to contribute to our understanding of what an action is, or, more practically, how does theology guide us as we struggle to emerge out of the vast effluvium of happenstance into imperfectly individuated characters? Let's accentuate that note of imperfection. The kickoff of Hauerwas's essay, "How to Be an Agent," is Austin Farrer's characterization of God's will as, well, God. Now here is a perfectly perfect will. Here there is not even a ghost of a metaphysical gap between a theorizing divinity, contemplating a possible course of action, and a demiurgic materializer, bringing a particular course of action to pass. There is only the eternally harmonious self-expression of the God whose relation to creation is necessarily unconflicted. Meanwhile we finite creatures, who find it impossible, perhaps gratefully so, to generate the material conditions of our own acting, are never, strictly speaking, self-possessed. Unlike the Being who made us, we always live at least a bit outside ourselves, and we cannot, without lapsing into self-deception, expect to live otherwise. We have here entered into the neighborhood of a radical imperfection, and theology, as the revelation of the difference between a radical and a redeemable imperfection, is our realtor. And in case you are keeping accounts, it is God who is doing the revealing.

In his suggestion that, in his words, "action is the basic metaphysical notion for any account of what it means for God to be God,"[1] Hauerwas joins ranks with Thomas Aquinas, Austin Farrer, and David Burrell. These are all theologians who are exquisitely attentive to the integrity of the difference between God and creation and who are consequently disinclined to render God into an exotic, and necessarily unique, object of theory. There would be only one instance of this kind of object, were God, as creator, some kind of object. But if giving an account of what it means for God to be God is not to indulge in groundless theoretical speculation, in this case a form of highbrow idolatry, what sense is left to the notion of giving an account? Where is the accountability in theology? Early in his essay, Hauerwas suggests that he can in fact come to know something about agency in relation to both God and self; he just needs to continue to do, even more intently, what he has done for most of his life: maintain his focus on the formation of Christian character; give testimony.

I concede that I have no confidence in my grip on a theistic metaphysics of action, though I have, throughout my academic career, affected to embrace some kind of Wittgenstein-inspired grammatical transfiguration of such metaphysics. Not that I would be so forward as to place myself in the ranks of Aquinas, Farrer, Burrell, and Hauerwas, but I do go to their home games, and when they are taking on their literal-minded opponents—scholastic metaphysicians, Reformed epistemologists, analytic theologians—I root for the home team to win. Still, I cannot help but think that in my case the long fascination with the theoretically unavailable God has mostly been my baroque way of reminding myself that no one I have managed to love, in however ragged a way, reduces down to one of hypothetically many of a desirable kind. I love my son and my daughter, and just because I do, I am not remotely tempted to think that I can sanely swap out either of them for a son or daughter of similarly good or improved character. The chiaroscuro of a developing character is not transferable. When I start to think that it is, I cease to see character; I see motion in a void.

When I say that my fascination for the untheorized God has mostly been my way of focusing, at a comfortable remove, on the singularity of a love, a focus that is not without its cost in intelligibility, I hold out the hope that God is more for me than the name of the love that mysteriously gathers particular beloveds, all one of a kind, into an increasingly articulate community, ultimately a choir of saints and angels. I would not be sorry, of course, for such a God to exist; my confession is that this God exists for me now mostly as an abstraction, and abstraction veers toward the idealization that threatens to eviscerate character. In book 4 of the *Confessions*, where Augustine confesses to a messy, semi-narcissistic grief over the relatively sudden loss of a childhood friend, he reports finding little consolation at the time in his faith; the dead friend was a great deal more real for him than the God whose existence he was trying, and not very well, to imagine (*conf.* 4.4.9). At the end of *Hannah's Child: A Theologian's Memoir*, Hauerwas tries to answer the query of a friend who had read the typescript draft and who wanted to know from Hauerwas what he had learned over the course of writing his rather singular book. Looking for a nonobvious answer, Hauerwas lands on a simple truth, that he is Christian, to which he appends the gloss, "How interesting."[2] In the abstract it is hardly surprising that a Christian theologian would turn out to be Christian, but if the God at issue is not some abstract distillate of ceaselessly mulled-over beliefs, then I suppose it might be especially surprising for a Christian theologian to turn out so. I certainly see the interest of the pronouncement "I am a Christian" as a personal realization, like waking up to discover that an ancient Nazarene rabbi, intimately infused with divine breath, has been long been a fixture at your family table. Now you cannot imagine your heart's genealogy apart from him.

Personally I don't feel that I know Jesus quite that well. But I know people who know him better than I do, and they know people. Where there is an element of dispossession in any affirmation of love of another, the undoing of possessiveness in the love of God in Christ—also the love of one particular human being—appears bottomless. It is an unsettling form of dispossession, feeling at times, on both sides of the love, like an abandonment. In Mark and Matthew, Jesus cries from the cross, "My God, my God, why have you forsaken me?," and in this way he voices the profoundest fear of God's people: that in singling them out, God has cast them off (Mark 15.34; Matt. 27:46). In Luke 23:34, Jesus seems alternatively to be reassuring God that his people, in their heart of hearts, have yet to betray him: "Father, forgive them; for they do not know what they are doing." In John, Jesus ends his life on the terse words "It is finished," but by then he will have already, from the vantage of his cross, reconstituted his family: his mother will move in with John, the beloved disciple, and the two of them will live, from now on, as mother and son (John 19:30). We are not to suppose that a simple substitution, of one son for another, is being suggested here, or that the reconstitution of a family, that of God's household, is finished. What is finished is the tyranny of a terrible fear, that one particular love demands the effacement of another, a sacrifice without issue. If that were true, then God's love for his one, only begotten Son would eclipse the light of any other love, and Trinitarian economy would require, from our darkened point of view, the perpetual undoing of particular human bonds. Human love would forever tend toward abstraction—as if that were a virtue.

I have no argument for my assertion, which I admit is rather naked, that the tyranny has been broken. I feel that I have, regrettably, overwhelming evidence for thinking that the fear persists. When Hauerwas, as a theologian, eschews a theory of God and yet insists on the possibility of practical reasoning, he is recognizing that there is, in fact, no argument for the saving work of a "cross-shattered Christ" beyond faithful witness to a less fear-hobbled love.[3] That, for Hauerwas, is a matter of attending to character, and he wonders how it is possible, given our lack of self-presence in so much of what we do, to get to the point of being able to account for ourselves. I feel the force of that question, and I readily concede the importance of character, but I also think that too pronounced a focus on accountability tends to privilege the ethics of care-giving and idealize adulthood, the time of having come of age. Like Oedipus before the Sphinx, I try to see life in the context of time's crucible, where metamorphosis is the rule and standing on one's own two feet no more defines a person than having to crawl to get around or having to lean on a cane. Unlike Oedipus, I have given up on thinking that a life bent by time and broken into pieces, imperfectly remembered, is a puzzle to be pieced back together and solved. Whatever the nature of the redemption that comes of holding fast to the one who enters time's crucible and finds himself fully there, it is not a redemption paid out in the coinage of intelligibility.

Hauerwas generously credits Alasdair MacIntyre, his longtime friend and fellow provocateur in the arena of revisionist ethics, for having rid him of a ground-level error in action theory, evident in his 1975 classic, *Character and the Christian Life: A Study in Theological Ethics*.[4] "The mistake," Hauerwas writes, "was to try to defend an account of agency to sustain what it means for us to take ownership of what we do on grounds that first-person avowals of action cannot be described in third-person language" (79). "I was, in short," he summarizes, "trying to defend action qua action as a logically primitive notion." The alternatively basic notion of action that Hauerwas takes over from MacIntyre is that of something intelligible. There is no such thing, on this revised way of viewing things, as a fundamentally unintelligible action. If not even the most meager modicum of an agent's capacity to frame an intention can enter into the description of what the agent has putatively done, then the agent really hasn't done anything; all we can say, echoing Samuel Beckett, is that something is taking its course. What is important to add here, to secure the appropriate distance from the old appeal to an irreducibly first-person perspective, is that no ascription of intelligibility can bypass altogether the broader networks of intelligibility, the narratives both implicit and explicit, that allow belief and desire to make sense to more than one person. The interpersonal element of action-ascription spells the end of first-person privilege. You may well understand what I do better than I do; I may, in fact, be largely clueless about what I have done. And God, being the Word that speaks us both into being and then becomes fellow flesh, presumably understands what we do far better, perhaps infinitely so, than you or I ever could, individually or together.

It strikes me that Hauerwas's shift in focus from action to intelligible action is not best cast as a shift in what he considers most basic. There is nothing reliably basic about the intelligibility of an action, and a theologian, or at least one of the serious, both feet in, no-hedging sort that Hauerwas always has been, is arguably in a good position to appreciate why. In book 2 of the *Confessions*, Augustine famously recalls his having joined up, in the sixteenth year of his life, with a crew of bored, backwater adolescents to steal pears from a neighbor's vineyard and throw the lot, untasted, to hogs (*conf.* 2.4.9). More than two decades after the fact, Augustine is still strangely bent out of shape about his motives for having acted this way. His repeated attempts to make retrospective sense of his petty crime all collapse under the burden of an undisclosed intelligibility.

"I stole pears," he tells himself. No doubt, but it wasn't pears you wanted. They weren't particularly good pears, and, as you freely admit, you weren't hungry for pears in any case. "I acted to impress my peers," he ventures next. Of course—Psychology 101. But why were you and your peers so impressed with pointless theft? They weren't any more in the mood for pear cuisine than you were. Ah, now the light goes on. "It was the sheer delight of transgressing," he recalls, "the delight of shaking free of alien authority, that captivated my covetous, but still unauthorized adolescent soul" (cf. *conf.* 2.4.9: *amavi defectum meum*). True enough—Psychology 102. But where is the authority figure in this picture? You and your peers stole the pears late at night, to assure that you wouldn't be discovered, and I assume that none of you left a note—a pretty anemic delight in transgression, if you don't at least leave a note. Augustine appeals finally to the God who is present to him even when he is, as in this crumbling memory of sin, absent from himself: "My soul was stepping out on you, God, seeking to give you the slip by ducking into an act void of good and so void of you" (inspired by *conf.* 2.6.14: *Ita fornicatur anima, cum avertitur abs te*).[5]

The most basic description of his act, the one that locks his soul into an imperfect love of God, is the least intelligible of the lot. For why would soul, the life of body, willingly break with God, the life of life, and suffer through an increasingly ruinous wound of separation? Augustine would have been better off sticking with peer pressure. That was the obvious motive. But in refusing to stick there, he rejects the intelligibility of a common form of worldly despair, where everyone is fated to come of age sequestered in self-exile and alone, and a good is a good only in the taking. The God from whom he can take absolutely nothing voids his theft and, at the same time, holds him accountable: Augustine cannot forever take refuge in the person he imagines himself to be. He will have to grow up in an unimagined way.

In the years I have been reading Hauerwas's writings and listening to him in conversation and when he lectures, I have never known him to confuse prophetic insistence on the distinctiveness of the Church, held apart from the world, with a claim about the superiority of the Christian narrative over worldly alternatives. It isn't the Christian narrative that saves, Hauerwas reminds us, but Christ. This is a distinction that speaks to a cataclysmic difference in redemptive power, yet within the context of any industry of words, it is a distinction that is easy to elide. Intellectuals especially, myself included, tend to idealize intelligibility, and even when we insist that no regnant form of narration or scheme of reason is ever final—call this an intellectual's faith—we are often still in the throes of a finality that works to render persons into a play of abstractions.

Take, for example, MacIntyre's case against J, *jemand*, in his essay "Social Structures and Their Threat to Moral Agency."[6] Hauerwas is undoubtedly right to point out that J, who cultivates indifference to the question of whether the trains he supervises are going to markets or to extermination camps, is an Eichmann-like character, if not a stand-in for Eichmann himself. To the question of whether we have grounds for holding J responsible for his cultivated indifference, MacIntyre works his way to a bloodless conclusion. We do have grounds in so far as we can fault Eichmann for failing to confront the possibility that he has absolutized an imperfect social order. Put otherwise, he has betrayed an intellectual's faith. What I find most unsettling about this particular construal of accountability is that it seems to confuse a monstrously retarded love of persons with a stubbornly shortsighted love of intelligibility.

Hauerwas politely takes his leave, not of MacIntyre himself, but of MacIntyre's tendency, epitomized by this J character, to dematerialize agency and thereby lend his philosophy an air of independence from the scandal of incarnation. In place of J, a stock figure for small-minded self-consistency, Hauerwas directs our attention to Dietrich Bonhoeffer, a flesh-and-blood martyr who is less sure of himself than of his love for the cross-shattered God and his suffering people. "By directing attention to Bonhoeffer, and in particular his poem 'Who Am I?,' I hope to show," Hauerwas writes, "what a life looks like when lived in a manner that would be unintelligible if the God we worship as Christians does not exist." The reference to the poem "Who Am I?," where Bonhoeffer confesses to having an irreparably broken self, puts in place the crucial qualification of Hauerwas's ambition. We will not be getting from Hauerwas (and how could we have expected otherwise?) the wager-like argument that Bonhoeffer's sacrifice makes sense only as his bet on the truth of his Christian beliefs. Instead we are offered a vivid reminder of the difference between the senseless coherence of imaginary love and the rupture of love's incarnation.

Hauerwas poignantly ends his essay with an allusion to book 10 of the *Confessions*, the part where Augustine appears to differentiate self-knowledge from self-possession. "For as long as I travel into your absence," he confesses to God (*conf.* 10.5.7), "I am more present to myself than I am to you." The implication of this confession is that Augustine's homecoming, a return to divine intimacy, is going to necessitate a form of self-estrangement. God will come between Augustine and himself and stay there, even at the high noon of revelation. I wouldn't conclude from this, as Hauerwas seems more inclined to do, that confessional love is without its element of self-knowledge. I prefer to think that knowledge of self, divinely mediated, is love of a stranger. I come to know myself in my love of others, and, being imperfectly triune, my love reflects back more than me. Such is the crack in selfhood that no divinity is meant to heal.

Notes

When these essays were first presented at the Symposium on Action at Duke University in 2014, a sustained response paper accompanied each essay. Of those, we include James Wetzel's response to Stanley Hauerwas here. Hauerwas's eminence in American theological circles is unique, and Wetzel's response was so exceptional that we felt that the conversation developed in this book is enhanced by its inclusion.—Eds.

1. From the opening of "How to Be an Agent," this volume.

2. Stanley Hauerwas, *Hannah's Child: A Theologian's Memoir* (Grand Rapids, Mich.: Eerdmans, 2012), 284.

3. The phrase "cross-shattered Christ" hails from John F. Deane's poem "Mercy." Hauerwas takes over the phrase to serve as the title for his Lenten meditation: *Cross-Shattered Christ: Meditations on the Seven Last Words* (Grand Rapids, Mich.: Brazos, 2004).

4. Stanley Hauerwas, *Character and the Christian Life: A Study in Theological Ethics* (San Antonio, Tex.: Trinity University Press, 1975). The book began its life as Hauerwas's doctoral dissertation at Yale, under Eugene TeSelle's direction. It was the first book I ever read of his, and I was thoroughly persuaded to embrace what Hauerwas is now calling the book's basic mistake.

5. In this paragraph, I am dramatizing an exchange with Augustine, not translating him verbatim. For the Latin that has inspired this exchange, see James J. O'Donnell, *Augustine: Confessions*, vol. 1: *Introduction and Text* (Oxford: Clarendon, 1992).

6. First published in *Philosophy* 74, no. 3 (1999): 311–29, reprinted as ch. 11 of Alasdair MacIntyre, *Ethics and Politics: Selected Essays*, vol. 2 (Cambridge: Cambridge University Press, 2006), 186–204.

CONTRIBUTORS

Sarah Beckwith is the Katherine Everitt Professor of English, Theater Studies, and Religion at Duke University. She is the author of *Signifying God: Social Relation and Symbolic Act in the York Corpus Christi Plays* (2001) and *Shakespeare and the Grammar of Forgiveness* (2011). She is now at work on a book on Shakespearean tragedy and ethics, and another on versions of *The Winter's Tale.*

Stanley Hauerwas is Gilbert T. Rowe Emeritus Professor of Divinity and Law at Duke University. He has written more than forty books, including *A Community of Character: Toward a Constructive Christian Social Ethic* (1991), *The Peaceable Kingdom: A Primer in Christian Ethics* (1991), and *Hannah's Child: A Theological Memoir* (2012). Hauerwas is best known for his role in the recovery of virtue ethics and his insistence on a Christian commitment to nonviolence.

Florian Klinger is an associate professor in Germanic studies at the University of Chicago. He works in philosophy and literature. His publications include *Urteilen* (2011) and *Theorie der Form* (2013), a revised English translation of which is forthcoming with University of Chicago Press.

John McGowan is Hanes Distinguished Professor of English at the University of North Carolina, Chapel Hill. His most recent book is *Pragmatist Politics: Making the Case for Liberal Democracy* (2012), and he is currently working on models of civility.

Christoph Menke is a professor in the Department of Philosophy at the Goethe Universität in Frankfurt am Main. His book publications in English include *The Sovereignty of Art: Aesthetic Negativity after Adorno and Derrida* (1998) and *Force: A Fundamental Concept of Aesthetic Anthropology* (2012).

Hina Nazar is an associate professor of English at the University of Illinois at Urbana-Champaign and an affiliate of the Unit for Criticism and Interpretive Theory. She is the author of *Enlightened Sentiments: Judgment and Autonomy in the Age of Sensibility* (2012) and has published widely on eighteenth- and nineteenth-century British literature and Enlightenment political theory. Her current book project offers a revisionist history of liberalism by tracing the ways in which liberalism's early discourse of rights and freedom became intertwined with questions of education and character development.

Oliver O'Donovan is an emeritus professor of Christian Ethics at the University of Edinburgh, where he served as a professor between 2006 and 2012, and an honorary professor of the University of St. Andrews. From 1982 to 2006 he was Regius Professor of Moral and Pastoral Theology and Canon of Christ Church at the University of Oxford, before which he taught in Oxford and Toronto. Recent books include *Common Objects of Love* (2002) and *The Ways of Judgment* (2005).

Thomas Pfau is the Alice Mary Baldwin Professor of English and Professor of German at Duke University, where he also holds an appointment in the Divinity School. The author of more than forty essays and articles, he has also published two monographs on English and European romanticism, numerous edited volumes and special journal issues, and translations of Hölderlin's prose and philosophical essays by F. W. J. Schelling. His most recent monograph is *Minding the Modern: Human Agency, Intellectual Traditions, and Responsible Knowledge* (2013). Currently, he is writing a monograph on the status of the image in philosophical, literary, and theological writing.

Gretchen Reydams-Schils is a professor in the Program of Liberal Studies at the University of Notre Dame. She holds concurrent appointments in the departments of Classics, Philosophy, and Theology and is the Director of the Notre Dame Workshop on Ancient Philosophy. She is the author of *The Roman Stoics: Self, Responsibility, and Affection* (2005).

Vivasvan Soni is an associate professor of English at Northwestern University. His book, *Mourning Happiness: Narrative and the Politics of Modernity* (2010), was the recipient of the Modern Language Association's eighteenth annual Prize for a First Book. He is working on a project that probes the long history of our discomfort with judgment, tracing its genesis in eighteenth-century discourses of empiricism and aesthetics.

James Wetzel is a professor of philosophy at Villanova University and holder of the Augustinian Endowed Chair. He is the author of *Parting Knowledge* (2013), a collection of essays on Augustinian themes, and the editor of the Cambridge Critical Guide to Augustine's *City of God* (2012). His current project explores the notion of Augustinian philosophy as a way of life.

Christopher Yeomans is a professor of philosophy and head of department at Purdue University. His most recent monograph is *The Expansion of Autonomy: Hegel's Pluralistic Philosophy of Action* (2015). He is currently working on German Idealist social and political philosophy.

Linda M. G. Zerilli is the Charles E. Merriam Distinguished Service Professor of Political Science and Professor of Gender and Sexuality Studies at the University of Chicago. Her books include *Feminism and the Abyss of Freedom* (2005) and *A Democratic Theory of Judgment* (2016).

INDEX